D1478564

STATE, RESISTANCE AND CHANGE IN SOUTH AFRICA

Edited by
PHILIP FRANKEL, NOAM PINES
and MARK SWILLING

CROOM HELM
London • New York • Sydney

© 1988 P. Frankel, N. Pines, and M. Swilling
Croom Helm Ltd, Provident House,
Burrell Row, Beckenham, Kent, BR3 1AT

Croom Helm Australia, 44–50 Waterloo Road,
North Ryde, 2113, New South Wales

Published in the USA by
Croom Helm
in association with Methuen, Inc.
29 West 35th Street,
New York, NY 10001

British Library Cataloguing in Publication Data

State, resistance and change in South Africa.
  1. South Africa — Politics and
  government
  I. Frankel, Philip H. II. Pines, Noam
  III. Swilling, Mark
  320.968   DT770

  ISBN 0-7099-4900-6

Library of Congress Cataloging-in-Publication Data

State, resistance, and change in South Africa

  Published in the U.S. in association with Methuen, Inc.,
New York, N.Y.
  Bibliography: p.
  Includes index.
  1. Apartheid — South Africa. 2. Government, Resistance
to — South Africa. 3. South Africa — Politics and government
— 1978- . I. Frankel, Philip H. II. Pines, Noam.
III. Swilling, Mark.
DT763.S7734 1988   968.06′3   87-20046
ISBN 0-7099-4900-6 (U.S.)

Printed and bound in Great Britain
by Billing & Sons Limited, Worcester.

Contents

Contributors

WILLIAM COBBETT	Research Fellow, Centre for Research in Ethnic Relations, University of Warwick
MICHAEL EVANS	Lawyer, Cape Town
DR PHILIP FRANKEL	Senior Lecturer, Department of Political Studies, University of the Witwatersrand, Johannesburg
DARYL GLASER	Department of Sociology, University of the Witwatersrand, Johannesburg
JEREMY GREST	Senior Lecturer, Department of African Studies, University of Natal, Durban
DR DOUG HINDSON	Senior Lecturer, Department of Sociology, University of the Witwatersrand, Johannesburg
PETER HUDSON	Lecturer, Department of Political Studies, University of the Witwatersrand, Johannesburg
DR TOM LODGE	Senior Lecturer, Department of Political Studies, University of the Witwatersrand, Johannesburg
COLLEEN McCAUL	Researcher, South African Institute of Race Relations, Johannesburg
MICHAEL MANN	Lecturer, Department of Political Studies, University of the Witwatersrand, Johannesburg
MARK PHILIPS	Faculty of Law, University of the Witwatersrand, Johannesburg
DR NOAM PINES	Senior Lecturer, Department of Political Studies, University of the Witwatersrand, Johannesburg
JEREMY SEEKINGS	Nuffield College, Oxford University
MARK SWILLING	Lecturer, Department of Political Studies, University of the Witwatersrand, Johannesburg
DR EDDIE WEBSTER	Professor, Department of Sociology, University of the Witwatersrand, Johannesburg

Abbreviations

ANC	African National Congress
Armscor	Armaments Corporation
ASI	African Studies Institute
ASRO	Atteridgeville-Saulsville Residents Organisation
ASSOCOM	Association of Chambers of Commerce
AWB	Afrikaner Weerstandsbeweging
AZACTU	Azanian Confederation of Trade Unions
AZAPO	Azanian People's Organisation
AZASO	Azanian Students' Organisation
BCM	Black Consciousness Movement
BLA	Black Local Authority
CASE	Community Agency for Social Enquiry
CBD	Central Business District
CCLGA	Council for the Co-ordination of Local Government Affairs
CNETU	Congress of Non-European Trade Unions
COSAS	Congress of South African Students
COSATU	Congress of South African Trade Unions
CP	Conservative Party
CUSA	Council of Unions of South Africa
CWIU	Chemical Workers Industrial Union
DAC	Defence Advisory Council
DCD	Department of Co-operation and Development
DCDP	Department of Constitutional Development and Planning
DET	Department of Education and Training
EAC	Ekangala Action Committee
EC	Executive Committee
ECC	End Conscription Campaign
ERAPO	East Rand People's Organisation
Escom	Electricity Supply Commission
FAPLA	Front for the Popular Liberation of Angola
FCI	Federated Chamber of Industries
FOSATU	Federation of South African Trade Unions
FWC	Ford Workers Committee
GBS	Gesaamentlike Bestuursentrum

GM	General Motors
HNP	Herstigte Nasionale Party
HSRC	Human Sciences Research Council
IBR	Institute of Black Research
ICS	Institute of Commonwealth Studies
JCI	Johannesburg Consolidated Investments
JMC	Joint Management Centres
JORAC	Joint Rent Action Committee
KLA	KwaZulu Legislative Assembly
KRO	Kagiso Residents Organisation
LMG	Labour Monitoring Group
MACWUSA	Motor Assemblers and Components Workers Union of South Africa
MAWU	Metal and Allied Workers Union
MOCA	Mohlakeng Organisation of Civic Associations
MPLA	Movement for the Popular Liberation of Angola
NAAWU	National Automobile and Allied Workers Union
NAFCOC	National African Federated Chambers of Commerce
NECC	National Education Crisis Committee
NF	National Forum
NP	National Party
NRDAC	National Regional Development Advisory Council
NSC	National Statutory Council
NUM	National Union of Mineworkers
NUMARWOSA	National Union of Motor Assembly and Rubber Workers of South Africa
NUSAS	National Union of South African Students
OVDB	Oranje Vaal Development Board
PAC	Pan-Africanist Congress
PC	President's Council
PEBCO	Port Elizabeth Black Civic Organisation
PEYCO	Port Elizabeth Young Congress
PFP	Progressive Federal Party
PWV	Pretoria-Witwatersrand-Vereeniging
RDAC	Regional Development Advisory Committee
RENAMO	National Resistance Movement (Mozambique)

RMC	Release Mandela Campaign
RSA	Republic of South Africa
RSC	Regional Services Council
SAAWU	South African Allied Workers Union
SACP	South African Communist Party
SACTU	South African Congress of Trade Unions
SADF	South African Defence Force
SAIRR	South African Institute of Race Relations
SAP	South African Police
SAPRHS	South African Plan for Research in the Human Sciences
SAYO	Saulsville-Atteridgeville Youth Organisation
SBDC	Small Business Development Corporation
SCA	Soweto Civic Association
SOMAFCO	Solomon Mahlangu Freedom College
SOYCO	Soweto Youth Congress
SSC	State Security Council
SWAPO	South-West African People's Organisation
SWATF	South-West African Territory Force
UAW	United Automobile Workers
UBC	Urban Bantu Council
UDF	United Democratic Front
UMMAWSA	United Metal, Mining and Allied Workers of South Africa
UN	United Nations
UNITA	National Union for the Total Independence of Angola
UWUSA	United Workers' Union of South Africa
UYCO	Uitenhage Youth Congress
VCA	Vaal Civic Association
VVPP	Vukani Vulahmelo People's Party
YSC	Youth Service Corps for Social Reconstruction
ZANU	Zimbabwe African National Union
ZAPU	Zimbabwe African People's Union

Journal abbreviations

AP	*Africa Perspective*
JSAS	*Journal of Southern African Studies*
RDM	*Rand Daily Mail*

Abbreviations

SALB	*South African Labour Bulletin*
SN	*SASPU National*
WIP	*Work in Progress*
WM	*Weekly Mail*

1

Introduction: The Politics of Stalemate

Mark Swilling

This book brings together a range of contributions on the fundamental dimensions of contemporary South African politics. While the first four papers analyse the changing nature and composition of dominant institutional, social and class interests, the last five address the organisational, social and ideological bases of black resistance to apartheid. The penultimate chapter discusses the various pathways that could lead to a post-apartheid dispensation. Written from a critical perspective, they show how the changing structures of racial and capitalist domination must be understood in relation to the severe challenges from below that dominant groups have had to face in recent years. They also show how the complex patterns of community, trade union and military resistance to apartheid have been shaped by the practices of ruling groups who have, since 1976, attempted in various ways to maintain, adjust and reform the social structures of domination.

The Soweto Uprising of 1976 was a watershed in South African politics. It brought home to dominant groups the realisation that if their interests were to be secured in the long term, existing structures of social control and political representation would have to be modified to cater for at least some sectors of the black majority. The Soweto Uprising also terminated a long period of apparent black political quiescence (notwithstanding the Durban general strikes of 1973) that began with the banning of the African National Congress (ANC) and Pan Africanist Congress (PAC) in 1960 and the brutal repression of the movements represented by these organisations during the early 1960s.

It is possible to periodise the last decade of South African politics into three phases:

1

(1) 1976–9, which was characterised by township rebellion and subsequent repression while conflicts within the state between 'verligtes' and 'verkramptes' were being fought out;
(2) 1979–84, which marked the genesis of the most important reformist strategies in the fields of industrial relations and urban policy under the rubric of 'Total Strategy'. At the same time, black responses in the workplace and communities emerged to pose a fundamental challenge to these reforms; and
(3) the post-1984 period, which saw the state move beyond Total Strategy to formulate reformist policies that dispensed with basic premisses of classic apartheid, while the nationwide black resistance that gathered momentum after the Vaal Uprising in September 1984 generated levels of conflict between the state and the black communities uprecedented in South African history.

1976–9: rebellion, repression and the emergence of new rulers

The township rebellion of the mid-1970s was largely the unintended consequence of apartheid urban policy. During the 1950s and through the 1960s, the state had systematically imposed its stringent controls on South Africa's black population. The basic objective was to rationalise controls over the African majority which had, since the 1920s, been defined as 'temporary sojourners' in the white cities. Their right to be in the urban areas was in theory meant to be determined by the labour requirements of white employers. Urbanised coloured and Indian populations, for their part, were steadily deprived of what scant representation they had in some municipalities, provincial councils and the Senate. Coupled to this was the often forced removal of these communities from their compact cultural enclaves in the inner-city areas to well-planned outer-city Group Areas. However, it was the effects of apartheid policies on the African communities that had the most politically significant implications.

During the 1950s, influx controls were rationalised to ensure that a relatively privileged minority of urban Africans was allowed to settle in the urban areas, while the large African majority was confined to impoverished rural bantustans and white farms.

2

Members of these marginalised populations were only allowed to enter the urban areas if their labour was required — a system of labour market segmentation that was regulated by the infamous labour bureaux. Expenditure on urban housing and services was directed into the new outer-city African townships created and built during the 1950s and 1960s to cater for the urban African minority. However, during the 1960s, apartheid planners realised that the natural increase of the African urban minority, and the relative stabilisation of this group that resulted from the practical application of influx control, was contradicting the basic theory of apartheid which envisaged the limitation of the size of the urban African population to the numbers required by white employers. Consequently, during the 1960s a range of measures was introduced to provide for the further tightening of influx control (see Bantu Laws Amendment Act of 1964 and the Bantu Labour Act of 1964). These and other measures froze the construction of housing for urban Africans, provided for the repatriation of redundant and surplus labour to the bantustans, and facilitated the removal of leasehold and other property rights and the reduction of expenditure on urban services.

These measures resulted in a qualitative decline in the living conditions of urban Africans. This was further exacerbated by the establishment in 1971 of the Bantu Affairs Administration Boards — white government appointed bureacratic hierarchies — to run townships according to the principle that expenditure on services and housing does not exceed income derived from rental, service charges and other commercial enterprises run by the Boards (e.g. liquor outlets). In this context, as Grest demonstrates, inefficient and illegitimate local government structures became the foci of grievance and resistance in the 1970s.

Meanwhile, coupled with the qualitative decline in living conditions by the early 1970s, worsened by the world recession, there was a similar deterioration in the quality of education. This was related to the changing composition of capital referred to by Webster. During the 1960s, South Africa had experienced sustained economic growth. By the end of the 1960s, however, the new production processes were resulting in a shortage of skilled educated labour. This resulted in a change in education policy which provided for an increase in the number of Africans being pushed through the Bantu education system without a corresponding increase in state expenditure in this area. Thus, larger numbers of students were catered for with the same level of resources. This led to a deterioration of educational facilities.

By the mid-1970s, townships were facing a crisis of reproduction: overcrowding, inadequate urban services, rising unemployment as a result of the recession, and declining real wage levels as inflation rose. The new generation of African youth was the product of the alienated environment of the sprawling impoverished townships; a system of education that was designed to train them for wage labour; an economy that could no longer provide them with sufficient job opportunities; and a culture of political quiescence that they had begun to reject. Stimulated by the psycho-iconoclastic discourse of the Black Consciousness Movement and inspired by the independence of neighbouring former Portuguese colonies after long armed struggles for national liberation, many elected to oppose their condition of oppression. The catalyst was to be the mandatory introduction of Afrikaans as the medium of instruction in the schools in 1976.

An equally important process of re-composition and resistance was evident in South Africa's workplaces. As Webster argues, the concentration and centralisation of ownership in the economy spurned a new 'massified' proletariat organised into large enterprises without any political or trade union channels to express grievances. The result was the expansion of the black trade union movement beyond the controls of the apartheid institutions. The 1973 general strikes in Durban and the failure of measures introduced both by state and employers to curb this movement, paved the way for the introduction of new labour policies.

The 1976 rebellions focused national and international attention on South Africa's political structures. Internationally, they were condemned and internally a moderate consensus emerged that accepted the necessity for reform. After the rebellions had been crushed, the stage was set for a re-alignment of the dominant institutional and class forces. As Mann argues, this assumed the form of proactive action by monopoly capitalist interests collected together in the Urban Foundation and the ascendance of 'verligte' political interests within the National Party under the leadership of P.W. Botha and backed by Afrikaner capital and the military. With the retirement of B.J. Vorster and the election of P.W. Botha as Prime Minister in 1978 with a clear reformist mandate, the state proceeded to restructure the foundations of urban regulation, workplace control, constitutional representation and coercion. This all-embracing reformist initiative took place under the rubric of Total Strategy.

1979–84: reform and resistance

Total Strategy was an aggressive reformist initiative with origins in the military, foreign affairs, and verligte organs of the state that rose to prominence after 'Muldergate' — the corruption scandal used by the 'verligtes' to oust the more conservative Vorster leadership. Based on a sophisticated 'hearts-and-minds' approach, Total Strategy contained four essential thrusts focusing on urban policy; industrial relations; the creation of a consociational/confederal constitutional framework to reorder the institutions of political representation at regional and central government level; and reorganisation of the security and intelligence apparatuses. The Riekert Commission was mandated to investigate urban policy,[1] the Wiehahn Commission was instructed to re-examine the industrial relations system[2], the President's Council investigated the various levels of the constitutional framework[3], and the military was in charge of reorganising the security system (see Evans and Phillips).

Organised business interests were initially dazed by the township conflicts, but slowly responded by demanding political reforms and giving support to extra-state reformist movements, e.g. the Urban Foundation. The politicisation of the business community and international pressure helped to foster a reformist climate within which verligte policy makers could proceed (see Mann, and Cobbett *et al.*).

The reforms, however, began to be introduced during the late 1970s when the balance of forces differed markedly from the 1976–7 period. The Black Consciousness Movement had been decimated by arrests, bannings, deaths and a mass exodus of activists fleeing the country. Although the trade unions were the only mass-based black movement capable of resisting the reforms at this stage, their relative weakness and absence of a political organisation prevented them from contesting the reforms outside the workplace. Consequently, the reforms were largely shaped by the new verligte elements represented by the P.W. Botha leadership and the more liberal demands of the business community. They were an attempt to re-constitute the means of domination on terms favourable to the ruling groups.

The Riekert and Wiehahn strategies should be seen as complementary. Giving urban blacks the right to live permanently in the urban areas needed to be complemented by rights that traditional apartheid had hitherto denied to 'temporary sojourners' in the areas of trade unionism, property, and local government. Superficial interpretations at the time presented these reforms as a major departure from traditional apartheid. However, as Webster, Grest, and Cobbett *et al.* suggest, they were constructed as part of a strategy to bolster the privileges of urban insiders at the expense of rural outsiders — a project designed to change the means of control without substantially altering the fundamental basis of apartheid. The Riekert Commission did not question the bantustan system and hence suggested that although urban blacks should obtain local political rights in municipal institutions and a range of urban rights (leasehold, commercial, intra-urban labour mobility and improved services), national political rights should still be expressed through the (independent) bantustans. The Wiehahn strategy, Webster argues, had a similar reform-cum-control objective: recognition of black trade unions coupled to the imposition of institutional checks and balances.

As for coloureds and Indians, the tricameral Parliament was intended to incorporate them into a 'consociational' central government structure without threatening the autonomy of the white parliamentary system. According to the President's Council reports, this consociational structure was seen as a component of a larger overarching 'confederal' structure that would link the various bantustan and South African governments. This solution, which was reached after reviewing and rejecting a number of options ranging from majoritarianism through non-racial consociationalism (or federalism) to total racial exclusivity, amounted to a 'consociational/confederal' alternative. It consisted of consociationalism for whites, coloureds and Indians within a tricameral Parliament, and confederalism to facilitate political and economic interdependence of 'separate' states — a vision frequently equated with the European Economic Community.

The confederal structure complemented the Riekert strategy in two ways. Firstly, during the early 1980s when policy makers were seeking a way to link up the non-bantustan based black local authorities (BLAs) established in terms of the Black Local Authorities Act of 1982 (see Grest) to higher forms of political representation, it was frequently suggested that this be done by creating 'city-states' with representatives in the central confederal decision-making body. Secondly, the confederal schema (initially articulated as the 'constellation of states' idea), provided the framework for the formulation of a new regional development policy based on the concept of 'economic interdependence and political independence' — what the Buthelezi Commission[4] described as the 'economic route' to power sharing. The regional development policy announced in 1979 (see Mann) was designed to ensure that the bantustans were viable confederal units capable of coping with the marginalised rural populations — an extension of the Verwoerdian scheme to limit the rate of urbanisation.

The confederal schema was designed to accomplish three aims: to legitimise the South African state by softening the meaning of 'separate' political development; to provide a framework for granting urban rights while simultaneously retaining bantustans as the only form of central political representation for Africans; and to rationalise industrial dispersal policy to slow down urbanisation. Whereas confederalism was aimed at streamlining the regional foundations of apartheid, the new labour dispensation and the Riekert-type urbanisation policies (i.e. tighter controls over rural-urban influx, greater mobility for urban insiders, improvement of urban living conditions and municipal representation in the BLAs) were designed to rationalise the new urban system.

As far as the security organs were concerned, the military spearheaded the formation of the State Security Council (SSC). The SSC is chaired by senior members of the security establishment and comprises several inter-departmental committees that discuss and formulate policy proposals for the Cabinet. It has several hundred regional and local organs that are co-ordinated by the National Security Management System. The function of this structure is two-fold: firstly, to maximise the ability of the state to monitor all facets of South African politics and to devise appropriate short- and long-term responses; and secondly, to monitor state practices and increase the efficiency of the state's ability to govern effectively in unstable conditions. The SSC, (see Evans and Phillips) amounts to a shadow government that specialises in crisis management.

The intentions of official policies, however, differ markedly from the way policies are implemented and the social processes to which they give rise. State policy cannot take account of all the structural forces that impinge on a given field of intervention, nor can the responses of a range of social actors be predicted. The fate of Total Strategy is a particularly illuminating example of how the combined effect of structural forces and social conflict can substantially inhibit the implementation of a reformist strategy and, in the final analysis, force government to change tack.

Although numerous political interests opposed the implementation of Total Strategy, their reasons were as varied as their agendas and practices. The most aggressive opposition came from the major trade union federations and community organisations. The oppositional position of these social movements was complemented to an extent by some bantustan leaders (see McCaul), the business community (see Mann) and the international community. The major achievement of the trade unions was to oppose the state's intention of excluding migrant workers from the trade unions. After refusing to register until the relevant clauses of the legislation had been removed, the government backed down soon after the legislation was passed in 1979. Consequently, migrant workers, who were the backbone of the new unions, began to organise and mobilise alongside urban insiders, thus undermining the Riekart strategy that attempted to divide the working classes along urban-rural lines. Trade unions have since given expression to the central political demand of migrant workers: the right to live and vote in the metropolitan political economies instead of being defined as members of a bankrupt bantustan.

Furthermore, according to Webster, by emphasising the need to establish strong democratic organisations, the unions thwarted the state's attempt to bring the unions under control by institutionalising industrial conflict. Instead, beginning in late 1979, the unions took advantage of the 1979–82 boom to wage protracted shopfloor battles to win recognition, wage increases, maternity rights, pension payouts, and a range of concessions that challenged, in the words of the head of Barlow Rand, 'management's right to manage'. Even during the subsequent recession, strike levels rose and union membership increased dramatically. The growth of the unions was significant for three reasons:

(1) the socialist leadership within the unions meant that workers were drawn into highly politicised organisations opposed to the perpetuation of apartheid;
(2) in many areas unions provided the organisational training for a new generation of community activists who subsequently played leading roles in powerful community organisations; and
(3) during 1979–82, the rolling general strikes that rocked the Eastern and Western Cape, Natal, and the East Rand forged

8

a space for the re-emergence of political organisations like the United Democratic Front (UDF) and National Forum (NF) in 1983.

Community organisations first emerged in Port Elizabeth and Soweto towards the end of 1979, and this was followed by the emergence of powerful student organisations in the Cape during the 1980 Capetown schools boycott. This boycott marked a turning point because its leaders repeatedly emphasised the need to 'learn from the mistakes of '76'. These were perceived by the leaders of the 1980 movements to be black exclusivism, student vanguardism, voluntarism, and the failure to recognise the leading role of the working class. Democratically organised neighbourhood-based 'civics' first emerged in Capetown in the wake of the 1980 boycott. Although community organisations also emerged in the other provinces, it was not until 1983 that they became the generalised phenomenon that Seekings examines. The re-emergence of mass-based community, student, youth and women's organisations during the early 1980s facilitated the formation of national political organisations.

Civics and youth congresses came to dominate the political terrain in the townships during the post-1983 period. The reasons for this were two-fold: the exclusion of Africans from the new constitution, and the failure of the BLAs. The BLAs that were introduced in 1983 were politically illegitimate largely because they were targeted by oppositional organisations who exploited the fact that these authorities were not linked up to higher forms of political representation. The boycott of the elections for the tricameral Parliament was explicitly coupled with the boycott of the elections for the BLAs because the UDF was keen to use the inadequacy of these structures to demand substantive political rights for all — an agenda that facilitated the re-emergence of the Freedom Charter.

Mobilisation around the demand for political rights alone would not have resulted in the mass-based community organisations that exist today. Equally important was the fiscal crisis of the BLAs and central state as the recession took its toll. In order to withdraw from the politically volatile task of providing the means of collective consumption, the central state built into the logic of 'self-government' the provision that BLAs should be self-financing. However, the townships do not have a viable tax base. Consequently, to improve township conditions, the BLAs were forced to increase rent and service charges, in some cases by 100 per cent. This triggered off, as

Seekings notes, dramatic township conflicts involving protracted rent boycotts, squatter movements, housing struggles and stayaways. The final result has been the total collapse of the BLAs as councillors resigned *en masse*, fled the townships in fear of their lives, or ceased to operate as intended. State officials now acknowledge that it was a mistake to give the BLAs inadequate fiscal resources.

At the central state level, the successful boycott of the elections for the tricameral Parliament in August 1984 was a severe blow to the reform strategy. This was compounded by the fact that prominent homeland leaders rejected the confederal schema, preferring a more integrated federal option as suggested by the Buthelezi Commission (see McCaul). Moderate and radical black political organisations were not the only groups that opposed the consociational/confederal solution. As the crisis continued well into the 1980s, Cobbett *et al.* argue, a growing caucus of disaffected Afrikaners in the National Party, the universities and certain branches of the state (e.g. Departments of Constitutional Development and Planning, Foreign Affairs and Finance) also began to admit that the bantustan system had failed and that blacks needed to be accommodated in new central government structures. This was reinforced by the vocal liberal intellectual community and organised commerce and industry who, Mann argues, took advantage of the cracks within Afrikanerdom and the bankruptcy of the reforms to demand far-reaching changes in a federalist direction.

1984–6: dimensions of the current crisis

The fundamental dimensions of the current crisis in South Africa include widespread sustained popular rebellion resulting in the collapse of civil government in many townships; a deepening recession (exacerbated by international economic pressure) that has simultaneously undermined the living conditions of the black majority and constrained the state's capacity to subsidise urban consumption (e.g. bread prices, transport costs, housing, education and services); increasingly effective international efforts to isolate South Africa at all levels; increasing tension between various reformist and conservative elements within the state and between the state and capital; and the steady disintegration of civil society's social and ideological fabric as rising levels of violence, poverty and disillusionment take their toll. Although the South African conflict has always confounded predictions that the collapse of the regime is imminent, there may be some truth in the popular view that the conflict is going through its last violent convulsive cycle. Much depends, however, on two important factors: the ability of the ruling groups to engineer a coherent and purposive reform programme on the one hand, and the ability of the national liberation, trade union and military movements to sustain a level of mobilisation effective enough to render the reform programme inoperable.

Since the Vaal Uprising in September 1984, South Africa has witnessed an upwelling of black protest and organised resistance unprecedented in South African history. From the small rural villages of the northern and eastern Transvaal, to the metropolitan agglomerations of the Witwatersrand, to the small towns and metropolises of the Cape, the communities, workplaces and schools have become the loci of black opposition and rebellion that has affected ever-widening layers of the black population. Workers through their trade unions, township residents in the civic associations, militant youths in the youth congresses, students in the student congresses and parents in the Parents Crisis Committees — all these constituencies have been organised and their efforts coalesced around a set of common demands frequently articulated by national organisations such as the United Democratic Front, National Education Crisis Committee and the major trade union federations.

Despite attempts to suppress this national uprising by detaining nearly 50,000 people since 1984, imposing two states of emergency, breaking up countless meetings and demonstrations, shooting peaceful demonstrators, banning and jailing political leaders, and limiting press freedom, the local and national resistance movements have succeeded in surviving. Although many have been weakened, they have not been broken. Nor is it likely — short of a massive repressive clamp-down similar to what happened in post-Allende Chile — that the state will succeed in wiping out the oppositional organisations. It is doubtful whether the state has the political resources for such a strategy, given the deeply divided nature of the ruling groups.

Three important reasons can be identified to explain the ability of the oppositional organisations to survive. Firstly, unlike the 1950s, contemporary black oppositional organisations are deeply rooted in most of South Africa's black communities. This entrenched power base is the product of a sustained period of political organisation and development that dates back at least to 1979, but with roots

11

in the 1973 strikes and 1976 rebellion. The current attempt by political activists to consolidate this power base by constructing embryonic 'organs of peoples' power' in the communities to complement the older shop steward structures in the workplaces that Webster describes, will critically affect the capacity of both the community and trade union organisations to survive the state's successive repressive unslaughts.

Secondly, South Africa's oppositional organisations have succeeded in articulating a common national political culture. This national political culture has roots in the long tradition of resistance to colonialism and racial oppression that exists in most black communities. However, its contemporary determinants are equally important. These include the persistence of social structures predicated on the denial of political rights to the majority and the domination of a capitalist economic system that enjoys very little support amongst black workers. Equally important has been the steady development of an alternative press; the consolidation of a political language complete with slogans, freedom songs and symbols; and a conceptual system that rests on a socialist interpretation of South African society and expressed in popular documents such as the Freedom Charter (see Hudson). Although local political cultures shaped by local conditions remain important, decades of urban concentration and industrialisation have enmeshed and integrated these local polities into larger entities that facilitate the articulation of national discourses, symbols and demands.

Thirdly, as Lodge argues, the role of the ANC as a 'state in exile' is pivotal in preserving an ideologically coherent movement that remains organisationally unaffected by the repressive actions of the state relative to the effects this can have on internal political organisations. Just as importantly, the ANC also plays a crucial role in ensuring that the oppositional activities of the internal organisations achieve an international legitimacy that they might not otherwise enjoy. This is significant, especially when it comes to winning support from disillusioned white political groups and business organisations. The moral authority commanded by both internal and external political organisations may well facilitate the building of a consensus over a post-apartheid future that will further weaken the state's ability to broaden its support base, which in turn will help to strengthen the political will of its opponents.

In short, the organisational entrenchment of the oppositional organisations in the political life of South Africa's black communities; the popular ideology and political culture they express;

and the national and international support they can command —
all of these factors will make it difficult for South Africa's rulers
to repress them successfully and still retain sufficient support,
internally and internationally, for reform strategies that require at
least a modicum of popular consensus to succeed.

South Africa's complex social conflicts did not determine state
policy in a structural vacuum. Nor are structural forces apolitical
processes moving relentlessly through history behind the backs of
human agency. Rather, new social conflicts bring into relief structural forces that were either hidden from view by discourses incapable of 'thinking' these processes, or else were simply ignored by
discourses that focused on 'more important' processes. Recent social
conflicts have focused attention on the 'urban question' precisely
because of the activities of the urban social movements (both union-
and community-based) which in turn reinforced the initiatives of
organisations like the Urban Foundation lobbying on behalf of big
capital. During the post-1984 period, the 'urban question' did not
refer to the narrow problem of how to incorporate 'urban blacks'
into a revamped apartheid structure, as was the case in the post-1976
era, but rather on how the entire urban and regional system of production and reproduction could be restructured to cope with the
'realities of urbanisation'. Before this issue is addressed, a brief
analysis of these structural forces is necessary.

The thrust of the argument in Cobbett *et al.* is that apartheid
policy inadvertently created regional patterns of population movement and industrial location that undercut what state policy and
analysts have hitherto assumed are the foundations of apartheid:
a dual economy, cheap labour power and de-urbanisation. Instead
it is argued that influx control and industrial dispersal policy have
combined to extend the metropolitan space-economies in a way that
enmeshes and incorporates populations located behind bantustan
boundaries into systems of production and reproduction that cannot be separated into rural-urban categories.

These extended metropolitan space-economies or regions have
not developed outside state policy. Recent shifts in state policy have,
per contra, been directly shaped by the exigencies of these spatial
forms. Some of the more important shifts are, firstly, the absolute
and relative quantitative decline of long-distance oscillatory migration and the massive increase in the number of 'cross-border commuters'. Development Boards have for some years now tended to
reduce the number of migrants employed in the metropoles while
simultaneously granting commuters 'administrative Section 10

rights', effectively giving rural outsiders (commuters) and urban insiders equal access to the labour market. This blurring of the distinction between rural and urban labour markets contradicts the logic of Riekert, who in any case virtually ignored commuters as a factor. Geographically, these new labour supply patterns correspond with regional rather than racial co-ordinates, giving rise to what Cobbett *et al.* call 'regional proletariats'. The new urbanisation policies, as articulated in the President's Council Report on Urbanisation and the 1986 White Paper on Urbanisation, are clearly designed to reinforce and rationalise this process.[5]

Secondly, industrial dispersal policy since 1982 has also been shaped by the need to manage the new metropolitan space-economies. Although rhetorical allegiance is still paid to traditional industrial decentralisation policy to satisfy demands of bantustan elites for 'development', in practice there have been two important shifts. Firstly, the focus is no longer on industrial decentralisation to outlying rural peripheries, but rather on industrial deconcentration to the metropolitan peripheries. Secondly, the number of Industrial Development Points has been scaled down to seven or eight key 'growth poles'. In short, industrial dispersal policy is firmly linked to the dispersal of industrial activities within the extended metropolitan space-economies, rather than acting as a component of the confederal schema based on spatially coherent bantustan economies. Once again, the geographical pattern that this produces corresponds with regional rather than racial co-ordinates — a process that is inscribed in the boundaries of the nine development regions.

Thirdly, the new Regional Services Councils Act of 1985 explicitly states that sections of the bantustans will be incorporated into the area of jurisdiction of these new multi-racial metropolitan governments. The RSCs, therefore, are the institutional expression of these extended metropolitan space-economies. They are aimed at providing substantial fiscal resources for restructuring and managing the metropolitan areas by cutting across traditional Group Area and bantustan boundaries — the so-called 'soft borders' approach (see Grest).

To sum up: significant structural changes have occurred, but state responses have not assumed the form of a new or coherent ideological package that could serve as an alternative to apartheid. Instead, the state is caught between the exigencies of structural needs that transcend traditional apartheid boundaries and the vicissitudes of the political terrain where it defends the need for 'orderly reform' — a euphemism for white and capitalist interests — against the right-wing pressuring for the retention of grand apartheid and the demands emanating from the large majority of South Africans for the transfer of power to those parties that represent this constituency.

South Africa is currently in the grips of an interregnum which consists of a social stalemate where 'the old is dying and the new cannot be born'.[6] The organisations and movements that represent the interests of the oppressed majority do not possess the organisational capacity, political power or coercive strength to overthrow the state. Nor does the state have the ideological and political resources required to re-establish its dominance without coercion. 'Where . . . the hegemony of a dominant class is persistently and strongly challenged', Miliband argues, 'the autonomy of the state is likely to be substantial, to the point where, in conditions of intense class struggle and political instability, it may assume "Bonapartist" and authoritarian forms, and emancipate itself from constraining constitutional checks and controls.'[7] This is where we are now: a social stalemate presided over by a defensive state constantly seeking to regain the initiative by liberating itself from the last remaining constitutional and political constraints on arbitrary power.

The demise of Total Strategy has been registered by key branches of the state (e.g. Department of Constitutional Development and Planning) that have since begun to formulate an alternative. However, unlike Total Strategy, current reforms have not been presented at the outset as a coherent set of strategies. This probably means that state policy is not systematically organised around a single guiding principle, but rather around a few power axes that correspond with different modes of formative action. There are at least four main power axes: the coercive apparatuses governed by the logic of maintaining 'law and order'; the traditional apartheid organs epitomised by the ailing Department of Co-operation and Development; some of the independent bantustans which are resisting threats to their sovereignty (e.g. Bophutatswana); and the reformist apparatuses concerned with the restructuring of the political economy (e.g. the Department of Constitutional Development and Planning). The State Security Council seems to preside over the points of intersection of these axes, attempting to retain the internal coherence of the state as the pressure builds up on the outside.

Although relationships between these different power axes depend on a range of subjective and objective factors, they essentially revolve around the conflict between officials genuinely committed to a substantial restructuring of political institutions and economic systems, and those who remain reluctant to face the fact that — to use the words of a prominent National Party ideologue, Willie Esterhuyse — 'a point has been reached where a clearer articulation of long-term goals and more daring thought about possible models have become essential.'

This ideological hiatus within the state as a whole explains its incapacity to transcend decisively the catch-22 position in which it currently finds itself: on the one hand, it wants to end political instability in order to create the conditions conducive for the imposition of reforms from above, while on the other, escalating repression fuels political instability. To escape from the paralysis of this internal crisis, the repressive and reformist branches have become increasingly 'autonomous' in order to break free from the fetters that proscribe certain actions, e.g. the more liberal demands of big business. Whether this will issue in real reform will depend on whether the actions of the reformist and repressive apparatuses begin to complement rather than contradict one another. The capacity of black resistance organisations to oppose state policy directly affects the relationship between the reformist and repressive apparatuses: the more opposition there is, the more repression is used, which in turn destabilises conditions for reform; as opposition diminishes, repression becomes increasingly functional to reform, and so the resulting greater unity of purpose within the state reinforces the chances of success of reformist initiatives. The former possibility, however, is more probable given the course of events over the last few years.

State policy, therefore, is a curious mixture of reformist and repressive practices. The most coherent reforms, however, are clearly moving in a federalist direction. These include the granting of citizenship to most Africans, replacing Provincial Councils with a number of multi-racial Executive Committees at second-tier level, the introduction of Regional Services Councils at third-tier level, official acceptance that blacks need to be incorporated into 'higher levels of decision-making', and all the talk of creating a 'unified' South Africa that transcends the cardinal principle of bantustan sovereignty. As McCaul suggests, the state is dusting the covers of the Buthelezi Commission and allowing white political parties and Inkatha to move towards establishing 'KwaNatal', reinforces the view that important sections of the state are willing to allow current reforms to move in a federal direction.

The ingenuity of these reforms lies in the fact that instead of beginning by restructuring the central state, policy makers are focusing on the third and second tiers of government — the so-called 'bottom-up approach' which lies at the heart of the state's strategy of repressive reform. The proposed structure of these tiers corresponds to the technical and managerial requirements of metropolitan and regional space-economies that have turned out to be the unintended consequence of years of influx control, industrial dispersal policy and bantustan development. In other words, the state can establish these apparatuses under the depoliticised rubric of consociationalism in order to administer what the new generation of technocrats define as the 'realities of change'. These changes are tightly controlled by the Department of Constitutional Development and Planning which presides over the nexus between regional development policy, constitutional planning and labour movement and settlement controls. The pace and nature of the reforms will depend to a large extent on whether this Department, under the leadership of Chris Heunis, can gain the strategic initiative within the state as a whole.

The state cannot choose the terrain on which it intends to impose reforms. It will continue to do battle with mass-based movements of the oppressed majority that are calling for completely different solutions to the crisis. One of the most significant alternatives to reform from above along federal lines is the vision of national democracy discussed by Hudson. If we consider the squatter and anti-removal movements, bus, consumer rent and school boycotts, stayaways, strikes, housing struggles, and the electoral boycotts of the tricameral Parliament and BLAs, we are talking about the mobilisation of enormous numbers around demands for change that affect the entire structure of civil society. There is little doubt that the extra-state political organisations and trade unions command substantial support. However, it remains to be seen whether these organisations can translate mass support into a movement capable of overthrowing the apartheid state. We can expect the current waves of township protest, mass strikes and military attacks to continue into the future. The community organisations and trade unions have recently begun to work more closely together and as the levels of conflict escalate, these organisations have begun to articulate a more radical conception of a liberated society as they become more deeply entrenched in the black communities. There is insufficient evidence to support the view that the state will be able to put an end to this resistance by using a combination of force and co-option. Nevertheless, the consistent application of repressive regulations and the continued detention of political leaders may well serve to prevent the black political and trade union organisations from mounting an offensive capable of overthrowing the state in the near future. The ANC is probably correct when it claims that it will still take ten years before South Africa has an ANC government.

If the state is to succeed in its reform-from-above policies, it will have to regain the strategic initiative and assume control of the mechanisms of social change that currently lie beyond its grasp. However, the levels of repression that this will require and the costs involved may well leave behind a society too ruined and devastated to support the kind of change required to redress the political and economic injustices stemming from decades of white minority rule.

In the final analysis, the social stalemate is likely to persist for the foreseeable future, as neither reform from above nor revolution from below decisively succeeds in altering the power balance at the heart of South African politics.

Notes

1. Republic of South Africa, *Report of the Commission of Inquiry into Legislation Affecting the Utilisation of Manpower* (Government Printer, Pretoria, 1979).

2. Republic of South Africa, *Report of the Commission of Inquiry into Labour Legislation* (Government Printer, Pretoria, 1979).

3. Republic of South Africa, *Joint report of the Committee for Economic Affairs and the Constitutional Committee on Local and Regional Government Systems in the Republic of South Africa* (Government Printer, Pretoria, 1982).

4. KwaZulu Legislative Assembly, *The Buthelezi Commission: the requirements for stability and development in KwaZulu and Natal* (H. & H. Publications, Durban, 1982).

5. See D. Hindson, 'Orderly urbanisation and influx control: from territorial apartheid to regional spatial ordering in South Africa' in M. Addleson and R. Tomlinson, (eds), *Industrial decentralisation and the South African state* (Ravan Press, Johannesburg, 1987).

6. A. Gramsci, *Selections from prison notebooks* (Lawrence and Wishart, London, 1978), p. 276.

7. R. Miliband, *Class power and state power* (Verso, London, 1983), p. 68.

2

A Critical Analysis of the South African State's Reform Strategies in the 1980s

*William Cobbett, Daryl Glaser, Doug Hindson
and Mark Swilling**

Introduction

Since the late 1970s the apartheid state has faced a sustained and deepening crisis of legitimation.[1] This crisis has been exacerbated by the attempt and failure to implement the post-Soweto 'Total Straregy' reforms — reforms wich left the territorial and political basis of grand apartheid intact. Since the end of the short-lived boom of 1979–82, the crisis of political legitimacy has been amplified by the slide into economic depression and the scope for concessionary economic reforms has been drastically curtailed.

For some time, the state has been caught up with the immediate threat of escalating opposition in the townships, the symptoms of the deepening economic crisis and spreading international hostility to apartheid. However, while this has been happening, elements within the ruling groups, both inside and outside the state, have been attempting to map out a longer-term strategic offensive aimed at defusing political conflict and restructuring the economy. Faced with a shrinking material basis for concessionary economic reform and growing mobilisation behind the demand for the extension of political rights, the country's ruling groups have begun the search for political solutions to the crisis. The schemes now being formulated take as their starting point the ultimate inevitability of political incorporation of black people into a single national state in South Africa. They aim to meet this in ways that ensure that

*A version of this article was published in *South African Review Three*, edited by South African Research Services (Ravan Press, Johannesburg, 1986). The authors wish to thank Ravan Press for giving permission to re-publish this article.

19

real power remains in the hands of the ruling classes.

The move towards political reforms for black people has gone beyond the stage of discussion and planning in certain areas of policy. Already an important pillar of the emerging strategy has gained expression in local government measures passed in 1985.[2] However, much of what is planned has so far only appeared in general policy statements. It is also evident that important facets of the strategy are still in the stage of formulation or are deliberately being held back for the moment. The fluidity of political conditions in South Africa is such that state strategy is the subject-matter of open debate and contestation and is usually susceptible to official reconsideration and reformulation. Nevertheless, we believe it is possible to identify the major contours of an emerging strategy which has been pursued with increasing determination by reformers within the commanding heights of the state since late in 1984.

This offensive is significant in that it goes well beyond the policy package associated with the Wiehahn and Riekert Commission reports, the Koornhof Bills, the new constitution and the confederation of ethnic states — it goes beyond the 'Total Strategy' formulated by P.W. Botha in the late 1970s.[3] In contrast to these policies, it abandons the political and territorial premises of apartheid, though not necessarily those of race or ethnicity, and envisages the eventual reincorporation of the bantustans into a single national South African state.

The manner in which this will occur is by no means clear or decided. However, this process of political reintegration of the bantustans is intended to result ultimately in the reorganisation of the territorial basis of South Africa's economic and political system. Central to the reform strategy is the conception that the present provinces and bantustans will be superseded by metropolitan and regionally-based administrative structures through a process of merging, absorption and cross-cutting of present geographical boundaries. It is this geographic outcome of the intended reform strategy that has led us to describe the complex of evolving measures as the state's regional strategy.

The aim of this chapter is to describe, anticipate and critically analyse the outlines of the emerging regional strategy. Its three major components are new controls on labour movement and settlement, regional development policies (notably industrial decentralisation), and local and second-tier government reforms and corresponding constitutional changes. We examine each of these three components and their interconnections.

These changes are a ruling-class response to escalating township struggles, the determined resistance of squatter communities to removal, the dogged efforts of unions to unite migrants and locals, and mass rejection of the new constitution. They have also been shaped by the operation of glacial forces which have produced a concentration of industry and population in and around South Africa's metropolitan industrial and commercial centres. The development of metropolitan-centred and wider regional sub-economies over a decade and more, we argue, has eroded the primary division between the 'white' and bantustan areas on which apartheid was constructed, and has eroded the dualistic spatial framework on which South Africa's political economy was based.

A central issue taken up in the chapter is the debate over the possible construction of a federal system in South Africa. We examine major alternative conceptions of the basis of federalism — geographic and ethnic — and show how they correspond to or contradict other plans to divide South Africa into metropolitan and wider planning and administrative regions. This chapter closes with an assessment and critical analysis of the regional strategy.

Industrial decentralisation and influx control policies

Labour movement and settlement controls

The basic aim of the urbanisation strategy set out by the Riekert Commission Report in 1979 was to resolve the township crisis by giving recognition to the permanence of urban Africans and to secure their economic welfare by making urban jobs even more inaccessible to the relatively impoverished rural work-force. The Commission drew a sharp distinction between insiders — 'settled urban Africans' with residence rights under Section 10 of the Urban Areas Act, and outsiders — Africans domiciled in the bantustans with temporary employment contracts in the white cities. While insiders were to be allowed to move freely within the urban areas subject to the availability of housing and employment, far stricter controls were to be applied to outsiders wishing to enter these areas. The new system of influx control was to be exercised by fortified labour bureaux called assembly centres.[4] What distinguished this policy from traditional apartheid was official acknowledgement of the right of a (narrowly defined) group of African city residents to remain in white South Africa. This right did not, however, include access to the political realm. Urban Africans would only be allowed to exercise national political rights within their designated bantustans.

Thus, the recommendations set out in the Riekert Report were framed within the basic political and geographical premises of traditional apartheid: that the majority of Africans could be contained within the bantustans and that even those who resided in white South Africa could be treated as citizens of independent, or potentially independent, black states.

In the six years since the publication of the Riekert Commission Report and the acceptance of its recommendations by the government, there have been repeated attempts to implement this policy through drafting new legislation and reorganising the administrative machinery of labour control. All attempts thus far have failed to give effect to the basic Riekert strategy of dividing the African population into insiders and outsiders and implementing the legislation necessary to maintain this division.[5] The breakdown of the Riekert approach was due to struggles waged against it by squatters resisting removal; by international pressure groups; and also by big capitalists (for example, through the propaganda exercises of the Urban Foundation). The organisational efforts of the union movement, which served to unite long-distance migrants, commuters and urban dwellers, contributed to the erosion of 'insider-outsider' divisions rooted in the 'white' South African-bantustan divide.

Traditional labour movement controls in South Africa were designed to regulate the flow of African workers from rural to urban, and from bantustan to 'white' areas. However, the *de facto* incorporation of parts of bantustans into the suburban peripheries of various metropolitan areas such as Durban and Pretoria over the last 10-15 years, together with rapid and relatively unrestrained migration within bantustans from the rural areas to these metropolitan peripheries within bantustans, constitutes an important structural factor underlying recent policy changes.

The crucial consequence of these structural changes is the massive increase in the size of the cross-border commuter labour force and the relative decline in long-distance labour migration.[6] Despite their formal legal status, commuter populations have become effectively indistinguishable from urban insiders, even though they are located on the peripheries of the metropoles. Recent legislation has recognised this by allowing commuters to retain Section 10 rights. What these processes amount to is the occupational and residential stabilisation of the African working class in and around the metropolitan areas — the formation of what we call new regional proletariats in South Africa.

The recognition of regional labour markets and the possibility of creating these was considered in the White Paper on the Creation of Employment Opportunities (1984). It approved of the policy, which '. . . pays particular attention to the need for creating more employment opportunities and places greater emphasis on dealing with labour matters in a regional context'.[7] Similarly, the Department of Constitutional Development and Planning (DCDP) has expressed the view that labour supply areas should be identified with specific regions.[8] This clearly cuts right across the Riekert conception in which rights of labour mobility were to be restricted to urban insiders within 'white' South Africa.

The distance of Port Elizabeth, the East Rand and, most importantly, Cape Town from bantustans has rendered cross-border commuting non-viable in these areas (the Bronkhorstspruit township called Ekangala which is sited in KwaNdebele is changing this picture in the case of the East Rand). Even in these cases the state has proved incapable of preventing the permanent urbanisation of people who previously would have been prevented from entering these areas except as long-distance migrants. State attacks on squatters have given rise to explosive situations — in particular at Crossroads. The resultant struggles received considerable international coverage and forced the state to accept the permanence of large informally settled African populations in Soweto-by-the-Sea (Port Elizabeth) and Crossroads; to build new townships in 'white' South Africa (as at Khayelitsha); and to grant leasehold rights to established Western Cape African townships such as Nyanga and Guguletu. This shift of policy is expressed in the recent scrapping of the 'coloured labour preference' policy in the Western Cape, which reserved jobs in this area for coloured workers.

Organised industry's recently intensified campaign against influx control involves, in part, a concern to defuse the types of conflicts that have beset Crossroads. Capital also recognises that, in one form or another, 'urbanisation' is taking place in spite of influx control,[9] and this makes the political costs of the system appear even higher. Nor are the costs of influx control only political: at a time of recession and inflation the administrative costs, the rigidities that influx control introduces into the labour market and its impact on urban wages have appeared excessive.

No doubt some businessmen hope that the exposure of organised labour to competition from a regional surplus population will put pressure on urban wage rates and thus erode the gains made by the independent trade union movement in the years immediately following the Riekert Report. Certainly, capital has called for greater play of market forces, involving a wider, more flexible definition of 'urban' and 'urbanisation' policy in an effort to counter the advance of militant unionism.[10]

The fundamental flaw of the urbanisation strategy set out by the Riekert Commission of 1979 was that it failed to address the twin issues of the urbanisation of the bantustans and African rural impoverishment inside and outside the bantustans. The success of its strategy of strengthening influx controls and segregating urban African 'insiders' from 'outsiders' hinged above all on securing the economic viability and independence of the bantustans as well as the legitimacy of their political systems. In fact the six years since the Riekert Report appeared have witnessed a mounting crisis of bantustan legitimacy. This has occurred through the exposure of desperate rural poverty, a flight from the countryside to the urban bantustan areas and into the peripheries of the white-controlled cities, increased reliance of Africans resident in the bantustans on incomes earned in the white-controlled economy through migration and commuting, and heavy dependence of the bantustan states on the South African treasury.

The failure of the Riekert strategy has led both the state and capital to reconsider and reformulate urbanisation policy within a framework which rejects the premises and objectives of traditional apartheid, and to replace it with a concept of 'orderly urbanisation'. In essence, the emerging policy of orderly urbanisation involves a widening of the official definition of 'settled urban' Africans to embrace sections of the *de facto* urban African population in and around the cities. This new definition of the metropolitan areas is expressed in the recent Regional Services Council (RSC) Act which provides for the inclusion of African townships within bantustan areas abutting metropolitan areas into the administrative ambit of these new local government structures. This last provision is a decisive break with the notion of the bantustans constituting independent economic and political units which underpinned the Riekert strategy. The new definition of a metropolitan area includes urban and (potentially) quasi-urban settlements within parts of the bantustans — those within commuting distance of the industrial and commercial centres of the country. These areas are now being seen as falling within the sphere of the Regional Services Councils.

In another move which corresponds to the shift in policy, some metropolitan Development Boards have, for over two years, given 'administrative' Section 10 rights to workers resident in commuter areas if they previously held such rights in the prescribed urban area concerned. More recently, legislation has been passed which enables Africans to retain Section 10 rights after they have been moved from a prescribed area into a bantustan.[11] In this way the meaning of 'local' labour has changed.

The state's current urban policy, which acknowledges the inevitability of African urbanisation, but seeks to control it, has been called 'orderly urbanisation'. This policy does envisage the incorporation of some previously excluded sections of the African urban population into the administrative and financial ambit of the new metropolitan regions. However, its aim is far from allowing unregulated rural-urban migration and settlement: rather, it aims to limit the growth of established townships in the core metropolitan areas and encourage homeless township families as well as some squatter families to move to new residential areas, called deconcentration areas, which are being established on the peripheries of the metropoles. These residential areas are to be linked to deconcentrated industrial and commercial centres which are intended to provide employment opportunities for the local residents.

There are undoubtedly limits to the ability of the metropolitan centres to generate employment and revenue to cater for growing numbers of African workers and their families leaving the countryside for the squatter settlements on their peripheries. Thus, inevitably, new forms and mechanisms of exclusion are being adopted to complement and make possible those of incorporation of the urban population already discussed.

Central among these mechanisms are the Regional Services Councils, which are being developed as powerful administrative and fiscal centres. The proposed employment and turnover taxes which are intended to generate revenue for the Regional Services Councils are clearly designed to increase the cost and reduce the incentive to employ African workers in the established metropolitan centres and encourage their employment in deconcentration areas and development points. If successful, these fiscal measures will gradually replace the overtly racist and repressive direct influx and pass controls presently exercised by the labour bureaux.

Incorporation of new sections of the urban African population under the jurisdiction of these councils necessitates at the same time the exclusion of others. Thus, while some sections of the urban population will be targeted as beneficiaries of redistributive expenditures within the RSCs, others will undoubtedly be excluded. Thus, a crucial unresolved issue is the formulation of criteria of inclusion and exclusion.

At the minimum, sections of the population resident in the rural areas within the bantustans will undoubtedly be deemed to have no claim on the revenues generated and controlled by the RSCs. If these people are to be prevented from migrating to the urban areas, and thereby increasing urban unemployment, measures must be designed to control movement within the bantustans between their urban and rural districts. In some areas in which the tribal labour bureaux have collapsed, the Development Boards are already operating mobile recruitment and registration units which selectively allocate employment and exclude some rural workers from urban employment.[12] Recent work done in the South-central areas of Bophuthatswana has exposed an apparently systematic attempt to harass non-Tswana people in squatter areas, people who commute to employment in Pretoria or the industrial areas of Brits-Rosslyn.[13] These examples point to the types of ethnically based physical movement and settlement controls that may be expected from the new dispensation.

The evolving system of movement and settlement controls is linked to an emerging housing and employment strategy. The Riekert Commission insisted that the right to move from one urban area to another should be qualified by availability of approved housing and employment in the area to which a person wished to move, and restricted this right to Africans with existing permanent urban residence rights under Section 10 of the Urban Areas Act. These principles are being modified to meet the aims of orderly urbanisation. While approved housing and employment remain necessary qualifications for movement and settlement, the standard of housing and employment deemed acceptable is being lowered.

Housing controls within established metropolitan townships have been relaxed to some degree and provision for some new sites made, largely for commercial housing construction and sale. Most expansion is, however, planned in the new deconcentration areas. Some of these areas, such as Soshanguve near Pretoria, may be incorporated into the bantustans, while others, such as Khayelitsha near Cape Town and Soweto-by-the-Sea near Port Elizabeth, will remain outside the bantustans.

The employment-linked movement and settlement controls

26

advocated by the Riekert Commission are similarly to be modified in order to allow for the accommodation of larger numbers of Africans in and around the metropolitan areas. The essence of this strategy is to deregulate economic activities in the urban areas and thereby foster the growth of 'informal sector' employment. This will entail the removal of health and safety regulations and exemptions from wage determinations in designated industrial areas.

The concept of 'orderly urbanisation' thus seeks to replace bantustan policy with measures designed to regulate population movement and settlement within newly defined spatial units which are centred on the metropolitan areas and embrace neighbouring bantustans or parts of bantustans deemed to fall within their labour supply catchment areas. The objective of this policy is to link such residential areas to industrial deconcentration points not subject to the stringent wage and health regulations and high tax structure of the core metropolitan areas, and to promote the growth of employment and income through the fostering of informal-sector activities.

Industrial decentralisation

Industrial decentralisation policy has sought for decades to lend economic and political credibility to the bantustans, and was as such predicted on the geographical division between 'white' South Africa and bantustans. When, in 1975, the physical planning branches of the state divided South Africa into 44 planning regions deemed to be geographically and economically 'functional', they were still forced to take as a starting point the continued centrality of bantustan development and 'homeland' policy.

In 1981, however, Prime Minister Botha unveiled a regional development plan premissed on a division of South Africa into eight development regions — the boundaries of which cut across bantustan boundaries, as part of what the Buthelezi Commission termed the 'soft-borders' approach. This entailed the planning of economic development within coherent regions free of the constraints imposed by political borders. Its corollary was the creation of the 'multilateral' decision-making structure to co-ordinate development between South Africa and the Transkei-Bophuthatswana-Venda-Ciskei (TBVC) states; the Development Bank of Southern Africa; and the establishment of Regional Development Advisory Committees (RDACs) to identify planning priorities within regions.

27

The eight regions are more than mere abstractions superimposed on the map of South Africa. Rather, they correspond to changes in the geographical patterns of capital location and labour settlement that have been developing since the late 1960s. These changes are in part the unintended result of previous decentralisation policies which, more from practical necessity than philosophical conviction, promoted surburban industrial development in places such as Hammarsdale, Brits and Rosslyn. They are also the legacy of the classical apartheid policy of limiting African urban settlement in 'white' South Africa and promoting growth of towns behind bantustan boundaries.

Industrial development in South Africa's metropolitan centres has been seen as evidence for the validity of spatially dualistic theories. In the radical literature, bantustans are believed to be the product of a process of underdevelopment, upon which the expansion of capitalist centres of industrial activity was based. Generalisations of this kind take as their starting point the notion that bantustans occupy a uniform position within a national division of labour. In reality, the bantustans are highly differentiated entities — if in fact they can be regarded as constituting coherent entities at all in economic terms.[14]

In our view, the expansion of the metropolitan space-economy since the late 1960s has entailed two facets: on the one hand, an urbanisation process that has enmeshed and integrated growing sections of the bantustan populations into the metropolitan industrial working classes; and on the other, the dispersal (in part through state inducement) to the metropolitan peripheries (on both sides of the 'borders') of productive activities that are closely tied to the central metropolitan economy through specialisation, the industrial division of labour and monopolistic relationships of ownership and control. It is this fundamental economic dynamic that we call integrative dispersal. This concept allows us to grasp the role that bantustans, metropolitan expansion, urban concentration and regional economies play in a new emerging division of industry and labour.[15]

The new industrial decentralisation policy takes cognisance of these changes in two ways. In the first instance, it seeks to ensure that the growth of metropolitan regions is not unnecessarily limited, and attaches considerable importance to deconcentration points. '. . . [It] will largely be necessary to rely on a process of deconcentration through which the benefits of agglomeration in the metropolitan areas will be spread over a wider area without aggravating pressure on the metropoles'.[16] In encouraging these trends, the state is acknowledging and attempting to build upon previous patterns of capital dispersal. Secondly, it is now encourging the dispersal of capital to the high-incentive Industrial Development Points (selected outlying areas with the potential for further growth) rather than primarily to remote industrial points in bantustan hinterlands (five to eight points, according to Croeser). This policy bases itself on the notion of 'balancing growth poles', which designates certain towns with proven growth potential as 'growth points'. Their expansion and development is encouraged in order to draw investment away from the traditional highly industrialised metropolitan centres. The designation of certain major towns as growth points themselves (Bloemfontein, East London, Port Elizabeth) is intended to facilitate this process.

The new official emphasis on deconcentration is one of several measures designed to encourage private participation in the regional development programme. Certain capitals have responded to the upgraded decentralisation incentives, but sections of organised industry continue to view the state's decentralisation programme as an artificial attempt to redistribute resources between regions, rather than allowing the regions to compete freely against each other. Free inter-regional competition could, in the view of the Federated Chamber of Industries (FCI), '. . . lead to the revitalisation of the South African economy',[17] whereas induced dispersal is viewed as imposing intolerable costs on industries based in the metropolitan heartlands — namely the Pretoria–Witwatersrand–Vereeniging (PWV) area, Durban–Pinetown, Port Elizabeth–Uitenhage and Cape Town. Industrialists have recently expressed opposition to the indirect fiscal controls which the state now intends using to encourage industrial dispersal and to strengthen the tax base of the Regional Services Councils.

State planners intended the new approach to regional development to provide the basis for the future political and economic map of South Africa, whether defined in federal or confederal terms. As the Buthelezi Commission remarked, '. . . through its new approach to regional development the government is taking the economic route to power sharing rather than the political one, which is unacceptable to its constituency'.[18] While the planning bodies associated with the development regions, like the RDACs, may not themselves evolve into administrative units, they are seen as a testing ground for 'co-operative decision-making' and future constitutional arrangements. Clearly there is no inevitability that the precise boundaries drawn up in the 1982 regional development policy will ultimately become the geographical boundaries of a second tier of government. What is apparent, however, is that the bantustans/provinces are no longer seen by policy makers as an adequate basis for a second tier of government and therefore new intermediate regional governmental units will be established.

Constitutional restructuring

Apartheid's racially exclusive democracy was predicated on a system that reproduced cheap and differentiated labour power.[19] We have argued that this system has broken down and is being replaced by the formation of regional proletariats and sub-economies. The combined effect of this process and the crisis of political legitimation generated by the mounting national struggles for non-racial democracy created the conditions for the ruling classes to rethink the question of African political representation.

During the course of extensive debates, key reformist groups have begun to perceive the metropolitan and development regions as providing the most appropriate geographic foundations for the construction of new local and regional authorities evolving towards a possible federal system. What follows is an examination of the institutional forms that the state introduced in 1984–5, followed by a discussion of the debate over how these structures may be built into a post-apartheid federal system.

During the last half of 1984 and 1985 the state restructured the third and second tiers of government to conform with the procedure laid down in the 1983 President's Council (PC) reports. This 'consociational' structure was originally designed to underpin the tricameral parliamentary system and hence excluded Africans. However, sustained nationwide resistance to the Constitution and popular revolts in the townships during 1984–5 forced the state to incorporate Africans into the RSCs (the upper level of the third tier of government) in November 1984, and to restructure those departments which control African affairs at first-tier level. This abandonment of the PC's consociational/confederal vision[20] has put federalism on the agenda for a wide range of reformists.[21] These include English-speaking liberals, bantustan leaders, influential Afrikaner verligte academics, ideologues and politicians, organised industry and commerce, and the coloured and Indian parliamentary parties.

The third tier

The third tier is composed of local authorities which deal with 'own affairs' for each racial group and the RSCs which cater for 'general affairs' at metropolitan level.[22]

RSC representatives will not be elected, but nominated by all the local authorities in a given metropolitan region, including the black ones. Each local authority will have one representative for every 10 per cent (or part thereof) of RSC-provided services that it consumes. None will be allowed more than 50 per cent of the votes on the RSC and a two-thirds majority is required for a decision. Thus, those authorities which use the most services (that is, the white ones where industry is located) will have the greatest say.[23]

The RSCs will become the most powerful bodies involved in the provision of public goods at the local level. The most important local authority functions will be transferred to them. Although RSCs are based on local authorities as defined by the Group Areas Act, they are in fact a form of local government that will govern across Group Area boundaries. In any case, Group Areas will probably be substantially modified once the new Demarcation Board replaces the old Group Areas Board. The declining importance of traditional boundaries is evident in the proposed establishment of 'grey' Central Business Districts (CBDs) as well as in proposals to place industrial areas under the jurisdiction of black local authorities (*Star*, 5 June 1985) and to place some 'homeland' areas under the jurisdiction of the RSCs.

RSCs are designed to be self-financing to facilitate the withdrawal of the central state from the provision of public goods and services. To this end, a new tax system incorporated into the RSC Bill is designed to raise R1.3 billion in the four main metropolitan areas. There will be two taxes: a regional establishment levy which is a tax on turnover; and the regional services levy which is a tax on wages and salaries.

The new tax system elicited a howl of protest from organised commerce and industry. The Association of Chambers of Commerce (ASSOCOM), the FCI and the SA Property Owners Association criticised the system as 'totally unworkable' (*Business Day*, 9 May 1985). They argued that the new tax would increase the number of bankruptcies, exacerbate unemployment and fuel inflation, and they have tried to stall the Act in order to allow the Margo Commission on taxation to review it.[24]

Despite these strong objections, the state is determined to find a way to resolve the urban crisis and meet the demands of its moderate African allies. Minister of Co-operation and Development Gerrit Viljoen admitted in May 1985 that it had been a mistake in establishing black local authorities without providing them with a viable revenue base (*Financial Week*, 19–22 May 1985). The RSCs, which were first mooted in certain inner-state circles in 1981,[25] are designed to overcome this weakness by accomplishing (at least in theory) three objectives:

(1) the substantial redistribution of resources from white to black areas. Instead of increasing rent and service charges to finance urban renewal, oppressed communities will in fact be paying for urban upgrading indirectly because the new taxes will increase consumer prices;

(2) the facilitation of the withdrawal of the central state from the provision of public services and the deflection of national political demands down to the local level;

(3) the tax on turnover and labour costs is intended to encourage decentralisation of economic activity from the metropolitan areas.

The redistributive and legitimising role of the RSCs is unlikely to succeed in the near future for three reasons:

(1) the third tier is in ruins in the African townships. In 1983, 34 black local authorities were introduced and by the end of 1984 there were meant to be 104. By April 1985 there were only three still functioning (*Rand Daily Mail*, 16 March 1985) as a result of mass resistance. Although this is unlikely to prevent redistribution, it will substantially undermine the legitimacy of the RSCs.

(2) the RSCs are extremely undemocratic, with the balance of power weighted in favour of big business and the petty bourgeoisie because voting capacity depends on 'user strength'. The democratic principle of proportional representation is totally absent, leaving the large impoverished communities politically powerless.

(3) the economic crisis currently facing the state and the debates between monetarists and redistributionists will continue to constrain supply of public services and hence the management of capitalist urban reproduction.

The second tier

In May 1985 the state announced that provincial councils would be scrapped as they subsequently were a year later. They will be replaced by strong executive and administrative committees appointed by the state president. They are fully multi-racial and deal only with 'general affairs'.

Although there are four regional Executive Committees (as they are now called), there is little doubt that four or five more will be created, based on the eight (now nine) development regions. A substantial planning infrastructure already exists on this level, including the RDACs, Regional Liaison Committees for those regions that include independent bantustans, the planning branch of the DCDP, and the Development Boards.

Most provincial council functions will be transferred to the first and third tiers, and the second tier will in the near future take charge of local government, regional development, labour movement controls and transport. Significantly, the FCIs demand that the second tier be given substantial powers to co-ordinate regional development strategies across bantustan boundaries within a federal framework has been granted.[26]

The Nata-'KwaZulu region is the most advanced as far as the politics of the second tier in an emerging federal order is concerned. Reformers of all persuasions, including elements in the National Party (NP) and the state, have suggested in recent months that the Buthelezi Commission and the Lombard Report[27] be used as a framework for consolidating Natal and KwaZulu into a single regional unit. In May 1985 the Cabinet considered a plan to implement this. It would involve consolidating KwaZulu into an area stretching from KwaMashu outside Durban to the Mozambique border, which would contain 'white' towns like Empangeni, Eshowe and Richards Bay. Natal would then stretch from the north of Durban and include the south coast and East Griqualand. In keeping with the Buthelezi Commission, the two parts would be governed by a central federal authority. In June 1985 the first step was taken when the New Republic Party and NP representatives in the Natal Provincial Council began to formulate a framework for establishing a statutory body to deal with 'general affairs' for Natal-KwaZulu as a whole, and since then an all-party 'indaba' has convened to hammer out a regional solution for Natal-KwaZulu.

The Buthelezi Commission called for a federal legislative

authority for all races in Natal-KwaZulu to be elected on a one person, one vote basis with proportional representation. The multi-racial executive should be co-chaired by the provincial administrator and KwaZulu Chief Minister Gatsha Buthelezi. Other recommendations were: a minority veto for 10 per cent of the legislature; that legislation should be tested by the courts; a Bill of Rights; and minimum group representation. Although these proposals were rejected by Finance Minister Owen Horwood in 1982, in May 1985 Co-operation and Development Minister Viljoen announced in Parliament that the Buthelezi Commission was in line with President P.W. Botha's policy that the only alternative to the complicated task of further consolidating KwaZulu was to recognise that Natal and KwaZulu are economically and hence politically interdependent (*Star*, June 1985). This announcement was followed by a meeting between P.W. Botha and Buthelezi which the press interpreted as another step towards the implementation of a regional federal solution for Natal-KwaZulu (*Sunday Times*, 19 May 1985).

Although the new second-tier system centralises power in the hands of the DCDP, this is designed to facilitate the transition to multi-racial regional authorities that cut across bantustan boundaries in the long run. The politicised nature of the old provincial councils (with the Transvaal moving increasingly to the right), would have prevented a technocratic top-down transition to multi-racial regional authorities in the manner envisaged by the Buthelezi Commission and Lombard Report. The fact that they have extensive powers suggests that the regions will be able to develop according to regionally specific economic, political and ideological conditions.

The first tier

There is a new consensus that 'no real progress in stabilising and normalising relations between people within South Africa or between South Africa and other countries can be made unless legal racial discrimination is removed in the political institutions of this country'. The future 'legitimacy of the Republic of South Africa both internally and externally depends on this issue'.[28] Stoffel van der Merwe, National Party MP and ideologue, wrote in a pamphlet approved by P.W. Botha that 'Now, in 1985, we have reached a stage where it [the national convention] can be postponed no longer[29].'

The state has not yet presented a coherent outline of what a future first tier will look like. Instead, the special Cabinet committee formed in February 1983 to investigate the 'urban black problem' established a multi-party negotiating forum in January 1985 and renamed the National Statutory Council in January 1986. This was meant to discuss with 'black leaders' ways to include Africans in 'higher levels of decision-making'. Commonly referred to as a 'mini-national convention', the forum generated a spate of declarations of intent, as various ruling-group interests tried to force the state to give it a clear federalist agenda. However, much to Buthelezi's chagrin, the state has refused to issue a declaration of intent, on the grounds that negotiations should remain open-ended. Instead, the state has introduced a range of reforms used by officials to demonstrate the state's good intentions. These include the repeal of the sex laws, the removal of the ban on multi-racial political parties, the announced moratorium on removals (subsequently broken), the repeal of the pass laws in June 1986, moves to deracialise CBDs and promises to incorporate blacks into higher forms of decision-making.

Stoffel van der Merwe's NP pamphlet maps out a corporate federal structure for the central state that would involve establishing a Black Assembly to deal with African 'own affairs' for 'non-homeland' Africans. This would then link up to a supra-parliamentary co-ordinating organ made up of representatives from the Black Assembly, the tricameral Parliament, and independent bantustan states. In this way the dual 'own affairs' structure would be replicated on all three tiers, leaving the NP's white power base intact — a model that P.W. Botha calls 'co-operative coexistence'. This has been interpreted by some observers as the first step towards a geographic federation (*Star*, 19 May 1985).

The regional or geographic federal alternative proposed by the Progressive Federal Party, the Labour Party, Inkatha and big business is critical of the racial federal model because it concentrates power in the central state. They call for the transfer of substantial power to democratically elected regional and local federal authorities, with KwaZulu/Natal as the first laboratory for a future geographic federation. This implies that the future form of the central state should be designed only after the lower tiers have been established.

In the mean time, powerful reformers in the state have substantially modified key central-state institutions. The Cabinet reshuffle in mid-1985 saw a significant shift of institutional power. The state under 'grand apartheid' controlled every aspect of African life in 'white' South Africa through a separate department (Native Affairs through to the present Department of Co-operation and Development — DCD) and by way of the 'homeland' states in 'black' South Africa.

The DCD is now virtually defunct. The following functions have been transferred to other departments over the last 18 months: African education to the Department of Education and Training, labour bureaux to the Department of Manpower, commissioners' courts to the Department of Justice, and relations with 'homelands' to the Department of Foreign Affairs. In the Cabinet reshuffle, responsibility for black local government and the Development Boards was transferred to the DCDP. This leaves the DCD in charge of trust land and development aid for the non-independent bantustans. The DCDP now controls the following: all local authorities and RSCs through the multi-racial Council for the Co-ordination of Local Government Affairs (CCLGA); the second tier which includes the new Regional Executive Committee, RDACs, Regional Liaison Committees, and significantly, the bureaucratic hierarchies that were once Development Boards and which have now been transferred to the Regional Executive Committees;[30] liaison with the bantustans through the multilateral co-ordinating bodies; 'homeland' consolidation; and group areas.

This Bonapartist concentration of power in the DCDP clears the way for a process of reconstruction that may have far-reaching implications for the federalist momentum. The fact that it works closely with capital in the RDACs, with the bantustans in the multilateral structures and with moderate urban Africans in the CCLGA means that it will be directly exposed to the combined demand of these interests for a more coherent geographic federation to ease South Africa out of the present interregnum.

The federalism debate

After 1979, reformers inside the state began to recognise that the Verwoerdian vision of parcelling South Africa up into independent ethnic states was unrealistic.[31] Those institutional pillars of apartheid, the bantustans, could not achieve either economic autonomy or political legitimacy. Their reintegration into a common economic planning and political framework was increasingly seen as inevitable, notwithstanding the granting of 'independence' to Venda in 1979 and Ciskei in 1981.

The concept of federalism has a long history in the English-speaking reformist community.[32] The Progressive Party advocated a federal formula as far back as 1962, following the recommendations of its internal Molteno Commission. The United Party adopted a federal programme in 1972, and its successor, the New Republic Party, has advocated a 'federal-confederal' option for South Africa.[33]

Both parties view African urbanisation as inevitable, and accept the corollary that sections of the African population must eventually be politically accommodated within central-state political institutions.

Set up by the KwaZulu legislative assembly, the 1982 Buthelezi Commission received strong support from English-speaking liberals in Natal. It argued for a single geographically based federal administration for Natal and KwaZulu.[34] The report hinted that a national federal system, in which Natal and KwaZulu together made up one of a number of regional units, provided a long-term solution to South Africa's problem of national political representation.[35]

Before the 1985 parliamentary session, the government was publicly committed to establishing a confederal system which required bantustan leaders to accept independence and then enter into an 'international' agreement linking them to South Africa. Some bantustan leaders — for example, Sebe of the Ciskei and Mphephu of Venda — supported the government's ethnic confederal blueprint and resisted the idea of geographical federation in which bantustans would lose their 'independence'.[36]

Other bantustans refused independence (KwaZulu, Lebowa, Kangwane, Gazankulu and Qwaqwa and more recently KwaNdebele), and two 'independent' bantustans (Transkei and Bophuthatswana) openly rejected Pretoria's schemes for confederation. In July 1983, the leaders of these bantustans, excluding Bophuthatswana, issued a declaration of intent in which they stated that, in the event of their opting for a constitutional arrangement, they would structure it on a regional non-racial and non-ethnic basis.[37]

There is considerable ferment among Afrikaner verligte reformers, both within and outside of the National Party (*Financial Mail*, 23 November 1984; 14 June 1985). Van der Merwe's pamphlet acknowledges that grand apartheid has met with insuperable problems and enumerates several new possibilities:

> The national states might obtain powers over some of the areas outside their borders; local authorities might be given considerably wider powers; local authorities might be linked together in authoritative structures encompassing larger areas; new bodies comparable to the white provincial councils might be established; a national assembly of black people outside the national states might be brought into being; some of these bodies might be involved in decision-making at the highest level in conjunction with the South African parliament and the governments of the national and possibly even the independent states.[38]

Two key features are present here: a search for means of incorporating Africans within central-state institutions, and retention of race or ethnic identity as the basis for political representation. This may lead to what has been termed a consociational federal option, in which membership of racial or ethnic group, rather than territorial location, defines the composition of a federating unit.

Another model has been proposed in reports sponsored by organised industry and commerce (notably ASSOCOM and the Sugar Association).[39] They call for a federation based on geographically rather than racially or ethnically defined units. ASSOCOM's report rejects corporate federalism on the grounds that it will be seen to be racist and calls instead for a geographic federation which can protect minority-group rights while simultaneously creating a single national state.

Federalism is seen by the ruling groups as resolving the problem of incorporating Africans politically, while retaining and strengthening a capitalist system. Both conceptions of federalism, consociational and geographic, have in common two basic features: the view that 'economic freedom and the private enterprise ethic — as well as the norms with which they are associated — are best entrenched in a future political system embodying the principles of federalism or confederalism';[40] and the belief that federalism is preferable to both apartheid and a majoritarian unitary state, because it allows for the creation of a new nation-state which grants political rights to all its subjects while 'protecting minorities'.

In fact, concern for group rights masks more fundamental fears. Firstly, that a state dominated by a black majority could begin building socialism, or at least impose a welfare state system that entails 'confiscatory taxation',[41] fiscal indiscipline, high minimum wages and nationalisation. (The latter is certainly implied in the Freedom Charter.) Secondly, the too rapid advancement of an inexperienced black elite into senior positions in the civil service, government and business could lead to managerial inefficiency and administrative 'chaos'.[42] The third fear is that ethnic conflicts under majority rule (including violence directed at whites) could lead to economic and political breakdown.

Proponents of federalism argue that the only way to prevent a black majoritarian state imposing socialism or a welfare state from above is to establish relatively autonomous local and regional political entities. These would hold sovereign power over limited coercive apparatuses and economic policies, fragmenting a national majority regionally. Federalism also lends itself to a system of institutional checks and balances, both regionally and within the central state. These include structures like an independent federal reserve bank, separate legislative houses, a separate legislature, executive and judiciary. Further entrenched constitutional provisions could protect freedom of contract, the status of the currency, minority veto rights, the rights to property, and so on. A federal system would thus limit any one group's access to political power.

A central government operating according to these principles might for example have to:

— accept unpopular monetary measures imposed by the (ostensibly apolitical) federal reserve bank; or
— secure acceptance of legislation from two legislative houses; or
— accept limits on its power to impose its policies on particular regions; or
— allow the constitutionality of its policies to be tested by an independent judiciary.

This is what Lombard and Du Pisenie call 'polycentrism'. Such 'division of sovereignty'[43] is a prescription for minimal or limited government, which leaves the state incapable of affecting radical changes. Reformers in the ruling groups hope a federal system would place the central state above political conflict, making it difficult to mobilise nation-wide forces around demands with national scope. A federal state would by default leave intact the foundations of the economy and relations of production, and expose only marginal or localised elements of the economic system to modification.

The meaning of 'group rights' and the theory of ethnic pluralism thus becomes apparent. The apartheid legacy of 'ethnicity' is now being used by many reformers as a rationale for a federal system which could provide the basis for a reconstituted capitalist political economy. Ethnicity need not necessarily be legally entrenched, because apartheid has ensured that racial and ethnic groups are already geographically separate.

The call for some kind of federal solution is rapidly becoming the cornerstone of consensus among those favouring a reformist solution in South Africa.

A critical analysis of regional federalism

This chapter has not attempted to provide a holistic analysis of the current period of crisis and restructuring in South Africa. Such an analysis would have required an examination of a number of developments that we have left out of our account, or have only superficially touched upon — namely, the economic stagnation of the 1970s and 1980s; the current recession; the resurgence of various forms of oppositional politics; the 1984–6 township rebellion, culminating in two states of emergency; and numerous other factors that have combined to make the present conjuncture extremely fluid and unpredictable.

We have argued that a consensus has emerged within the reformist elite about the need to implement changes that go well beyond the 'Total Strategy' initiatives of the late 1970s and early 1980s. In part this further metamorphosis of the reform process is the outcome of increasingly intense conflict between the regime and its opponents — in particular its failure to establish legitimacy for the new black local authorities and the tricameral Parliament and more recently, its inability to curb the wave of popular demonstrations, boycotts, strikes and other civil disturbances that began early in 1984. It was these events which forced the government to include Africans in the RSCs, to re-examine the question of African political participation in the central state, and to consider substantial modifications to its influx control policies.

However, we also argue that the necessity for and tendency of state restructuring in these areas can only be fully understood in relation to changes in South Africa's reproductive economy. By this we mean the development of new patterns of capital and labour location, in particular the dispersal of capital from metropolitan heartlands to metropolitan peripheries and other regions; the enmeshing of certain bantustan labour supply areas into the process of metropolitan urbanisation; and the crystallisation of regional economies and regional proletariats. These processes, which have drained of meaning the conventional dichotomies of bantustan-white South Africa and urban-rural, have informed thinking about the RSC concept as well as debates around second-tier regional structures in a future federation. They have also directly shaped the regional development strategies. Finally, they have influenced aspects of the emerging policy of 'orderly urbanisation'.

We have shown, briefly, how the devolution of power, the partial 'de-racialisation' of administration and the proposed federalist system are being developed as an alternative to 'majoritarianism' and all that the ruling groups fear would accompany majority rule: bureaucratic breakdown, social disruption, intercommunal conflict, welfare statism, socialism. The more immediate purpose of these initiatives is to help the state reimpose 'law and order', secure a degree of popular quiescence and regain control of the pace and direction of political developments. The 'reforms' are consciously designed to arrest, rather than promote, rapid and fundamental change. They are therefore unlikely to satisfy crucial popular demands.

The reform initiatives will face popular pressure for rational economic planning to reduce unemployment and inflation and for improved provision of basic services. The restructuring process involves a curious combination of 'free market' and 'redistributive' policies. On the one hand, the central state, confronted by a fiscal crisis and committed to a monetarist economic programme, is cutting back its role in the provision of welfare services (as, for example, in the case of bread and transport subsidies). At the same time, the state is confronted by a political crisis in the urban areas, and recognises that it has to improve the quality of life of black townships in order to restore stability there. Its solution is to force the RSCs to subsidise expenditures in the townships through their payroll and turnover levies.

The logic seems to be three-fold. First of all, such a programme (theoretically) allows the central state to insulate itself from

41

competition over the allocation of resources, thereby localising these conflicts. Secondly, devolution of fiscal responsibility forces capitalists to choose between subsidising metropolitan services or relocating their investments to decentralisation growth points. In other words, business men cannot have it both ways: if they insist upon the desirability of urbanisation, they must be willing to pay for it.

Finally, since the total resources available for redistribution remain limited, especially in a period of economic stagnation, it is impossible for the state to satisfy every locality's claims on social resources. Given that this is so, it makes sense for the central state to allow local and metropolitan governments to rely on their own fiscal resources, however unequal these may be. The likely result is increased inequality between metropolitan regions. To offset this (and its potentially explosive political consequences in areas like the Eastern Cape) the state is relying on persuading capital to relocate to less developed regions in response to incentives offered there. These incentives form part of a decentralisation programme that is itself expensive, at least in the short to medium term.

Whether these various objectives — central state withdrawal, metropolitan upgrading and regional development — can be accomplished simultaneously, especially in a period of low economic growth, remains very doubtful. Consider the dilemma facing the metropolitan authorities. Since the RSCs would enjoy a minimum of financial support from the central state, the only way they could hope to deliver adequate services to the black urban areas would be by raising metropolitan taxes and levies beyond the levels presently envisaged. If they raise taxes beyond a certain point, they could provoke either a capital flight to regions offering better incentives, or else an investment slowdown that would further reduce economic growth in the economy as a whole.

If they choose to spend beyond their means the RSCs could generate a series of local fiscal crises, forcing the central state to bail out troubled councils in an *ad hoc* way. The state's overall borrowing requirements would have to expand (whether it is the central state or the metropolitan authority that does the borrowing), and this in turn could swell the national debt, create inflationary difficulties or force interest rates to rise. The alternative would be to cut back on the provision of services, or increase rents and service charges in the black townships. However, both these measures would have

42

dire political consequences, particularly in the light of the current rent boycott that is affecting 54 townships countrywide.

If the RSCs cannot provide goods on a scale that meets the increasingly insistent demands of poor and working people in the urban areas, they could be forced into a game of 'divide and rule', playing off some recipients of social goods against others. With considerably more goods available for distribution in black townships than in the past, metropolitan authorities could, in some cases, play such a game quite effectively. They — and the central state — would thus acquire new resources of social control.

Faced by increasingly sophisticated techniques of co-option, popular organisations will have to rethink their own tactical and strategic responses. Under these circumstances it will be more important than ever to reiterate the demand for democratically determined social welfare priorities, and for services that address the needs of the poorest regions and social strata within regions. These demands will have to be backed up by an increasingly articulate call for strategies to promote economic recovery in ways that are not detrimental to the interests of the working class.

The reforms cannot satisfy popular demands for democratic participation in the reform process. Political restructuring is proceeding in a top-down managerial way, with at best a small circle of influential reformers and black collaborators being drawn into decision-making. The public language of ruling-group reformers is framed in the imagery of the free market economy, technocratic rationality, devolution of power, consensus and consultation. Its private agenda — where such an agenda exists — is shrouded in deliberate secrecy. Public deception is central to the timing and delivery of reforms; it is seen as crucial to defusing opposition from both the right and the left. If it should fail to contain popular opposition effectively, the state is more ready than ever to resort to repression. It seeks reform, but as a precondition for that it demands tight control.

Reformers will maintain constant vigilance against all political initiatives not amenable to state manipulation. They are determined to force others to conform to their own plans. This requires that they negotiate only from a 'position of strength' — which means ensuring the weakness of community organisations, trade unions and political groupings seeking fundamental change through grass roots struggle. Deception and repression are thus the constant companions of 'reform'.

Reformers in the state cannot satisfy popular demands for

43

democratic political representation. While accompanied by talk about the 'devolution' of power, the reorganisation of the state system involves a combination of centralising and decentralising tendencies. Crucial functions — for example, security, the formulation of the reform programme, and foreign policy — are being concentrated in executive organs insulated from electoral pressures and public scrutiny. These organs include the Office of the President, top officials in a few key departments (like Constitutional Development and Planning), and the State Security Council. These are the commanding heights of the authoritarian-reformist state that the Botha leadership has set in place.

At the same time, second- and third-tier structures will be given genuine powers, but mainly (it seems at this stage) of an administrative kind. Thus, for example, while the RSCs are likely to command considerable resources, their sole function will be the management of certain kinds of 'hard' services at the metropolitan level. At the same time an attempt is deliberately being made to remove the RSCs from the field of political contestation, to present them instead in a neutral, technical visage. They will also be predicated on indirect, rather than direct, representation and on the over-representation of wealthier municipalities. Devolution of power along these lines does not involve real democratisation.

The final demand that the 'reforms' cannot satisfy is the demand for national democratic rights — for the effective transfer of sovereignty to the representatives of the majority of South Africans. The emerging federal framework is intended to prevent national democratic forces from mobilising against the central state and, should they come to control that state, it is designed to prevent them from effectively using it to bring about radical social and economic changes.

The ideological rationale for anti-majoritarian federalism lies in the argument that minority rights need to be protected from 'majority domination': and, indeed one can readily concede that minorities should have 'rights' — rights to freedom of speech, press, association, religion, petition, to practise their own culture, to equal political rights, and to safeguard their material well-being. However, minorities do not have the 'right' to entrench their political and economic privileges at the expense of the majority.

In South Africa the right of the majority to rule — whatever form that rule may take — remains non-negotiable. This is the basic right demanded in the Freedom Charter and other popular manifestoes, and is implicit in the programme of the workers' movement.

Conclusion

The fate of the 'reform' process is extremely uncertain. Whether or not it gains any substance will depend on the outcome of struggles within the ruling party and in reformist circles; it will also depend on struggles between reformists and their opponents both on the right and in the popular movements; finally, it will depend on the state of the economy. Yet it would be wrong to dismiss the restructuring process as simply cosmetic. It could prove real enough to reshape, in important ways, the terrain upon which struggles over fundamental change are being played out.

The 'reforms' could have a considerable impact on, for example, the resources available for the co-option of sections of the black population. They could also affect the international saleablity of South Africa's constitutional order. These are but two of the many areas in which their influence could be felt. How far the restructuring process 'succeeds' will depend on how seriously it is taken by its opponents. To dismiss the 'reforms' in advance as illusory or unworkable, or to suppress discussion of their content and direction, would automatically enhance their effectiveness as weapons in the hands of the ruling groups.

The claim that the 'reforms' are cosmetic is likely to carry less analytical and moral force as time goes by. A much more powerful criticism would be one that exposes the real motives behind the 'reforms', decodes the discourse and shows, concretely, why — and where — they are unlikely to satisfy key popular demands. We have commenced, but by no means completed, this task. We should not assume, however, that the entire 'reform' process is so pervaded with repression and authoritarianism, or that it so uniformly expresses the will of the ruling class and the imperatives of class domination, or that it is so immutable, that some of its elements are not open to transformation into something more democratic and into something capable of advancing certain popular objectives.

The 'reforms' are complex and varied: some offer more spaces and opportunities than others. We need to seriously examine these spaces and opportunities, both to assess their importance to short- and medium-term strategy, and in order to determine what elements, if any, can be built upon in the struggle for a radically different order.[44]

If we accept that the process of building democratic structures must begin in the here and now, and that certain progressive reforms are possible prior to the achievement of full democratic rights, then we must ask whether, and to what extent, the reform process is generating resources and openings that can be utilised as a part of a 'politics of transformation'.[45] Can some of the emerging structures be utilised by organisations seeking to institutionalise genuinely democratic practices? Can they be used to secure material concessions that in turn could help to bolster the credibility and power of those organisations?

It may be wrong to adopt a principled but purely rejectionist response, in advance, to everything that the restructuring process delivers: what is needed instead is the capacity to buttress rejection with rigorous critical analysis, and to modify rejection, where necessary, with a careful assessment of new strategic opportunities.

Postscript

The foregoing chapter was completed in mid-1985, and although its basic argument is still valid, there have been some important subsequent developments that warrant discussion.

As far as labour movement and settlement controls are concerned, the state has moved rapidly to consolidate and clarify the meaning of 'orderly urbanisation'. In August 1985, the President's Council published a report entitled *Report of the Committee for Constitutional Affairs on an urbanisation strategy for the Republic of South Africa*. This was followed by the presentation to Parliament in April 1986 of a White Paper entitled 'An urbanisation strategy for the Republic of South Africa'. These key policy documents led finally to the scrapping of the pass laws in terms of the Abolition of Influx Control Bill in June 1986. The PC Report, White Paper, subsequent legislation and recent speeches by state officials have made it clear what officials mean when they say influx control is being replaced by 'orderly urbanisation'.

Influx control relied primarily on documentary controls and secondarily on access to housing and employment (in terms of the Riekert reforms) to regulate the movement and settlement of Africans. The policy of orderly urbanisation intends to replace this direct form of coercive control with new indirect controls over access to land, services and housing. The aim is to prevent Africans settling in the metropolitan heartlands by using South Africa's stringent vagrancy, slum clearance and housing laws. Since the repeal of the pass laws, the state has used these laws to move against several well-known squatter camps (e.g. Crossroads in Cape Town, Langa in

Uitenhage, Soweto-by-the-Sea in Port Elizabeth and Duncan Village in East London). The objective is to destroy the squatter settlements because they do not constitute what the White Paper called 'approved accommodation' and force the residents into either formal townships where they are told to rebuild their shacks in controlled site-and-service schemes, or alternatively to move into regulated (i.e. approved but unserviced) squatter areas on the very peripheries of the metropolitan areas. This relocation and dispersal of squatter areas is now being coupled to a move to privatise housing in the formal townships, thus forcing out the poorer urban residents and cultivating a middle stratum of employed houseowners.

In short, at least three types of urban settlement are being created to prepare the way for the predicted influx into the metropolitan areas: formal inner townships for the relatively privileged houseowner; controlled site-and-service schemes for the slightly less well-off residents located alongside the formal townships and on the metropolitan peripheries; and regulated squatter areas for the most impoverished urban dwellers who can serve as important reserve armies of labour.

As always, the intentions of state policy are always mediated by South Africa's intense social conflicts. Consequently, to realise its objectives, the state has to do battle with highly organised squatter and housing movements that will require very high levels of repression if they are to be prevented from thwarting government policies. This has already served to escalate township conflict and triggered off a nation-wide rent strike that is effectively immobilising the new urban policy before it has even got off the ground. However, since the 1986 State of Emergency was declared in June, two squatter areas have already been smashed, i.e. Langa and Crossroads. Nevertheless, it remains to be seen whether the organised black communities are strong enough to resist the implementation of 'orderly urbanisation' on a national scale.

As far as constitutional restructuring is concerned, a number of important developments have taken place. Firstly, the Provincial Councils were scrapped in May-June and replaced with appointed Executive Committees (ECs). Although there are still four ECs, state officials admitted that more will be created in the future, thus reinforcing the view that in future these executive organs of second-tier government will be based on the development regions. Secondly, the Development Boards were disbanded when the pass laws were scrapped in June and the 12,000 bureaucrats that previously staffed the Boards put under the authority of the ECs. Thirdly, the government has passed enabling legislation that will allow the KwaZulu-Natal initiative being led by Inkhata to go ahead to form a politically integrated federal authority for the entire KwaZulu-Natal region.

Fourthly, despite widespread opposition from business, parliamentary and extra-state organisations, the state is proceeding with the RSCs. However, due to complex bureaucratic problems relating to the specific mechanics of these structures, the state has repeatedly delayed installing them. Nevertheless, the central Witwatersrand and the Eastern Cape region centred around Port Elizabeth have been chosen as the first regions to get RSCs. There is no evidence, however, that the state has made any progress overcoming the twin problems of political illegitimacy and fiscal unviability that the proposed RSCs are going to face.

Finally, the state seems to have made very little progress at central-government level. The renaming of the National Forum as the National Statutory Council in 1986 and as the National Council in 1987 has not, despite many claims by state officials to the contrary, elicited any black support. Even Gatsha Buthelezi has made the release of Nelson Mandela a precondition for participating in the Council. Nevertheless, Cabinet Ministers continue to drop hints about the creation of an elected Black Assembly linked in some way to a supra-parliamentary 'Council of State' made up of bantustan leaders, urban black representatives and the tricameral Parliament. How this clumsy representative monstrosity will work, however, has never been revealed — probably because no one in the state knows the answer. It is significant, however, that the National Council Bill that was considered but not passed by Parliament in 1987, recommended that the National Council be elected by constituencies defined in terms of the nine development regions.

In short, despite the imposition of two States of Emergency in 1985 and 1986, the state has been unable to seize the strategic initiative it requires to make its reform policies work. Instead, the coercive branches of the state, and in particular the State Security Council controlled by the military, have become increasingly dominant as state action degenerates into defensive initiatives designed to retain control of South Africa's volatile social forces. As repression has replaced reform as the primary activity of the state, the state has lost important allies in the private sector, in the international community and even amongst its moderate black supporters. In the final analysis, as the crisis deepens, it becomes increasingly unlikely that reforms can succeed, nor is it likely that sheer brute force will restore

the state's authority in a way conducive for reforms to be implemented from above. In the meantime, the calls for federal solutions
from ruling-group reformers located outside the state have reached
new levels of intensity. However, even these elements acknowledge
that no solution can work without a ceasefire as the prelude to genuine
negotiations with the true representatives of the black majority.

Mark Swilling

Notes

1. See, for example, J.S. Saul and S. Gelb, *The crisis in South Africa. Class
defence, class revolution* (Monthly Review Press, New York, 1981); G. Moss,
'Total Strategy', *Work in Progress*, II, 1980; D. O'Meara, 'Muldergate and the
politics of Afrikaner nationalism', *Work in Progress*, no. 22, 1982; D. Glaser,
'The state, the market and the crisis', *Work in Progress*, no. 34, 1984, pp. 32-8.
2. See the Regional Services Councils Act no. 109 of 1985.
3. Commission of Inquiry into Legislation Affecting the Utilisation
of Manpower, RP 32/1970 (Riekert Commission); and Commission of
Inquiry into Labour Legislation, RP 47/1979 (Wiehahn Commission).
4. D.C. Hindson, 'The role of the labour bureaux in South Africa:
a critique of the Riekert Commission Report' in D. C. Hindson (ed.), *Working papers in Southern African studies volume 3* (Ravan Press, Johannesburg,
1983), pp. 149-73.
5. D.C. Hindson and M. Lacey, 'Influx control and labour allocation: policy and practice since the Riekert Commission' in South African
Research Services, *South African Review One* (Ravan Press, Johannesburg,
1983), pp. 97-113.
6. See BENBO, *Statistical survey of black development* (1982), part 1, tables
24 and 26.
7. White Paper on *A strategy for the creation of employment opportunities in
the Republic of South Africa*, 11 (2.32) (1984).
8. Department of Constitutional Development and Planning, submis-
sion to the National Regional Development Advisory Council (NRDAC),
2 August 1984 (c).
9. G. Relly, 'Influx control and economic growth' in H. Giliomee
and L. Schlemmer (eds), *Up against the fences* (David Philip, Cape Town,
1985), pp. 296-304.
10. Relly, 'Influx control'; M. Swilling and J. McCarthy, 'Transport
and political resistance: bus boycotts in 1983', *South African Review Two*
(Ravan Press, Johannesburg, 1984), pp. 25-44.
11. S. Bekker and R. Humphries, *From control to confusion: the changing
role of the Administration Boards in South Africa, 1971-1983* (Shuter and Shooker,
Pietermaritzburg, 1984).
12. S.B. Greenberg and H. Giliomee, 'Labour bureaucracies and the
African reserves', *South African Labour Bulletin*, vol. 8, no. 4 (1983), pp. 37-51.
13. J. Keenan, unpublished mimeo, Sociology seminar University of
Witwatersrand (1985).

14. This point was made by J. de Villiers Graaff in 'Homeland function and dependency: a case study of reformist potential', paper presented to the Development Society of Southern Africa, University of the OFS (1984).

15. The transformation of South Africa's spatial economy cannot be understood by those who remain trapped within two key assumptions that, until recently, pervaded the literature on apartheid: firstly, the assumption that South Africa can be understood as a spatially dualistic society differentiated into two coherent but radically different entities called bantustans and 'white' South Africa; and secondly, that these spatial entities correspond exhaustively to distinct, even if interconnected, forms of social reproduction.

16. Summary of Report of the Study Group on Industrial Development Strategy (Kleu Report) (1983), 21, 10.8.

17. G. Maasdorp, 'Coordinated regional development: hope for the Good Hope proposals?' in Giliomee and Schlemmer (eds), *Up against the fences*, pp. 213-34.

18. National Party pamphlet, '. . . and what about the black people?' (1985), p. 9.

19. D. Kaplan, 'The South African state: the origins of a racially exclusive democracy', *The Insurgent Sociologist*, vol. X, no. 2 (1980), pp. 15-29.

20. NP pamphlet, '. . . and what about the black people?'.

21. See J. Lombard on *Sunday Times*, 3 March 1985; and M. Forsyth, *Federalism and the future of South Africa* (South African Institute of International Affairs, Johannesburg, 1984).

22. The RSC Bill went through its second reading in early 1984, after which it was referred to a parliamentary select committee where its controversial tax system and racial composition were reviewed. It was passed by Parliament in June 1985.

23. At this stage the provincial administrator will appoint the chairperson, decide on the number of representatives and can make ruling on decisions that are not supported by a two-thirds majority.

24. The Margo Commission into the Tax System in South Africa has not yet reported.

25. Interview with G. Croeser, Deputy-Director of Finance.

26. See FCI Memo, 'Regional development in South and Southern Africa', submitted to the meeting of the National Regional Development Advisory Council (2 August 1984).

27. J. Lombard, *Alternatives to the consolidation of KwaZulu* (Natal) (University of Pretoria, 1980).

28. ASSOCOM Memorandum, *Removal of discrimination against blacks in the political economy of the republic of South Africa*.

29. See NP pamphlet, '. . . and what about the black people?', p. 9.

30. There is evidence that these boards are to be phased out. See *Star*, 6 June 1985.

31. NP pamphlet, '. . . and what about the black people?'.

32. The possibility of uniting South Africa on a federal or confederal basis was first raised in a serious way by Lord Carnarvon's confederation scheme in the 1870s and was raised again by the proposal of Milner's

Kindergaren that South Africa be united on the basis of federation rather than union.

33. B. Hackland, 'The economic and political context of the growth of the PFP in South Africa, 1959-78', *Journal of Southern African Studies* (October 1980). On the NRP, see *Star*, 9 March 1985.

34. Buthelezi Commission, *The requirements for stability and development in KwaZulu and Natal*, vol. 11, 4.2.1, 76.

35. Buthelezi Commission, vol. 11, 5.4, 111-15 and 6.6.2, 126.

36. The term is borrowed from Fleur de Villiers, *Sunday Times*, 23 May 1980.

37. South African Institute of Race Relations, *Survey of race relations in South Africa* (Johannesburg, 1983), p. 316.

38. NP pamphlet, '. . . and what about the black people?', p. 13.

39. ASSOCOM Memorandum, *Removal of discrimination*; and Lombard, *Alternatives to consolidation*.

40. ASSOCOM Memorandum, *Removal of discrimination*, p. 2.

41. ASSOCOM Memorandum, *Removal of discrimination*, p. 24.

42. NP pamphlet, '. . . and what about the black people?'.

43. ASSOCOM Memorandum, *Removal of discrimination*.

44. G. Adler, 'The state, reform and participation', paper presented to the Contemporary Studies Seminar, Sociology Department, University of the Witwatersrand (31 July 1985).

45. A. Erwin, 'On unions and politics', paper presented to ASSA Conference, University of Cape Town (July 1985).

3

The Giant Stirs: South African Business in the Age of Reform

Michael Mann

In 1977, Andreas Wassenaar, a pillar of the Afrikaner establishment, and the chairman of Sanlam, the second largest conglomerate in South Africa, published a stinging attack upon governmental economic policy. The title of his book, *Assault on private enterprise: the freeway to communism*, expressed his understanding of the nature of political intervention in the economy. Wassenaar reflected: 'Why are democratic governments in some countries bent on nationalisation? Why do they disown private enterprise? Why is the RSA so prominent in this respect? . . . The answer must lie in an almost inexplicable antipathy to the profit motive.'[1]

Wassenaar's sentiments, however, were not without an element of irony, since his criticisms were levelled against precisely those policies which, in the 1950s, had facilitated the rapid growth of Sanlam. Indeed, one of the effects, if not the objectives, of governmental intervention in the economy after 1948 has been the advancement of Afrikaner corporate interests. For at least six decades, the South African state has been a vigorous actor in the economy. From the 1920s onwards, it played a major role in fostering secondary industrial development by means that included tariff protection and direct investment in heavy industry. After 1948, it strengthened its presence in the economy through the elaboration of a complex system of reproducing and controlling African labour. In other spheres too, such as managing the money supply and administering prices through agricultural boards and public corporations, state regulation has become the norm. Of course, the state has not only participated in the economy, narrowly defined, but also in society at large. To the end of achieving a degree of social stability, it has extended political and material concessions to the white community, whilst, at the same time, subjecting the African majority to a vast

52

array of bureaucratic controls and repressive measures.

Historically, the South African state has therefore been structured for the performance of interventions on a massive scale. It was the legitimacy of this legacy that Wassenaar's broadside threatened, at least to some extent, to erode. By the 1970s, Afrikaner business had come of age, and the larger concerns were capable of surviving without much of the patronage that their earlier development had required. The class project of Afrikaner nationalism, Dan O'Meara has argued,[2] had come to fruition. The growth of powerful Afrikaner economic enterprises, together with the increasing concentration and centralisation of the 1960s, laid the foundation for the emergence of a newly dominant monopoly capital.

If the boom of the 1960s facilitated the consolidation of the economic ascendancy of monopoly capital, it was the crisis of the 1970s which led to a convergence of hitherto partially diverse and conflicting social forces. By 1978, South Africa was experiencing the worst recession in its history. The real growth rate was negative in the first half of 1976, and zero in 1977. The volume of manufacturing output fell during these years, whilst the total outflow of capital was some R121 million.[3] Moreover, there were mounting balance-of-payments difficulties, inflation was rising, and by the end of 1976 African unemployment stood around the two million mark.[4] Ironically, in the face of such unemployment, the shortages of technical workers in the economy became more acute.

Accompanying and exacerbating the economic crisis was a rapid intensification of working-class and popular struggles. From January 1973 to mid-1976, over 200,000 Africans engaged in strike action.[5] Political stability was further shattered by the Soweto Uprising in 1976 and the intensification of a guerrilla war fought inside South Africa co-ordinated by Umkhonto we Sizwe, the armed wing of the African National Congress (ANC). The latter half of the 1970s also saw the collapse of Portuguese colonialism; the defeat of the South African army in Angola; and the ongoing military campaign in Namibia.

It was in this context that the military outlined its programme of a 'Total Strategy' as the appropriate response to the 'total onslaught' allegedly being waged against the state on every front. As P.W. Botha, then Minister of Defence, wrote in 1977:[6]

The resolution of a conflict in the times in which we now live demands interdependent and co-ordinated action in all fields

53

> — military, psychological, economic, political, sociological,
> technological, diplomatic, ideological, cultural etc . . . (W)e
> are today involved in a war . . . The striving for specific aims
> . . . must be co-ordinated with all the means available to the
> state.

Such 'co-ordinated action in all fields', though, was not construed
as a mere defence of a static *status quo*. In the words of Magnus
Malan, the then Chief-of-Staff,[7] 'The lesson is clear. The SADF
[South African Defence Force] is ready to beat off any attack . . .
but we must take into account the aspirations of our different
population groups. We must gain and keep their trust.' An article
in *Paratus*, the military journal, rendered explicit the fundamental
aim of the Total Strategy. It was 'a guarantee for the system of
free enterprise'.[8]

The doctrine of Total Strategy, then, in its emphasis upon the
protection of 'free enterprise', created the basis for an alliance
between the military and monopoly capital. By 1978, O'Meara
observes,[9] with the important exception of agriculture, big business
was agreed on the need for significant reforms in economic and
political policy. The military also argued that changes had to be
implemented, with blacks being offered a stake in the capitalist
order. They would have to begin receiving such 'benefits' as 'higher
standards of living'[10] if the threat of Marxism was to be countered.
Hence, by the late 1970s, the paths of the military and the most
powerful sections of business were intersecting at a point of common
awareness that various reforms were crucial if the survival of South
African capitalism was to be ensured. In the aftermath of Soweto,
leading businessmen became directly and stridently involved in a
campaign for change. Indeed, as O'Meara notes,[11] in the climate
of economic and political crisis, business-funded pressure groups
proliferated, as the capitalist class engaged in a desperate flurry of
open politicking on a hitherto unprecedented scale. However, the
government of Prime Minister John Vorster, rent by paralysing
internal divisions, appeared incapable of accommodating the
demands being voiced. Indeed, Wassenaar's public entry into the
fray, and his condemnation of governmental economic policy, construed as endangering the very existence of 'private enterprise',
elicited an extremely hostile state reaction. Stung by the ingratitude
of the chairman of Sanlam, who seemed to be biting the hand that
had fed his company, Vorster sounded a warning to business men
to 'keep out of politics'.

The impasse was broken by the 'Muldergate' scandal of the late 1970s, which resulted in the election of P.W. Botha as leader of the National Party and Prime Minister. The events of 'Muldergate', as O'Meara has argued,[12] catalysed significant shifts in the alignment of forces both in the National Party and in the state. By the 1970s, the class composition of Afrikaner nationalism, which in 1948 represented an alliance of the Afrikaner petty bourgeoisie, white workers, fractions of industry, commerce and finance as well as farmers, had been transformed. The ascent of big Afrikaner business, which was finding common cause with the giant English and foreign concerns, was the decisive moment in this process. With the rise to power of the Botha faction, large-scale Afrikaner capital established itself as the hegemonic element in Afrikaner nationalism as organised by the National Party. Botha is a product of the Cape National Party machine, which has been dominated, almost since its inception, by the Afrikaner financial institutions of the province, especially Sanlam.

As Minister of Defence, though, Botha's power base was also in the military. His accession to the premiership thus provided the political conditions for co-operation between this group, Afrikaner business and other monopoly capitalist interests. Under the banner of the Total Strategy, Botha has institutionalised a military and business presence within the state. Membership of the executive is no longer restricted to parliamentarians, and various senior military officers and prominent business men nominated by Botha have been directly absorbed into key roles in government through inclusion on the Cabinet Committees that have all but replaced the previous ministerial system of decision-making. The up-front collaboration between these particular social actors is a distinguishing feature of the initiative launched by the state under the rubric of the Total Strategy.

From the outset, the proponents of the Total Strategy seemed to realise that their capacity to defend the society from external attack was to a significant extent dependent upon internal threats to its reproduction being reduced, and the subordinate classes, or sections thereof, developing a vested interest in its perpetuation. The Total Strategy, from a military perspective, involved a recognition that internal conflict defied any simple military solution: that it was vital to win the 'hearts and minds' of a nascent fifth-column population. Business, in its turn, clamoured for the creation of a 'black middle class' that would, as the *Financial Mail*, a leading organ of capitalist opinion, put it, 'have a stake in stability and provide a counter to the process of radicalism'.[13] Central to the Total Strategy was, it appears, an understanding that the crisis of the 1970s was such that increases in the scope and sophistication of repression alone would not contain it. Coercion would, increasingly, have to be supplemented by formative, productive actions if Africans were to be drawn into what the *Financial Mail* described as 'an alliance with capitalism'.[14]

This is not to suggest that repression had no place in the Total Strategy, for as popular resistance to the innovative measures intensified, the state came to rely more and more heavily upon the *modus operandi* to which it has always been most, although not exclusively, accustomed in its dealings with the African majority. Yet it was also perceived by business and the military that any attempt to 'gain and keep the trust' of the subordinate communities had to encompass more than coercion: the question was how such an endeavour was to be undertaken. The doctrine of the Total Strategy, as formulated by the military, envisaged the state as intervening 'at all levels of planning and execution'.[15] This implied, in one sense, a more active state, co-ordinating efforts in all fields, and extending its influence in areas in which it had previously constituted at most a marginal presence.

An instance of this was the case of academic research. The 1980 South African Plan for Research in the Human Sciences (SAPRHS) represented a revision of the method of functioning of the Human Sciences Research Council (HSRC), which had been established by an Act of Parliament in 1968. The SAPRHS provided for the creation of machinery through which 'existing and future national problem areas can be identified and arranged in order of priority' so that they can be 'systematically investigated and such research stimulated, co-ordinated, financed and controlled'.[16] The emphasis was placed upon projects that were 'directed towards the needs of the decision-taker',[17] and whose findings were 'of optimum use'[18] to those engaged in the framing of policy. This meant, in effect, the harnessing of the human sciences in the service of the Total Strategy.

However, whilst the Total Strategy entailed a greater state participation in certain endeavours, it also came to be associated with the idea of a reduced governmental role in, most importantly, the economy. As such, the Total Strategy was, to an extent, part of the global anti-statist crusade that has, in the era of Reagan and Thatcher, been popularly described in terms of 'monetarism'. What is distinctive, though, about monetarist policies in South Africa is that they have been applied in the context of a reformist initiative. In the United States and Britain, as Stephen Gelb and Duncan Innes have noted,[19] monetarism has involved the attempt to effect a decisive shift in the balance of social forces in favour of capital. To this end, efforts have been made 'to smash the power of trade unions directly, as well as to weaken them by inducing recession and high unemployment.'[20] Jeremy Keenan endorses such an analysis. The aim of what he calls the 'New Right' has been[21]

> to roll back past working class gains; to reverse the political and economic advances made by labour during the post-war expansionary phase of capitalist development. The method of achieving this was not simply to beat inflation . . . but in so doing to destroy the institutional strength of labour and thereby to restore a greater responsiveness of workers to market forces.

In South Africa, however, the flirtation with monetarism has accompanied the Total Strategy, which has had, as perhaps its principal objective, the granting of some of those economic and political benefits which, in the United States and Britain, are being at least partially withdrawn. Gelb and Innes interpret monetarism as the response of the state and leading business sectors to the economic crisis confronting South Africa. The monetarist approach, they declare, seeks to arrest long-term economic decline through 'intensifying social oppression and class warfare'.[22] Yet whilst monetarist solutions to the economic woes of the country may necessitate the increased repression, both direct and indirect, of the working class, the political logic of the Total Strategy has tended to work against such a development. This, it is suggested, is the actual source of the double bind of South African monetarism: its proposals for resolving the economic crisis have been largely at odds with various measures designed to secure political stability. Monetarism, then, has been articulated, in a contradictory fashion, with other facets of the Total Strategy. This may help to explain why the monetarist experiment has been such a limited one in South Africa.

The central features of neo-liberal economic thought, of which monetarism is one brand, are its endorsement of less governmental activity, especially in the market place, which is viewed as the basic mechanism for allocating resources and establishing political freedoms; its advocation of cuts in both taxes and state expenditure; and its support for the deregulation of controls on production, which are seen as raising the price of products.[23] In South Africa, as elsewhere, monetarists have singled out state interventionism as the major cause of inflation, which is in turn regarded as the foremost expression of the economic crisis. Yet demands for the withdrawal of the state from certain spheres cannot, in the South African situation, merely be construed as emanating in strict conformity with monetarist reasoning. Thus, calls by white capital and state organs for the deregulation of controls on production cannot simply be explained in terms of a lowering of costs. They are, more importantly, related to a perceived need to stimulate the informal sector, and to remove restrictions on small businesses in general and African enterprises in particular in order to foster 'the participation of members of the . . . lesser developed population groups' in the 'market economy'.[24]

Hence, it would be misleading to interpret all appeals for diminished governmental intervention as issuing from monetarist premises, and entailing heightened oppression of the working class through the displacement of various economic and social responsibilities of the state on to the market. The welfare system that is under partial assault in the United States and Britain is absent in South Africa, and so also is the degree of popular acceptance which those societies enjoy. In South Africa, the state has, historically, not acted to incorporate the majority of the population within welfarist arrangements, and therefore has not extended to it those advantages which capitalism in the United States, Britain and elsewhere has been able to deliver. Rather, it has sought to prevent such developments from occurring. Given these peculiar circumstances of South Africa, it has been possible for some to argue that less state involvement would free the capitalist economy from its political fetters, enabling it to spread its benefits more widely, and, in this way, to provide for its own legitimation.[25]

These criticisms of the dysfunctional intrusions of the apartheid polity upon the economy have long been voiced by adherents of the 'conventional wisdom' of South African liberalism. Wassenaar's attack, from the very citadel of Afrikaner business, upon governmental interference in the economy, conceived as an irrational 'antipathy to the profit motive', linked him with this tradition. Yet whereas the 'conventional wisdom' did not doubt the existence of capitalism in at least the territorial bulk of South Africa, even if in a form distorted by extraneous politico-ideological factors, Wassenaar suggested an alternative understanding, one which was to be elaborated in naïve monetarist argumentation. The *Financial*

Mail testified to a growing sentiment when it commented in 1980 that it was no wonder 'some argue that the extreme legal restraints on blacks, who constitute the majority of the population, disqualify SA as a free enterprise society'.[26] Leon Louw, director of the Free Market Foundation of Southern Africa, reflected this position most forcefully when he declared, in a 1979 conference on Free Enterprise and the Individual, that blacks, in so far as they were subject to stringent governmental controls, laboured under a 'socialist regime'.[27]

The logic of such a perception of South African society called into question the hugely interventionist role historically performed by the South African state. Yet, the specific conditions of South Africa meant that a retreat by the government from certain areas might not simply be negative or repressive, leading to heightened social oppression, but might have a productive power: for if capitalism, defined, in extreme ideal-typical terms, by the existence of free markets, was to survive in South Africa, it was imperative, in the words of Harry Oppenheimer of Anglo American, the biggest conglomerate in South Africa, that 'all the apartheid regulations which get in the way of the private enterprise system are removed'.[28] The Wiehahn Commission, reporting in 1979, recommended that the statutory definition of 'employee' be amended to include Africans, so that their trade unions could be officially registered if certain stipulations were met. The state introduced legislation to this effect, thus furnishing the legal framework and space for the rapid consolidation of the African labour movement. Hence, the repeal of racial restrictions on the recognition of trade union rights has served to strengthen, rather than weaken, the working class.

The state has also acted to scrap job reservation. In addition, in accordance with a proposal of the Riekert Commission, which advocated the reinforcement of divisions within the African population between permanent urban 'insiders', with relatively privileged residential, educational and employment opportunities, and temporary 'outsiders', over whom controls were to be intensified, constraints on the intra-urban movement of the former group were loosened. Furthermore, since 1975, legal disabilities affecting African entrepreneurs have been progressively abolished.[29] Some of the above measures, such as those relating to job reservation, might be seen as addressing the economic crisis, a component of which was the shortage of categories of skilled personnel. Yet they are sought to go beyond mere coercion, so as to generate elements of the African community supportive of 'free enterprise', some of the 'benefits' of which, like industrial citizenship, could be provided, at least in part, by a reduction in such forms of state interventionism as statutory or bureaucratic restraints.

In dismantling certain apartheid controls, the state was given eager encouragement by representatives of big capital. In November 1979, at the Carlton Conference in Johannesburg, the inauguration of a new epoch of formal co-operation between the government and business was solemnised. Addressing some 350 leaders of the 'private sector', the Prime Minister pledged his commitment to a 'policy of strengthening the free enterprise system and introducing orderly reform'.[30] 'The reciprocal channels of communication being created', he declared, would enable the government and business 'to work as a team on those things on which we can agree'.[31] One of the points of accord was the need for rapid economic growth. 'The greatest good in South Africa', Botha asserted, 'is not stability *per se*, or order for its own sake. A system in which material welfare is limited to a few within a sea of poverty is not only indefensible, it is objectionable.'[32] Rhetoric notwithstanding, it was evident that such a 'system' was 'objectionable' only in so far as it no longer seemed defensible by principally repressive means. If the 'stability' of the capitalist order was to be secured, segments of the subordinate population would have to be won over to the cause of 'free enterprise' through an enhancement of their 'material welfare'. For this to occur, it was argued, sustained economic growth was required.

In a 1985 interview, Gavin Relly, chairman of Anglo American since 1983, highlighted the relationship between economic growth and the process of reform. The former was perceived not simply as boosting profitability, but as having repercussions of a political nature:[33]

> In South Africa our problem is essentially one of the cake not being big enough to go around. That is why the politics of reform are absolutely and directly related to the impact which industry and commerce can make on the gross national product.

If the 'cake' were to be made 'big enough to go around', economic growth was vital, and the best way this could be achieved, both the government and business proclaimed, was through the promotion of 'private enterprise'. 'We have embarked', Relly noted, on 'a most important era of agreement between government and business — that free enterprise should be the motif of our society'.[34] This common affirmation of the system of 'free enterprise', and of the urgency of reform, rendered possible, in principle, the *rapprochement* of the state and capital.

At a follow-up summit with business men in November 1981, known as the Good Hope Conference, Botha declared: 'If we differ, let us differ on the merits of matters. But let us co-operate in those matters on which we really agree.'[35] He further observed:[36]

> I assume, therefore, that the promotion of a regional order in which real freedom and material welfare can be maximised and the quality of life of all in Southern Africa can be improved, is still our common goal on which agreement does exist.

To give effect to this shared objective, it was, Botha asserted, 'the Government's serious intention to expand further the system of free enterprise'.[37] However, he warned that 'Instability is bound to follow if reforms are tackled which do not allow for balance between spheres of interest.'[38] At the previous meeting in November 1979, there was, Botha remarked, consensus that it should be[39] '. . . possible for all in South Africa to participate effectively, individually and within the group context, in processes affecting their lives and expectations'. Yet, on

> . . . exactly how this is to be achieved the political parties in this country differ, and I assume that there was or is not agreement among those who participated in the Carlton Conference on the way in which an effective political voice for all should be sought.

Since no 'agreement' on this question was to be had, the government could legitimately claim exclusive jurisdiction over 'political' affairs — that is, over the formulation of a new constitution for South Africa. Partnership between the state and capital was therefore perceived as applying only 'in the spheres of spiritual and social welfare as well as material welfare'.[40] In these areas, no issue was beyond the rightful concern of business. 'Political reform'[41] or the determination of constitutional change, was, though, the prerogative of the government alone, even if it might choose, in practice, to solicit advice from business men in this regard.

Hence, concluding his speech at the Good Hope Conference, Botha urged the 'private sector' to help 'solve the development problems in Southern Africa',[42] whilst the Governor of the Reserve Bank, presiding over the meeting, asked the delegates to keep politics out of the proceedings.[43] Business men expressed their willingness to oblige on both fronts, but the support they offered Botha was more cautious and conditional than had been the case two years previously. Indeed, a feature of that occasion, as the *Financial Mail* commented at the time, was the 'uncritical attitude'[44] displayed by the business community, brought in from the cold to which it had been consigned under the Vorster administration. Thus, Botha could 'hardly be blamed' for believing that he had been given 'an endorsement of his strategy'. Yet, the *Financial Mail* continued, apart from 'an apparent willingness to look more tolerantly on the claims of private enterprise, it seems that SA business has received very little in exchange'.[45] Despite such misgivings, however, the *Financial Mail* itself shared in the euphoria with which business men greeted what it described as Botha's 'most spectacular *coup* since reaching the premiership'.[46] It named him 'Man of the Year' for 1979 on account of 'a driving resolve on his part to move away from the narrow, sectarian approach which has characterised the regimes of other NP Prime Ministers'.[47]

In August 1981, in an article entitled 'Reform in limbo', the *Financial Mail* posed 'the question concerned businessmen are asking' — namely, 'Is the very basis of what has been called the "Carlton Contract" being shredded?'[48] Business men, it declared, wanted, in return for their succour to Botha, 'the *quid pro quo* of a relaxation of the economic stranglehold of apartheid . . . Why has it not been forthcoming?'[49] The answer, as business men perceived it, lay in the opposition by elements within the ruling National Party to a process of reform. Yet as Oppenheimer had noted a year earlier, 'Time is running dangerously short and if our problems are not faced now they will have to be faced in a much aggravated form in the future'.[50] It was doubtless to allay the fears of business, impatient at the lack of 'significant progress' made by the government 'toward realising the hopes that were . . . raised'[51] at the Carlton Conference, and to re-establish his *bona fides*, that Botha convened the Good Hope Conference.

Responding to Botha's speech at the Good Hope Conference, Oppenheimer, whilst reaffirming the qualified backing he had given to the Prime Minister two years previously, voiced the 'sense of disillusionment' felt by business men at the results of the first meeting. 'It is really only in the field of industrial relations', he asserted, 'that major solid progress has so far been made.'[52] Other areas demanding attention were the mobility of African labour, restricted by governmental influx controls, education and housing. Mike Rosholt, chairman of Barlow Rand, the biggest industrial group in South Africa, declared that business men were 'very much concerned with those aspects in our system which obstruct or delay' economic growth. 'In the main these are socio-economic and not political, although inevitably these days the lines tend to become more and more blurred. It is in any case', he observed, 'not necessary for government and business to be in a state of confrontation, even on those matters which border on political issues.'[53]

These remarks revealed some of the understanding of 'politics' possessed by business men, and the way in which they defined their relationship to the state. It was recognised that politics was imping-ing upon economics, such that it was in practice becoming increas-ingly difficult to distinguish sharply between the two. This was because various governmental interventions, such as influx control, had an influence upon economic performance. The field of opera-tion of business was thus, as Rosholt put it in a 1983 interview, 'a very grey area' in which 'politics and business overlap'.[54] At the same time, as Relly contended, a commitment to 'free enterprise' had 'major implications for the politics of the country because it means basically that nobody should be excluded from any processes who has the wit, ability or education to participate in them'.[55] Yet although these 'processes' were constitutional as well as economic ones, this linkage, Relly asserted, should not[56] 'be pushed to the point where either businessmen set out to determine the politics of the country or politicians set out to control business according to the image they believe in'.

This insistence upon a delimitation of spheres of competence left sole authority over the creation of a new constitutional dispen-sation in the hands of the state. As Oppenheimer declared,[57]

I don't think one ought in one's capacity as a head of a big public company to plunge into the details of party politics but I think if you are running a large company in what is, after all, still a comparatively small country, you can't help finding yourself operating in the grey area where politics and business mix.

Warren Clewlow, executive director of Barlow Rand, observed,[58]

63

I have had to rethink my approach. I belonged to the old
school which held that business and politics were separable.
As soon as I had to face the issues of the day, I started to
realise that my ideas were not right, but wrong. I still regard
myself as apolitical.

Such statements, it is suggested, expressed the desire of business
to distance itself from what it acknowledged as a proper domain
of the state — namely, the supervision of constitutional reform. On
how this task was to be performed, as Botha noted at the Good Hope
Conference, the various political parties disagreed. Thus,
Oppenheimer, a traditional supporter of the opposition Progressive
Federal Party, could avoid the 'plunge into the details of party
politics', and the risk of compromising his political principles, since
the collaboration between the government and business was viewed
as excluding constitutional matters. Clewlow could also describe
himself as 'apolitical'. However, there was also an acute consciousness of the fact that, in another sense, business was deeply
political, both in that it was so affected by state regulations, and
in so far as it could contribute to social stability — hence the notion
of 'the grey area where politics and business mix'.

At the basis of the 'Carlton Contract', as re-endorsed two years
later, then, was, it is argued, an acknowledgement by the state and
capital of the sovereignty of the former in the constitutional domain,
and of a partnership in the promotion of 'free enterprise'. The
interrelationship between the constitutional and the other dimensions of reform was recognised by business. As Oppenheimer contended,[59] 'Racial discrimination and free enterprise are basically
incompatible, and . . . failure to eradicate the one will ultimately
result in the destruction of the other.' This was not simply because
'racial discrimination', as institutionalised in the structures of the
apartheid state and elsewhere, was held to have a negative impact
upon economic performance. There was also, as a business
spokesman declared, the 'real danger' — hardly surprising, given
the historical complicity of racism and capitalism in South Africa
— of the latter being 'rejected for its perceived support of oppression and apartheid'.[60] Capitalism was thus redefined as 'free enterprise'. 'I am not keen', Relly asserted, 'on calling ours a capitalist
society because I think capitalism in certain circumstances is not
very free.'[61] 'Free enterprise', in contrast, entailed liberty, 'both
economically and politically',[62] and was therefore 'incompatible'
with racial domination, not only as effected by governmental

interventions in the economy, but as manifested in the existence of an apartheid polity.

However, the constitutional changes to accompany the reform process were to be the unilateral responsibility of the state. This reflected, it seems, the unwillingness of the government to share command over what it regarded as its natural province, the inexperience of business men in this respect as well as the disagreement between some of the participants in the Carlton and Good Hope Conferences, whose party-political affiliations diverged, as to the form constitutional development should take. Where there was consensus, though, as Relly later put it, was on the idea that 'free enterprise should be the motif of our society'.[63] Rhetorically, both the state and capital defended 'free enterprise' in principle. It ensured, as Piet Koornhof, then Minister of Co-operation and Development, remarked, the 'attainment of a large measure of political and personal freedom'.[64] In the words of Rosholt, it involved 'the freedom of the individual to use his personal enterprise'.[65] Simultaneously, 'free enterprise' has been explicitly upheld as a system of co-option and control. Botha described it as a way of creating 'a middle class among the nations of South Africa', and thereby laying 'the foundation for resisting Communism'.[66] For Relly too it was a mode of generating amongst the subordinate population 'an increasingly stable and hopefully contented middle class'.[67]

This pragmatic, technocratic understanding of 'free enterprise' was thus co-present with an alternate conception in the discourse of both the state and capital. Deborah Posel has contended that,[68] since 1978, the South African state has had increasing recourse to a technocratic ideology for the legitimation of its practices. In accordance with such technocratic rationality, its policies are justified, not by their substantive ends or the ethical values they enshrine, but by the efficiency of their means. Its actions, then, are defended on instrumental grounds, as the sole, incontrovertibly necessary responses to the 'facts' of the case. What precisely constitutes 'social actuality' can be established beyond dispute by 'experts'. The effect of technocratic rationality, as Posel observes, is to depoliticise politics by depicting it as a purely technical reaction to objective 'reality'. It is consequently viewed as ideologically or politically non-contestable, and hence closed to public discussion and ratification.

As Posel declares, technocratic ideology has doubtless facilitated the centralisation of state power in the hands of the executive, reducing its accountability to Parliament, on the one hand, and to the National Party rank and file, on the other. Opposition in both these quarters to a reformist initiative has prompted efforts to create, to the side of the terrain of democratic participation and the conventional state structures, institutions, most notably the Cabinet committees, which are insulated from the arenas of conflict. This development, Posel maintains, has been portrayed by the state as a move towards 'effective government', which involves administering 'objective' solutions to 'national' problems in a spirit of 'realism'. In this fashion, large areas of decision-making have been defined in technical terms, as outside the proper scope of popular and partisan political debate.

A technocratic language, then, has been employed to assist in the isolation of policy formation from sites of resistance, and to sanction a role for the military and business in various spheres of government. Leading business men, as Posel observes, have been incorporated into Cabinet Committees in their capacity as 'specialists' in such matters as economic development, industrial decentralisation, labour relations and inflation. In addition, teams of business and state representatives have been established to address such issues as urban African housing. It might be added that the post-1978 period has also witnessed a heightened reliance upon commissions of inquiry in the formulation of policy. Frequently proclaiming their 'scientific' credentials, they have allowed space for the reformist input of capitalist interests.

However, it would be entirely misleading to suggest, as Posel does, that the collaboration between the state and capital has been defended by the former purely on the grounds of expediency, with 'free enterprise' construed simply as an 'effective' part of the Total Strategy: for the government has also voiced, at the Carlton and Good Hope Conferences, amongst other occasions, its principled support of 'free enterprise', as a system maximising 'real freedom'.[69] One might be inclined to perceive this affirmation of the value of 'free enterprise' as a mere rhetorical sop to the business community, designed to enlist its co-operation; yet it has, in addition, afforded the state a discursive means by which to pursue, at least in certain instances, its own legitimation. Its announcements concerning the dismantling of influx controls in their present form were a case in point. The government claimed that, in allowing the freer play of forces in the African labour market, it was enhancing liberty.[70]

With respect to business too, its alliance with the state in the advancement of 'free enterprise' was endorsed on the basis of principle as well as pragmatism. Hence, it was possible for business men to enter the partnership whilst at the same time being able to criticise violations by the state of precepts of 'free enterprise' to which it had pledged adherence. The logic of a justification of 'free enterprise' in terms of the norms implied by a 'free market' order entailed a diminution in the scope of state interventions: for such values as liberty and justice were, allegedly, contingent upon the opening of markets and a reduction in the governmental regulations which constrained individual freedom. The market was also seen as the most efficient mechanism for allocating resources. To the extent, then, that this particular 'free market' rhetoric has been employed by capital, it has been to call for the removal of various state restrictions and to distance business from some of the more odious governmental practices.

Thus, the *Financial Mail* warned in a 1984 editorial that the 'free market cannot credibly continue to co-exist with forced removals and influx control'. Prominent business men such as Relly, Anglovaal's Basil Hersov and others, it asserted, are 'telling government that influx control and removals are immoral, counter-productive, unjust, economically disastrous and internationally damaging'.[71] Business could hence defend its association with the state in so far as this resulted in a loosening of governmental controls, whilst reserving the right to condemn, when it chose to do so, actions deemed contrary to the supposedly beneficial and effective operation of the 'free market'.

However, the promotion of 'free enterprise' encompassed a great deal more than a mere retreat by the state from certain activities: for it was realised by both the government and business that the withdrawal of the former from various areas, and the liberation of the forces of the market, would alone be unable to produce within the subordinate communities those social elements that might tilt the balance of power in favour of the continuation of capitalism. Consequently, whilst lessening its involvement in some spheres, the government has extended its presence in others. Its field of influence, as has been noted, has expanded to embrace business men and the military through such structures as the Cabinet Committees and the State Security Council.

The alliance between the state and capital, it is suggested, was in part necessitated by the fiscal crisis confronting the government. Owing to its lack of sufficient financial resources, it was obliged to seek the aid of business in order to make available material concessions designed to affect the allegiances of at least sections of the dominated population. At the Carlton Conference, Botha called for a new 'development strategy', which included the participation of the 'private sector' in the establishment of small businesses, especially amongst Africans. In 1980, the Small Business Development Corporation (SBDC) was founded as 'a partnership between private sector and State' aimed at encouraging 'entrepreneurship amongst all population groups' and providing additional job opportunities. This was viewed as contributing towards 'maintaining a free market economy' and securing 'political stability, particularly in times of unemployment'.[72] Upon registration as a public company in 1981, the SBDC had an authorised share capital of R150 million. By 1985, this figure stood at R200 million. The shareholding was equally divided between the government and business, the latter being represented by over 90 of the major concerns in South Africa.[73] The SBDC has attempted to advance small businesses by offering loans, facilities such as buildings and industrial parks at reasonable rentals, training, advisory and after-care services, and by underwriting bank credit.[74]

In other instances too, the state, with or without corresponding support by capital, has increased its interventions in the service of its reformist initiative. In an effort to generate a degree of legitimacy for the system of African schooling, and to defuse conflict in what has in the past decade become a prime site and focus of political resistance, the government has raised the budget of the Department of Education and Training, which is responsible for African education, by over 700 per cent since 1978–9, from R143 million to R1,148 million in 1986–7.[75] At the Good Hope Conference, Botha unveiled a revised economic decentralisation programme, and appealed to business to co-operate in 'creating job opportunities and decent living conditions in . . . rural areas'.[76] In order to achieve a more even geographical distribution of industry, an upgraded package of decentralisation incentives was announced. However, the financial pillar of the regional development strategy was to be the Development Bank of Southern Africa. It was formally opened in 1983, and the government has committed itself to supplying R1,500 million for its Development Fund between 1984 and 1989. By 1986, over R400 million had been given.[77]

Moreover, in 1985 the government declared its intention of spending R1,000 million during the next five years to improve infrastructure and facilities in 'underdeveloped towns and cities'.[78] In response to the enormous socio-political problem posed by soaring unemployment, it also allocated an additional R600 million for job creation. However, it is unclear as to precisely how much of this amount has been used to alleviate unemployment specifically amongst Africans.

As regards business, it has likewise been active in ways which contradict 'free market' or monetarist doctrine. It too has understood that the cause of 'free enterprise' could not be furthered simply by abolishing certain state regulations. Although the emancipation of markets might, in various cases, have a productive impact, this was inadequate on its own, and had to be complemented by greater interventions in particular fields. The most important of these have been in relation to African education and housing, with the endeavours of business spearheaded by the Urban Foundation. In 1976, the year of the Soweto Uprising, the Urban Foundation was formed by a group of large white business corporations to 'improve the quality of life' of Africans, especially 'in urban communities'.[79] This task was viewed as motivated by considerations that transcended the narrowly economic. As Jan Steyn, executive director of the Urban Foundation, noted, what was 'at stake' was nothing less than the very survival of the capitalist social order: for if 'free enterprise' was to be saved, it was imperative that business men were seen to dissociate themselves from racially discriminatory practices 'in areas where they do have some choice',[80] such as education and housing. Capitalism, then, had to be perceived as rendering these 'benefits' accessible to everyone, irrespective of colour.

Between 1977 and 1983, the Urban Foundation launched or participated in 620 projects to the value of R47 million. It financed or was involved in over 250 educational undertakings, constituting an investment of over R17 million of business funds. In the sphere of housing, it expended some R19 million on 80 schemes, mainly in the home-ownership and self-help fields. In addition, some R30 million was mobilised from abroad to assist purchases of homes by Africans under 99-year leasehold. Another R60 million was raised, mostly internally, to promote infrastructural and residential development.[81]

The efforts of big capital, however, go beyond its sponsorship of the Urban Foundation. In 1982, the Chairman's Fund of Anglo American was described as 'South Africa's Other Government,'[82] because of the amounts of money it was channelling into, amongst other areas, African education and training. In its 1985 annual report, Anglo American noted that in the year under review, the

Chairman's Fund and its Educational Trust had together spent over R25 million, of which 74 per cent had been devoted to secondary and tertiary educational projects.[83] In 1986, the American oil company Mobil announced that it would be allocating R40 million for African education, small business and rural development in South Africa.[84]

These initiatives by capital in the provision of education and training have not, as Linda Chisholm has argued,[85] been simply designed to meet its economic need for technically qualified manpower. The purpose, she declares, has been as much to wed workers more firmly to capitalist values in an attempt to win the 'hearts and minds' of Africans. Through the interventions of business, and the state, limited upward mobility, facilitated by the removal of job reservation, might come to be regarded as a possibility, if not a reality. Thus, belief in the apparent advantages of 'free enterprise' might also be fostered, with failure to succeed in such a situation, in which education and training are available to all, being viewed as lying with the individual and not the social system.

At the Good Hope Conference, Botha noted that the government had accepted the proposal of the Viljoen Committee, which was a joint undertaking between the state and business, that the 'private sector' shoulder a greater part of the burden of 'solving Black housing problems in South Africa'.[86] This was 'an essential condition for a happy and contented labour force',[87] and the 'public sector' did not possess 'the financial means' to tackle the enterprise alone. Hence, in 1983, for example, the Standard Building Society made available R1.5 million for housing in Mamelodi near Pretoria.[88] By June 1984, the total cost of the housing programme initiated by Volkswagen of South Africa had reached R2.9 million, although not all of this amount had been spent on Africans.[89] Anglo American has contributed substantially towards urban African housing, whilst in 1986 Coca-Cola declared that R20 million would be used to create new South African foundations to open opportunities for Africans in housing, business and education.[90]

Such conduct by these leading members of the business community testified to an awareness of the limitations of the market in the South African context. Rosholt remarked:[91]

I am concerned about the survival of the free enterprise system in South Africa. It has disappeared completely in some countries to the north. And the writing is on the wall for us.

If we don't give blacks the opportunity to share we make that
omission at our peril.

What was required, though, was considerably more than state
withdrawals and an unfettering of the market — hence the doctrine
of 'social responsibility', as preached and practised by dominant
elements of capital in such spheres as education, housing and the
development of small businesses. 'The question', Peter Searle,
managing director of Volkswagen of South Africa, asserted, 'for
South African business is no longer whether it should be spending
money on its social . . . responsibility — the question is rather how
much?'[92]

'Social responsibility', as Tony Bloom, chairman of the Premier
Group, recognised, conflicted with the tenets of 'free market' or
monetarist discourse.[93] This school of thought, as he observed,
considered the manager of a business to be an employee of the
owners, with an overriding duty to maximise profits for the
shareholders. For Milton Friedman,[94] 'few trends could so
thoroughly undermine the foundation of . . . free society as the
acceptance by corporate officials of a social responsibility other than
to make money for stockholders.' In South Africa, however, the
behaviour of various sections of business has not been exclusively
oriented towards the short-term pursuit of economic gain. This is
not a reflection of altruism, but rather of a desire to guarantee the
long-term survival of capitalism. Monetarism envisages the individual as making provision for his own well-being through purchases
on the market. In South Africa, in contrast, particular interventions by business, and some by the state, have had as their object
the subsidisation of the welfare of at least segments of the subordinate population. The costs, then, of certain services, rather than
being 'privatised' and devolving upon the wage earner, have been
increasingly met by corporate profits and, in instances such as
African education, tax revenues.

Hence, in so far as the alliance between the state and capital
has not merely involved a retreat by the former, but also heightened
participation by both actors in a number of arenas, it has not been
open to justification purely through an invocation of the justice and
efficiency of the 'free market'. Thus, for example, when expressing
his cautious approval of the revised industrial decentralisation
programme outlined by Botha at the Good Hope Conference,
Rosholt depicted and defended the new policy in technocratic terms.
It showed, as he told the Johannesburg Chamber of Commerce,

'a stronger economic and less ideological approach', signalling 'a welcome realism by the government, and an acceptance by it of the vital role of private enterprise. It . . . warrants our careful consideration and attention'.[95] In a situation, therefore, in which what was demanded was an expansion rather than a contraction of interventions, it was obviously not possible to rely upon a 'free market' rhetoric; instead, an appeal was made to pragmatic 'realism'.

In this fashion too, collaboration with the state could be upheld by business as non-'ideological', thus minimising the danger of undermining its political credibility within the wider society. By depoliticising its co-operation with the government in various endeavours, and portraying these as matters of practical, objective necessity, it could keep its principles intact, and affirm them in other contexts, such as through criticisms of state practices regarded as incompatible with the values of the 'free market'. Hence, Rosholt could denounce influx control 'from the standpoint of free-enterprise convictions', which emphasised 'the freedom of the individual to use his personal enterprise'.[96]

The coexistence, therefore, of both technocratic and 'free market' strains in the discursive repertoire of business has in a sense enabled it to have its cake and eat it: for in so far as its partnership with the state has served the purpose of reducing the functions of the government, it has been justifiable in terms of the norms and effectiveness of the 'free market'. At the same time, this has permitted business, when it saw fit, to make whatever political capital was to be had from censuring violations by the state of 'free market' precepts.

A technocratic language, on the other hand, has allowed business to represent joint actions with the state as exercises in non-partisan 'realism'. Its party-political allegiances, and its standing within the community at large, consequently stood less risk of being compromised: for its growing involvement with the government in certain ventures was not seen as deriving from an 'ideological' or political affinity, but instead as a set of technical interventions divorced from affairs of principle. Of course, technocratic rationality could also operate as a critique of whatever state policies were judged to be 'at loggerheads with the facts of life'.[97] In this manner, then, through its employment, in differing circumstances, of technocratic and 'free market' discourses, business could reap the benefits of association with the state and simultaneously attempt to ensure that it was not perceived, in the words of Relly, as being 'in bed with government as part of a political system'.[98]

A technocratic rhetoric has therefore been articulated with a 'free market' one, and both have been utilisable, in divergent contexts, in the service of reformist measures. In so far as 'free market' ideology is concerned, it was suggested earlier that its application in the particular conditions of South Africa meant that in specific cases it might have a productive impact. This is not to deny, however, that orthodox 'free market' or monetarist policies have been adopted at times by the South African authorities, and have led, in various instances, to intensified social oppression of the working class. Care must be taken, though, to distinguish cause from consequence. Monetarist responses in South Africa, it is contended, represented an attempt to remove the drag of high inflation and thereby lay the foundations for sustained economic growth, vital to boost profitability and to enlarge the economic cake so as to permit a greater claim by the subordinate population upon material resources. One of the effects of monetarist practices was a weakening of the position of the working class in certain respects, most notably in relation to unemployment.

Some of the monetarist activities of the South African government have included, as Gelb and Innes have noted,[99] the 'privatisation' of the state enterprise Sasol through the offering of share ownership to private interests; the reduction in the provision by the central authorities of a range of services, such as white education, municipal facilities and health care; the exposure of elements of the local economy to increased foreign competition; and the easing of financial restrictions through lifting exchange controls on overseas residents and allowing the currency to float on international markets. Thus, subsidies on items such as transport fares and bread have also been cut, but it can be argued that withdrawal in these areas, which especially affects Africans, necessitates additional spending on the police and the military. Indeed, with the escalation of conflict in South Africa, and the ongoing war in Namibia, expenditure on defence has risen to R5.12 billion or 13.7 per cent of the 1986–7 budget.[100]

Hence, the decrease in governmental spending in some spheres has, it seems, merely freed those revenues for use elsewhere, particularly in defence, African education, industrial decentralisation and small business development. Monetarism, then, has not profoundly challenged the traditionally interventionist nature of the South African state, for governmental expenditure has soared, from 22.9 per cent of the gross domestic product in 1975 to 29.2 per cent in 1985.[101] The principal factors accounting for this have been the costs of a reformist programme and its accompaniment by ever fiercer popular resistance, and thus a growing financial commitment on the part of the state to repression. The events of the last few years have shown that the government has lost none of its mastery of violence.

However, it would be misleading to interpret coercive reactions to the unrest in South Africa, which culminated in the declaration by the government of a State of Emergency on 21 July 1985, and its reimposition in June 1986, as a movement away from reform. Rather, the Emergency has been required, as Mark Swilling contends,[102] in order to destroy African opposition to reform, and to regain the strategic initiative needed to introduce measures designed to restabilise the capitalist system. The government has not proclaimed its abandonment of its reformist goals: on the contrary, it has reaffirmed them, in both Botha's so-called 'Rubicon' speech in August 1985, and in his address at the opening of Parliament in January 1986. The business community, evidently believing that the first Emergency was a prelude to the announcement of significant changes, cautiously welcomed it.[103]

The continuing process of reform, with the objectives and fiscal outlays it encompasses, together with the expenses of repression, have sabotaged any attempt by the government to lower permanently its share of total spending, and have rendered impossible any consistent pursuit of monetarist policies. In August 1984, in an effort to combat inflation by squeezing 'excessive demand' out of the economy, the authorities raised interest rates to unprecedented heights.

The immediate result, as Innes observes,[104] was to drive the economy deeply into recession. The crippling cost of credit caused consumer expenditure to drop sharply and inhibited company borrowing, thereby placing businesses — particularly small ones — as well as the state-owned corporations, under pressure to curtail expansion plans and to contract production.

During the course of 1985, the monetarist package of the previous August took its toll, with serious damage being inflicted upon the industrial base of the country. For the first five months of the year, insolvencies were 105 per cent higher than for the corresponding period in 1984, when the recession was already under way. Moreover, in the first half of 1985, company liquidations increased by 27 per cent over the last six months of 1984.[105] Nor was it just the smaller enterprises that were battered: virtually every major manufacturing and commercial concern suffered losses of some sort. Yet the impact of the recession upon capital was uneven: the mining houses earned record profits from the dramatic erosion of the value of the South African rand, and, as was the case with certain financial institutions and insurers, swallowed up a number of struggling firms, to expand their holdings.

As regards the working class, the recession exacerbated African unemployment, currently estimated at around 50 per cent of the economically active population.[106] Between October and December 1984 alone, 43,000 jobs were lost in manufacturing, mining, construction, electricity and transport.[107] Furthermore, between December 1984 and December 1985, the number of Africans registered as jobless, who constitute only a fraction of the whole, rose by 63.6 per cent.[108] Until the middle of 1985, however, the fight against inflation remained the declared economic priority of the state, and most business spokesmen voiced their support of the August 1984 austerity measures, despite the price being paid by some sectors of capital: for as André Hamersma, economist of the Standard Bank, put it, 'Inflation must be fought. In the long run, when overspending has been controlled, the economy will be healthier. But once we decide to live with inflation, we will become a banana republic.'[109]

As 1985 unfolded, though, inflation soared whilst unemployment also increased alarmingly. The intensification of social conflict as the year progressed indicated that those groups, workers and the poor in general, who experienced such developments most acutely were not inactive. By mid-1985, it was also becoming apparent that the process of reform was severely threatened by the inability of the state to devise political or constitutional changes that would bring it widespread legitimacy amongst Africans, thus helping to defuse the escalating unrest. The system of African local government which it had established towards the end of 1983 lay in ruins two years later as a result of mass opposition in the townships.

The upsurge in popular resistance fed the anxiety of business leaders about international perceptions of South Africa as an unstable and hence high-risk 'banana republic'. In the light of the considerable degree of dependence of the country upon overseas trade, investment and finance, such worry as South African business men may have felt was compounded by an increasingly successful and respectable disinvestment campaign, especially in the United States. As it was, what was to emerge as the chief source of concern was the foreign debt. As Innes notes,[110] an important outcome of the August 1984 austerity package was the sharp growth of foreign debt, as South African companies, banks and even the state sought loans abroad, where interest rates were significantly lower. Overseas debt rose to 26.8 per cent of the gross domestic product by the end of 1984, compared with 8.4 per cent in 1980.[111] Still worse, much of this borrowing was short term, and would fall due within a year.

The South African economy was therefore in an extremely vulnerable condition by the middle of 1985. Not only was it in the grip of a profound recession, but the devaluation of the rand in the latter half of 1984 had meant that debt and service charges on overseas borrowing virtually doubled. In a situation in which 66 per cent of the total debt burden consisted of short-term loans,[112] the loss of international financial confidence in the wake of the swelling unrest in South Africa dealt the economy a devastating blow. The proclamation of the Emergency in July was succeeded by the 'Rubicon' speech in mid-August, in which it was hoped by business that Botha would outline a plan of constitutional reform that would address the major, political dimension of the conflict in the country. On 31 July, after the imposition of the Emergency and of economic sanctions by France, Chase Manhattan Bank had decided to freeze all of its unused credit lines, and to call in its loans as they matured. Other American banks resolved to follow suit, and to refuse to roll over the billions of dollars of short-term debt that would be due for repayment in the coming months. The 'Rubicon' affair, which offered nothing in the way of serious proposals for political change, delivered the killer punch to the credit rating of South Africa.

The torrent of banks and investors withdrawing from South Africa became a flood. This massive vote of no confidence in Botha's political policy precipitated the collapse of the currency, so that trade on the foreign exchange and stock markets was suspended for a few days, and capital was prevented from being moved out of the country through the sale of shares. Moreover, the financial rand, abolished in 1983 as part of a monetarist programme, was reintroduced to impede the repatriation of foreign assets. Furthermore, on 2 September, South Africa unilaterally declared a moratorium on repayments of principal on its overseas debt, to enable officials to negotiate a settlement.

In response to the debt crisis, the government, in an attempt to contain the soaring unemployment that was contributing to the heightened African militancy and hence to the erosion of investor confidence, increased the additional R100 million it had already assigned in 1985 for the purpose of job creation by another R500 million. To finance this, a 10 per cent surcharge on imports was levied. The state has subsequently depicted the primary aim of its economic policy as the combating of unemployment rather than inflation, and has lowered interest rates accordingly. Thus, in presenting the 1986–7 budget, the Minister of Finance described it as meeting 'just claims to social upliftment' as well as 'the need for upgrading of the security services', and ensuring 'the moderate stimulation of the economy'.[113]

The set of reflationary measures introduced after August 1985 has been construed by some as a total economic volte-face; as a rejection, in favour of Keynesianism, of a monetarism which has failed disastrously.[114] It is, however, the contention of this chapter that it would be extremely misleading to interpret this as a complete 'turnaround':[115] for to do such is to imply that monetarism was pursued steadfastly up until this time, so that developments thereafter represent its final abandonment. In contrast, it is argued that monetarism has never been resolutely applied in South Africa, and consequently recent governmental actions should not be seen as a surrender of a hitherto firmly held position. Of course, a variety of state practices can be referred to as 'monetarist', and certain of these at least have been reversed. Yet it would be wholly incorrect to view the entirety of previous economic policy as exclusively reflecting a monetarism which has at present been swapped for an equally coherent Keynesianism.

The special circumstances of South Africa guaranteed that monetarism could not be consistently implemented. The local economy was too small, weak and open to sustain successfully such experiments as the floating of the rand on international currency markets, with the huge devaluations which accompanied this. More importantly, the social conditions necessary for the single-minded imposition of a monetarist programme — namely, a degree of stability and material security — were lacking in South Africa. Indeed, it was these which the reformist strategy sought to create, and the emergence of which various monetarist activities tended to frustrate.

What was peculiar, therefore, about the manner in which monetarist measures were adopted in South Africa was not only that they might, in particular instances, have a productive or generative power, but also that, where their impact was negative or repressive, they were co-present with a number of other elements intended to achieve the opposite effect. Thus, for example, whilst the monetarist austerity package aggravated unemployment, money was being diverted to the SBDC to counter this trend. The costs of greater interventions in the cause of 'social upliftment' as well as the 'upgrading of the security services' have thwarted any endeavour by the state to reduce its overall expenditure. Following the debt crisis, the government has pledged itself to 'the moderate stimulation of the economy' so as to attain the growth required to defuse the powder keg inside the country. Whilst its initiative on the constitutional front has faltered and lurched towards paralysis, its efforts in other areas of the reform process have continued. Indeed, in the 'Rubicon' speech, in which the bankruptcy of official thinking on the subject of political change was revealed, Botha announced that R1,000 million would be spent during the coming five years on improving underdeveloped cities and towns, and the policy of decentralisation would still be actively pursued.

Until the time of the foreign debt crisis, most of the business community stood squarely behind Botha. His willingness to confront the right wing of the National Party, and to force the showdown which precipitated the breakaway of the faction led by Andries Treurnicht and the formation of the Conservative Party in 1982, had been hailed by business as a demonstration of Botha's reformist credentials. 'The image of the Prime Minister as a "winner" ', the *Financial Mail* proclaimed in 1982, 'has never been stronger'. Now that 'a substantial component of the Right has been purged', the 'dalliance between the NP and business sector is on again'.[116] A number of prominent business men publicly expressed their support for the introduction of the tricameral parliamentary system, incorporating whites, 'coloureds' and Indians. The 1983 referendum held amongst whites, and endorsing the new Constitution, was described by even as outspoken a critic of governmental policy as Bloom as giving 'an overwhelming mandate for change which will also hopefully be used to establish a trend towards a more just society.'[117]

Enthusiasm in business circles about Botha's performance in office verged on euphoria in the first half of 1984, with the signing of the Nkomati Accord with Mozambique in March, and the official visit to several European countries a few months later. Commenting on the latter event, the *Financial Mail* noted that it might be the beginning of the road to 'SA's re-admission to the world community', for it signalled 'a recognition that, within the constraints of ideology, SA has moved towards change'.[118] In a 1984 interview, Rosholt, in an assessment of relations between the state and capital in the Botha era, declared, 'There has been remarkable change. Government accommodates the business point of view, and even invites assistance.'[119] Chris Saunders, chairman of the Tongaat-Hulett Group, concurred, adding that 'President Botha has shown great courage and political ability' in his manner of leadership.[120] In his 1985 statement to shareholders, Relly observed that considerable socio-political reforms had occurred, and the tricameral Parliament had had 'surprising success' in its first year.[121]

Such optimism as many eminent businessmen may have felt concerning the Botha administration did not, of course, imply an absence of conflicts between capital and the state. One involved the announcement by the authorities of a tax on company perquisites ('perks'). After an outcry from business, the government diluted its initial proposal. A more serious antagonism has emerged with respect to the Regional Services Councils (RSCs). A bill providing for the creation of RSCs was enacted by Parliament in June 1985. The RSCs have been interpreted as an attempt by the state to ensure a substantial redistribution of resources from white to black areas.[122] Business has bitterly opposed the RSC system, since the RSCs, which are to become the most powerful bodies involved in the supply of public goods and services at the local level, are to be financed by two new taxes, both levied upon employers. The first will be a tax upon turnover, and the second upon wages and salaries.

The hostility of organised industry and commerce to the establishment of the RSCs stems from a perception that the additional funds capital will be obliged to contribute will deepen the economic recession and further erode business confidence by increasing bankruptcies, unemployment and inflation.[123] It should not be assumed, however, that capital thus wishes to deny its share of responsibility for sponsoring the process of reform. Indeed, since the debt crisis, it has repeatedly reaffirmed its commitment in this regard, contingent upon, as always, its capacity to afford the outlays on such projects as African education, housing and small-business development, as well as upon its being treated as a partner by the state. Hence the resentment of business at the manner in which, in a situation in which, it was argued, many enterprises were hard-pressed already, the RSC system was unilaterally imposed upon employers by the government.

However, such a violation by the authorities of the Carlton and Good Hope Contract did not, it is suggested, cause its dissolution. That happened as a result of another issue. The foreign debt crisis had spurred South African business leaders on to the offensive, in open confrontation with the state. In particular, it was the standstill of 2 September which touched business men directly, by removing their access to overseas credit, and, indirectly, by making the outlook for the whole economy even bleaker. This promised to affect profits more severely, and also, in this way, to have a detrimental impact upon reform. The *Financial Mail* articulated the 'terrible paradox facing SA' in the aftermath of the moratorium. The economy 'has to grow to restore political stability';[124] yet such a development was crucially dependent upon international loans, which would not be forthcoming until relative 'political stability' prevailed.

It was evident that the withdrawal of banks and investors from South Africa was in reaction to the heightening domestic conflict, the principal aspect of which was the inability and reluctance of the Botha regime to devise a constitutional order satisfactory to the African majority. The debt crisis forced upon local business men the awareness that the flow of fresh capital from abroad would not resume as before so long as the state of affairs in the country remained explosive. If the violence was to be contained, business contended, it was imperative that the government go much further than it had hitherto contemplated in implementing political reforms. As a prominent economist was to put it: 'Political change is a prerequisite for sustained growth. Growth through economic stimulation won't ease political unrest and disturbances, and therefore uncertainty.'[125]

Never, for business, had its very functioning been so intertwined with constitutional matters. It was, to an important degree, in the hands of politics, in this latter sense, that the performance of the economy rested. The government, however, seemed incapable of anything more than minor gestures of change. Its intransigence in this respect, as exemplified in Botha's 'Rubicon' address, drove capital on to the attack, and the selfsame voices that, but a year earlier, had sounded Botha's praises, now led his denunciation. 'Having lost the opportunity to be a statesman', the *Financial Mail* fulminated, 'the State President has no option but to turn his job over to more capable people — and resign. Everyone will cheer'.[126] Even Afrikaner business men like Anton Rupert and Louis Luyt joined the chorus of criticism.[127] Chris Ball, managing director of Barclays National Bank, urged business to overcome its traditional passivity, and to take to 'the political dance floor'. The politicians, he asserted, had brought the country 'to the desert', and

the success of government in this exercise has had the result
that we are now economic as well as political pariahs. Politicians are purveyors of power and it is the inappropriate use
of that power that we have to challenge.[128]

This strong rhetoric was matched by action. A full-page
advertisement, signed by 91 industrialists and financiers, was placed
in a national Sunday newspaper. It called for the lifting of the State
of Emergency, the end of racial discrimination, 'the granting of
full South African citizenship to all our people', and negotiations
with 'acknowledged black leaders about power sharing.'[129] This
was intended to do more than influence the state. 'We wanted to
show black and union leaders that we are not part of the government', said Raymond Ackerman, chairman of the largest supermarket chain in South Africa, who had helped organise the
advertisement. 'And we had to tell overseas companies who invest
here where we stand.'[130] Ackerman was also one of a number of
businessmen to become involved in the 'Convention Alliance', a
grouping incorporating representatives of capital, the opposition
Progressive Federal Party and the Inkatha movement. Its aim was
to gather all political forces around the same table to formulate a
new Constitution.

Overall, therefore, capital was making plain its disillusionment
with the inability of the state to introduce the necessary political
changes. In September 1985, Relly and several other business men
flew to Zambia to conduct discussions with the exiled African
National Congress. Their mission was reputedly supported by such
giants of the Afrikaner business establishment as Rupert and Fred
Du Plessis of Sanlam.[131] In the mean time, demands for reform
grew more strident. 'It becomes daily more imperative', the *Financial Mail* urged, 'that Nelson Mandela be released.'[132]

Then, in January 1986, the South African Federated Chamber
of Industries (FCI), which represents the majority of the manufacturing sector in the country, issued its so-called 'Business Charter
of Social, Economic and Political Rights'. Robin Lee, managing
director of the Urban Foundation, endorsed the FCI initiative on
behalf of his organisation,[133] whilst the Association of Chambers
of Commerce of South Africa (ASSOCOM) voiced its backing for
'the basic theme of the FCI Business Charter'.[134] The content of
the FCI document is unremarkable, for the vision of South Africa
which is outlined is a mere application of classical liberal *laissez-
faire* principles to the social, economic and constitutional spheres.

What is of immense significance, however, is the fact that the Business Charter appeared: for the manner in which it emerged constituted a violation of the terms of the agreement concluded between the state and capital at the Carlton Conference and re-initialled two years later. In August 1985 ASSOCOM had published its own version of constitutional alternatives in South Africa, opting for a federal formula.[135] Yet this had been at the express request of the Minister of Constitutional Development and Planning. In contrast, the FCI Business Charter was unsolicited by the government. Hence, in presenting its set of political proposals, however vaguely defined, the Business Charter flouted a fundamental clause of the Carlton and Good Hope Contract — namely, the exclusive jurisdiction of the state over constitutional affairs.

Although the government could, and did, as in the case of ASSOCOM, invite the opinions of business on constitutional questions, it had hitherto retained the prerogative to initiate or prevent such dialogue. Thus, the Business Charter, which was issued independently of the state, struck a blow at the heart of the relationship between capital and the authorities. It hence had a meaning deeper than simply a desire to restore the credibility of business in the wider society or to pressurise the government to change. It also signalled that business, or at least important sections of it, would no longer be bound by previous allegiances, and would be free to seek political allies elsewhere. This awakening of capital as an autonomous political force is perhaps the most decisive consequence of the Business Charter, and carries ramifications that could become far-reaching.

As 1986 dawned, the state found itself confronting not only a battered economy and a haemorrhage of support to the far right, but an erstwhile partner upon whose loyalties it could no longer rely. It was doubtless in recognition of this, and in an attempt to negotiate a new settlement following the collapse of the old, that the government organised a third meeting with business men in November 1986.

Notes

1. A.D. Wassenaar, *Assault on private enterprise: the freeway to communism* (Tafelberg, Cape Town, 1977), p. 145.
2. See D. O'Meara, *Volkskapitalisme* (Ravan Press, Johannesburg, 1983).

3. D. O'Meara, ' "Muldergate" and the politics of Afrikaner nationalism', *Work in Progress*, no. 22 (April 1982), p. 3.

4. See R.W. Johnson, *How long will South Africa survive?* (Macmillan, London, 1982), p. 205.

5. See B. Hirson, *Year of fire, Year of ash* (Zed Press, London, 1979), p. 133.

6. Quoted in G. Moss, 'Total Strategy', *Work in Progress*, no. 11 (February 1980), p. 7.

7. Quoted in ibid., p. 3.

8. Quoted in ibid., p. 8.

9. See O'Meara, ' "Muldergate" '.

10. Paratus, July 1979, quoted in Moss, 'Total Strategy', p. 8.

11. See O'Meara, ' "Muldergate" '.

12. See ibid.

13. Quoted in J.S. Saul, and S. Gelb, *The crisis in South Africa* (Monthly Review Press, New York, 1981), p. 45.

14. Quoted in ibid., p. 2.

15. Magnus Malan, quoted in Moss, 'Total Strategy', p. 7.

16. *South African Plan for Research in the Human Sciences* (Human Sciences Research Council, Pretoria), 1979, p. 1.

17. Ibid., p. 32.

18. Ibid., p. 10.

19. S. Gelb, and D. Innes, 'Monetarism's double bind', *Work in Progress*, no. 36 (April 1985), p. 36.

20. Ibid., p. 37.

21. J. Keenan, 'Free markets, ideology and control', in J. Clammer (ed.), *Beyond the new economic anthropology* (Macmillan, London, 1987).

22. Gelb and Innes, 'Monetarism's double bind', p. 32.

23. Keenan, 'Free markets, ideology and control'.

24. Report of the Committee for Economic Affairs of the President's Council, 'Measures which restrict the functioning of a free market orientated system in South Africa' (1984).

25. See the discussion of this issue in A.W. Stadler, 'Shifting bases of legitimacy' in *On the political economy of race, proceedings of the Conference on Economic Development and Racial Domination, vol. 2* (University of the Western Cape, October 1984).

26. *Financial Mail*, 2 May 1980.

27. *Financial Mail*, 23 November 1979.

28. Quoted in the *Financial Mail*, 28 March 1980.

29. See P. Hudson, and M. Sarakinsky, 'Class interests and politics' in South African Research Services, *South African Review Three* (Ravan Press, Johannesburg, 1986).

30. *The Good Hope Plan for Southern Africa* (Department of Foreign Affairs and Information, Pretoria, 1981), p. 9.

31. Ibid., p. 6.

32. Quoted in *Leadership South Africa*, vol. 1, no. 1 (Autumn 1982) p. 15.

33. *Leadership South Africa*, vol. 4, no. 3 (1985), p. 13.

34. Ibid., p. 13.

35. *The Good Hope Plan for Southern Africa*, p. 14.

36. Ibid., p. 16.

37. Ibid., p. 17.
38. Ibid., p. 28.
39. Ibid., p. 15.
40. Ibid., p. 28.
41. Ibid., p. 28.
42. Ibid., p. 28.
43. See the *Financial Mail*, 20 November 1981.
44. *Financial Mail*, 30 November 1979.
45. Ibid.
46. Ibid.
47. Ibid.
48. *Financial Mail*, 14 August 1981.
49. Ibid.
50. See the *Financial Mail*, 18 July 1980.
51. Ibid.
52. See *The Good Hope Plan for Southern Africa*, p. 32.
53. See ibid., p. 34.
54. *Leadership South Africa*, vol. 2, no. 4 (Summer 1983), p. 16.
55. *Leadership South Africa*, vol. 4, no. 3. (1985), p. 13.
56. Ibid., p. 13.
57. *Leadership South Africa*, vol. 1, no. 4 (Summer 1982), p. 7.
58. *Leadership South Africa*, vol. 3, no. 4 (1984), p. 64.
59. See the *Financial Mail*, 18 July 1980.
60. Jan Steyn, executive director of the Urban Foundation, in *Leadership South Africa*, vol. 1, no. 1 (Autumn 1982), p. 16.
61. *Leadership South Africa*, vol. 4, no. 3 (1985), p. 13.
62. Gavin Relly, in ibid., p. 13.
63. Ibid., p. 13.
64. Quoted in the *Financial Mail*, 23 November 1979.
65. A.M. Rosholt, 'Urbanisation and the private sector: the need for a new approach' in H.Giliomee and L. Schlemmer (eds), *Up against the fences* (David Philip, Cape Town, 1985), p. 284.
66. Quoted in D. Posel, 'Language, legitimation and control', *Social Dynamics*, vol. 10, no. 1 (June 1984), p. 4.
67. *Leadership South Africa* vol. 4, no. 3 (1985), p. 16.
68. See Posel, 'Language, legitimation and control'.
69. See *The Good Hope Plan for Southern Agfrica*, pp. 6 and 16.
70. See, for instance, the *Sunday Star*, 27 April 1986.
71. *Financial Mail*, 9 November 1984.
72. *Services to small business* (Small Business Development Corporation, April 1985), pp. 3 and 4.
73. Ibid., p. 5.
74. See Hudson and Sarakinsky, 'Class interests and politics', p. 179.
75. *South African Digest*, 11 April 1986, p. 304.
76. *The Good Hope Plan for Southern Africa*, p. 64.
77. See A. Hirsch, 'Banking on discipline' in *South African Review Three*.
78. *Manifesto for the future* (Department of Foreign Affairs, Pretoria, 1985), p. 6.
79. *Leadership South Africa*, 'Human resources' (1984–5), p. 34.
80. *Leadership South Africa*, vol. 1, no. 1 (Autumn 1982), p. 16.

81. *Leadership South Africa*, 'Human resources' (1984–5), pp. 34–5.
82. The *Star*, 28 October 1982.
83. 1985 annual report of the Anglo American Corporation.
84. See *South African Digest*, 11 April 1986.
85. See L. Chisholm, 'Redefining skills', *Comparative Education*, vol. 19, no. 3 (1983).
86. *The Good Hope Plan for Southern Africa*, p. 18.
87. Ibid., p. 20.
88. See Posel, 'Language, legitimation and control'. p. 16.
89. *Leadership South Africa*, 'Human resources' (1984–5), p. 123.
90. See *South African Digest*, 4 April 1986.
91. Quoted in the *Financial Mail*, 'Top companies supplement' (4 May 1984).
92. *Leadership South Africa*, 'Human resources' (1984–5), p. 122.
93. See *Leadership South Africa*, vol. 1, no. 1 (Autumn 1982).
94. Quoted in *Leadership South Africa*, vol. 4, no. 2 (1985), p. 106.
95. Rosholt, 'Urbanisation and the private sector', pp. 289–90.
96. Ibid., p. 284.
97. See ibid., p. 290.
98. *Leadership South Africa*, vol. 4, no. 3 (1985), p. 18.
99. See Gelb and Innes, 'Monetarism's double bind'.
100. *Financial Mail*, 21 March 1986.
101. The *Star*, 14 April 1986.
102. See M. Swilling, 'Stayaways, urban protest and the state' in *South African Review Three*.
103. See the statement issued by the two largest employer organisations in South Africa on 21 July 1985.
104. See D. Innes, 'Monetarism and the South African crisis' in *South African Review Three*.
105. See ibid., p. 295.
106. See the *Star*, 12 September 1986, and the *Daily Telegraph* (London), 15 September 1986.
107. See K. von Holdt, 'The economy: Achilles heel of the New Deal', in *South African Review Three*, p. 314.
108. The *Star*, 14 April 1986.
109. *Financial Mail*, 9 November 1984.
110. See Innes, 'Monetarism and the South African crisis'.
111. See ibid., p. 292.
112. See ibid., p. 297.
113. *Business Day*, 18 March 1986.
114. See, for instance, Innes, 'Monetarism and the South African crisis'.
115. See ibid., p. 300.
116. *Financial Mail*, 5 March 1982.
117. See the *Financial Mail*, 16 November 1984.
118. *Financial Mail*, 1 June 1984.
119. See the *Financial Mail*, 'Top companies supplement', 4 May 1984.
120. *Leadership South Africa*, vol. 3, no. 3 (1984), p. 61.
121. See the *Financial Mail*, 12 July 1985.
122. See W. Cobbett *et al.*, 'South Africa's regional political economy', in *South African Review Three* (1986), pp. 137–68.

123. See, for instance, the *Star*, 19 May 1986.

124. *Financial Mail*, 20 September 1985.

125. See the *Financial Mail*, 28 February 1986.

126. *Financial Mail*, 6 September 1985.

127. See, for instance, ibid.

128. See 'Investment in 1986', supplement to the *Financial Mail*, 29 November 1985.

129. *Sunday Times*, 29 September 1985.

130. Quoted in *Euromoney* (December 1985), p. 79.

131. See the *Financial Mail*, 20 September 1985.

132. *Financial Mail*, 27 September 1985.

133. See the *Star*, 23 January 1986.

134. See the *Financial Mail*, 24 January 1986.

135. J.A. Lombard and J.A. du Pisanie, A Memorandum for ASSOCOM, *Removal of discrimination against blacks in the political economy of the Republic of South Africa* (Bureau for Economic Policy and Analysis, University of Pretoria, 1985).

4

The Crisis of Local Government in South Africa

Jeremy Grest

Introduction

This chapter discusses the current reorganisation of local government in South Africa, with a view to assessing the nature, extent
and possible future implications of the reform measures presently
being introduced at the local level. It begins with an overview of
the development of the local government system, focusing on major
trends and key moments in the process, with the emphasis on its
post-1948 apartheid phase. It provides a detailed analysis of the post-
Soweto 1976 attempts by the state to rebuild its system of urban
control, and to accelerate the pace of reform using local-level
structures. It discusses the major restructuring of local government
introduced in the wake of the 1983 constitutional reforms, and the
resistance to these reforms culminating in the declaration of a State
of Emergency in July 1985. It closes with a discussion, in the context
of the state's strategy of 'orderly urbanisation', of the Regional
Service Councils, and some speculation as to their likely impact
on the highly politicised local arena.

The discussion starts from the position that the current crisis of
local government has to be understood in terms of the historical
development of the system as a whole. Although the political
separation of local government structures along racial lines is one
of the hallmarks of the system's development, too narrow a focus
on the separate political structures obscures the underlying
coherence of the social relations underpinning them. The chapter
aims to illustrate, within an historical framework, the specific
place occupied by local government within the overall framework
of political domination and capital accumulation.

Separate structures dealing with local government and administration for the variously defined racial groups have been created and developed over time. Their uneven emergence has been a reflection of the differential incorporation of the various groups into the racial division of labour and of the differing needs of the state for administrative controls over urbanisation during its various phases. Control over African urbanisation was an early priority, leading to the emergence of uniform state policy in the 1920s. Coloured and Indian people, as minorities, faced concerted state action on the local level starting in the 1940s.

The absence of any meaningful representation in bodies whose decisions govern daily living has led to a lack of legitimacy which over time has reached crisis proportions as apathy has turned into outright rejection and active, violent opposition. This lack of any political legitimacy of local structures of representation for all South Africa's dominated groups has its material basis in state urban policy which has created segregated dormitory areas starved of even the most basic infrastructural resources. These areas have no independent fiscal base which could be used to finance the work necessary to create a more tolerable living environment. The bulk of industry and commerce has been developed in 'white' areas and pays taxes to the relevant local authority. The state's policy until recently of preventing the emergence of a property-owning urban African petty bourgeosie has further exacerbated the financial position of the townships' local administrative structures. The development of Indian and 'coloured' Group Areas has had similar overall financial effects on local administration, where property ownership has tended to be limited to a relatively small stratum in the population, and is certainly not general in the working class.

Running counter to the tendency towards full ethnic institutional separation has been a different logic which dictates, through cost structures, a limit to this process. Given that it is the business of local government to ensure the provision of services in the sphere of collective consumption and urban reproduction, a range of 'technical' consideration[5] relating to cost factors, economies of scale, etc. have begun to make themselves felt very forcibly, especially in the context of the serious economic and fiscal crisis of the last few years.

Current state strategy is aimed at dealing with the effects of the crisis it faces at the local level through the implementation of two major principles. The maximum devolution of authority and self-determination at the local level is designed to recreate the former structures of control on a new footing with a firmer indigenous base. The commitment to private enterprise at the local level effectively lays the foundation for the state's withdrawal from key areas of urban reproduction, leaving the local communities to carry the costs of services, and opening further avenues for private accummulation.

The new structures of local government have been conceived as operating on a regional level. This is in accordance with the state's developing strategy for regional development (see Cobbett *et al.*, 1986) and follows the dominant trends of capital accumulation in the last decade (Bell, 1985). The regional form taken by the new structures also reflects the reality of uneven development in South Africa, and the regionally specific nature of the struggles currently being fought at the local level.

Local government: from Union to Soweto

One of the most salient features of local government in South Africa has been the underlying continuity of the structures that have developed since Union. The basic features of the system of administration and control are outlined in order to provide a context for the evaluation of the post-Soweto reforms introduced in response to a developing challenge to the previously hegemonic structures.

At Union in 1910 a centralised unitary state was created, with provincial councils in each of the former British colonies and Boer republics exercising a range of subordinate powers, including control over local government.[1] A federal drive, emanating from Natal, had been debated and set aside at the time. The provincial structure represented a concession to federal sentiment, and since Union it has been subject to sustained erosion of its powers by an increasingly centralised state.[2] The provincial structure was headed by a politically appointed chief executive officer which further ensured central political control. Political participation at the provincial level was progressively confined to whites after Union.[3] All four colonies had established systems of local government at the time of Union. Municipal affairs were controlled by the provincial councils, which were empowered by Parliament to pass ordinances for their regulation.[4]

The 1923 Urban Areas Act provided the framework for a uniform national system of 'Native Administration' (under central government control) in which municipalities had a key role as the local agents of the central state. Central to the administrative structures created was the principle that the urban areas were a 'European' preserve and that Africans were temporary sojourners, there to serve the economy as long as they were needed, but no longer.

The administrative framework consolidated in the 1920s laid the foundations upon which the apartheid state was built from the 1950s. Residential segregation was enforced by the municipal authorities which were delegated the power to build and administer 'native locations' and to control African housing. The regulation of entry into urban areas and registration of service contracts was also a municipal responsibility. The costs of urban African administration were met from a separate Native Revenue Account, financed from the proceeds of the sale of sorghum beer under municipal monopoly. Local administration of Africans was expected to be self-financing, and municipalities were generally reluctant to consider any subsidy by transfers from the general rates account to which white voters contributed. African freehold property rights in urban areas were circumscribed and in time totally prescribed. In addition, there was a refusal to grant any further political rights to urban Africans. Provision was made for municipalities to create purely consultative Advisory Boards for the articulation of urban African interests. Municipalities proved reluctant to take even this limited step and often failed to give any real weight to the opinions expressed by these bodies. Advisory Boards were powerless bodies with low credibility, often attracting opportunists to their ranks.[5]

Although the municipalities acted as agents of the central state, they did so within a broadly defined set of legislative parameters which accorded them a measure of administrative autonomy. When the apartheid state was introduced in the 1950s, the central-local relationship was substantially restructured. The National Party victory in 1948 happened at a time of a growing urban management crisis for the dominant classes. A combination of factors, including the rapid development of secondary industry during the war, the relaxation of pass laws, low agricultural wages and the growth of rural landlessness, led to an intensified and uncontrolled urbanisation process.

The development in the major urban centres of a militant challenge to the established mechanisms of accumulation and control led to a debate over urban strategy within the ruling class. The United Party's Fagan Report of February 1948 argued that the urbanisation of Africans was inevitable and that the process needed overall supervision and control by the authorities; whilst the National Party's Sauer Report of the same year, representing the interests of agricultural capital and the white working class, outlined the basis of the subsequent apartheid strategy.

Under Verwoerd's control, the Native Affairs Department became the leading arm of the state apparatus charged with the implementation of apartheid in South Africa. Its interventions in the field of municipal African administration became much more direct as the central government took greater powers and exercised detailed supervision at the local level. The implementation of the influx control provisions of the 1952 Urban Areas Act by the major municipalities under United Party control, particularly Johannesburg, became a source of conflict between central and local authorities. The housing crisis which had built up in the 1940s was also a result of the shortage of municipal funds — a direct consequence of the reluctance of local authorities to subsidise African housing from their general rates funds. The state dealt with this through further centralisation of control over the provision of municipal housing and the development of the model township.

Popular resistance to the state's urban policies of the 1950s was crushed by savage repression in the 1960s. The development of the bantustan strategy meant that urban African administration was progressively linked to this idea. Its general effect was to limit further the resources available for urban administration, especially the provision of housing. In 1961 an Urban Bantu Council (UBC) system replaced the former 'Advisory Boards' as a vehicle for local consultation in a move which linked the selection of representatives more closely to the bantustans. The UBCs, like the Advisory Boards, were purely advisory bodies which acted as agents of the local authorities. They were equipped with some additional powers, none of which gave them any greater credibility in the community.

By the late 1960s the process of centralisation of administrative power by the Department of Bantu Administration and Development was far advanced, with the main thrust of its policies being directed towards urban control rather than the provision of services to the population. The municipalities lost all control over local administration in 1971 with the creation of 22 Bantu Affairs Administration Boards, constituting a separate specialised branch of the state directly responsible to the Department of Bantu Administration and Development. The Boards had a wider geographical area of jurisdiction than the municipalities, and also took in rural areas within their boundaries. Their creation represented the high watermark of apartheid in urban administration. With the increasing focus on bantustan development in the

1970s' the Boards became active agents of bantustan urbanisation, apart from tightening central control over almost every aspect of the daily lives of township dwellers. For urban Africans the advent of the Boards meant increasingly stringent influx control measures, coupled with attacks on Section 10 qualifications. Township services were badly ignored and from 1968 there was an effective freeze on family housing construction.[6]

The Boards as an institutional expression of Verwoerdian-style apartheid were created at the end of a long phase of capital accumulation which had been underwritten by the repression of the 1960s and the disorganisation of the popular classes in the townships. It has been argued that their creation was a response to pressures from industrial capital in particular for a restructuring of the relations of production and of reproduction of the working class. The wider areas of jurisdiction of Boards were a response to calls for greater labour mobility, but their labour allocation function was subordinated to the state's influx control strategy. They emerged as monolithic structures of control without any form of democratic representation for township-based interests (Hindson, 1985a).

Local government for coloured and Indian people

The system of local government for coloured and Indian people reflects the intermediate position these groups have come to occupy in the racial division of labour, as well as the specific regional dynamics of accumulation in South Africa. Local government structures developed after Union were not uniform in the space they allowed for the representation of the interests of the dominated groups.

In the Cape, with its 'liberal' tradition, coloured and Indian people were able to enrol as voters in municipal elections until 1971. In Natal Indians were disenfranchised at the local level in 1924, whilst coloured voters remained on the same municipal roll as whites until 1956. There was no local representation for either group in the Orange Free State or the Transvaal.

The contrast between the local government systems developed in Cape Town and Durban illustrates the complexity and variety of local forces and underlines the dangers of oversimplification. The 'liberal' tradition tended to give greater salience to discrimination based on wealth and was less overtly racist in its ideology. The Cape Town City Council had five (out of 45) coloured city councillors by 1949, but at the same time frequently raised its voting qualifications, based on property ownership, effectively excluding a greater proportion of coloured people from the franchise. When the Group Areas Act was passed in 1950 the City Council resisted its implementation (Todes *et al.*, 1986). In Durban racist anti-Indian sentiment was strongly articulated from an early stage following the settlement of Indians in the 1860s, based on perceived threats of commercial competition and residential infiltration. The Durban City Council, as the local representative of ruling white interests, acted as one of the chief architects of the Group Areas Act (Grest, 1985).

The present system of local government for coloured and Indian people has its origin in the Group Areas Act. As one of the foundation stones of apartheid, it demarcated separate zones in which only white, coloured or Indian people could live and own property. The newly designated group areas for coloured and Indian people fell directly under the administrative control of the white local authorities until 1962 when the Act was amended to create a system of separate local representation. It was envisaged that this would lead to the eventual creation of autonomous local bodies (Hughes and Grest, 1983).

The various provincial authorities then passed a series of ordinances setting up the new system. From these ordinances developed a series of consultative, management and local affairs committees whose powers, functions and development were structured by the various provincial authorities through the promulgation of provincial notices and regulations.

These committees began as partly nominated and partly elected bodies, evolving over time into fully elected bodies. They emerged as purely consultative organs, enjoying no legislative powers whatsoever. The system was created at a time when the leading coloured and Indian political organisations which were associated with the national democratic struggle had been severely repressed, and popular organisation was virtually non-existent. In this context these bodies lacked popular legitimacy and were met with a general apathy or suspicion on the part of potential voters committed to the restoration of a single municipal franchise.[7]

Soweto and beyond: towards crisis

By the mid-1970s state policy governing the control and reproduction of the labour force in the African townships had created the preconditions for the Soweto Uprising of June 1976.[8] Conditions of daily living in the townships deteriorated under the Administration Board regime as the housing shortage grew, rents increased, services remained uniformly poor and urban controls were tightened, all in the context of the diversion of state resources into the developing bantustan programme in which the Boards played an important role.

The downturn in the economy from 1972 contributed to urban unemployment at a time when the African working class was re-emerging as a militant and organised force following the Durban strikes of 1973.[9] The Black Consciousness Movement's development from the late 1960s had created a heightened political awareness amongst certain strata in the urban population, notably students and the petty bourgeoisie. Students in particular were increasingly conscious of the links between Bantu education and the subordinate role they were expected to play in an economy which was no longer able to provide work. Events in Southern Africa, culminating in the collapse of the Portuguese colonial regime and the accession to power of the MPLA and FRELIMO, contributed to a growing sense that minority domination was not unassailable.

The violence which broke out in Soweto spread to other urban centres in the country and continued through 1977, with attacks on Administration Board buildings and liquor outlets as the most visible symbols of state rule in the townships. In Soweto the UBC collapsed under popular pressure after it had agreed to an unpopular rent increase announced by the Administration Board.

The state's response to the urban revolt of 1976 and 1977 was a strategy aimed at dividing and controlling the popular classes under the guise of the twin policies of 'reform' and 'development', coupled with coercion where other measures failed. For its part, monopoly capital created the Urban Foundation as a private sector body designed to make strategic interventions in the field of state urban policy. The Foundation emerged out of the growing significance of monopoly capital in the state and the economy and from the perceived necessity for an urban reproduction policy more in keeping with its particular needs.

In 1977 Community Councils were created to replace the moribund UBCs and Advisory Boards. They were to function as representative bodies with greater executive powers operating alongside the Administration Boards. Their creation was aimed at co-opting a section of the urban population as agents for the state at the local level through the extension of a limited range of concessions (Bloch, 1982).

Ministerial power over community councils was total: the Minister established the councils, allocated powers, made regulations in regard to elections, period of office, conditions of service, conduct of meetings, employment, finance, and any other matters affecting their operation. The Community Councils were designed to take over some of the responsibility for the provision and management of housing from the Boards at a time when the state was looking for ways of shifting the burden of costs of provision of services increasingly on to the working class. They emerged both as an effect of the struggles in the townships and as an attempt to defuse them.

Relations between Councils and Boards were a source of some controversy. The relationship was cast by the Boards as one of principal and agent: the Council as principal taking decisions and making recommendations and the Board as agent carrying these out, by virtue of its access to resources, staff and expertise. In practice the Boards continued to wield management power in the townships and were reluctant to relinquish it. Councillors for their part found themselves in the front line, taking responsibility for decisions over which they felt they had no immediate control.

Influx control and labour allocation remained under the control of the Boards in conjunction with the police and commissioners' offices and courts, and it was made clear that this function would not be handed to Community Councils. In the late 1970s, state strategy as outlined in the Riekert Report moved towards a limited relaxation of controls on urban 'insiders' and a tightening of prohibitions against the 'outsiders' — that section of the population not considered 'established' in the towns. At the same time the state was busy whittling away Section 10 urban qualifications (Hindson, 1983).

By 1980 about 224 Community Councils had been established in the face of large-scale rejection of the system by the vast majority of township residents all over South Africa. Where elections were held, polls were generally low, and Councils lacked political legitimacy from their inception. Councillors were not generally regarded as the 'real' leaders of the communities they claimed to represent and acquired a reputation for corruption and using their positions for self-enrichment (Labour Research Committee, undated).

One of the problems contributing to the fiscal crisis in the townships was their lack of a tax base, owing to the small number of businesses located within them, and the state's suppression of private property rights for urban Africans. From the late 1970s the state's commitment to 'private enterprise' as an ideology of legitimation saw attempts being made to foster 'free enterprise' in the townships. Restrictions on traders and business-men were lifted, but freehold was still not granted at that stage. The former Postmaster-General, Louis Rive, was appointed to a Soweto Planning Council to plan and develop Soweto in conjunction with the Community Councils for the area. One of the main objectives was to foster business development. When in 1979 'white' capital was allowed into the townships (one of Riekert's recommendations), the Community Councils were empowered to supervise this process — one which led to struggles between councillors and excluded local business men, and their alienation from the council system.

One implication of the Community Councils' control over township housing and services was that they became responsible for implementing unpopular increases in rents and service charges. When the Boards took over from the municipalities, their main sources of finance were rents, profits on beer and alcohol sales, which amounted to over 50 per cent of their income, and levies from employers. Nearly all of the Boards inherited healthy revenue accounts from the municipalities, but within a short space of time their position was transformed and the Boards began to experience serious financial problems. The major cause of the deterioration of Board finances was the loss incurred on housing and services and the failure to match income with increased expenditure in the 1970s (Bekker and Humphries, 1985). To compound their difficulties, the monopoly on beer sales in the townships came under popular attack in the late 1970s and further threatened the financial base of the Boards. Their response was to begin to introduce 'economic' rentals and service charges based on actual cost of delivery and progressively to phase out the previously built-in subsidies. The question of increased rents and charges was rapidly politicised as township residents mobilised against them on the grounds that current wage levels, already under attack from inflation, could not meet the increases.

From 1979 a series of township struggles over rent (and transport, which was not controlled in any way by Community Councils) led to the creation of community-based organisations which mobilised against the Community Council system.

In 1980 three Bills were introduced by the Minister of Co-operation and Development, Dr Koornhof, intended to give effect to the state's new urban strategy as articulated in the Riekert Report. The Bills were withdrawn in the face of widespread opposition and resurfaced in 1982 as the Black Communities Development Bill, the Black Local Authorities Bill and the Orderly Movement and Settlement of Black Persons Bill (Hindson and Lacey, 1983).

By 1982 the Community Council system had all but collapsed. Elections scheduled for 1980 had been twice postponed at the request of councillors themselves. The new legislation was intended to give effect to the state's strategy of gradual withdrawal of central state control over the townships and its replacement with a decentralised structure under the control of developing black local authorities (BLAs).

The Black Local Authorities Act provided the mechanism for the conversion of the discredited Community Councils into a system of local government similar to that operating for whites. In terms of the legislation, the 232 Community Councils in the 299 townships in 'white' South Africa were to be phased out and replaced with Town or Village Councils. The Act conferred certain powers directly on the new local authorities, giving them a greater status and a longer measure of autonomy than the Community Councils whose powers were subject to much wider ministerial discretion. The new local authorities were vested with a range of powers which were previously the functions of the Administration Boards.[10] A large degree of control remained in the hands of the Minister of Co-operation and Development, however, including financial decisions. The Administration Boards, which under the Black Communities Development Bill were to become Development Boards, remained under the control of the Department of Co-operation and Development. The Department continued to control township and housing development. This was regarded as a critical function since the third Koornhof Bill on Orderly Movement and Settlement of Black Persons made 'approved' accommodation a necessary requirement for permanent urban residential rights for Africans in townships in 'white' South Africa. The Boards were also to maintain their influx control functions, although it had been accepted in principle that they would lose these at some future stage.

Elections were held in November and December 1983 for the first 26 Councils to be upgraded under the new Local Authorities Act against a background of growing popular resistance, and increasing violence in the townships. Bomb attacks on councillors, death threats, court cases alleging fraud, murder, theft and assault punctuated the business of many Councils (Grest and Hughes, 1984). The majority of the new Councils were created in the Transvaal urban areas, where an Anti-Community Councils Election Committee was formed to co-ordinate rejection of the new system. Voting figures showed a 21 per cent overall turnout, compared with 30 per cent in 1978. The Soweto poll was 10.7 per cent — a clear indication that the 'new deal' had failed to attract the broader support for which the government was hoping (SAIRR, 1984, p. 259).

Coloured and Indian local government after Soweto

The question of representative structures for coloured and Indian people has been a problem for the ruling group for some time. To the extent that it has been the intention to win their political allegiance and prevent an alliance from being formed with the African majority, the state's problem has revolved around the creation of separate structures sufficiently attractive to co-opt sufficient participants to make its strategy workable. The pattern of reform has involved a process of gradually increasing the political stakes and providing the incentives for participants to put themselves forward.

Initially there does not seem to have been much urgency attached to the question, as twelve years elapsed after the passage of the Group Areas Act before it was amended in 1962 to create the basis of the present system of separate representation. By 1976 no coloured municipalities existed, and only two Indian town Boards had been created in terms of the Act. The Theron Commission, reporting in 1976, drew attention to serious weaknesses in coloured local government structures. It found that the state had failed to create the necessary capacities to provide adequately for the needs of local coloured communities. It listed as reasons a range of factors which pointed on the one hand to the political rejection of the system by the majority of the population and resistance to its implementation by the established white local authorities. On the other hand, it listed a set of apparently more 'technical' or 'administrative' factors — such as the geographical fragmentation of coloured areas, the fact that services were tied in to white municipalities, that they were not financially viable — and experienced shortage of trained personnel and of potential councillors of 'calibre' (Todes *et al.*, 1986).

The local committees were met in the 1970s with a widespread lack of enthusiasm and support from their constituents and they do not seem to have been taken very seriously by the white 'parent' bodies. The general neglect of services in coloured and Indian areas was a further problem. The state was aware of the issues in the 1970s but took no action either to improve the financial position or to force the issue of autonomous local government for coloured and Indian people. It is probably that the failure to implement its plans at that stage was a combination of a lack of urgency and the unco-operativeness of both white local authorities and the management and local affairs committees. The inability of the National Party to implement a policy which in practical terms would have required some multiracial co-operation was a further brake (Todes *et al.*, 1986).

The impact of events in Soweto forced an acceleration in policy implementation and a redirection of state goals, at least to some extent. The Black Consciousness Movement posed the threat of black unity in an alliance involving Indians and coloureds. At the same time changes in the class structure of the coloured and Indian population with the growth of a more substantial petty bourgeoise demanded a new attitude towards the question of representative structures.

From the mid-1970s the state embarked on a process of 'reform by commission'. A series of committees investigated various aspects of local government relating to coloureds and Indians. The Yeld Committee published two reports in 1978 on the feasibility of establishing autonomous coloured local authorities. It found that no single coloured area was capable of becoming a viable autonomous local unit without further state assistance. It also reported that racially separated local authorities were generally unacceptable, and that attitudes had hardened with Labour Party-controlled management committees rejecting the idea of separate coloured municipalities (Republic of South Africa President's Council 1, 1982, p. 33).

The Schlebusch Report of 1978 looked at ways and means of providing management committees with additional powers and of raising their status generally. Schlebusch found that the members of his committee representing management committees were adamant that any adjustments made to local government arrangements should lead to direct representation on white councils. He also found that the management committee system had become politicised and deprecated this, considering that it prevented the performance of the 'proper tasks' of the system. He also referred to a general feeling that these committees had been imposed on coloured people and lacked real power (ibid., p. 25).

The Slater Committee reported in 1979 on four selected Indian group areas in Natal and the Transvaal where Local Affairs Committees (LACs) were in operation. The aim was to determine whether autonomous local authorities could be established there. They found a unanimous rejection by Indian bodies of separate local authorities and a demand for mixed town councils (ibid., p. 34).

The Browne Committee Report of 1980 looked at local government financing in a comprehensive fashion. It recommended a system of transfer payments from white municipalities to coloured and Indian local authorities as a method of solving their financial problems. This solution was unacceptable to the municipalities and was not implemented. What was made clear by Browne was that local government financing is heavily influenced by South Africa's unequal income distribution, since the levying of rates on fixed property is the single most important source of tax revenue for local authorities (ibid., p. 91).

The twin problems of the absence of political legitimacy for the state's structures at the local level, and how these bodies are to emerge as financially viable entities, have continued to exercise the minds of the ruling group. Given the perceived inadequacy of the Browne Report on financial reform measures, an *ad hoc* working group headed by the Director-General of the Department of Finance, Gerhard Croeser, was set up to re-examine the question of financing. The Croeser Committee's work has had a decisive impact on state thinking, and has been embodied in the Regional Services Council structure which has emerged as the framework within which the state will attempt to contain the overwhelming problems of urban management which confront it.

The 1982 President's Council Report on Local and Regional Management Systems provided the basic parameters for the current phase of restructuring at the local level. Adopting a self-consciously reformist stance, the Council sought to tackle the problem of how potentially autonomous separate local authorities could gain greater political legitimacy and finance the provision of services in the context of a general fiscal crisis. The committee proposed a universal franchise at the local level, weighted in favour of property ownership. Tenants could receive single votes, property owners could have several.

Regarding the provision of services, the committee drew a distinction between 'hard' services (such as water, electricity, roads, waste disposal, etc.), which were susceptible to economies of scale and used by all groups in a community, and 'soft' services. The latter included parks, libraries, swimming baths, etc., as specific to an area and 'culturally sensitive'. The committee proposed that 'hard' services be taken over by metropolitan boards upon which local authorities would be represented, and that 'soft' services remain the responsibility of the various local bodies. The committee proposed that financial reforms be implemented to widen the fiscal base of these local authorities which would then progress upon the road to autonomy (ibid., pp. 87–95).

The President's Council (PC) solution lay in the separation of 'hard' and 'soft' services, the creation of a new overarching structure of control at the local level, broadening the fiscal base of coloured and Indian local authorities and launching them into autonomy where they would assume financial responsibility for services which were currently a drain on white local authority coffers.

Two alternative proposals for the future of second-tier government were outlined. The first involved the complete phasing out of provincial government as an intermediate level between central and local state and the creation of a series of metropolitan or area authority service corporations linking both levels. The second alternative, which has come to be the option pursued by the state, envisaged the retention of the provincial level with revised powers and metropolitan or area authority structures as a link to the local level.[11]

Public reaction by participants in coloured and Indian local structures was negative, but characteristically their reluctance to accept the new structures as formulated by the state did not prevent them from negotiating for improvement and concessions.

The new Constitution, insurrection, and local government

The introduction of the new Constitution in 1983 has had far reaching effects on politics at both the national and local levels. The inception of the tricameral Parliament provided a certain purchase for the government's junior coloured and Indian allies within the state apparatus, whilst firmly excluding African participation. It also led to greater unity of opposition forces and the emergence of national groupings committed to challenging state policy (Barrell, 1984).

The key political distinction between 'own' and 'general' affairs within the Constitution made local government an 'own affair' where it affects members of one race group only. When a local government matter affects the interests of more than one group, it falls under 'general affairs'. The notion of 'own' and 'general' affairs has in effect been duplicated at the local level through the distinction between 'hard' and 'soft' services. The structures that are being developed at the local level similarly seek to entrench minority ruling interests whilst allowing for a limited degree of multiracial management.

Given the importance of local government within the overall reform strategy, it has been a central area of state initiative since the introduction of the new Constitution. The Promotion of Local Government Affairs Act of 1983 made provision for a Co-ordinating Council and Municipal Development Boards, whilst also setting out measures to improve communications between coloured and Indian committees and white local authorities.[12] The Co-ordinating Council's task is that of a 'think-tank' for the Department of Constitutional Development and Planning which has removed ultimate jurisdiction over local affairs from the provincial structures and has centralised power in the hands of the Minister. The Municipal Development Boards are composed of technical specialists whose job it is to facilitate the necessary conditions for the creation of autonomous local authorities as soon as possible.

Management committee elections in the Cape in 1983 showed that the Labour Party's participation in the tricameral Parliament was unacceptable to a majority of urban voters who heeded the stay-away call from the UDF. The Labour Party's hold on rural areas in both the Western and Eastern Cape remained firm. Both participants in local committees and their opponents, increasingly well organised in urban civic associations, have made repeated calls for direct representation on white City and Town Councils. By 1983 there was an increasing trend for civic organisations to bypass the management committees which they regarded as powerless bodies, and to negotiate directly with white local authorities on housing-related issues. In Johannesburg the state's strategy for local authorities led to a protracted struggle between the Lenasia committees and the civic association, culminating in Lenasia being granted 'autonomy' by the City Council under instruction from the Province. The experience of the Natal Indian Town Boards which have autonomous status suggests that this has not enabled the development of a self-regulating system, and that continued administrative intervention by the province has been necessary due to the frailty of the economic base on which autonomy was erected (Grest and Hughes, 1984). The civic associations reject autonomy on the grounds that residents will have to bear very heavy increases in service costs.

In 1984 the state's strategy for the restructuring of local and regional government began to emerge much more clearly, the groundwork having been prepared by recommendations from a series of state organised investigations.[13] The state's guidelines for local authorities as set out by the Minister of Constitutional Development and Planning were based on the principles of maximum devolution of power and decentralisation of administration to the local level, and of minimal administrative control over local authorities. Local authorities were to be established for the various population groups on a territorial basis, subject to their financial viability. Joint services would be provided at metropolitan or regional level by purpose-created bodies, the Regional Services Councils (RSCs).

Local government reorganisation has increasingly come to be seen as an important tool of conflict management through its potential buffering effect on central structures. The state aims to use the local arena as a training ground for collaborative political leadership, and to depoliticise local government through the creation of a series of technical management bodies controlling the provision of essential local services. At the same time it is withdrawing its fiscal support at the local level and encouraging the privatisation of local government services, arguing that this is the most efficient way of cutting costs and increasing efficiency.

The Regional Services Councils Act of 1985 incorporated most of these strands of state policy. Its effect will be the division of each of the provinces into a number of regions which will in turn be divided into local government areas. Each region will have an RSC, on which each local government area will be represented by a recognised primary local authority such as a city council, management committee or other representative body. The state's original formulation excluded African areas from direct representation but it was subsequently announced (in December 1984) that African Town Councils would be represented. The Act empowers the administrator of a province, after consultation with recognised local authorities, to establish an RSC in any region. The RSCs will have the function of a local authority but will not be empowered to levy rates on property. Each primary local authority in the RSC's jurisdiction will be allocated votes in proportion to the services paid for by that authority, with a limit of 50 per cent. This effectively allows the larger urban local authorities to retain control over these bodies whilst incorporating African, coloured and Indian representatives into a 'multiracial' decision-making framework.[14]

RSC finances are to be created from two new sources of revenue suggested by the Croeser Committee. These are both taxes on capital: a Regional Establishment Levy, not exceeding 0.1 per cent of business turnover, and a Regional Service Levy, not exceeding 0.25 per cent of total wages payroll. The state's intention is to use the RSCs to upgrade the standard of basic infrastructural services in the segregated African, coloured and Indian local authority areas lacking an independent fiscal base through taxing capital on a regional level.

The Local Government Bodies Franchise Act of 1984 provided for uniform franchise qualifications for whites, Indians and coloured people in the election of local authorities. It restricted the franchise to registered parliamentary voters, and specific separate voters' rolls and votes for separate local structures for the various groups. It also provided for property owners to exercise a vote in a local authority area in which they owned such property, thus giving additional weight to property owners' political participation at the local level. The Local Authority Loans Fund Act of 1984 expanded the borrowing power of local authorities, but centralised control over funding, a move seen as being designed to further control policy implementation through financial means. In a further centralising measure the Minister of Constitutional Development and Planning took power to establish or dissolve a local authority, to change its area of jurisdiction and to classify it according to a grading system. The effect of the measure was to further diminish the powers of the provinces over local government (SAIRR, 1984, p. 152). The Remuneration of Town Clerk's Act of 1984 removed from local authorities the power to set their own rates of remuneration and vested it in the hands of the Minister of Constitutional Development and Planning. In future town clerks' salaries will be determined according to the grading of the local authority as determined by central government. The effect of the measure is to blur the former distinction of the town clerk's role as a municipal employee rather than a central government civil servant (Evans, 1985).

Whilst the state moved rapidly to restructure local government for whites, Indians and coloured people after 1983 it was faced with a far more intractable set of problems regarding the administration of the African townships. Its attempts to reorganise African local government contributed to a series of grievances deeply felt by township dwellers, which culminated in the outbreak in 1984 of civil violence more widespread than any experienced since Soweto in 1976. Persistently high inflation rates and deepening unemployment, a continuing educational crisis and rejection of the tricameral parliamentary structures created a volatile environment in the townships.

Against this background the state moved ahead with its plans. The Black Communities Development Act of 1984 began the process of redefining the role of the notorious Administration Boards. They were reconstituted as Development Boards, still under the control of the Department of Co-operation and Development, but with a new accent on the promotion of the 'viability, development welfare and autonomy' of urban African communities. It was intended that powers of township administration would devolve to the BLAs being developed by the state, and that the Department Boards would confine their activities to the establishment of housing schemes and the training of personnel for local authorities (SAIRR, 1984, p. 161). The transition in roles was not a smooth one, reflecting the tensions inherent in the process of converting a well developed repressive apparatus into a more facilitative mould. It became clear that a hard-fought struggle was being waged within the state apparatus itself between its various branches; and that the 'reformist' wing led by the Department of Constitutional Development and Planning was set upon dismembering the once-powerful Department of Co-operation and Development.

The Development Boards were annually sinking deeper into debt, and were under severe parliamentary criticism for their financial profligacy and unrepresentativeness. At the same time their relations with the emerging BLAs were subject to strain over issues relating to the activities of seconded white personnel, transfer of land and property formerly held by the Boards, and the projected sale by the Boards of liquor outlets which further threatened the fiscal base of the BLAs.

The majority of Town Councils were rapidly running up deficits: between March and September 1984, 14 councils on the Witwatersrand announced rent and service charge increases. The response of the various civic associations to these increases was to call for their scrapping and for the resignation of the town councillors. Resistance to rent increases, linked with educational and political grievances, led to township rebellions in the Vaal Triangle between September and November 1984, which later spread and became generalised in large parts of the country, reaching a particular intensity in the Eastern Cape between February and May of 1985. Town councillors, their homes and businesses, became prime targets of attack. Several were killed and many went into hiding. The intensity of the attacks led many councillors to resign, leaving councils on the Witwatersrand and the Eastern Cape without a quorum, thus renderng them temporarily unworkable.[15] Several councils suspended the rent increases in the wake of the violence, but began to create paramilitary community guard forces in terms of powers they held under the Black Local Authorities Act of 1982.

The conflict in the townships began to take on the dimensions of a civil war in late 1984. Resistance to the BLAs was widespread, being spearheaded by youth and community organisations, but increasingly drawing in the progressive trade union movement as well. In July of 1985 a State of Emergency was declared in 36 magisterial districts, largely in the Witwatersrand-Vereeniging area and in the Eastern Cape. The state attempted to counter the increasing ungovernability of the affected townships through armed occupation by the military, coupled with police action aimed at the destruction of organised opposition through mass arrests and detentions.[16] The State of Emergency was lifted in March 1986 for a brief period, before being reimposed in a more stringent form on a national basis in June.

Black local government has been in disarray at least since 1984. Its crisis is deepest in the Eastern Cape where 30 out of 50 local authorities do not have a quorum, but nowhere in the country can it be said that it is functioning as intended by the state.[17] Where councils no longer exist or no longer function, white administrators have been appointed to manage these bodies. In the Eastern Cape and to a lesser extent on the Witwatersrand 'street committee' structures and 'people's courts' have been created as organs of people's power to take the place of the moribund and discredited local authorities. Whether they will remain coherent and disciplined bodies in the face of continued repression of organisations and individuals opposed to the state is an open question.[18] The state has arrested several thousand community leaders, activists and trade unionists. With the leadership either in detention or in hiding, the distinction between political violence and criminal activity has become increasingly blurred in many townships.

Whilst the forces ranged against the state's agents in the townships have succeeded in making the townships 'ungovernable', the point has not yet been reached where any coherent counter-vailing community-based power structures can exist to lay the basis for new forms of local self-government. The repressive power of the state, coupled with the increasing presence since the first Emergency of right-wing vigilante groups, serves to prevent this occurring. Rent boycotts are taking place in 28 townships across the country, some of them dating from September 1984 (*Natal Mercury*, 18 July 1986).

The widespread violence, the rapid decline of the economy and the lack of visible progress by the government towards a political settlement capable of stabilising a deteriorating situation have together brought on a crisis of confidence in the business community at large. Significant sections of capital have distanced themselves from state strategy and have begun to look for political alternatives more in keeping with their own needs for long-term stability and continued accumulation. Faced with a protracted and crippling consumer boycott in the Eastern Cape and the collapse of civil administration in the townships, businessmen began to negotiate with community leaders, calling on the government to abolish all discriminatory legislation, to introduce participation on all levels of government by the elected or recognised leaders of all races, and to re-establish the rule of law (*Financial Mail*, 25 April 1986). Parliamentary opposition representatives blamed the collapse of the Eastern Cape Development Board on the reluctance of the government to negotiate acceptable structures with popular black leaders (*Financial Mail*, 14 February 1986). Attempts by the state to force employers to deduct money owing to BLAs from workers' pay packets in the face of rent boycotts have been strongly resisted by employers (*Daily News*, 17 April 1986).

Capital's response to the RSCs, due to be introduced in October 1986, has been highly critical. It has been argued that the taxes imposed to finance their operation will not affect metropolitan-based industries equally, and that they will tend to drive businesses out of the metropolitan areas, thus hindering the growth of the cities and impeding their ability to manage the process of urbanisation (*Business Day*, 29 May 1985). ASSOCOM argued that the inclusion of BLAs, with their lack of legitimacy and revenue base, would prejudice the successful operation of RSCs from the outset. It called for uniform enabling legislation on local authorities, based upon the free market, common-law principle of voluntary contract rather than administrative compulsion (ASSOCOM, 1985).

The general view of black community groups is that the RSCs are bound to fail because they are to be based upon the discredited and collapsing Community Councils (*Sowetan*, 4 March 1986). The RSCs are rejected by both participants and non-participants in the tricameral Parliament as being based on racially separate primary local authorities (Durban Housing Action Committee, 1985; *Sunday Tribune; Eastern Province Herald*, 29 June 1986). Chief Buthelezi has warned that in Natal they cannot work without the co-operation of KwaZulu, and their introduction has been frozen because of the reluctance of KwaZulu authorities to participate in them (*Natal Mercury*, 1 July 1986).

White municipalities have displayed considerable anxiety over the fiscal and political implications of their involvement in the RSCs. Debate at the United Municipal Executive's annual conference in April saw Eastern Cape municipalities expressing grave reservations and calling for more acceptable forms of representation to be introduced (*Eastern Province Herald*, 18 April 1986). The Progressive Federal Party (PFP) has rejected RSCs and is to campaign against their introduction and in favour of 'non-racial, viable and cost effective' local government (*Daily News*, 28 April 1986). The Urban Foundation, as an important policy research body for capital, is currently investigating non-racial local government alternatives for the future.[19] It is clear that resistance is mounting against the introduction of RSCs in their present form. Their implementation has been delayed and evidence suggests that there is a high degree of bureaucratic incoherence and confusion over the process (*Natal Mercury*, 1 July 1986).

The Department of Co-operation and Development was formally dismantled at the end of August 1985, marking the end of an era in which that particular arm of the state apparatus, in its various guises, had shaped state strategy and dominated the lives of millions of black South Africans. Both the Development Boards and the BLAs had previously been removed from its jurisdiction and placed under the Department of Constitutional Development and Planning. The Development Boards were dismantled in June 1986 by the Abolition of Development Bodies Act and their 12,000 white employees absorbed by the various Provincial Administrations in the 'largest and most complex operation ever undertaken in the public sector' (*Natal Mercury*, 23 June 1986). Thus, the personnel from 'the most hated bodies in the country' have been relocated in the restructured provincial organisation amid demands for members of the House of Delegates and Representatives and the PFP that they should not be given the same positions of power which they formerly held (*Natal Mercury* and *Daily News*, 26 June 1986).

The latest development in the state's post-Riekert urban policy has been the abolition of influx control following the President's Council report on urbanisation, published in August 1985[20] (RSA, 1986).

The White Paper confirms the state's intention to maintain separate residential areas (4.3.5), but the Group Areas Act is currently under scrutiny by the President's Council and a report is expected later in 1986 (*Financial Mail*, 2 May 1986). East London City Council has voted to cease administering the Act, and Durban has called for its abolition, failing which it has requested the authorities to decide on how it should be applied locally (*Natal Mercury*, 20 May 1986). The indications are that the government may allow 'local options' to be exercised with the effect of 'privatising' apartheid in terms of residential areas and amenities (*Financial Mail*, 14 March 1986). The piecemeal reform of the Act would still leave intact the racially based primary local authority system which the state intends using as the framework for local government in the future.

It remains to be seen whether the state's local government plans in the form of the RSCs will become viable. The intention is that these bodies should perform a redistributive function by extending basic infrastructural services to the areas of greatest need — those administered by BLAs. However, these bodies are in deep financial crisis: the debt owed to the 13 Development Boards increased by 25 per cent in the year to 30 June 1985 (*Financial Mail*, 27 June 1986). The state's commitment to the privatisation of local government services and the ending of subsidies will mean increased user costs at a time when the ability of black communities to pay is being seriously eroded by unemployment and inflation.

To carry through its programme, the state has centralised power away from the local level, and the indications are that it has not yet unleashed its repressive power against popular resistance to anything like its full potential. The military is well integrated into regional government structure through the Regional Development Advisory Committees, which are regarded as essential components of the RSC system (*Sunday Tribune*, 22 June 1986). The military is becoming more involved in local government structures — and this integration should be seen as the ultimate guarantee of their maintenance in the face of increasing popular rejection.

Conclusion

The crisis of local government is intimately linked with, and forms an important part of, the national crisis in South Africa. The crisis at the local level has developed its own particular dynamic and content, which varies from region to region, but it is increasingly determined by the state's national reform strategy and the popular struggles being waged against it. The effect of the top-down reform strategy adopted by the state has been to place local government in the forefront of national political struggles. The political separation of local government structures developed under apartheid is being reworked, with the current reorganisation involving the RSCs and the provinces. The various local government components which were formerly separate are being brought together in new structures, with interesting implications.

The white local authorities have traditionally operated as democratic structures answerable to a racially exclusive electorate. They have been insulated until now from the direct political effects of the widespread rejection of the BLAs, management committees and local affairs committees. They have also benefited from the apartheid-style financing system which has ensured that white ratepayers enjoy a high level of services based on jealously guarded revenue accounts. To the extent that these bodies remain responsive to a racially exclusive electorate, they do not suffer from the acute fiscal and legitimacy crisis experienced by the majority of other local authorities. However, it is probable that participation by white primary local authorities in the RSC structures will render them less accountable and therefore less responsive to their local constituents. Voters will not elect representatives to the RSCs directly — the elected local authorities will perform this function. As a further step away from the limited democracy practised by white voters, it is likely to lead to increasing apathy and loss of legitimacy by white primary local authorities.

A further distinction may be drawn between the larger well-established metropolitan-based primary local authorities, with a highly developed infrastructure, and those which, because of size or newness, are not as well endowed infrastructurally and financially. The latter will be entering the RSCs in a much weaker position and will in effect be competing directly with the other primary local authorities for basic infrastructural resources. The necessity of sharing pooled resources may place the white local authorities in a worse position than formerly. In this sense the fiscal crisis of the various BLAs may well be experienced by smaller white bodies as a relative impoverishment leading to a lower level of service provision in their areas.

The coloured and Indian management and local affairs committees with their origins in the Group Areas Act are widely discredited as representative bodies, and will bring with them into the new structure the lack of legitimacy associated with the tricameral Parliament. In addition, they are not financially self-sufficient and it is hard to envisage how the new dispensation will dramatically alter this, despite the powers allocated to the Provincial Administrator to redraw boundaries of primary local authorities to include industrial areas within them. One of the likely effects of their participation will be the opening of new avenues of accumulation at a regional level for locally based interests, and the emergence of new patterns of strategic bargaining and alliances mediated by the bureaucratic structures developed. To this extent the new local government dispensation will materially influence local class-formation and potentially foster the emergence of a new stratum of bureaucratically based entrepreneurs controlling access to strategic local government resources.

The BLAs are at the heart of the township crisis by virtue of their strategic location as local agents of the state. They will bring the RSCs their legacy of bankruptcy, political rejection, corruption and violence. Viewed from this perspective, the chances for the successful functioning of RSCs are not good. Given their origins, it is likely that the RSCs will be widely rejected before they begin their work. However, it is clear that they have not been designed as democratic bodies and the lack of popular consent is unlikely to prevent their development as a bureaucratic mechanism by an increasingly militarised state carrying through a process of reform from above.

The limits to the state's ability to introduce new structures at the local level and to manage them without popular consent are to be found in the nature of the crisis it confronts nationally. The ability of the state to govern is based on its role as guarantor of continued capital accumulation, apart from questions of political legitimacy. The collapse of its urban management policies in the context of economic recession and popular struggle has placed this in question in the minds of leading capitalist interests, which now perceive the necessity of a political solution to the crisis. The racially based nature of the new local government structures has come to be perceived as the fundamental flaw preventing the emergence of a more democratic and politically legitimate dispensation at the local level.

To that extent at least, there is a convergence of interests between the state's capitalist critics and its popular democratic opponents. However, the state's withdrawal from fiscal involvement in the provision of local services and the increasing intervention of capital in this sphere of urban reproduction cannot hope to meet the increasingly urgent popular demand for affordable shelter and services. The ability of local government to meet these needs will ultimately be governed by the form of state which emerges at the national level as the outcome of the current struggle.

Notes

1. The most important provincial powers were those over education, health and hospital services, roads and bridges, public works and local government.
2. The provincial councils lost control over coloured education in 1953, and Indian education in 1965 when these functions became centralised. Autonomous powers of provincial taxation have been progressively removed. The provincial share of total government spending fell from 45 per cent in 1950 to less than 22 per cent in 1980 (Mercabank, 1985). By 1971 the provinces depended on central government for approximately 80 per cent of their income on revenue account (President's Council 1, 1982, p. 23).
3. In the Cape, African voters were put on a separate roll in 1936. They elected white representatives to the Provincial Council, House of Assembly and Senate. This system was abolished in 1959. Coloured voters in the Cape were placed on a separate roll in 1958 to elect white representatives. This form of representation ended in 1970. In Natal, Indians were deprived of the parliamentary franchise in 1898, and coloured voters were removed from the common roll in 1956. In the Transvaal and Orange Free State, coloured and Indian people had no franchise whatsoever at any level of government.
4. The powers of local government included: the construction and maintenance of roads, electricity and water supply, traffic control, the provision of housing, refuse collection, health services, public libraries, public transport, parks and recreation facilities, city and town planning, abattoirs, fire-fighting, business and vehicle licensing, sewerage, cemeteries and crematoria.
5. See Bloch and Wilkinson (1982) for a useful summary of state urban policy from 1920 to 1970.
6. See Bekker and Humphries (1985) for the most comprehensive account available of the activities of the Administration Boards.
7. See Todes and Watson (1984) for a detailed analysis of local government restructuring from 1948 to 1984.
8. For accounts of Soweto 1976, see Kane-Berman (1978), Hirson

(1979), and Brooks and Brickhill (1980).

9. The most comprehensive analysis of the Durban strikes is in Institute for Industrial Education (1976).

10. Powers of the black local authorities (BLAs) included: waste disposal, sewerage, electrification, preventive health, sport and recreation, housing administration, including the prevention of illegal occupation, welfare services, construction and maintenance of roads, and employment of staff. Source: SAIRR, 1984, p. 253.

11. The provincial structures as operating from 1 July 1986 have no 'elected' representation, and are directed by a nominated executive committee headed by an appointed administrator.

12. For the composition of the Council, see SAIRR, 1984, p. 246.

13. Apart from the President's Council Report, and evidence presented to the Schlebusch and Browne Committees, there was also the work of the Croeser Committee, and that of the six sub-committees of the Co-ordinating Council for Local Government Affairs working under the Department of Constitutional Development and Planning (see References.)

14. For discussion of the RSCs, see Dewar (1985), Hemson (1986) and Indicator Project South Africa (1986).

15. For a list of councillors who have resigned since 8 March 1985, see Hansard, 23 May 1986, cols 1906–18, and 1936–40.

16. In 1985 over 35,000 troops were used in 96 townships throughout South Africa. Source: Hansard, 6 May 1986, col. 1641.

17. For a survey of the number of Community Councils and other BLAs presently constituted and their official status, see Hansard, 7 May 1986, cols 1661–72.

18. For a discussion of township conditions since the Emergency, see *Work in Progress*, nos 40 and 41.

19. The work of the Urban Foundation on influx control was highly influential in shaping state strategy: see Giliomee and Schlemmer (1985). It is likely that their proposals for alternative local government structures will receive the state's careful attention.

20. For incisive comment on this Report, see Hindson (1985a).

References

ASSOCOM (1985) *Removal of discrimination against blacks in the political economy of the Republic of South Africa. A memorandum by J.A. Lombard and J.A. du Pisanie.* Bureau for Economic Policy and Analysis, University of Pretoria

Barrell, H. (1984) The United Democratic Front and National Forum: their emergence, composition and trends. In South African Research Services, *South African Review Two*, Ravan, Johannesburg, pp. 6–20

Bekker, S.B. and R. Humphries (1985) *From control to confusion. The changing role of Administration Boards in South Africa 1971–1983.* Shuter and Shooter, Pietermaritzburg

Bell, R.T. (1985) 'Is industrial decentralisation a thing of the past?'. Paper presented to a conference on South Africa's Regional Policy: Industrial Decentralisation and the Apartheid State, University of the

Witwatersrand, August

Bloch, R. (1982) 'All little sisters got to try on big sister's clothes: the Community Council system in South Africa!'. Unpublished paper presented to the African Studies Institute Seminar, University of the Witwatersrand, April

—— and P. Wilkinson (1982) Urban control and popular struggle: a survey of state urban policy. *Africa Perspective, 20*

Brooks, A. and J. Brickhill (1980) *Whirlwind before the storm*. International Defence and Aid Fund, London

Cobbett, W., D. Glaser, D.C. Hindson, and M. Swilling (1986) South Africa's regional political economy: a critical analysis of reform strategy in the 1980s. In South African Research Services, *South African Review Three*, Ravan, Johannesburg, pp. 137–68

Council for the Co-ordination of Local Government Affairs (CCLGA), (1984a) *Report and recommendations of the Committee of Enquiry into Municipal Electoral Qualifications, no 1* (Chairman J.C.G. Botha). April

—— (1984b) *Report and recommendations of the Committee of Enquiry into the Demarcation of Geographical Areas of Jurisdiction of Local Authorities, no. 2* (Chairman O.A.W. Van Zyl). April

—— (1984c) *Report and recommendations of the Committee of Enquiry into the Establishment of Criteria for Viable Local Authorities, no. 3* (Chairman W.A. Cruywagen). April

—— (1984d) *Report and recommendations of the Committee of Enquiry into Control over Local Government Authorities* (Chairman L.J. Botha). April

—— (1984e) *Report and recommendations of the Committee of Enquiry into Personnel for Local Authorities* (Chairman D.M.G. Curry)

Croeser Working Group (1982) *Report of the Committee of Enquiry into the Finance of Local Authorities in South Africa*. Cape Town, 6 May

Dewar, Neil (1985) Municipal government under the new South African Constitution: who gets what, where, who decides and who decides who declares? *Social Dynamics, 11* (2), pp. 37–48

Durban Housing Action Committee (1985) 'Regional Service Councils: an introduction'. Unpublished notes for seminar, 9 November

Evans, S. (1985) The remuneration of Town Clerks' Act no. 115/1984. In W.A.J. Coetzee (ed.), *Orientation of municipal councillors and leading municipal officials in a new dispensation for local authorities. Proceedings of a Symposium*. University of Durban-Westville, Durban, 9–11 April

Giliomee, H. and L. Schlemmer (1985) *Up against the fences: poverty, passes and privilege in South Africa*. David Philip, Cape Town

Grest, J. (1985) 'The Durban City Council and "the Indian problem": local politics in the 1940s'. Paper presented to the Conference of the Association for Sociology in Southern Africa, Cape Town, July

—— and H. Hughes (1984) State strategy and popular response at the local level. In South African Research Services, *South African Review Two*, Ravan, Johannesburg, pp. 45–62

Hemson, C. (1986) 'Impact of the Regional Services Councils on Indian and African areas'. Paper presented to the progressive Federal Party Seminar on RSCs, Johannesburg, 26 April

Hindson, D.C. (1983) The role of the Labour Bureaux in South Africa: a critique of the Riekert Commission Report. In D.C. Hindson (ed.),

Working papers in South African studies, Volume III, Ravan Press, Johannesburg

—— (1985a) 'Orderly urbanisation and influx control: from territorial apartheid to regional spatial ordering in South Africa'. Paper presented to the Conference on South Africa's Regional policy: Industrial Decentralisation and the Apartheid State, University of the Witwatersrand, August

—— (1985b) 'The pass system and differentiated labour-power'. Paper presented to the Conference of the Association for Sociology in Southern Africa, Cape Town, July

—— and M. Lacey (1983) Influx control and labour allocation policy and practice since the Riekert Commission. In South African Research Services, *South African Review One*, Ravan Press, Johannesburg, pp. 97–113

Hirson, B. (1979) *Year of fire, year of ash*. Zed Press, London

Hughes, H. and J. Grest (1983) The local state. In South African Research Services, *South African Review One*, Ravan Press, Johannesburg, pp. 122–41

Indicator Project South Africa (1986) *Servicing the nation: local and regional government reform*. Centre for Applied Social Sciences, University of Natal, Durban

Institute for Industrial Education (1976) *The Durban strikes 1973*. Ravan Press, Johannesburg

Kane-Berman, J. (1978) Soweto: *black revolt, white reaction*. Ravan Press, Johannesburg

Labour Research Committee (undated) *Ruling the townships: housing, services, influx control and local government*. Braamfontein

Mercabank (1985) *The logic of the federal option. Focus no. 37*. Compiled by the Bureau for Economic Policy and Analysis, University of Pretoria, edited by Professor J.A. Lombard, December

Republic of South Africa President's Council (1982) *Local and regional government systems in the Republic of South Africa, Joint report of the Committee for Economic Affairs and the Constitutional Committee*. Government Printer, Cape Town, PC1/1982

Republic of South Africa (RSA) (1985) *Report of the Committee for Constitutional Affairs on an Urbanisation Strategy for the Republic of South Africa*. Cape Town, 21 August

—— (1986) *White Paper on the Report of the Committee for Constitutional Affairs on an Urbanisation Strategy for the Republic of South Africa*. Cape Town, 23 April

South African Institute of Race Relations (SAIRR) (1984) *Annual survey 1978–1983*. SAIRR, Johannesburg

Todes, A. and V. Watson (1984) 'Restructuring local government. The state and local government in South Africa 1948–1984'. Urban Problems Research Unit UCT, University of Cape Town Centre for African Studies, Africa Seminar, October

—— and P. Wilkinson (1986) Local government restructuring in South Africa: the case of Western Cape. *Social Dynamics, 12* (1), pp. 49–68

Union of South Africa (1948) *Report of the Native Laws Commission 1946–8* (Chairman Fagan). U.G. 28–1948

Newspapers and periodicals

Cape Times, Cape Town
Daily News, Durban
Eastern Province Herald, Port Elizabeth
Financial Mail
Indicator SA, Durban
Natal Mercury, Durban
Sowetan, Johannesburg
Star, Johannesburg
Sunday Tribune, Durban
Weekly Mail, Johannesburg
Work in Progress, Johannesburg

5

Intensifying Civil War: The Role of the South African Defence Force

Michael Evans and *Mark Phillips**

On the night of Saturday 6 October 1984, South African Defence Force (SADF) troops entered Joza township outside Grahamstown. By the next morning they had moved into Soweto outside Johannesburg as well. Their presence was more than a mere show of strength, for in Grahamstown at least the soldiers were equipped with sjamboks (South African police whips) and were used to quell a 'riot situation'.[1]

Within two weeks Operation Palmiet was launched. At 4 o'clock in the morning a 7,000 strong contingent of policemen and soldiers entered the Vaal township of Sebokeng outside Vereeniging. While troops cordoned off the streets, the police conducted house-to-house searches in an attempt, as Law and Order Minister Louis le Grange put it, to 'root out revolutionaries'. By the end of the day they had arrested 350 residents for pass law offences, contravention of influx control regulations and certain minor statutory crimes such as possession of dagga and pornography.[2]

Over the next two months army troops moved *en masse* into Boipatong, Daveyton, Atteridgeville, Tembisa, Fingo Village, Evaton and Vosloosrus. A new phase of conflict in South Africa had begun: a phase in which the lines of battle shifted from the borders of Namibia to the black townships of South Africa, and in which the SADF was deployed for the first time in South Africa's history on an ongoing and national basis inside the country.

This marked a watershed in South African history, as the struggle

*The authors, who are both members of the End Conscription Campaign, would like to thank local committees of the Campaign for their help in the preparation of this chapter.

between the apartheid state on the one hand, and the broad-based forces of opposition on the other, reached new levels of intensity. It is our concern to examine the particular role of the military in this growing civil conflict. To understand its changing role, an examination of the SADF's immediate history is necessary — of the way in which the Defence Force both expanded its size and sphere of operations and at the same time began to move to the centre-stage of South African state policy formation.

The SADF and the South African state

The permanent deployment of SADF troops in combat situations in Southern Africa began in 1973 when, in the context of the Namibian miners' strikes, the stepped-up military activity of the South West African People's Organisation (SWAPO) and the imminent defeat of Portuguese colonialism in Angola, the SADF replaced the South African police (SAP) as the directors and main protagonists of South Africa's war in Namibia.

The conflict which the military entered in northern Namibia was a distinctly political one. Commitment of greater fire-power and the exercise of military force alone were insufficient for victory. South African military officers were well aware that experience elsewhere — Algeria, Malaya and Vietnam, for instance — had taught that success in this type of conflict was best achieved through denying the enemy the political allegiance of the civilian population. As General Magnus Malan, then chief of the SADF, put it:[3]

> Bullets kill bodies not beliefs. I would like to remind you that the Portuguese did not lose the military battle in Angola and Mozambique, but they lost the faith and trust of the inhabitants of those countries. The insurgent forces have no hope of success without the aid of the local population.

The clearest manifestation of a more than simply military strategy of warfare in Namibia was the civic action initiative introduced into the operational area from 1974. By deploying doctors, teachers and agricultural experts as well as soldiers in the war zone, the army hoped to win the allegiance ('the hearts and minds') of the civilian population — or at least exhibit a different, less hostile image than the hitherto exclusively combative one. The lessons of this type of warfare in Namibia were not lost on the South African military in the popular uprising that swept across South Africa in 1976 and 1977. Mass resistance to apartheid and signs of a return of the African National Congress (ANC) to the forefront of South African politics required, it was felt, a more 'total' strategy than had hitherto been employed to outmanoeuvre, rather than simply overwhelm, the mounting forces of opposition to apartheid structures.

'Total Strategy' was publicly defined for the first time in the 1977 White Paper on Defence as an integrated national action which 'demands interdependent and co-ordinated action in all fields — military, psychological, economic, political, sociological, technological, diplomatic, ideological, cultural, etc'.[4] The 'striving for specific aims' it was stated, 'must be co-ordinated with all the means available to the state'.[5] Crucial to the success of this Total Strategy was the choice of a definite political line to be followed, a line which would help meet the need for co-ordinated action across all spheres of state activity. Military strategists had to start to become political analysts.

Yet no coherent political project — that is, no Total Strategy — was possible while the military remained removed from the centre of state policy formulation. Policy formulation under the Vorster administration had been characterised as 'random and low pro-file'.[6] It suffered from internecine conflict between the country's various security arms, particularly between the various police branches and the Department of Information on the one hand, and the military on the other. The Vorster government, moreover, with a mass base in the white working and middle classes, saw little point in a restructuring of apartheid which might threaten the privileged position of a section of its electorate. The strong reformist pressure emanating from both Afrikaans and English big capital and from a military concerned to develop a militarily defensible state policy[7] was blunted by right-wing opposition to any refashioning of the structures of white privilege.

It was the Information Scandal of 1978 which brought about the collapse of the Vorster government and the beginnings of a change in state policies. The election of Minister of Defence P.W. Botha as Prime Minister facilitated a shift of military and overall strategic thinking from the wings of decision-making to its centre. Under Botha the SADF had undergone a thorough process of expansion and rationalisation. His organisational and managerial abilities and the technocratic and hierarchically disciplined methods of the military itself were quickly brought to bear upon the disorganised and sometimes moribund structures of political decision-making which he inherited. The entire state security apparatus was reorganised and streamlined and its component parts centralised into a revitalised Cabinet committee known as the State Security Council. Formed in 1972 as an advisory body, it was only after P.W. Botha had come to power that the State Security Council began to play a central role in co-ordinating a 'total national strategy'.[8]

The State Security Council is the only Cabinet committee which is chaired by the Prime Minister, now State President. The Council's secretary is a senior SADF officer, and as many as 70 per cent of the initial complement of the secretariat was drawn from the SADF.[9]

The State Security Council directs and co-ordinates the activities of 15 inter-departmental committees, for example a manpower committee concerned with matters such as 'labour unrest'.[10] It is averred that 'SADF representatives now take part in all inter-departmental meetings regardless of their subjects or whether direct SADF interests are involved'.[11] The Cabinet's role in ratifying State Security Council decisions is largely a formal one, the Security Council itself being often characterised as an inner Cabinet.

Security Council policy and decisions are implemented at regional and local level by Joint Management Councils (JMCs). More commonly known by their Afrikaans name, Gesaamentlike Bestuursentrums (GBSs), their function is to assess the security situation in each region and recommend to the authorities appropriate 'solutions', ranging from security force action to the upgrading of living conditions.[12]

The JMCs, and their sub-structures or mini-JMCs, are made up of representatives from business, community councils, ex-development board officials, the SAP and the SADF. Their areas of jurisdiction correspond exactly with the area commands of the SADF.[13] Of the 13 JMCs, twelve are at present headed by military officers and one by a police officer. Together they comprise the regional units of the National Security Management System.

The precise composition and functions of these bodies, as well as their relationship to other organs of local and regional government, are well-kept secrets, but what is clear is that they are becoming increasingly involved in township matters. The clearest example of this is their role in attempting to break the rent boycott which began in the Vaal area in mid-1984 and which two years later was continuing in at least 31 townships in the Transvaal, Eastern Cape and the Orange Free State.[14]

One researcher observed that with the establishment of the JMCs 'the state is preparing to shift the administration of the country at a regional level into the hands of the security forces'.[15] This shift was again apparent in the passing of the amendment to the Public Safety Act in June 1986, which gave the Minister of Law and Order the power to declare any area an 'unrest area' and hand over effective control of that area to the local security forces.

What does seem clear, despite the veil of secrecy maintained over these bodies, is that behind the civil 'façade' of the tricameral Parliament, the Cabinet, the President's Council, the provincial administrators and executives, the Regional Services Councils and other local authorities and the Community Town Councils, all with their token black and brown faces, lies another, more powerful level of government. This level is not subject to public scrutiny, it is not unwieldy and unworkable like the tricameral system, and it operates outside the ambit of constitutional debate. The State Security Council (dominated by the SADF), the National Security Management System and the Joint Management Councils (dominated by the security forces), and other structures, such as the Regional Development Advisory Committee[16] together form a parallel level of government. It is a level which in general functions as an unseen shadow administration, but which during times of more intense crisis can be expected to surface and to play a more overt co-ordinating and directive role, all in the interests of 'national security and stability'.

The military-industrial complex

As much as it has been concerned to cement its ascendency within a restructured state, the military has ensured the development of an extensive and symbiotic relationship between itself and the business community. With the establishment of the Armaments Corporation (Armscor) in 1968, and increasingly since the imposition of a mandatory arms embargo in 1977, virtually all of South Africa's leading corporations, the subsidiaries of many multinational corporations and some 6,000 smaller business operations and subcontractors have enjoyed what one source has euphemistically labelled 'the not inconsiderable benefits of the armaments industry'.[17]

As both internal and external pressure on the South African state has increased since the 1970s, so Armscor has grown to one of the largest industrial undertakings in South Africa, directly employing over 35,000 workers and providing work for 100,000 people through its subsidiaries and some 3,000 private subcontractors. By 1983 South Africa was said to be the world's tenth largest arms producer.[18]

The military's formal partnership with capital has been carefully structured under the tenure of P.W. Botha, first as Minister of Defence and subsequently as Prime Minister and State President. In 1973 a Defence Advisory Council (DAC) was established as a subsidiary of the Defence Command Council — the supreme command body in the SADF. The DAC brings together leading representatives of the military and of all the country's major corporations. It has emerged 'as a primary institution for the exchange of opinions between the elites of government, the State Security apparatus and the representatives of capital'.[19] A Defence Manpower Liaison Committee has been established to facilitate communication between the SADF, the Department of Manpower Utilisation and the major employers of white labour. (There is ongoing potential conflict between a defence force relying on conscription of white men and an economy experiencing shortages of skilled labour.) A Defence Research and Development Council exists to channel specialist knowledge in the private sector into defence research and development (R & D) activities.[20] Legislation such as the Petroleum Products Amendment Act and the Atomic Energy Act require that firms do not disclose certain data about their operations. In addition, the National Supplies Procurement Act gives the Minister of Defence the power to order any person producing or processing vital goods 'to manufacture, produce, process or treat and to supply or deliver or sell it to the Minister'. This power was first used in 1975 when companies were ordered to produce tents for the troops in Angola.[21] Commenting on the implications of this Act, a 1977 General Motors (GM) memorandum recognised that 'in the event of a national emergency there is little doubt that control of GMs South African facilities . . . would be taken over by an arm of the Ministry of Defence'.[22]

Another indication of the significance of the Defence Force within the South African economy is the amount budgeted to it each year. This has risen from only R44 million in 1960-1 to over R5.2 billion for the 1986-7 financial year. While the official defence budget has not risen above the rate of inflation in recent years, real defence expenditure is in fact considerably higher as many items are budgeted under other accounts. Intelligence gathering, for example, falls under the Treasury, while much military infrastructure comes under the Community Development, Manpower and Public Works Accounts. Both Armscor and the South-west African Territory Force (SWATF) are excluded from the Defence budget vote and a considerable proportion of defence expenditure is actually laundered through a secret Defence Special Account which is beyond the realms of state audit.[23] 'Independent' homeland defence expenditure also lies outside the official defence budget. It has been estimated that 1986–7 defence expenditure may be closer to R7 billion, representing between 20 per cent and 25 per cent of the total national budget (or R20 million) per day.[24]

Winning the hearts and minds?

It is clear that much of the relationship between the SADF and the South African political and economic establishment is cloaked in secrecy. This secrecy extends from the functions of the State Security Council and Joint Management Centres through the provisions of numerous Acts to the size of the defence budget itself. There are some activities, however, which SADF promotes in far more public fashion. This is particularly so in the case of its 'hearts and minds strategy', developed in the Namibian War, which it transferred to South Africa from 1978. Most prominent in its civic action pro-gramme has been the use of white soldier-teachers (many of them conscripts) in black schools. In the words of the one-time com-mander of the Namibian War zone, Major-General Charles Lloyd, 'We want the national servicemen to teach the black man whilst his rifle is standing in the corner of the classroom'.[25] Acting on the somewhat peculiar logic that 'a healthy civilian population is a sure bulwark against Communism,'[26] military doctors have been exten-sively used in drought-ridden and cholera-infested regions of South Africa's homelands. Other Civic Action Programme workers have been used as engineers, legal, agricultural and financial advisors, dentists, vets, lecturers, administrative personnel and even as traders and directors of tourism.[27]

There are essentially two interrelated rationales for the Civic Action Programme. The first is a psychological one, legitimising the increasingly ubiquitous military presence and undercutting support for the ANC by demonstrating to the local population that the army 'is there to help and protect them and not to harm them'.[28] Though universally condemned by black community and political organisations, the programme appears to have enjoyed some degree of success, particularly in parts of the Namibian operational zone (such as Caprivi) and in certain rural areas in South Africa.

Its second rationale is an intelligence-gathering one, and in this case success is more difficult to assess. Many Civic Action recruits are expected to collect and pass on information relating to the populations they are supposedly serving. One national serviceman involved in the programme cites pressure to gather intelligence while working as a defence-force doctor in Ciskei as contributing to his decision to conscientiously object to any further service in the SADF.[29]

The Civic Action Programme has been further undermined in both schools and hospitals by more overtly military SADF activity. Poorly paid nurses and hospital workers at Baragwanath hospital in Soweto went on strike in 1985 after being physically attacked by hospital security officials for demanding higher wages. One thousand troops were sent into the hospital for two weeks to intimidate and temporarily replace the striking staff. The Army has also been extensively used against boycotting pupils across the country. More than anything else, the directly repressive use of the SADF has made a mockery of the reformist intentions of the Civil Action Programme.

A somewhat different role is played by the SADF in the country's white schools. Here it has overseen the establishment and progressive extension of a 'youth preparedness' programme and a cadet system designed to prepare the pupils for compulsory military training. At their most rudimentary, cadet programmes involve regular marching and drill sessions. In their more developed form they extend to marksmanship, first aid, map reading, camouflage and concealment, and camps where boys are taken through mock battles and lectured on the nature of the onslaught facing the nation.[30] Once young men graduate to military service itself they provide a captive audience for a military system at pains to ensure their 'cultural enrichment' and 'spiritual defensibility'. The content of the SADF internal education programme designed to achieve this has been aptly characterised as 'vigorous in its use of crude racial and ideological stereotypes, dangerously selective in its interpretation of historical data and fundamentally hostile to any information critical of either the Nationalist Party or its apartheid policy'.[31]

While young white men are conscripted into the SADF (usually beginning their two-year period of initial service at the age of 18, to be followed by a further two years of camp duty, spread over twelve years), no such policy applies to black South Africans. The 'hearts and minds' emphasis of the military leaders, however, has led them over the past decade to put much energy into the recruitment of blacks into the SADF.[32] Besides assisting the SADF's civic action work, an increased number of black volunteers is seen as part of the process of 'deracialising' the war (a process similar to that employed in pre-independence Zimbabwe). In the words of Commandant Swanepoel of the Lenz-based 21 Battalion,[33] 'with blacks in SA army uniforms, you can say "heck, this proves this is not a white man's struggle anymore" '. A further motivation for this policy has been the recognition by the SADF of the need to expand its ranks in order to meet the minimum manpower requirements of Total Strategy projected into the indefinite future.[34]

In a period of economic recession, and considering the significant perks offered by the SADF, the military's recruitment programmes have been only partially successful. A two-pronged strategy has been adopted: the recruitment of blacks into the SADF and, in accordance with the SADF's stated support for the government's separate development policy, the creation of bantustan units. By 1979 a total of 12,000 blacks were being trained and deployed by the SADF, with coloureds and Indians making up 10 per cent of the Permanent Force.[35] In 1985, 4,010 coloureds, 667 Indians and no Africans volunteered for national service. Of these 1,897 coloureds and 297 Indians were accommodated.[36] In addition, the SADF remains centrally involved in the defence forces, national guards and ethnic units of both the 'independent' and non-independent bantustans.

In a separate category, is the SWATF, which, while officially autonomous from the SADF, remains effectively under the latter's control.[37] Here, black recruitment — and since 1981, black conscription — has proceeded apace, so that by 1982, 40 per cent of the forces in the operational area were black.[38]

With the ushering-in of the new South African Constitution in 1983, and in the Coloured and Indian elections which followed, the issue of the possible conscription of Coloureds and Indians was frequently raised by proponents of Total Strategy. Joint power-sharing, it was argued by Nationalist Party leaders, meant joint obligations to defend newly acquired 'rights'.[39] Although mass resistance to the racially demarcated and politically inconsequential 'rights' bestowed by the 1983 Constitution persuaded government leaders to shelve the issue for some time,[40] it was reiterated in the 1986 Defence White Paper that 'White males can no longer bear the security burden alone without harming the economy. The SA Defence Force will therefore be increasingly reliant on other man-power resources'.[41] The introduction of a selective national service system is envisaged before compulsory national service can be considered. The White Paper recognises that voluntary service of Coloureds and Indians will have to suffice 'at present'.[42] Yet as the civil conflict intensifies, and as the necessity to professionalise and deracialise the defence force increases, so the recruitment of blacks is likely to be treated with growing vigour. Already, in early 1986, the SADF was opened to 'coloured female' volunteers for the first time, and the establishment of a second military base in the rural Karoo was announced.[43]

SADF and Southern Africa: regional destabilisation

The military's predominent role in the determination of state strategy is perhaps most publicly evidenced in its actions beyond the country's borders. Here, behind a veil of deceptions and lies directed at both the South African and international public, the military has embarked upon an aggressive and violent policy of both direct and indirect intervention in the affairs of all of South Africa's neighbouring states. The SADF's regional destabilisation has tied in with the South African government's wider strategy of perpetuating Southern African dependence on the South African economy, of making its neighbours' socialist experiments appear unworkable, and of attempting to 'break' the ANC.[44]

Since the invasion of Angola by the SADF in 1975 (an operation concealed from the South African public for much of its duration), parts of that country have been almost permanently occupied by South African forces. In addition, Jonas Savimbi's UNITA move-ment, in conjunction with the SADF's 32 Battalion (comprising mercenary former FNLA and other mercenary troops) has done its utmost to destroy the economic infrastructure of southern and eastern Angola and has constantly engaged Angolan government troops. Since 1984 UNITA and 32 Battalion have been unable to hold their own against joint government and Cuban troop cam-paigns, necessitating the commitment of regular South African divisions and, increasingly, of the South African Air Force.[45] Acts of long-distance sabotage of strategic installations in Angola, though claimed by UNITA representatives in the capitals of the Western world to be the work of their movement, have on occasion been embarrassingly revealed to have been carried out by specialised South African reconnaissance units. Two South African soldiers were killed and one captured in 1985 during an attempt to sabotage the US-owned Gulf Oil installation in Angola's northern enclave, Cabinda. The three carried UNITA propaganda material and the surviving soldier candidly admitted that if successful, the operation was to have been claimed by UNITA.[46] Few observers believe that UNITA would be able to lead an independent existence without South African — and now US — aid.

In similar fashion, the military, through its Special Operations arm, has provided support and assistance to the National Resistance Movement (RENAMO) in Mozambique, and allegedly to the Mushalala group in Zambia, dissident former UANC and ZAPU troops in Zimbabwe and to the Lesotho Liberation Army.[47] According to the Progressive Federal Party MP Graham McIntosh, the SADF itself refers to these groups as 'surrogate forces'.[48] They have wreaked varying degrees of havoc in their respective operational areas. In Mozambique RENAMO — 'no longer a movement, but a collection of different gangs armed by South Africa'[49] — has undermined the FRELIMO government's control over most of the country and severely inhibited economic reconstruction.

The use of proxies has been complemented by direct SADF strikes in Botswana, Lesotho, Zimbabwe, Zambia and Mozambique which, although ostensibly directed at ANC targets, have left many civilians dead. South African soldiers on so-called 'unauthorised missions' have died in clashes in Zimbabwe against the country's army. SADF and ex-SADF and National Intelligence Service personnel were responsible for an abortive *coup* attempt in the Seychelles, using SADF weapons.[50] There are in addition persistent allegations of SADF complicity in assassinations and assassination attempts throughout Southern Africa.[51]

Meanwhile South Africa's occupation of Namibia — illegal in terms of international law — continues, seemingly indefinitely. Because SWAPO enjoys majority support in the territory,[52] all South African concessions in the direction of genuine independence have been essentially cosmetic, with the establishment of the Multiparty Conference in 1983 being the latest in a series of attempts to stall the inevitable SWAPO victory. In the interim, Namibia remains — in the words of one writer — 'a virtual military fiefdom',[53] with the entire northern zone under effective military occupation and the economy totally geared towards the war effort.

Though the military component of South Africa's external policy has been emphasised here, it is essential not to overlook its character as an element of a broader 'Total' Strategy. Parallel to a generalised pattern of what is euphemistically known as 'destabilisation' has been a set of policies that can loosely be classed under the term 'formative action' — 'the attempt to create a new network of regional economic and social relations which would persuade Southern African states that it is in their interests to cooperate with South Africa.'[54] The carrot on the one hand and the stick on the other appeared for a brief period in 1984 to have generated the sort of breakthroughs for which strategic planners had hoped. The ANC appeared to have been effectively denied a military presence in both Mozambique and Swaziland, while great pressure continued to be exerted on Botswana and Lesotho. Swaziland had secretly signed a non-aggression pact with South Africa in 1982, while March 1984 saw the very public signing of the Nkomati Accord with Mozambique. The momentum of this and a temporary cease-fire with Angola (through the signing of the Lusaka Agreement) was carried through to a highly publicised diplomatic tour of Western Europe by P.W. Botha in June of that year. Within three months, however, the momentum of South Africa's regional and international offensive was to falter upon the twin crises of political illegitimacy and a decade of economic stagnation within South Africa itself.

Troops in the townships: intensifying the civil war

September 1984 marked a distinct turning-point in South Africa's history. On the one hand it showed the spontaneous unity of township residents in challenging the structures of apartheid domination. This challenge, which began as a protest against rent increases in Sebokeng, has become the daily experience of millions of South Africans country-wide. It has demonstrated the bankruptcy of the government's claims to be implementing meaningful political reform, and has marked the failure of the more enlightened aspects of Total Strategy.[55]

On the other hand, September 1984 marked the beginning of the involvement of the combined SADF–SAP security forces on a continuous and country-wide basis in suppressing township resistance. It is significant that on its own, the police force was unable to cope with the intensifying and spreading resistance. On 5 October, at the Transvaal National Party Congress in Alberton, Law and Order Minister le Grange announced plans to increase co-operation between the South African Police and the SADF, with the latter playing a greater role in supporting the police in various areas, including 'unrest' situations.[56] SADF and SAP co-operation in itself was nothing new: between April 1983 and March 1984, for instance, 43,000 soldiers had been used in police work, 27,000 of them being deployed at road blocks.[57] On a more overtly political level, the SADF had, together with the SAP, been used forcibly to resettle entire black communities, demolish squatter shacks, conduct pass raids and break strikes. It has even, in a crude implementation of petty apartheid, been used to keep black people off Port Elizabeth's 'whites only' beaches.[58] By October 1984, however, a more permanent relationship involving joint action to contain internal unrest appeared to be necessary. Within 24 hours of le Grange's announcement, the SADF and SAP moved jointly into Joza township outside Grahamstown.

In the following 18 months the military was deployed in at least 96 townships around the country, sometimes operating from temporary police bases, sometimes establishing its own bases within, or in close proximity to, black townships.[59] National servicemen, citizen force members and commandos drawn from all four arms of the defence force have been used. Within a month of their first deployment, a blanket ban was issued on the release of any information relating to the use of troops.[60] However, Minister Malan did indicate the extent of SADF deployment when he stated that to draw up a list of the occasions on which troops were used to control unrest and monitor townships 'would take months to compile' and would run 'to hundreds of pages'.[61] Parliament has been told only that in total 35,372 SADF troops were deployed in townships during 1985.[62] Similarly, accurate figures of the number of deaths resulting from defence-force action are difficult to obtain. Law and Order Minister le Grange announced in early 1986 that between September 1984 and December 1985, the security forces were responsible for the death of 628 people in township unrest.[63] Independent researchers put the figure considerably higher.[64]

Mere statistics, however, do not reflect the substance of defence-force involvement. Affidavits collected throughout the country have been remarkably consistent in their allegations of rape, assault, murder, theft, the besieging of schools, the disruption of funerals and church services and the demolition of shacks,[65] and the providing of assistance and a line of defence for right-wing vigilantes in their attacks on members of political, community and labour organisations. Many of these allegations have been laid before the courts in civil cases against the Ministers of Law and Order and Defence.[66]

Within a week of the declaration of South Africa's second State of Emergency on 21 July 1985, the allegations of Defence-Force misconduct had reached 'alarming proportions', according to a Port Elizabeth newspaper.[67] It was alarming enough for the Defence Force itself to take notice: by September, in an attempt to 'clear its name', the SADF announced a public relations programme which would include investigating allegations of troop excesses in black areas.[68]

The programme, however, turned out to be little more than just that — a public relations exercise. After the first week the SADF director of Manpower Liaison, Brigadier Chemaly, remarked: 'The 28 complaints centres opened last week have not received a single complaint. Nobody is coming in'.[69] Yet the allegations continued. In a random survey of residents in Port Elizabeth's black townships, a morning newspaper found that 27 per cent of people interviewed claimed to have been assaulted by members of the security forces. Many alleged that they had been sjambokked, struck with rifles and kicked, yet none had registered complaints.[70] Their reasons for failing to go to the complaints centres were echoed throughout the country: fear of the consequences of registering complaints and lack of confidence in the effect of complaining. As two residents in the East Vaal township of Katlehong expressed it:[71] 'It is fruitless to lay complaints to men you are accusing . . . I fear that the very people who beat people up could be the ones behind the counter'.

When complaints were registered and followed up, the actual sentences received by those convicted did little to encourage confidence in the whole procedure. Eight soldiers found guilty of assault with intent to do grievous bodily harm after assaulting a man, branding his legs with a hot iron and stoning him received fines of R200 (US$80) each.[72] In another case, an SADF sergeant was found guilty of assaulting three journalists and a shebeen owner after they alleged they were beaten with rifle butts, slapped, kicked, punched and had a dog set on them. His fine of R100 (US$40) was suspended for three years.[73] In addition, this State of Emergency, in common with the third, nation-wide State of Emergency declared eleven months later, indemnified all security force members from any civil prosecution for any action committed in 'good faith' anywhere in South Africa. In other words, as long as the soldier believed he was acting within the broad bounds of his authority, he was indemnified. Nevertheless, despite all these limitations, over 500 complaints had been lodged against members of the security forces by early 1986, 40 of them against national servicemen.[74]

The second aspect of the SADF's public relations programme involved an attempt to distance SADF activities from the poor image of the SAP. The defence force likes to think of itself as less prone to unauthorised brutality than the SAP, more concerned with winning the 'hearts and minds' of the people (the 80 per cent of the battle) and more answerable, through conscription, to the general public. In the early stages of township involvement, the distinction was possibly valid. Generally, the Defence Force would cordon off streets, while members of the SAP would go door to door. Most of the early accusations of brutality were made against the SAP, and by May 1985 the SADF had 'only been officially responsible for the death of five township residents.'[75]

However, as the conflict intensified, so the distinction became more blurred. As one Grahamstown resident expressed it:[76]

Initially the police thought they could just crush the resistance, while the army appeared to have a more thought-out programme. They seemed more concerned with the hearts and minds. But as resistance increased, so the army became more and more brutal. Any distinction the township residents had made between the army and police collapsed completely.

This seems to have been the experience in other parts of the country as well. In Port Elizabeth, the United Democratic Front publicity secretary, Stone Sizane, went as far as to suggest that the residents were more antagonistic to the army than to the police.[77] And in Cape Town, a teacher in a coloured school related the perception of her students:[78]

The army is seen no differently from the police and the students with whom I have contact certainly do not differentiate between the two. In fact, the only difference I have heard expressed is that the army are the ones who wear brown uniforms "and who carry those big guns".

Possibly the clearest statement of this blurring of roles was made by a national serviceman in Port Elizabeth, who recalled his experience in the townships:[79]

> Almost throughout these four months the army has been mixed in with the police, with a couple of policemen in each Buffel [an SADF vehicle] and usually a few more SADF members in the police vehicles. So for the black population, there has never been an opportunity to differentiate between the two forces, and the SADF almost immediately inherited the lack of credibility and bad reputation of the police. Not that there is always that much to choose between the forces, discipline and things like communication control are greatly superior in the army, but the separation of troops in small allocated units has often allowed SADF members to get into the spirit of being a law unto themselves, and mirror the behaviour of the police, not only their attitudes.

The implications of these statements are grave. We have shown in this chapter how the Defence Force's role has gone well beyond the primary role of any defence force — that of protecting a nation from external threat. We have shown how it has been involved in the civilian arena at the level of the formulation, implementation and defence of apartheid policies. Moreover, we have shown how, when the SADF did in the past engage in internal police work, it was usually in a support capacity whether it was involved in crime prevention, relief from natural disasters such as the Laingsburg floods or the recent locust plague, or in staffing police road-blocks. Yet through all this the SADF managed to maintain an image distinct from that of the SAP, with the latter having the dubious distinction of being the major repressive apparatus of the state at the level of the containment of internal resistance.

Since 6 October 1984, that situation has changed. Even if the authorities have attempted to maintain the distinction at the level of command structure (for example, the divisional commissioners of police were the ultimate authorities in each district for the duration of the State of Emergency), at the level of perception the SADF and SAP are seen in the townships as a single force, colloquially and derogatively labelled 'the boere'. The state itself meanwhile, in its regular official reports on 'unrest', no longer differentiates between the roles of army and police, but refers only to the 'security forces'.

Yet while these activities indicate a blurring of military and police functions, the relationship between these two state institutions has not always been entirely harmonious. We have already pointed to the conflict between defence force and police leadership during the period leading up to the Information Scandal. There is also evidence to suggest that both SAP leadership and rank and file have not always accepted the reformist initiatives in which the military has played an important conceptualising role. In a revealing interview the head of the Civic Action Programme in Cape Town, Major Brits, stated:[80]

> In 1981, just after the schools boycotts, we went out there in the townships unarmed and soon the people began to see us as protectors whereas the cops [police] are seen as pro-secutors — and sometimes by the way they behave towards black people, I'm not surprised. In the platteland black people run like hell from military vehicles and this is usually because they've had a problem with some difficult police sergeant.

However, as the resistance to apartheid has intensified, and as the maintenance (or establishment) of 'law and order' has increasingly become an absolute government priority, so the military and the police have developed a close working relationship, a relationship which has been cemented in the series of events since September 1984. The effect of this has been that the lines of battle in South Africa's civil conflict have become more clearly drawn. The state has come to be seen more monolithically, with the SADF, the SAP and the local Community Councils and vigilante groups being seen as a single oppressive force. In addition, the township-based community, labour and political organisations, despite any other differences that may exist between them, have united in their call for the withdrawal of troops from the townships. An independent survey conducted by the Women for Peace organisation in late 1985 found that over 90 per cent of blacks in the Witwatersrand area wanted the troops to be withdrawn from the townships, with the majority identifying 'apartheid and related oppression' as the 'main cause of the unrest'.[81]

In Port Elizabeth, the withdrawal of the troops from the townships in November 1985 was strongly welcomed by all the extra-parliamentary political organisations, the English-language churches, the Progressive Federal Party and even by the local Chamber of Commerce.[82] In fact, throughout the Eastern Cape, local business men have called for troop withdrawal following highly successful consumer boycotts in which one of the major demands has been that troops be withdrawn from the townships. Possibly the most significant effect of the impact of the SADF presence in the townships, however, was the little-publicised parliamentary announcement by Defence Minister Malan that during the whole of 1985, not one African volunteered for military service[83] — and this during a year in which unemployment reached new heights.

The overlapping roles of the military and police received legislative acknowledgement in a December 1985 amendment to the Defence Act. In short, all police powers were extended to the SADF, independently of the existence of a State of Emergency. Soldiers were given the right to search, seize articles, disperse crowds and man road-blocks without police assistance. Any Defence Force member with rank equivalent to that of a warrant-officer would now be entitled to prevent a prohibited gathering, disperse an unlawful gathering and order the detention of anyone.[84] The legislative machinery for the implementation of these regulations had existed since the Defence Act was amended in May 1984, but this was the first time that regulations had been promulgated to give full effect to that legislation. As one newspaper editorialised, there was now a situation of 'martial law in all but name'.[85]

Resistance to conscription

The use of the SADF in this internal repressive role has had a further effect — one less anticipated by the military authorities than township-based resistance. Since the mid-1970s, an increasing number of conscripts had conscientiously objected to service in the SADF. Religious and political grounds had been advanced by the various objectors. The state attempted to put a lid upon the increasing publicity these objectors were receiving through the passing of a 1983 amendment to the Defence Act. On the one hand, the amendment made concessions by creating a category of people who could be recognised as objectors and by granting religious pacifists the possibility of six years alternative service. On the other hand, the prison sentence for those yet to render service who objected on political or non-religious grounds was lengthened from two to six years.

The legislative changes played an important part in prompting the launching of the End Conscription Campaign (ECC) in late

1983, a campaign which was significantly boosted by the activities of the SADF in South Africa's townships. By early 1986 the ECC had grown into a national umbrella body representing over 50 organisations, and with branches in nine centres.[86] The dramatic growth of the campaign, and the wide-ranging public debate it generated, reflected increasing strains within the white power bloc. Yet while the ECC gave direction to growing discontent within the white community with the system of conscription and the role of the SADF, it was the army itself which most starkly posed the dilemmas for those affected by conscription.

Reports are increasingly being received of growing dissatisfaction amongst white conscripts with the system of compulsory national service. Increasing numbers are evading the call-up altogether, while others within the military are refusing to be deployed in the townships.[87] Between July 1984 and July 1986, 936 conscripts applied to the Board for Religious Objection to be recognised as objectors.[88] At the same time trials of conscripts who fail to report for SADF camps have indicated that about 25 per cent of those called up for camps do not turn up.[89] Military concern is evidenced by the Minister of Defence's refusal to release figures to Parliament of the number of conscripts who failed to report for military service in 1985–6.[90]

As the country slides into a state of unofficial martial law, the always tenuous unity of the apartheid state is being rent asunder. Its once exclusive and largely supportive white base is starting to fracture. While this has been most visible in the growth of a vociferous ultra-right wing which urges the annihilation of popular organisation and black resistance, it has also been visible in the growing number of whites who have recognised the prohibitive cost of the repressive and militaristic path which the government has chosen. It is this latter group of whites and its organisations such as the ECC which (along with thousands of black South Africans) have suffered at the hands of the government's repressive policies since the declaration of the third State of Emergency on 12 June 1986. Indeed, included in the emergency regulations was one making it an offence to incite the public to discredit or undermine the system of compulsory military service.[91] Yet though supressed, desertion has not been eliminated, and from internal military seminars to public 'passing-out' parades, a growing concern is being expressed with the state of troop morale.

The strains within the power bloc are also being felt in less obvious ways. The number of people emigrating from South Africa rose by 64 per cent between 1984 and 1985.[92] At the same time the growing unemployment of returning national servicemen is causing concern to military authorities. The officer commanding the SADF's orientation service said that of 400 servicemen polled at the end of 1985, 26 per cent had no employment waiting for them.[93]

Cumulatively, these factors induced the military to consider the previously non-negotiable question of compulsory conscription as the basis for participation in the SADF. The authorities are acutely aware that a partially dissatisfied conscripted army poses problems at the levels of both security and efficiency. Conscription was one of a number of issues examined during 1984–5 by a high-ranking committee of enquiry headed by the Chief of the Defence Force, General Jannie Geldenhuys. However, the report of the Committee, released in April 1986, rejected any concessions to objections to the system of compulsory national service on the revealing grounds that such concessions would 'result in the Defence Force being reduced to inefficiency'. The Committee recommended the maintenance of the SADF's reliance on conscription of white males, while urging increased efforts to counter the anti-national service campaign.[94] Some of these efforts were manifested in the first two months of the third State of Emergency when 49 ECC members country-wide were detained without trial.

The SADF on South Africa's borders

While the situation in South Africa's major urban centres may have reached a stage of 'martial law' by 1985, on South Africa's borders a low-intensity war has been waged for the past decade.

From 1976 onwards thousands of young black South Africans (and a few whites) began leaving the country for military training in the armed wing of the ANC, Umkhonto we Sizwe. By 1985 the ANC was reliably estimated to have 10,000 trained guerrillas.[95] They were responsible from 1979 onwards for a series of bomb and guerrilla attacks which hit all South Africa's major cities and many outlying areas and which prompted Defence Minister Malan to speak of a 'second front' within the country and of 'area-based warfare'.[96] The northern, western and north eastern borders of the Transvaal are regarded as the 'first line of defence' against guerrilla insurgents. As early as 1978 the Defence Act was amended, empowering the SADF to enter private property within a 10 km zone of the border, and to demolish or erect buildings or structures without the consent of the owner. In 1984 the 10 km strip was extended to 50 km.[97]

More importantly, during 1982 the Defence Act was amended to enable the Defence Force to call on a large reservoir of auxiliary manpower 'so that no area in South Africa will be vulnerable to attack'.[98] Besides lengthening the citizen force (camp duty) requirements of national servicemen from 240 days over eight years to 720 days over twelve years, the amendment empowered the military to call up all white males to do commando duty for twelve days a year up to the age of 55.[99] The number of potentially mobilisable men was thus doubled to over 800,000, and the military could now use people with specialised knowledge of local terrain to counter locally based resistance.[100] Under this new system commando units (some of which had only 5 per cent of their quota when they operated on a volunteer basis) were able to be adequately staffed for the first time. Though the amendment was particularly directed at strengthening border defence capabilities, it also provided for urban and industrial commandos, as well as rural commandos with wide-ranging duties including protection of 'key points', intelligence, counter-insurgency and patrol work.[101] By 1985, six months after the beginning of the Vaal resistance, 'Dad's Army' commando units had been established throughout the northern, eastern and western Transvaal, the eastern Cape and Border, the northern Orange Free State and Natal. Provision was being made for similar commandos in the western Cape and on the west coast.[102] Significantly, a Coloured commando unit was established in Queenstown in December 1985, when 93 volunteers were given a week's training in shooting, urban patrols, road-blocks drill and military discipline so that they could be used operationally with immediate effect.[103]

In addition, the Civil Defence Section of the SADF has been actively involved for 15 years in helping City and Town Councils, Community Councils and other local authorities 'to provide for the protection of the Republic and its inhabitants in a state of emergency and in other incidental matters'.[104] By the end of 1983 there were 646 civil defence organisations, of which 86 had achieved the 'highest preparedness rating'.[105]

A major area of concern to the military has been the ongoing depopulation of the border areas. In 1978 the Steyn Committee, appointed to investigate precisely this issue, found that 44.6 per cent of the farms in the border areas were not occupied by whites,[106] and by 1986 the figure had risen to 67 per cent.[107] The government responded by passing legislation which provided the farming community with military and financial perks as rewards for remaining in or returning to strategically important areas.[108] At the same time the deputy Defence Minister, Kobie Coetsee, announced recommendations for a 'ring of steel' to counter Umkhonto we Sizwe incursions. This included the establishment of fortified strong points where farmers would be able to sleep at night. According to Coetsee, South Africa's borders would be secured by a 'chain of protected villages doubling as military bases'. The farmers, acting in collaboration with existing commandos, would therefore form part of a security network. Training bases would also be provided.[109] These plans were extended with the building of a high-voltage electrified fence along South Africa's northern and north eastern borders, which have already caused a number of deaths. There is also talk of electrified fences between black 'homelands' and white farm lands, particularly in the strife-torn Sekukhuneland area of Lebowa in the northern Transvaal.

The implications of this strategy are clear. The border agricultural sector has become the military's front line of defence. This is the background to the ANC's intensified activities in the northern Transvaal in late 1985, when land-mine blasts killed a number of local farmers. These attacks prompted Major General Charles Lloyd to tell farmers in the Messina district that the Minister of Defence was 'giving the Soutpansburg military a higher priority than Namibia'.[110]

The upsurge in guerrilla activity in the border areas also reflects the failure of the Nkomati Accord and other security agreements to curb ANC guerrilla activity. This is born out by the figures of ANC guerrilla attacks within South Africa. According to Pretoria's Institute for Strategic Studies, the number of attacks rose from 31 in 1983 to 44 in 1984 (the year in which the Nkomati Accord was signed between South Africa and Mozambique), to 136 in 1985.[111] Of the 1985 attacks, 40 involved the assassination or attempted assassination of members of the security forces or state witnesses and 17 involved attacks on SADF and other government buildings.[112] What is clear from these figures is not only the escalation of attacks, but also the extent to which the security forces have been a major target. This will no doubt be a major site of battle in the future, occurring parallel, and often in complementary fashion, to the mass struggles being waged by township and rural residents.

Conclusion — towards military rule?

The declaration, on 12 June 1986, of South Africa's third State of Emergency under Nationalist Party rule was an indication of the increasing fragility of white minority rule. Yet by declaring the Emergency and in choosing to respond with repression, the government was not abandoning its programme of reform, which has been haltingly implemented over the past decade. Three weeks after the Emergency was declared, the pass laws were formally removed from the statute books, and government Ministers continued to promote the establishment of a black advisory council, independent 'city-states' and racially integrated Regional Services Councils. Rather, the Emergency represented a tacit admission on the part of the government that its reform programme to date had been reduced to tatters. In particular, the overwhelming rejection of the tricameral Parliament, a nation-wide popular uprising of over two years duration and the collapse of the black local authorities had shown the government's failure to win significant support amongst the black population.

The Emergency also represented the government's refusal to allow the failure of the reform programme to jeopardise the overriding concern with the question of national security. Indeed one of the immediate effects of the declaration of the Emergency was to strengthen the role of the security forces in formulating and implementing state policy and to confirm the shift towards the regionalisation and militarisation of political power.

The powers granted to the security forces by both the emergency regulations and the 1986 amendment to the Public Safety Act have assisted the building of a shadow state behind the contention-ridden civilian façade. Established along regional lines, the structures of this shadow state parallel and sometimes actively overlap with the already sophisticated and effective structures of area and regional command of the security forces. It is not an exaggeration to suggest that the groundwork has been laid for the implementation of a Gauleiter option — a strategy employed by the Nazis in the 1930s in which significant authority and control was vested in military authorities at the regional level. The connotation of the shadow state clearly validates the assertion of a number of writers that a 'silent' or 'creeping' *coup* is occurring.[113]

An alternative power structure and a sophisticated system of control, however, do not necessarily ensure Pretoria's long-term security. Over the past decade, brute force coupled with a faltering reform programme have not managed to slow the tide of growing black resistance. As some more far-sighted business men, and even some members of the Nationalist Party, have realised, unless the state can attract black allies on a large scale (not merely from among the discredited coterie of 'sell-outs'), its defence problems could soon become unmanageable, especially once sanctions and disinvestment take hold.

The government's reliance on the support of the 15 per cent of the population who are classified white is in itself a major defence problem, particularly as the civil war moves beyond the stage of sporadic low-level outbursts of violence. If South Africa moves closer to a 'siege scenario', the problem will be exacerbated. The severing of overseas commercial and industrial links will shrink the economy. At the same time an increasing percentage of the GNP will be spent on defence, requiring greater taxation and thus reducing confidence in South Africa's future. The emigration figures will continue to escalate, further weakening the skills-base on which the economy is reliant. This in turn will limit the state's potential to meet basic black economic needs of housing, health, employment and education, thereby weakening its potential to win over long-term allies.

So the government has placed its only hope on breaking the black resistance which has intensified dramatically over the past two years. If the resistance can be smashed (at whatever cost in international and local support), the government hopes that the resultant stability will lead to a reversing of the ebb of business confidence. Cabinet Ministers have frequently asserted that economic growth will enable the economy to meet basic material needs and will open the way for the securing of moderate black support. For this scenario to have any chance of even short-term success, a highly co-ordinated national security strategy is necessary. It is this strategy which has begun to unfold in the period since mid–1984, and which has relied significantly on the increased powers granted to the security forces by the two states of emergency.

Thus, in the short term, whether this strategy succeeds or fails, we can anticipate the SADF and the other security forces playing a far greater role than previously. If the strategy succeeds in the short term, the military will have to ensure that widespread resistance does not resurface. Failure could provide a short cut to fully fledged martial law which will confer an even greater role on the SADF. Either way, the distinct possibility of some form of *de facto* military rule over the next few years looms large.

What the government strategy ignores, however, is the fact that those involved in the struggle against apartheid are not merely concerned with questions of material need, and will certainly not be pacified by offers of piecemeal economic advancement. Masses of black South Africans are today raising the fundamental question of political power. On this question the government and military strategy is doomed to failure: for the central areas of contention — race classification and a universal franchise in a democratic and unitary state — are non-negotiable for the government and the military as well as for most representatives of big business.[114] Yet these demands unite all anti-apartheid forces across the ideological spectrum.

For those who wish to look beyond the daily toll of death in the country's townships, it could be said that South Africa is in a state of civil war to the extent that the terms upon which the present state can survive, and the terms upon which the grievances of the country's people can be resolved, are mutually incompatible. This is why the siege solution chosen by the government and military leaders can only alleviate the country's problems on a short-term basis. In the long term, such strategies cannot hope to block the southward path of Africa's decolonisation.

Notes

1. *Cape Times*, 8 October 1984; *Sunday Times*, 14 October 1984.
2. *Cape Times*, 23 October 1984; *South African Outlook*, April 1985, p. 52.
3. Cited in *Daily News*, 13 June 1979.
4. White Paper on Defence and Armaments Supply, 1977 (henceforth Defence White Paper). On the question of Total Strategy, see Philip Frankel, *Pretoria's Praetorians: civil-military relations in South Africa* (Cambridge University Press, Cambridge, 1984); Richard Leonard, *South Africa at war* (A.D. Jonker, Cape Town, 1983); Kenneth Grundy, *The militarisation of South African politics* (I.B. Tauris, 1986); Deon Geldenhuys, *The diplomacy of isolation: South African foreign policy making* (Macmillan, Johannesburg, 1984).
5. Defence White Paper, 1977.
6. Frankel, *Pretoria's Praetorians*, p. 34.
7. The French general and military strategist, André Beaufre, whose theories have had a major influence on the South African defence leadership, refers to the need to develop policies which 'cut the ground from under the feet of the malcontents'. See Frankel, *Pretoria's Praetorians*, p. 52.
8. Defence White Paper, 1979.
9. On the composition and functions of the State Security Council, see the readings listed in note 4, and K. Grundy, *The Rise of the South African security establishment: an essay on the changing locus of state power* (SAIIA, Bradlow Series no. 1, Johannesburg, 1983).

10. *Argus*, 21 September 1983.

11. *Financial Mail*, 2 April 1982.

12. *Weekly Mail*, 1 August 1986.

13. Frankel, *Pretoria's Praetorians*, p. 106.

14. *Weekly Mail*, 1 August 1986. The document entitled 'Strategy for the collection of arrear rental and service charges' was submitted to a meeting of the Lekoa Town Council on 4 November 1985.

15. K. Melliker, 'Local government in South Africa and the government's proposed changes'. Paper delivered at the Non-Racial Municipality Conference, Grahamstown (April 1986).

16. Very little is known about the Regional Development Advisory Committees. It appears that the first RDACs were set up from 1982, and that 250 of these bodies are planned across the country. They appear to have a business/academic/military membership.

17. *Financial Mail*, 11 September 1981. Among the more prominent multinational firms supplying components to the SADF are Fuchs, Siemens, AEG Telefunken, Messerschmidt and IBM in the electronics and communications spheres, and motor manufacturers Ford, Mercedes Benz and Toyota. Shell and BP are both active as sources of oil products.

18. Grundy, *South African security establishment*, pp. 13–14. See also Simon Ratcliffe, 'Forced relations: the state crisis and the rise of militarism in South Africa' (unpublished dissertation, Witwatersrand University, 1983 and Defence White Paper 1986).

19. Frankel, *Pretoria's Praetorians*, p. 74.

20. Ibid., p. 80.

21. *Financial Mail*, 26 November 1976.

22. Cited in B. Sjollema, *Isolating apartheid* (World Council of Churches, 1982), p. 19.

23. Frankel, *Pretoria's Praetorians*, p. 74.

24. *Weekly Mail*, 21 March 1986.

25. Charles Lloyd, *The importance of rural development in the defence strategy for South Africa and the need for private sector involvement* (Urban Foundation, Johannesburg, 1979). See also Gavin Evans, 'SADF and the Civic Action Programme', *Work in Progress*, no. 29 (1983).

26. *Paratus*, February 1982.

27. Lloyd, 'Rural development, Defence White Paper', *Paratus* (June 1978).

28. Ibid.

29. Dr Ivan Toms, address to End Conscription Campaign public meeting, Cape Town, October 1984.

30. Gavin Evans, 'The role of the military in education in South Africa' (unpublished dissertation, University of Cape Town, 1983). See also National Union of South African Students, *Total war in South Africa: militarisation and the apartheid state* (Allied Press, Cape Town, 1982).

31. Frankel, *Pretoria's Praetorians*, p. 97. Citing Parliamentary Debates of 22 April 1975.

32. See Kenneth Grundy, *Soldiers without politics: blacks in the South African Armed Forces* (University of California Press, Berkeley, 1983); and Gavin Evans 'SADF and Civic Action: blacks in the defence force', *Work in Progress*, no. 28 (1983).

33. Quoted in National Union of South African Students, *In whose defence? Conscription and the SADF* (Esquire, Cape Town, 1984), p. 42.

34. This has also influenced the attempted recruitment of women. See NUSAS, *Total war*, pp. 28–30; and Frankel, *Pretoria's Praetorians*, p. 109.

35. South African Institute of Race Relations (SAIRR), *Annual survey 1979*, p. 83.

36. *Business Day*, 13 February 1986.

37. See Defence White Paper, 1986, part 8, which also asserts that 51 per cent of the soldiers deployed in the Operational Area are members of SWATT.

38. *Sunday Express*, 30 May 1982. See also Catholic Institute of International Relations, *Desert conflicts* (London, 1981).

39. Transvaal National Party leader, F.W. de Klerk quoted in *Cape Times*, 24 August 1982. See also NUSAS *Total war*, p. 36; and Michael Evans 'Restructuring: the role of the military' in South African Research Services, *South African Review One* (Ravan Press, Johannesburg, 1983), pp. 42–9.

40. The United Democratic Front slogan 'Fake Votes for Real Bullets' won support in communities which registered percentage polls as low as 5 per cent in the 1984 coloured and Indian elections.

41. Defence White Paper, 1986, p. 17.

42. Defence White Paper, 1986, p. 19.

43. *Star*, 14 May 1986.

44. P.W. Botha, as quoted in *Beeld*, 22 May 1986.

45. Journalist Alistair Sparks has pointed to evidence of an extensive air strike against Angolan army (FAPLA) columns advancing on UNITA in September 1985. UNITA has no Air Force, and the Angolan government alleged that its Army had been repeatedly attacked by South African Air Force bombers: *Weekly Mail*, 11 October 1985.

46. *Business Day*, 30 May 1985 (*Cape Times*, 23 May 1985). For an excellent survey of South African destabilisation tactics in Angola and elsewhere in Southern Africa, see Phyllis Johnson and David Martin (eds), *Destructive engagement — Southern Africa at war* (Zimbabwe Publishing House, Harare, 1986).

47. Grundy, *South African security establishment*, p. 31; and Graham McIntosh, Parliamentary Speech, 28 May 1985.

48. McIntosh, Speech.

49. Landeg White, 'Review article: the revolutions ten years on', *Journal of Southern African Studies* (JSAS), vol. 11, no. 2 (1985), p. 322.

50. According to *coup* leader Colonel 'Mad' Mike Hoare, the SADF provided half his 50 men with funding from the National Intelligence Service. Hoare stated that he was informed that the State President, P.W. Botha, had personally approved of the raid (*Citizen*, 14 July 1986; *Star*, 14 July 1986).

51. See, for example, Rob Davies's letter to Deon Geldenhuys, *JSAS*, vol. 12, no. 2 (1986), p. 315.

52. See Southern African Catholic Bishops' Conference Report on Namibia (Pretoria, 1982). The finding of the Catholic Bishops that SWAPO enjoys majority support in Namibia has been confirmed by both the Anglican Bishops and a delegation from the British Council of Churches.

53. Frankel, *Pretoria's Praetorians*, p. 104.

54. Robert Davies and Dan O'Meara, 'Total Strategy in Southern Africa: an analysis of South African regional policy since 1978', *JSAS*, vol. 11, no. 2 (1985), p. 184.

55. See End Conscription Committee, 'The "Internal Enemy" — civil war in South Africa', *South African Outlook* (April 1985), pp. 59–61.

56. *Cape Times*, 6 October 1984.

57. *Cape Times*, 19 May 1984.

58. The SADF has been involved in removals in the following areas: the Zimbabwe and Venda border areas; St Lucia, where an SADF missile base was built; Mafekeng to Zeerust; Ditakwaneng in the northern Cape; Maremane area — now Lohatla — the site of Operation Thunderchariot in 1984; Kosi Bay to Ingwavuma. It has been involved in the breaking of strikes at the Impala Platinum Mine and at Baragwanath Hospital, Johannesburg, both during 1985.

59. House of Assembly, Parliamentary Question no. 878, 1986.

60. *Rand Daily Mail*, 7 November 1984.

61. Parliamentary Questions, quoted in *EEC Calendar*, vol. 1, no. 3 (1985).

62. House of Assembly, Parliamentary Question no. 878, 1986.

63. See End Conscription Committee (ECC), *Evidence submitted to the United Nations Special Committee Against Apartheid* (New York, 21 March 1986).

64. See, for example, SAIRR figures published regularly in the *Weekly Mail*.

65. ECC Evidence.

66. See, for example, the Witwatersrand Local Division case, *Krugersdorp Residents Association and Others v Minister of Law and Order and Others*.

67. *Weekend Post*, 2 August 1985.

68. *Sunday Star*, 15 September 1985.

69. *Argus*, 18 September 1985.

70. *Eastern Province Herald*, 13 November 1985.

71. *Star*, 25 September 1986.

72. *Cape Times*, 4 November 1985.

73. *Cape Times*, 11 December 1986. Such sentences should be compared with prison sentences of up to ten years meted out to children convicted of public violence (which often involves no more than stone-throwing).

74. *Cape Times*, 12 December 1986.

75. Parliamentary Questions, quoted in *EEC Calendar*, vol. 1, no. 3 (1985).

76. *Report to the End Conscription Committee National Conference* (Durban, February 1986).

77. Interview in 'Out of step', quoted in ECC Evidence.

78. ECC Evidence.

79. *Guardian Weekly*, 15 September 1985.

80. Gavin Evans.

81. *Citizen*, 16 October 1985.

82. *Eastern Province Herald*, 23 November 1985.

83. *Cape Times*, 13 February 1986.

84. *Star*, 20 December 1985.

85. *Star*, 3 January 1986.

86. See End Conscription Committee, 'Conscription into the SADF

— 25 years of resistance', *South African Outlook* (April 1985), pp. 53–7.

87. Most cases of individual soldiers who refuse to go into the townships are generally handled internally, with local Commanding Officers at times allowing such refusal. One case that did receive significant publicity was that of Alan Dodson, who in August 1985 was found guilty at a Natal court martial of having disobeyed his orders to go on a vehicle patrol in the townships. He was fined R600 (US$250).

88. *Cape Times*, 25 August 1986.

89. ECC Evidence.

90. *Argus*, 13 February 1986.

91. Emergency Regulations 1 (vii) (b) (v).

92. *Weekly Mail*, 7 March 1986.

93. *Star*, 11 December 1985.

94. Defence White Paper (1986), pp. 9–10.

95. International Institute of Strategic Studies, *The military balance* (London, 1985). See also Tom Lodge, *Black politics in South Africa since 1945* (Ravan Press, Johannesburg, 1983), and Lodge's regular articles in *South African Review*.

96. *Rand Daily Mail*, 5 June 1982. See also Defence White Papers, 1982 and 1984.

97. Development of Designated Areas Act, *Citizen*, 12 December 1984.

98. *Financial Mail*, 15 January 1982. See also Grundy, *The rise of the South African security establishment*, p. 8.

99. Act 103 of 1982.

100. *Cape Times*, 19 April 1982.

101. Evans, 'Restructuring: the role of the military', p. 43.

102. Defence White Paper, 1984; *Natal Mercury*, 6 September 1985; *Cape Times*, 24 January 1986.

103. *Daily Despatch*, 16 December 1985.

104. Civil Defence Act, 1974.

105. Defence White Paper, 1984.

106. SAIRR, *Annual survey 1979*, p. 89; *Star*, 21 July 1979.

107. *Business Day*, 5 June 1985.

108. Promotion of the Density of Population in Designated Areas Act, 1979. See NUSAS, *Total war*, p. 48, and Frankel, *Pretoria's Praetorians*, p. 136.

109. SAIRR, *Annual Survey 1979*, p. 89; *Financial Mail*, 9 March 1979; *Rand Daily Mail*, 3 March 1979.

110. *Sunday Star*, 22 December 1985.

111. See T. Lodge in *South African Review Two* (1984), pp. 21–5 and *South African Review Three* (1986), pp. 226–47. These figures do not include attacks in the 'independent homelands'.

112. ECC Evidence.

113. See Dan O'Meara, 'Muldergate and the politics of Afrikaner nationalism', *Work in Progress*, no. 22 (1982), and Frankel, *Pretoria's Praetorians*, p. 173.

114. To date the only representative of a major South African corporation who has been prepared to admit the inevitability of 'one person, one vote' majority rule is Gordon Waddell of Johannesburg Consolidated Investments (see *Star*, 15 September 1986, and *Business Day*, 15 September 1986).

6

The Wild Card: Inkatha and Contemporary Black Politics[1]

Colleen McCaul

Inkatha Yenkululeko Yesizwe, led by Chief Mangosuthu Buthelezi, has emerged as a major conservative force in black South African politics. At a time of widespread social upheaval and growing political polarisation, the white establishment has invested in Inkatha its hopes for a negotiated political settlement capable of arresting pressures for fundamental social change and counteracting the increasingly successful mobilisation of the black population by rival and more radical political groupings. However, Inkatha is no mere tool of the ruling group. As an autonomous and even unpredictable force, with its own political agenda for change, the organisation, as Shula Marks has recently commented, is immersed in the politics of ambiguity.[2]

Described by one analyst as 'Janus faced',[3] the movement simultaneously presents a liberal programme for change, while showing itself a master in the manipulation of traditionalist instruments and networks of patronage and control. Opposed to the use of violence in the furtherance of the liberation struggle, its adherents frequently use and threaten violence against their opponents. Inkatha describes itself as a movement of 'workers and peasants' but it is in firm alliance with capitalist interests. Portraying itself to blacks as a political organisation in the traditions of the founding fathers of the African National Congress (ANC), it is also a Zulu nationalist movement, often exhibiting extreme Zulu chauvinism. While it regards itself as a 'liberation movement', it is entrenched in the power structures of the KwaZulu bantustan, all members of the KwaZulu Legislative Assembly (KLA) being Inkatha members:[4] so, while something of a mass movement, Inkatha simultaneously wields power in a regional adjunct of the South African state as a one-party administration.

How are these apparent 'contradictions' to be understood? Firstly, as Marks has pointed out,[5] there are certain echoes of the ambiguity that has historically characterised black politics in Natal: the opposition to, and dependence upon, the white state; an attachment to Zulu traditions and the Royal house, coupled with a commitment to progress and Western civilisation; and a regionalist rivalry with black political movements elsewhere. There are certain continuities between Inkatha and its early 1920s precursor, Inkatha ka Zulu. Founded by Chief Buthelezi's late uncle, King Solomon ka Dinuzulu, it was designed, as Marks writes, by the Zulu aristocracy and the African petty bourgeoisie in Zululand, to gain state recognition for the Zulu king, and to collect funds for the Royal Family. To African landowners and the petty bourgeoisie, the Royal Family, unlike the subordinate chiefs recognised by the Natal administration, could play a pan-Zulu nationalistic and self-consciously modernising role. On the other hand, the early Inkatha was encouraged and regarded as useful by representatives of capitalist farming interests in Zululand and the idealogues of segregation as a bulwark against the dangers of sharpening class conflict and major strains in Zululand at the time.[6] Likewise today, in the face of widespread social upheaval, the Inkatha movement is regarded by sections of the dominant bloc as being crucial to the task of countering growing mass radicalisation and finding moderate constitutional solutions to the 'problem' of the political incorporation of the African majority.

Secondly, while Inkatha is committed to Natal/KwaZulu as its most secure base (it is here that it is powerfully entrenched in regional and local state structures, controls the networks of patronage, enjoys the support of traditional chiefs, and has a certain degree of popular support, particularly in the rural areas; and it recognises KwaZulu's limitations as a base for any movement with national political aspirations), the bantustan is impoverished, and extremely fragmented, and bantustan policy is politically discredited. The movement is therefore impelled outwards to seek alliances and bases in strata and regions outside of Natal/KwaZulu, and has committed itself to mobilising a large and disciplined following. Inkatha's membership has grown rapidly (to a claimed 1.2 million people),[7] constituted in youth and women's wings and general membership, and evidenced in part in the huge crowds it attracts to rallies both in Natal and on the Reef. In mobilising this mass base, in a changing and increasingly ideologically competitive political environment, and in establishing its own distinctive identity, Inkatha has become somewhat uncomfortably straddled across its different constituencies, audiences and bases, and must play to different mobilising themes: on the one hand, it exhibits assertive anti-apartheid reformism, maintains a critical distance from the state, appeals to the traditions of the ANC and the liberation struggle and asserts a broad African nationalism; while on the other hand, it appeals to traditionalism, ethnic loyalties, patriarchal and hierarchical values, discipline and a Zulu nationalism.

Thirdly, at a time when the trade union movement is growing and consolidating and there is an increased popular receptiveness to socialist appeals, Inkatha has sought class compromise between capital and labour, and committed itself to free enterprise and individual advancement, equating liberation ideologically with the attainment of economic benefits in a deracialised capitalist system. It thus forms alliances with capital and political groupings committed to reformed capitalism and supports the formation of conservative trade unions to challenge the Congress of South African Trade Unions (COSATU). In order to compete effectively against more radical unions and ideologies, Inkatha has to appear to be on the workers' side, hold out the promise of gains and appear to challenge exploitation, while at the same time giving a guarantee to capital of harmonious and relatively strike-free relationships in the workplace. The commitment to a reformed, deracialised capitalism also reflects the concerns of those sections of the black petty bourgeois elite within Inkatha (particularly those whose interests are, to a certain extent, vested in the existence of the KwaZulu bantustan): traders, chiefs, headmen, town councillors, business men, KwaZulu civil servants, small agricultural and industrial entrepreneurs and professionals.

All these factors place the movement in tension, constituting it in its many contradictions.

Inkatha membership and support

Since its revival in 1975 (the early Inkatha had become defunct by the late 1920s), Inkatha has mobilised a claimed membership of 1.2 million people organised in more than 2,000 branches.[8] The Secretary General of Inkatha, Dr Oscar Dhlomo, said in mid-1985 that 38 per cent of the membership was accounted for by Inkatha's youth brigade, 34 per cent by the women's brigade, and 28 per cent by general membership.[9] Membership claims should be treated with circumspection as figures have been found to include not only paid-up members, but also those who have resigned, died or failed to renew subscriptions.[10] Nonetheless, Inkatha's membership is clearly substantial.

Its stronghold is KwaZulu/Natal, particularly rural KwaZulu (of the 1,200 branches in 1982 the majority were still in the rural areas), and members elsewhere are generally in areas with large numbers of Zulu-speaking people, with support strongest there among migrants and hostel dwellers — notably Soweto and the East Rand in the Witwatersrand complex. The majority of Inkatha's members are Zulu-speaking (between 80 per cent and 95 per cent in 1979), but exact statistics are unavailable as Inkatha does not keep ethnic statistics.[11] (The 1975 Constitution was amended in 1979 to remove numerous references to KwaZulu and officially open membership to all Africans.)

The strong rural base of Inkatha was in 1980, by Professor Lawrence Schlemmer, who has a long involvement with Inkatha, ascribed to the 'active co-operation' of chiefs who established branches within their own constituencies. As automatic members of the KLA, he said, they 'could fairly readily be persuaded to mobilise their constituents. Inkatha enables chiefs to become involved as key figures in a modern political organisation.'[12] Roger Southall has claimed that the chiefs used their coercive powers to entrench Inkatha within their own areas, describing tribal chieftaincy as 'a motor power behind the rapid growth of Inkatha' and questioning whether party dues assumed the character of tribal levies.[13] In their crucial role in 'mobilising their constituents', KwaZulu chiefs have considerable powers of patronage and an Inkatha Institute official admitted to the writer that this 'affects Inkatha support a lot', the perception of Inkatha's rank and file being that Inkatha membership eased access to resources (such as land, jobs, housing and pensions).[14] Given the powerlessness of rural inhabitants, the difficulties in gaining access to basic resources and evidence of corruption and control at tribal authority level,[15] it is probable that Inkatha membership is a welcome asset (at only R3 a year), given the perception that it eases access to patronage.

Rural KwaZulu members may also be attracted by Inkatha's self-help and self-reliance ideology and activities (the latter handled by its development office, which sets up co-operative bulk-buying schemes and credit unions, and women's brigade, which organises vegetable gardening, sewing groups, and so on).[16] Inkatha adopted a rural upliftment strategy in 1979, Buthelezi describing Inkatha as the 'economic arm' of the KwaZulu administration and the instrument for 'mobilising the peasantry' for rural development.[17]

Youth brigade membership has grown from 1,000 in 1976 to a claimed half a million in 1986, and many young members are recruited in KwaZulu schools — targeted by Inkatha as recruiting grounds.[18] In 1978 a programme of 'education for nationhood', including a weekly hour of instruction on the aims and principles of Inkatha, was introduced in all KwaZulu schools. The Inkatha syllabus is known as Ubuntu/Botho (meaning humanism/communalism/good citizenship) and pupils are taught, *inter alia*, about Inkatha's history and organisation, the conduct of Inkatha members, the 'role of leaders and led', the liberation struggle, African culture, rural and urban life, and the need for African business enterprise.[19] Inkatha aims to have a youth brigade branch in every school and Inkatha documents are sent to all KwaZulu teachers. Youth brigade officials are generally granted time to talk about Inkatha to pupils, and school time is allowed for brigade activities.[20] Buthelezi has referred to the importance of teachers' being imbued with the spirit and principles of Inkatha for 'our cultural and political survival' and Dhlomo has threatened that non-Inkatha teachers would be regarded with suspicion and might not be 'entrusted with the future of our children'.[21] A recent study found evidence of obligatory youth membership in some KwaZulu schools and that in at least one school the membership fee was automatically added to school fees.[22]

Schlemmer has remarked that Inkatha has used 'the sanctioning power of the KwaZulu administration to nudge teachers, civil servants and others into co-operating'. While denying on occasion that civil servants were penalised for not joining, Buthelezi has also said that their 'standing in Inkatha would be taken into account when they were assessed for promotion'.[23] A survey of the large township of KwaMashu in KwaZulu in 1980 of 255 male household heads found that while most of the 41 per cent who were Inkatha members claimed to have had a desire to join anyway, 81 per cent of them also said that the organisation had 'helped them in their employment or career', and 75 per cent that membership had been 'necessary in obtaining it'.[24]

Sitas has referred to Inkatha's strong base in the urban areas of KwaZulu/Natal amongst sections of the African petty bourgeoisie — traders, township business men, teachers and civil servants (bantustan self-government caused their rapid numerical expansion) — who defend their political interests through township local authority structures, and who have created a tight patronage system in the townships. Sitas locates Inkatha's 'significant worker support' in the townships in its offers of 'moral rearmament'; the restoration of Zulu dignity, pride and prowess; continuity with the past; and a social identity. This must have resonance for Natal workers, many of whom are newly urbanised (one survey found that 75 per cent of a large township sample still had active links with the rural areas) and who have been through the upheaval of relocation which had forced rural people into wage labour over the previous two decades. Inkatha was also part of a 'moral rearmament' process under way in the townships which featured the revival of ancestral rituals, traditional forms of justice, an attempt by elements of the community to police their own neighbourhoods, a reinvigoration of traditional familial relationships, and a belief in discipline.[25]

Buthelezi's own personal charismatic appeal has been significant in attracting members to Inkatha. Teague has commented that within Inkatha there is a 'form of hero worship, where he is revered and beyond reproach. This idolisation cannot be underestimated'.[26] Buthelezi returned to Zululand in 1953 from the University College of Fort Hare, where he was an ANC Youth League member in the 1940s and early 1950s, to become chief of the Buthelezi people and advisor to King Cyprian, and in 1972, the first executive councillor of the new territorial authority of KwaZulu. Thwarting the imposition of bantustan policy on Zululand and ultimately forcing a change in the legislation, 'he established a reputation as a major opponent of apartheid and a fearless champion of African interests'.[27] Buthelezi rejects charges of collaboration, pointing out, firstly, that his position in KwaZulu as Chief Minister is hereditary (he is the nephew of King Solomon ka Dinuzulu and his family were traditionally 'Prime Ministers' of Zululand) and not bestowed on him by the government; and secondly, that his participation in bantustan structures was encouraged and approved by the ANC. Equally skilled in a discourse of Zulu ethnicity and chauvinism as that of national liberation, Buthelezi, in the words of one writer,[28]

> makes reference to his Zulu ancestors at the same time as reminding people that he was a member of the ANC Youth League. He has successfully integrated the popular democratic traditions of struggle in South Africa with the Zulu tribal traditions, and maintains that Inkatha was built on the same principles as those of the 'founding fathers' of the ANC.

Ideologically situated by its leadership as filling the vacuum left by the ANC's banning, Inkatha has also adopted ANC songs and slogans and the Inkatha uniform bears ANC colours. This may be a further factor in Inkatha's appeal.

Despite claims of huge membership, recent opinion polls have indicated that Inkatha's and Buthelezi's popularity is diminishing rapidly outside the traditional rural KwaZulu stronghold. Opinion surveys by Professor Fatima Meer among Africans in the Durban area found that Buthelezi's support had fallen from 45 per cent in 1979 to 5 per cent in 1985, while a survey in September 1985 by Orkin and the Community Agency for Social Enquiry and the Institute for Black Research (CASE/IBR) of urban African support (all urban areas) for major political tendencies found only 8 per cent support for Inkatha and Buthelezi. (The sample was 800 African respondents over 16 years of age proportionately spread over all ten major metropolitan areas.) Orkin cites surveys conducted in 1977 (Hanf *et al.*) and 1981 (Schlemmer) to show a decline in support for Buthelezi and Inkatha from 78 per cent to 48 per cent in Natal townships, and from 28 per cent to 17 per cent in the Pretoria/Witwatersrand/Vereeniging (PWV) area between those years respectively. The CASE/IBR Survey (1985) revealed support of only 33 per cent (Natal) and 5 per cent (PWV) respectively. Among Zulu speakers the proportions were 34 per cent and 11 per cent in the two regions. In all areas, even in Natal, a greater proportion of Zulu speakers supported the radical groupings and leaders than Inkatha and Buthelezi.

Orkin suggests that the data reveals strong regional and ethnic effects at work, Buthelezi's support diminishing 'as one moves out of the Natal region and the Zulu-speaking group'. Among urban dwellers, 'his laager largely keeps non-Zulus out, whereas it by now keeps only a minority of Zulus in.' He concludes that 'In sum, across the metropolitan areas of South Africa, Buthelezi has basically lost the battle for popular support, and the decline in his showing can be expected to continue.'[29] This is especially likely if the level of political conflict carries on rising and radical rival groups continue to maintain a high capacity for popular mobilisation.

Inkatha and the politics of negotiation

In a recent speech Buthelezi said,[30]

> Inkatha has been massing power for the people of South Africa
> and it is now indisputably the largest black political consti-
> tuency ever seen in the history of this country . . . We [have]
> evolved a power base which will yet become compelling
> around the negotiating table.

In its attempt to buttress its essentially conservative reformist
demands, Inkatha has mobilised a mass base, whose main use has
been to provide substance to Buthelezi's as yet unfulfilled threats
of a display of consumer and worker power, and to make Inkatha
a 'compelling' force 'around the negotiating table'. At a time when
South African society has become increasingly conflict-ridden and
polarised, the Inkatha leadership has remained committed to the
slow manoeuvrings of the politics of 'negotiation' and compromise.
Along with this, it rejects the armed struggle and revolutionary
violence as political strategies on the grounds that they have no
chance of success, and would destroy the economy. It also opposes
'protest politics' and consistently responds negatively to spontaneous
popular mass action. (The CASE/IBR survey[31] found that only a
third of Buthelezi's urban supporters supported direct action —
strikes, boycotts and protests — compared with four-fifths of United
Democratic Front (UDF) and ANC supporters. While more than
half of ANC supporters backed the armed struggle, less than a tenth
did so in the Inkatha camp. However, peaceful negotiation as a
strategy for social change was supported by 80 per cent of supporters
of all political tendencies, indicating that non-Inkatha supporters
do not see support for protest politics as contradicting the negotiation strategy: Inkatha draws a stark distinction between the two.)

As an alternative to protest politics, Inkatha advocates the
strategy of 'infiltrating the economy' as a liberation strategy —
where liberation is synonymous with upward mobility for blacks,
greater bargaining power in the market-place and the equality of
opportunities and facilities. Buthelezi refers to African economic
advancement as freeing African political power, to the establishment of black businesses as striking blows for the liberation struggle, and to school children who persist through school — defying
school boycott calls — as having a chance to lead 'liberation battalions in the market place and in the factories'.[32]

Rejecting protest politics, Inkatha emphasises to its members the
need for order and discipline, one official comparing Inkatha
discipline — through which members had learned to 'wait' till the
time was ripe — to 'military high discipline where you command

your regiment "left, right, stop, turn" '. Buthelezi has said that
the battle for liberation would succeed only if all people formed a
disciplined task force for change, that peaceful solutions required
the prevention of chaos, and that Inkatha was committed to
'eradicating disorder' in black politics.[33]

Buthelezi's emergence as a leader of 'moderation' committed
to stability and reform within the existing capitalist relations, backed
by a substantial mass following, has won him the regard of powerful sections of the dominant bloc. The Inkatha leadership has been
prepared to compromise on the issue of 'one person, one vote' —
which 'might not be realistic' or could 'lead to civil war' — and
to seek alternative constitutional solutions (principally federalism).
Accordingly, they increasingly speak the language of power sharing,
rather than that of black majority rule. They allay white fears with
promises of checks and balances to protect 'minority rights'. They
frequently state their commitment to capitalism, and ardently
campaign against sanctions and disinvestment on diplomatic trips
abroad, at mass rallies, on state-controlled South African televi-
sion and even, along with 2,000 supporters, in the garden of the
US Consul-general's Durban home.

Vis-à-vis the white regime, Buthelezi has played an artful game.
He has rejected numerous of the state's reform initiatives and
boycotted meetings between the government and homeland leaders
over the years. Inkatha, for example, launched successful action
against government plans to incorporate KwaZulu's Ingwavuma
district into Swaziland in 1982. It also waged a vigorous campaign
against the new South African Constitution in 1983 and 1984,
advocating both a 'no' vote in the white referendum on the
Constitution and a boycott of the elections for the new tricameral
Parliament. Buthelezi has also indicated that he would consider
participation in the National Statutory Council (NSC) proposed
by the State President in 1986 only if the government committed
itself to scrapping the tricameral Parliament, allowed the NSC to
negotiate a new Constitution, and freed jailed leaders, so that they
and their constituencies could participate.[34] However, Buthelezi
continues to endorse the concept of change through reform and to
oppose violent change (generally siding with the forces of law and
order during conflict), thereby revealing himself as a critical but
also potentially co-operative negotiating partner. Referring to
Buthelezi's emergence as 'the Great White Hope', Sutcliffe and
Wellings have commented:[35]

As South Africa descends yet further towards a state of civil war, there seems a greater likelihood that Buthelezi's dominance of the moderate terrain in black politics could secure him some kind of limited, probably regionally confined, power sharing deal from an embattled white regime, desperate for muscular black allies.

While relations between Inkatha and the major black South African opposition groupings have been largely hostile, Inkatha has formed alliances with, *inter alia*, moderate black leaders, the Progressive Federal Party (PFP), and capital, in line with its commitment to a non-violent, negotiated compromise settlement with the white regime. The South African Black Alliance was formed in 1978 between Inkatha, the (coloured) Labour Party, the (Indian) Reform Party and, later, the leaders of two other bantustans, QwaQwa and KaNgwane. This alliance has largely disintegrated with the 'defection' of the Labour Party to the tricameral Parliament, and the visit of KaNgwane leader Enos Mabuza to the ANC (Buthelezi accused him of stabbing him in the back and of irreparably damaging the cause of black unity).[36] Inkatha and many homeland leaders held 'unity talks' during 1983 with the aim of blocking the state's envisaged confederation in favour of a federal formula. This alliance, however, appears to have come to naught. Regarding the PFP, talks with Inkatha in Ulundi in March 1980 led to the PFP's acceptance of Buthelezi's proposal of a political partnership, and in 1982 they agreed to co-operate on the grounds of their mutual opposition to the incorporation of Ingwavuma (a portion of KwaZulu) into Swaziland and the new constitutional proposals, as well as their joint acceptance of the recommendations of the Buthelezi Commission.[37] Inkatha and the PFP shared various platforms in their campaign against the new Constitution during 1983, and in 1985 they together started an initiative towards the setting up of a national convention — the Convention Alliance.[38] The initiative, aimed at bringing about a non-violent dismantling of apartheid and the negotiation, through a national convention, of a Constitution based on one citizenship in one country, subsequently collapsed.[39]

Regarding sections of capital, their support for Inkatha has taken concrete form in the search for a 'Natal option'. While Inkatha is committed to the politics of negotiating compromise solutions with the white regime, there are various factors circumscribing the potential for negotiating room at the level of the central state. These include the discrediting of participation in government institutions, coupled with Inkatha's own commitment to having all the major political groupings present at any negotiations (it recognises that any settlements without their participation would be untenable), and the state's evident lack of serious commitment to genuine compromise on the question of majority political rights. Added to this Inkatha's largely KwaZulu/Natal-bound strengths, the organisation has pursued the politics of negotiation at the regional level. From as early as 1974, Buthelezi has endorsed a geographic federal formula as a constitutional option for South Africa. This envisages the maximum devolution of power to component regions, with a central state controlling only residual functions such as defence and foreign affairs. In 1980, Inkatha's support for a federal formula and its search for stability manifested itself in the appointment of the Buthelezi Commission, subtitled *The requirements for stability and development in KwaZulu and Natal*, and has culminated in the search for a 'Natal option'.

While both the ANC and the National Party turned down invitations to participate in the Commission, participants included, besides Inkatha, the PFP; conservative coloured and Indian parties; powerful capitalists including Harry Oppenheimer; representatives of the Natal sugar industry and of the national chambers of commerce and industry; and a wide range of foreign and local 'experts'. Glaser has commented that 'the commission thus represented the entire range of dominant bloc interests, excepting the government itself'.[40] The Commission's Report in 1982 proposed for Natal/KwaZulu a consociational formula involving a legislative assembly based on universal franchise, proportional representation (combined with minimum representation for minority groups, and a 10 per cent minority veto in matters concerning cultural and individual rights); an executive coalition (made up of the KwaZulu and Natal provincial executives and Indian and coloured representatives); a bill of rights, and an independent judiciary. Group representation would partially be retained but defined culturally, and units of representation defined geographically rather than ethnically.[41]

While the government rejected the Report for a number of years, it was in 1985 in the midst of a nation-wide uprising and its own restructuring of second-tier government (in terms of which the Provincial Councils were abolished), that it began to give affirmative signals regarding the Report, and to indicate that in Natal/KwaZulu — which it regarded as unique — a distinctive regional solution might be possible. In early 1986, it indicated its readiness to accept a multiracial joint executive and administrative authority in Natal/KwaZulu, but not, however, a joint legislature.

The search for a Natal option began in earnest in late 1984 with a series of meetings between the executive committee of the Natal Provincial Council and KwaZulu Cabinet, during which a three-phase proposal was formulated involving, firstly, the implementation of joint planning between the two administrations; secondly, a joint executive authority for the region; and finally, a joint elected legislative assembly. The initiatives culminated in 1986 in the KwaNatal indaba to which all major political groupings were invited. Among others, the ANC, UDF, Azanian People's Organisation (AZAPO) and COSATU turned down invitations, while the National Party took observer status. The deliberations of the indaba have not yet been made public. The Buthelezi Commission Report, however, serves the basis of Inkatha's contribution to the deliberations.[42]

Glaser has situated the pursuit of a Natal option in the wider context of the dominant bloc's project of regionalisation (restructuring the state at and around the regional level of government in order to create a part of the institutional basis for a future reformist dispensation) and points out that as conservative reformers are turning more and more to 'regionalisation', Natal/KwaZulu has become an increasingly important testing ground for constitutionally and politically reorganising at the second tier of government.[43]

While the objectives of the KwaNatal initiative are far more ambitious than state reformers are currently willing to accept, Glaser points out that it itself remains conservative in so far as it retains safeguards against the redistribution of wealth; continues to attach importance to the political representation of distinctive cultural segments; and in general, seeks to avoid majority rule in a unitary state. In addition, there is also a great deal that is elitist and secretive about the way in which the outlines of the future regional dispensation are being formulated. These various conservative premises, as well as Inkatha's dominant position in the initiative, stand to limit its capacity to achieve popular legitimacy.[44]

'Eradicating disorder' in black politics

Engaged in the manoeuvrings of compromise and negotiation in the terrain between a tenacious state and an increasingly powerful, militant and broad-based opposition, Inkatha has constituted the diverse components of its mass membership as a major conservative force. The movement has, in its ideology and practice, sought to amplify and build upon the most conservative and traditional aspects of African political culture.

Inkatha's eleven years of existence have coincided with three periods of protracted social conflict — the 1976 Soweto Uprising, the 1980 schools boycotts, and the nation-wide unrest which began in September 1984 — as well as with the rapid growth and strengthening of an independent trade union movement. In so far as these periods of social conflict have featured youths' outrunning their working parents in terms of militancy, the failure of some elements associated with radical organisations to consult fully with adult and working people, and their use of coercion and intimidation (in enforcing stayaways or consumer boycotts for example), Inkatha has had fertile ground available to it. This it has artfully exploited with its appeals to a patriarchal discipline and a concern with order. Inkatha has been able to present itself as a force of community cohesion and order to sections of the townships' population. It has done this, in part, through consistently responding negatively to radical mass action — unrest, school boycotts, work stayaways — which it presents as unplanned, or as attributable to 'agitators', 'intimidators', 'criminals', and 'youth gone mad'.[45] Inkatha has urged, rather, the 'employment of anger in an orderly fashion', appealing during the 1976 Uprising for an end to unrest and on 'responsible elements' to group together to protect township property from militants; during school boycotts in KwaMashu (KwaZulu) in 1980, Inkatha called for the creation of vigilante groups to 'shoot and kill' those attacking property. During the current phase of unrest, Buthelezi has appealed to adults as the 'suffering silent majority' and victims of the politics of protest which 'destroy the things you have strived for'.[46]

In presenting itself as a force of cohesion and order, however, there has been a certain coalescence between a nation-wide right-wing backlash spearheaded by the violent vigilante groupings which have sprung up in the African townships, and the activities of Inkatha adherents in Natal/KwaZulu. Inkatha adherents have attempted to neutralise radical elements, leaving the way free for Inkatha to maintain a political dominance in the region it defends as its own. Alleged Inkatha 'vigilantism' has exacerbated already-present antagonisms between the organisation and major opposition groupings. The following section explores these processes, looking at how Inkatha has sought to counter the influence of radical organisations among youth and working people, and to mobilise elements from these strata as a conservative force in township politics.

Inkatha's appeals to patriarchal and hierarchical values and discipline are particularly evident in its relations with the youth — within and without its ambit. The Inkatha youth brigade, established in 1976 and numbering almost half a million by 1986,[47] is ascribed in Inkatha's Constitution 'the vanguard role of upholding and consolidating the gains of the movement'. However, the Constitution also stipulates that the brigade act at all times in accordance with the directions of Inkatha's President or central committee and approved policy, and carry out all duties as directed by Inkatha's President.[48] In her study of the youth brigade, Teague concluded that 'the task Inkatha sets for itself with regard to the youth is to contain the militancy — existing or potential — of the youth and to assert its conservative ideology'.[49]

Occasional signs of strain between the Inkatha leadership and Inkatha youth are reflected in the former's references to youth militancy and to the youth's perception that their leaders are not aggressive enough, and to the 'generation gap' as an 'ongoing problem'. The Secretary General of Inkatha, Dr Oscar Dhlomo, has said: 'The youth are pushing the leadership — we accept the militancy of the youth as a natural fact. . . It is difficult to say how far the leadership is willing to be pushed.'[50]

The containment of this potential militancy, not only in its own youth membership but more especially of militant youth beyond its ambit, has taken on a variety of forms. Firstly, Inkatha's women's brigade take seriously their task of 'upbringing of the children towards the objectives of the movement' and monitoring youth activities in their sphere of influence. They resolved in 1977, for example, that they would not abdicate power to their children, and to 'rehabilitate recalcitrant students and deviant youth'. The ageism and reinforcement of patriarchal values reflected here is prevalent in various Inkatha statements, Dhlomo insisting during the unrest of 1980, for example, that Inkatha was 'not prepared to be led by children', and that 'we do not believe that children have the intellect to devise strategies under which the black man is to be liberated'. This ageism is part of the process of keeping young members 'in their place' and has many echoes historically in earlier Zululand society.[51] Youth brigade members have been expelled for wishing to push Inkatha into 'spectacular mass action' and 'senseless violence'.[52]

Secondly, since 1978, KwaZulu's youth have been inculcated with Inkatha ideology in the schools (as already mentioned). The participation of 36 KwaZulu schools (out of 2,000) in the 1980 schools boycott and the 'recalcitrance' of University of Zululand (Ngoye) students in the same period, however, signified to Inkatha a chink in its armour and elicited hysterical speeches about the failure of 'our teachers to inculcate in our youth the right attitude to our struggle' and the need for Inkatha to be able to control riots, 'to establish training camps where branches and regions are schooled in the employment of anger in an orderly fashion', and to 'create well disciplined and regimented impis in every Inkatha region'.[53] Vigilantes restored 'order' to KwaMashu and rooted out 'agitators', and the 'ringleaders' were abducted by armed men and taken to a KLA session in Ulundi. (They were subsequently granted a Supreme Court interdict against Buthelezi and other Inkatha members, preventing them from assaulting or threatening to assault them, or inciting others to assault them.) During the boycotts, Inkatha gave no recognition to the legitimacy of the pupils' grievances and blamed the unrest on agitators.[54]

The seeds were sown in this period for an increasing emphasis on the paramilitary organisation of the youth (a further feature of Inkatha's approach to the youth): an Inkatha conference resolved on the immediate introduction of paramilitary approaches to Inkatha activities and on the establishment of a Youth Service Corps for Social Reconstruction (YSC). The first trainees in the first camp of the YSC were admitted in 1982 for training in rudimentary rural development skills. They were organised into army-like structures and wore uniforms symbolising, according to one Inkatha youth official, unity and loyalty to the President. In the words of this official, 'Our youth is getting out of hand. The youth need to be united and disciplined, otherwise they could be used by other people for their own ends'.[55] Teague has argued that this trend towards paramilitarism provides Inkatha with the means of substantiating Buthelezi's constant threats that Inkatha will 'pick up the gauntlet' thrown down by its enemies, and is a further attempt by Inkatha to contain and channel the youth's militancy in a direction of use to the movement.[56]

A fourth feature of Inkatha's relations with youth has been a quickness to retaliate against those who do not fit in with the movement's patriarchal vision of how the young should conduct themselves or who challenge the movement — as demonstrated during the KwaMashu schools boycott. One case in point has been

Inkatha's interventions at the University of Zululand (Ngoye). Conflict from 1976 onwards between Inkatha and its students — 'a vital group', as Teague points out from which future civil servants and professionals can be drawn into the movement, and among whom Inkatha had consistently failed to win substantial support — culminated in the Ngoye massacre of October 1983 when, Teague concludes, 'Inkatha took a decision to show a massive display of force and to attempt finally to assert hegemony at Ngoye'.[57] Student attempts to secure a court order restraining Buthelezi from addressing a campus meeting (as they feared violence) were unsuccessful, and on the day of the meeting, armed Inkatha supporters, many from far afield, arrived at Ngoye, and according to student accounts, attacked hostels, singling out anti-Inkatha students, leaving five dead and 113 injured. Buthelezi, while deploring the violence, accused the students of plotting it, and of provoking youth brigade members by abusing him. He warned that if the 'provocation' continued, 'Inkatha youth will demonstrate their strength and prowess. The abuse of me must now cease. Continuing to label me as a sell-out is going to have ugly repercussions.'[58]

The Inkatha youth appear to have remained impervious to the trends in black youth organisations elsewhere, reflected, for example, in their shunning any alliance with militant youth groupings, choosing instead to forge links with a moderate Afrikaans student movement, the Afrikaanse Studentebond, and in Natal's being largely unaffected by the 1984–5 school boycotts.[59] According to its President, Musa Zondi, the youth brigade saw one of its tasks as 'fighting for the rights of children to attend schools and to protect teachers at the schools'. Referring to its relations with other youth groupings, he said: 'We already have a battle situation in some areas.'[60]

With regard to workers, the other numerically large component of Inkatha's membership, it is of significance that the movement's existence has coincided with the greater part of the period of the independent trade union movement's emergence and consolidation. While Inkatha has sought class compromise between capital and labour, it has had to compete effectively against more radical unions and ideologies. Inkatha's ideology reflects these concerns: the organisation's leadership characterises Inkatha as a movement of 'workers and peasants', regards the mobilisation of worker power and consumer power as the most powerful of non-violent liberation methods, recognises the right of workers to a public holiday on 1 May, supports the formation of trade unions, and objects (rhetorically) to exploitation.[61] It also provides for trade union affiliation (although only the National Sugar Refining and Allied Industries' Employees' Union, regarded by many as a sweetheart union, has affiliated).[62] At the same time, Inkatha's ideology and practice reflect a concern to neutralise the antagonistic potential of the capital-labour relationship, portraying it as an essentially harmonious one, and workers' interests as synonymous with the attainment of a living wage. Inkatha's leaders have generally been hostile to strikes and stayaways, and are vehemently opposed to the politicisation of the trade union movement, having accused various Natal unions of 'exploiting black workers for political ends' and serving as 'surrogates of certain exiles'.[63] Inkatha's leadership also offers its unqualified support to capitalism.

Inkatha's ideological message to workers is encapsulated in a 1982 speech by KwaZulu chief labour officer to members of the northern Natal branch of the Federation of South African Trade Unions (FOSATU), in which he said that the KwaZulu administration 'acknowledges and protects' workers' rights 'because it is committed to the free enterprise system' and because 'it believes that harmonious relationships will be guaranteed by the co-operation of industrialists and trade unionists'. He added, 'I wish to sound a warning that if trade unionists do not train their subscribers on how to go about in negotiations with their employers, strikes will never cease to occur. I also wish to advise the employers to train their workers on what to expect in an ideal trade union that will perfectly suit their requirements.'[64]

Given Inkatha's control of the KwaZulu legislative assembly, the KwaZulu administration's own labour relations record is of relevance. Like all bantustans, KwaZulu has a number of industrial decentralisation points where the central government offers various incentives to those who invest there, and where one of the main attractions to employers is the lower cost of labour. Industrial council agreements and minimum wage determinations in South Africa are inapplicable in the bantustans, enabling employers to pay workers less there than in the metropolitan areas. KwaZulu, where there were 116,420 people employed in manufacturing in 1980, passed an Industrial Conciliation Amendment Act in 1981, amending South Africa's Labour Relations Act of 1956.[65] The Act provides for the establishment of an industrial court and the concept of an unfair labour practice. It also provides for unions to join or assist political parties (unlike the South

African legislation which it amended). This provision was presumably designed with Inkatha as the political party in mind. However, the legislation does not provide for the minimum wage or industrial council agreements in 'South Africa' to cover KwaZulu industry.

Cooper has pointed to problematic cases of interventions by the KwaZulu authorities in labour disputes. During a 1982 strike at a Bata Shoe Company plant in KwaZulu, for example, the National Union of Textile Workers appealed to the KwaZulu authorities to intervene. KwaZulu officials failed to bring about constructive negotiations and Bata fired the work-force and relocated its plant. The union accused the KwaZulu labour official of having gone secretly to the factory and appointing his own committee among the strike breakers, so bypassing the union. Similar claims were made by the union in a dispute in 1984 with the same company.[66]

The Inkatha leadership's frequent threats to use consumer boycotts and worker action as strategies for change have not come to fruition (with the exception of a white bread boycott in KwaZulu in 1982). On the contrary, Inkatha has been opposed to strikes and work stayaways, and a FOSATU-organised consumer boycott of white-owned Howick/Pietermaritzburg shops in August–September 1985 had to be called off following extreme opposition from Inkatha. This is attributed by Sutcliffe and Wellings to both Inkatha's desire to extend and strengthen its alliance with business interests, and a determination to weaken organisations which challenge its authority.[67]

Affiliates of FOSATU in Natal had thousands of members who at the same time found their political home in Inkatha. Accordingly, FOSATU kept a low political profile in Natal, and in the words of one official, if Inkatha 'raised something about FOSATU, we used to go and discuss it at Ulundi' (the KwaZulu capital). In accord with its cautious approach, for example, FOSATU obliged a KwaZulu administration request in 1982 not to organise its civil servants.[68]

While FOSATU may have had an uneasy yet working relationship with Inkatha, the new 500,000-member union superfederation, COSATU, into which it was absorbed in late 1985, took the union movement more overtly into the political realm, criticised Buthelezi, 'totally rejected' the bantustan system, and condemned federalism as 'fraudulent and undemocratic'. Buthelezi denounced COSATU as an 'ANC pawn' interested only in political agitation, and claimed that its formation was hardly directed against Pretoria, rather against Inkatha.[69] A few months later, Inkatha 'drew the battle lines' with COSATU. On May Day 1986 a rival union — United Workers' Union of South Africa (UWUSA) — was launched under the auspices of Inkatha and the KLA at a rally drawing between 60,000 and 80,000 people. Children carried a coffin bearing the words, 'COSATU is dead' and one writer commented that several employers were on the stage for the UWUSA launch, 'lending credence to COSATU claims that UWUSA will be a sweetheart union formed with the active backing of employers'.[70] Adding to this impression is the fact that UWUSA General Secretary Simon Conco is a successful Ulundi business man, chief whip in the KLA and chairman of an Inkatha labour committee (the latter two positions he resigned to take the UWUSA position). Other executive members include another Umlazi business man, a personnel relations officer, and a township superindendent. The former regional chairman of FOSATU in northern Natal, however, is also on the executive.

Conco has declared his opposition to strikes and boycotts (except as 'a very last resort'), and UWUSA has rejected disinvestment, supports free enterprise, supports the political aspirations of Inkatha, and is committed to non-interference in both business and labour matters by political organisations.[71] While UWUSA was formed on the initiative of the former chairman of a FOSATU affiliate who led a group of workers — dissatisfied with alleged anti-Inkathaism and undemocratic practices in their union — to Inkatha in January 1986, requesting a new union, Conco claimed that 'our battle to establish a union has been going on since the early 1970s'. COSATU regional secretary in northern Natal Jerry Ntombela has said that the conflict with Inkatha predated COSATU, adding that FOSATU 'had problems with them since we started operating in this area'.[72]

Fearing the incorporation of its members into a rival organisation with a political agenda very different from its own, and committed to sustaining moderation amongst workers and curbing militancy, Inkatha has entered the fray at shop-floor level, where it has had no experience whatsoever. Within months of UWUSA's formation, there have already been numerous reports of violent conflict between UWUSA and COSATU, court interdicts restraining members on both sides, and COSATU allegations (rejected by Inkatha) of Inkatha and police harassment of its unionists, attacks by armed Inkatha adherents, disruptions of its meetings, and assaults and killings of its unionists.[73]

In its commitment to class compromise and 'reform', its opposition to protest politics, and a fear of other organisations which challenge its authority, Inkatha has developed a series of antagonistic relationships with opposition groupings in the country. This is despite a rhetoric which advocates black unity. In addition, it has acquired a notoriety for repressive vigilante action against its opponents, which has exacerbated these hostile relationships.

There are indications of Inkatha's fear of political competition in Natal/KwaZulu as far back as 1975, when the central government received a KLA request that it empower KwaZulu to control or forbid the formation of political parties in the territory. The government refused, giving the KwaZulu administration a lecture on democracy.[74] Buthelezi has also been quoted as saying that opposition forces in KwaZulu were a 'luxury' and would 'lead to needless bickering'.[75]

The earliest of Inkatha's acrimonious relations was with the Black Consciousness Movement (BCM). Hostilities with the BCM — a fierce critic of collaboration in state structures — culminated in Buthelezi's near death at the hands of militant youths at the funeral of Pan Africanist Congress leader, Robert Sobukwe, in March 1978, and Dhlomo's assertion in that year that the BCM's elimination was a precondition for the success of the liberation struggle.[76] Relations with the BCM's heirs, such as AZAPO, have remained hostile.

Despite an evidently cordial beginning, Inkatha's relations with the ANC deteriorated steadily after an ANC/Inkatha meeting in London in November 1979. While Buthelezi claimed that the ANC had recognised Inkatha's role and sanctioned its non-violent strategy and participation in bantustan structures, the ANC evidently accused him of claiming endorsement from what was merely dialogue. Relations soured further in the context of Inkatha's increasingly moderate political proposals, its reformism, its response to the KwaMashu school boycotts, the 1983 events at Ngoye and Buthelezi's outspoken stand against the armed struggle and the disinvestment campaign. The ANC has said that Buthelezi's actions were not those of someone genuinely supporting the struggle, that he had always publicly attacked the very pillars of the ANC, and that he had increasingly identified himself with the government.[77] Despite numerous public criticisms of the ANC and claims that it plotted the violent elimination of Inkatha and Buthelezi, Inkatha's leaders have paradoxically continued to claim that they and the ANC have no political differences, only strategic ones, and that

Inkatha is the 'largest representative of the ANC tradition'.[78] However, as Sutcliffe and Wellings have commented, Buthelezi's strategy appears to be one of promoting Inkatha as a moderate alternative to the ANC to both local and international audiences.[79]

The United Democratic Front (UDF) brought under its wing a large number of local and some national black organisations (although not the trade union movement) after its formation in 1983, and has become a major force in opposition politics. Inkatha and the UDF have launched numerous public attacks on each other, Buthelezi claiming that the ANC had set up the UDF as an 'internally based surrogate' to destroy Inkatha. A UDF President, Archie Gumede, refused a KLA invitation to address it on the grounds that the UDF would be compromised and that the KLA was an instrument of coercion.[80] Buthelezi has tended to hold UDF 'intimidation' responsible for all student protest and unrest, and supporters of the Congress of South African Students (COSAS) and the Azanian Students' Organisation (AZASO) (UDF affiliates) are allegedly now being excluded from KwaZulu educational institutions. Buthelezi has also threatened to dismiss KwaZulu civil servants who work for the UDF.[81]

Sitas and De Villiers have pointed to major UDF organisational weaknesses in Natal/KwaZulu's African townships, both referring to a weak presence in Umlazi, KwaMashu and the Inanda informal squatter areas. A UDF affiliate, the Joint Rent Action Committee (JORAC), however, enjoyed strong support in a number of townships, particularly Lamontville and Hambanathi. JORAC, however, became involved in escalating conflict with Inkatha and local councillors, conflict which was fuelled by the impending incorporation of a number of African townships into KwaZulu. Sutcliffe and Wellings argue that for Inkatha, incorporation meant that it would be 'significantly easier to extend its influence in the townships once they fell under the control of KwaZulu'. For residents, however, incorporation meant, *inter alia*, that social services would be provided by an impoverished administration.[82] At least twelve people died during the ensuing violence between Inkatha and JORAC supporters in Lamontville and Hambanathi during 1984, and when JORAC refugees returned in April 1985, armed mobs of alleged Inkatha adherents, led by community councillors, moved through Hambanathi, forcing them to flee once more.[83]

A 'bloody fortnight' in Durban townships in August 1985 left 64 people dead and 1,000 injured. Many shops were looted and burnt and many homes destroyed.[84] The events were sparked off by the assassination of 1 August of a prominent political attorney, Victoria Mxenge, in the wake of which COSAS and AZASO planned school and university boycotts. In the process of organising these, violence broke out, and serious unrest in KwaMashu, Umlazi and Inanda followed. There was much arson and looting, particularly in Inanda, where a criminal subgroup appeared to take advantage, looting and attacking Indian shops, businesses and homes. Some 1,000 Indians fled the area. In KwaMashu and Umlazi, more overtly political targets were also attacked.[85] A commemoration service for Mxenge on 7 August in Umlazi ended in 19 deaths and 100 people injured following an attack by an assegai and stick-wielding impi, reportedly from Lindelani.

Sitas comments that from this point, councillors' regiments and Inkatha began gaining the upper hand.[86] Amabutho — assegai-bearing warrior mobs rallying to the traditional Zulu battle cry 'Usuthu'[87] and mainly consisting of rural people, migrants and hostel dwellers — began arriving in Durban's townships from various parts of Natal. By 9 August Inkatha local branches had organised vigilante groups to conduct house-to-house searches for looters and to patrol the streets (on one occasion in a group of some 1,000 people). According to Sitas, many men in the affected townships willingly joined them. Haysom comments, however, that the amabutho seemed intent on using the opportunity to attack UDF and COSAS members, and that these attacks, sometimes savage executions, continued for some weeks. Ten to twelve people died in attacks by a Lindelani impi on a crowd in Inanda.[88] During this show of force, the police and army reportedly stood by, 'satisfied that events were under control'.[89] On 11 August, Oscar Dhlomo asserted that Inkatha was fully mobilised and had taken control of the townships to restore order and protect property.

When factory shop stewards tried to take some initiative to intervene in this intolerable situation, they were, according to Sitas, 'stopped in their tracks by a pro-Inkatha backlash in many factories. Inkatha was being seen by large numbers of workers as having acted in an exemplary way as peacemakers, and any co-operation with youth groups, which were seen as hooligans, was not to be allowed.' Sitas comments, however, that while Inkatha won acclaim for its 'peacemaking' endeavours, the methods used by its power bloc in hounding out opposition in subsequent weeks 'stretched beyond elasticity Inkatha's legitimacy'.[90] In the words of one writer,[91]

With the police turning a blind eye, Inkatha has burnt out and harassed UDF supporters in all major townships in and around Durban. Inkatha has secured Umlazi and KwaMashu by appealing to the older members of the community, and promising to discipline the youth and restore law and order. [To belong to the UDF] now almost certainly means having your home burnt down and possibly death.

Inkatha's notoriety as a movement quick to use violence against its opponents stems from these events and various others. Regarding the nature of the relationship between the Inkatha leadership and the amabutho, it must be pointed out that Buthelezi has on a number of occasions explicitly called for the formation of vigilante groups (as mentioned earlier). Furthermore, he has often condoned the violence of his supporters with comments such as 'whoever challenges me challenges the people who will deal with them', and threats that while he 'deplores' violence, he may not be able to contain the 'people's anger'. He has frequently blamed the victims for provoking the violence by criticising Inkatha. Thus, while distancing himself from the violence against his detractors, he holds out suggestions of further unrestrained violence against them. Added to this, in a region with a bleak history of inter-communal conflict, Inkatha's Zulu chauvinism — expressed in the ethnic tones of its threats to its opponents (whether Swazi, Xhosa or Indian) — is both reactionary and irresponsible. Referring to the August events as well as to subsequent attacks on Mpondo workers in southern Natal by tribal impis, Marks has commented that[92] 'Whether or not Inkatha has been directly implicated, these tragic events reveal starkly the reactionary and conservative repercussions of "cultural organisations" which serve to glorify ethnic identity and heighten ethnic consciousness.'

Haysom has commented that the existence of links between Inkatha and the amabutho cannot be contested in the sense that some Inkatha supporters and leaders have been the driving force behind the vigilantes.[93] The claimed leader of Durban's impis, Thomas Mandla Shabalala, has been extremely explicit on the relationship between Inkatha and the amabutho. He is an Inkatha central committee member and leader of the 9,000 shack Lindelani settlement — reportedly the headquarters of the most notorious impi combatants. He claimed that it had been decided that Inkatha branches should set up groups to 'stamp out UDF-created unrest' and that the impis were Inkatha's 'brainchild'. He referred to Lindelani as 'Inkatha territory' and to virtually compulsory Inkatha member-ship there. A Lindelani Amabutho leader, E Khanyile, said: 'I long for the day when there will be an open war between the UDF and Inkatha — it will prove who is who in the political battle.'[94]

Other accounts would indicate a more ambiguous relationship — Marks commenting that some of Inkatha's own members have suffered at the hands of the amabutho and that central committee members appear unable to control them. Inkatha's leaders, however, have done little to denounce publicly, or to curb, the amabutho's actions, except to warn their leaders that they were acting without the support of the central committee.[95] Sutcliffe and Wellings point out that they do not have much of an option, for a public condemnation carries the risk of Inkatha's losing a substan-tial portion of its support base, while support of these groups would be seen as their condoning mob violence.[96]

However, whatever the precise view adopted by Inkatha's leader-ship regarding the violence of its supporters, the fact remains that Inkatha has asserted its dominance in the major Durban townships.

Concluding comments

Inkatha will undoubtedly be an important actor on South Africa's political stage in the years ahead. With black politics becoming increasingly radicalised, Inkatha is likely to become the hinge around which the very possibility of a reformist settlement will turn. The organisation's indisputably large popular following, its vast institutional resources, and the support it is likely to receive from a wide spectrum of domestic and international actors, ensures that the movement will be a formidable force for a long time to come, rather than simply evaporating into the vacuous 'middle ground' vacated in the course of growing political polarisation. Nonetheless, the organisation is under severe challenge: its national support base appears to be shrinking, while political organisations to its left — notably the ANC — have been increasingly successful in projec-ting themselves as the likely future government of South Africa. Inkatha's ability to withstand challenges of this kind will be decisively tested as the KwaNatal initiative proceeds. A regional settlement would, as Glaser has argued,[97]

> allow Inkatha to solidify alliances with local white business
> and political groups, create an embryonic Inkatha-dominated

multi-racial state on a regional scale, and ensure that the organisation would be well placed to bargain for future entry into the central state.

On the other hand, the failure of this regional initiative, in which Inkatha has vested so much, would seriously undermine the organisation's — and Buthelezi's — credibility. All this suggests that Inkatha's home region — Natal/KwaZulu — could become a crucial battleground in the deciding of South Africa's future.

Notes

1. I should like to thank Daryl Glaser for reading and commenting on the various drafts of this chapter.
2. Shula Marks, *The ambiguities of dependence in South Africa: class, nationalism and the state in twentieth century Natal* (Ravan Press, Johannesburg, 1986).
3. John D. Brewer, 'The membership of Inkatha in KwaMashu', *African Affairs*, vol. 84, no. 334 (January 1985), pp. 111–35.
4. Colleen McCaul, *Towards an understanding of Inkatha Yesizwe* (SARS/DSG Dissertation Series number 2, Johannesburg, 1983).
5. Marks, *The ambiguities of dependence.*
6. Marks, 'Natal, the Zulu Royal Family and the ideology of segregation', *Journal of Southern African Studies*, vol. 4 (1978), pp. 172–94.
7. Figures over the years were 30,000 in 1976; 120,000 in 1977; 150,000 in 1978; 250,000 in 1979; 300,000 in 1980; 411,000 in 1982; 750,000 in 1983; 984,000 in 1984; and 1,155,000 in 1985. (South African Institute of Race Relations (SAIRR), *Survey of race relations* for various years; *Clarion Call*, vol. 3 (1985); Vicki Cadman, 'Inkatha' (first draft), South Africa Beyond Apartheid (SABA), Boston meeting, 12-15 June 1986, p. 2; McCaul, *Towards an understanding*, p. 7.)
8. Cadman, 'Inkatha', p. 2.
9. *Clarion Call*, vol. 3 (1985), p. 14.
10. SAIRR, *1982 survey of race relations*; John Kane-Berman, 'Inkatha: the paradox of South African politics', *Optima*, no. 30 (1982), cited in Cadman, 'Inkatha', p. 2.
11. Cadman, 'Inkatha', p. 2; McCaul, *Towards an understanding*, p. 5; SAIRR, *1979 survey of race relations*, p. 322; Kane-Berman, 'Inkatha', cited in Brewer, 'The membership of Inkatha', p. 114.
12. Professor Lawrence Schlemmer, 'The stirring giant: observations on Inkatha and other black political movements in South Africa' in Robert M. Price and Carl G. Rosberg (eds), *The apartheid regime: political power and racial domination* (David Philip, Cape Town, 1980), pp. 99–126.
13. Roger J. Southall, 'Buthelezi, Inkatha and the politics of compromise', *African Affairs*, vol. 80, no. 321 (October 1981), p. 457.
14. Interview with a professional officer at the Inkatha Institute, Clarissa

Fourie, by the writer, 7 March 1983, cited in McCaul, *Towards an understanding*, p. 9.

15. A recent study based on research in eight KwaZulu rural districts revealed that most chiefs or local headmen demanded cash payments for 'privileges' such as the use of fields or allocation of sites, and 40 per cent of the respondents revealed that it was common practice to bribe indunas before pension applications were proceeded with. Chiefs also commonly demanded contributions from their subjects. (P.M. Zulu, 'The rural crisis: authority structures and their role in development' in Hermann Giliomee and Lawrence Schlemmer (eds), *Up against the fences: poverty, passes and privilege in South Africa* (David Philip, Cape Town, 1985).)

16. McCaul, *Towards an understanding*.

17. SAIRR, *1979 survey of race relations*, p. 42.

18. Peta Ann Teague, 'A study of Inkatha Yesizwe's approach to the youth with specific reference to the movement's youth brigade'. (Unpublished Bachelor of Arts Honours dissertation, Cape Town, 1983), p. 18; *Weekly Mail*, 13–19 June 1986.

19. Teague, 'A study of Inkatha'; 'Natal education boycott: a focus on Inkatha', *Work in Progress*, no. 15 (1980); DSG/SARS, cited by McCaul, *Towards an understanding*, p. 17.

20. Teague, '*A study of Inkatha*', p. 23.

21. SAIRR, *1978 survey of race relations, 1979 survey of race relations*; Teague, 'A study of Inkatha', p. 32.

22. Cadman, 'Inkatha', p. 3.

23. SAIRR, *1978 survey of race relations*; McCaul, *Towards an understanding*, p. 13.

24. Brewer, 'The membership of Inkatha', p. 123.

25. Ari Sitas, 'Inanda, August 1985: "Where wealth and power and blood reign worshipped"', *South African Labour Bulletin* (SALB), vol. 11, no. 4 (February–March 1986), pp. 90–5.

26. Teague, *A study of Inkatha*, p. 12.

27. Marks, *The ambiguities of dependence*, p. 116.

28. Teague, *A study of Inkatha*, pp. 10-11.

29. Mark Orkin, *Disinvestment: the struggle and the future. What black South Africans really think* (Ravan Press, Johannesburg, 1986), pp. 40–2; Paul Wellings and Michael Sutcliffe, 'The widening rift, Inkatha and mainstream black opposition politics in South Africa', *Transafrica Forum*, vol. 2, no. 3 (1986).

30. Chief Buthelezi's presidential address at Inkatha's annual general conference, 29 June 1985, Ulundi.

31. Orkin, *Disinvestment*, pp. 50–1.

32. SAIRR, *1984 race relations survey*; Teague, 'A study of Inkatha, p. 37. Speech by Buthelezi, 5 August 1977; Interview with Fourie, cited in McCaul, *Towards an understanding*.

33. Interview with Inkatha's Natal regional organiser, David Masomi, by the writer in 1983, cited in McCaul, *Towards an understanding*, pp. 54–5; SAIRR, *1980 survey of race relations*, pp. 51–2.

34. *Weekly Mail*, 11–17 July 1986.

35. Sutcliffe and Wellings, 'The widening rift', pp. 1 and 4.

36. Cadman, 'Inkatha', p. 12.

37. SAIRR, *1980 survey of race relations; 1982 survey of race relations*.

38. SAIRR, *1983 survey of race relations*; Cadman 'Inkatha', p. 12.

39. Cadman, 'Inkatha'.

40. Daryl Glaser, 'Regionalisation: the case of KwaNatal', paper presented at the Association for Sociology in Southern Africa Annual Congress, Durban, 1986, pp. 5–6.

41. Ibid., p. 6.

42. SAIRR, *1985 race relations survey; Business Day*, 6 August 1985.

43. Glaser, 'Regionalisation', p. 1.

44. Ibid.

45. SAIRR, *1984 race relations survey*, p. 15.

46. Ibid.; McCaul *Towards an understanding*, p. 74; Teague, A study of Inkatha', pp. 41–2.

47. *Weekly Mail*, 13–19 June 1986.

48. Teague, *A study of Inkatha*, p. 18.

49. Ibid., p. 75.

50. McCaul, *Towards an understanding*, p. 18; Interview with Dr Oscar Dhlomo by Teague, November 1983, cited in Teague, 'A Study of Inkatha', p. 28.

51. See, for example, Marks, 'Patriotism, patriarchy and purity: Natal and the politics of Zulu ethnic consciousness', *African Studies Institute (ASI) Seminar Paper*, University of the Witwatersrand, Johannesburg (4 August 1986).

52. SAIRR, *1978 survey of race relations*.

53. Speeches by Buthelezi in June 1980, cited in Teague, 'A study of Inkatha', pp. 44 and 67.

54. Teague, 'A study of Inkatha', pp. 38–9, 42.

55. Interview with a professional officer in the Youth Affairs Division, Sandile Makhanya, by Teague in November 1983, cited in Teague, 'A study of Inkatha', p. 72.

56. Teague, 'A Study of Inkatha', pp. 67–72.

57. Ibid., p. 56.

58. Speech by Buthelezi, cited in Teague, *A study of Inkatha*, p. 63.

59. *Clarion Call*, vol. 2 (1985).

60. Shaun Johnson, 'The student web that spans South Africa', *Weekly Mail*, 13–19 June 1986.

61. SAIRR, *1979 survey of race relations*, p. 42; *Clarion Call*, vol. 2 (1985), p. 17.

62. Sutcliffe and Wellings, 'The widening rift', p. 24.

63. SAIRR, *1981 survey of race relations*, p. 194.

64. Z.A. Khanyile, 'What is a trade union?', speech to FOSATU, February 1982, *SALB*, vol. 8, no. 1 (September 1982).

65. Carole Cooper, 'Homelands and trade unionism', *SAIRR, Topical Briefing*, PD 7/84 (16 July 1984).

66. Ibid.

67. Sutcliffe and Wellings, 'The widening rift'.

68. *SALB*, vol. 11, no. 5 (April–May 1986).

69. Sutcliffe and Wellings, 'The widening rift', p. 28.

70. *Weekly Mail*, 2–8 May 1986; Philip van Niekerk, 'Inkatha and COSATU drawing the battle lines', *Work in Progress*, no. 42 (May 1986).

71. *Weekly Mail*, 2–8 May 1986; *SALB*, vol. 11, no. 5 (April–May 1986), p. 50; *Clarion Call*, vol. 2 (1986).

72. *SALB*, vol. 11, no. 5 (April–May 1986).

73. *Weekly Mail*, 13–19 June 1986; *SALB*, vol. 11, no. 5 (April–May 1986).

74. SAIRR, *1975 survey of race relations*.

75. Cadman, 'Inkatha', p. 5.

76. SAIRR, *1979 survey of race relations*, p. 45.

77. SAIRR, *1980 survey of race relations*, pp. 52–3.

78. SAIRR, *1984 survey of race relations*, p. 13.

79. Sutcliffe and Wellings, 'The widening rift', pp. 21–2.

80. SAIRR, *1984 race relations survey*, p. 530.

81. Sutcliffe and Wellings, 'The widening rift', p. 23; *The Citizen*, 20 December 1985.

82. Sitas, 'Inanda'; Richard de Villiers, 'UDF under attack: Inkatha and the state', *Work in Progress*, no. 34 (October 1985); Sutcliffe and Wellings, 'The widening rift', p. 34.

83. Sutcliffe and Wellings, 'The widening rift', p. 30.

84. De Villiers, 'UDF under attack'.

85. Nicholas Haysom, *Mabangalala, the rise of right-wing vigilantes in South Africa*, Centre for Applied Legal Studies, University of the Witwatersrand, Johannesburg, Occasional Paper, no. 10 (1986), p. 87.

86. Sitas, 'Inanda'.

87. Haysom, 'Mabangalala', p. 84.

88. Ibid.

89. Sitas, 'Inanda', p. 111.

90. Ibid., p. 112.

91. De Villiers, 'UDF under attack'.

92. Marks, 'Patriotism', p. 2.

93. Haysom, 'Mabangalala', p. 97.

94. *City Press*, 1 June 1986.

95. Marks, 'Patriotism', p. 2; Haysom, 'Mabangalala', p. 99.

96. Sutcliffe and Wellings, 'Attitudes and living conditions in Inanda: the context for unrest', November 1985, cited in Marks, 'Patriotism', p. 2.

97. Glaser, 'Regionalisation'.

7

The Rise of Social-movement Unionism: The Two Faces of the Black Trade Union Movement in South Africa*

Eddie Webster

There is a widespread view that the emerging black trade union movement is 'coming of age'. The idea that trade union development goes through certain stages of growth, rather like a child or adolescent, becoming mature when they reach a certain age, has deep roots in popular views of trade unionism. In fact, Richard Lester's classic study of American trade unionism was titled *As unions mature*.[1] In sum, Lester proposed that as a union's growth begins to curve off, subtle changes occur. They are two-fold. Firstly, as democracy declines, rank-and-file participation disappears, and a division of labour takes place whereby a core of professional leaders emerges within a centralised and bureaucratic structure. Secondly, the old idealism and militancy declines as a new leadership emerges which is more moderate, accommodating and 'responsible'. A process of goal displacement occurs as union leadership moves closer towards the articulation of the interests of its supposed adversaries, and further away from the articulation of the implicit interests of the membership.

This thesis, which has become something of an orthodoxy in industrial relations, goes on to suggest that where management learns to tolerate conflict and recognises the union, and management and union come to work together, rules of the game are developed which both sides are keen to retain. Conflict, in other words, becomes institutionalised.

This theory, which has been labelled pluralism, became popular

---

*Part II of this chapter is based on joint work done during the past 18 months by members of the Labour Monitoring Group at the University of the Witwatersrand, in particular Stephen Gelb, Jon Lewis and Mark Swilling. I alone am responsible for this particular version of our argument.

174

in managerial circles in South Africa in the post-Wiehahn period. It has been drawn largely from the experience of Western Europe and North America during the period of economic prosperity after the Second World War. With economic decline in recent years, this industrial relations system has come under increasing strain. However, with these qualifications, it can be said to fit the history of trade union development of Europe and North America, and to a certain extent, the established, predominantly white unions in South Africa.

The orthodox theory breaks down, however, when applied to black trade unionism in South Africa. Observers have been impressed with the growing professionalism of union leadership — and by the negotiating sophistication that trade unions have developed with limited formal training. Many managers have successfully established good working-relations with shop stewards and organisers. Furthermore, for many unions their development has moved beyond the struggle for recognition, and towards maintaining and administering an agreement. Inevitably, this has involved both sides developing certain common interests in retaining the 'rules of the game'; but these examples do not imply that internal democracy has declined. Indeed, a recent study shows that as shop steward structures have taken root in the workplace, the degree of shop floor penetration has deepened.[2] Similarly, and more importantly, it cannot be argued that militancy has declined — in fact, the opposite has occurred. After eschewing involvement in politics and concentrating on the shop floor, trade unions have broken with economism and have become actively involved in non-factory issues.

The question arises, then, as to why the orthodoxy does not fit the development of the black trade union movement in South Africa. The most common response is that it takes time for unions to 'mature': black unions are in an immature stage in their development, and they are, in other words, emerging unions and as such, are still learning the rules. I shall argue that this viewpoint is both patronising and wrong. It is patronising, as I show in the first part of this chapter, because it ignores the long history of black trade unionism that does not simply date back to 1973, but to the First World War. More significantly, it is wrong because it fails to recognise that the emergence of what some have called 'political unionism', but which I prefer to call social-movement unionism.[3] This kind of unionism is a response to economic and political conditions facing South Africa that diverge significantly from those

175

faced by unions in the First World during the economic boom. These conditions, and the growing union involvement in political struggle, are discussed in the second part of the chapter.

Research on these unions over the years suggests that a unidimensional conception of their chief function as that of raising wages is seriously misleading. This is of course an important objective, especially during recession, but in addition to increasing wages, unions have significant non-wage effects which influence diverse aspects of modern industrial life. This interpretation of trade unionism is suggested by recent research in the United States by Richard Freeman and James Medoff.[4] They argue that by providing workers with a voice, both at the workplace and in the political arena, unions can positively affect the functioning of the economic and social system. As a voice institution, moreover, unions also fundamentally alter social relations in the workplace. Most importantly, a union constitutes a source of worker power in the firm, diluting managerial authority and offering members access to law through the grievance procedure.

The point is that unions have two faces, each of which leads to a different view of the institution. One, the economic dimension, is that of a union trying to win increases and improvements in living conditions; the other is that of a voice institution, i.e. a social and political institution. Where, as in South Africa, the majority does not have a meaningful voice within the political system, unions will inevitably begin to play a central role within the political system. However, it was the decline in living standards accompanying the economic recession that brought the two faces of unionism together. It is this fusing of the economic with the political — the two faces of unionism — that began to take place after November 1984, that I call social-movement unionism.

The rise of shop floor unions — the economic dimension

Until 1979, South Africa had a dualistic structure of industrial relations: a legalistic, formal guarantee of certain industrial rights to white, coloured and Indian workers through the 1924 Industrial Conciliation Act, and a repressive labour regime for African workers, resting since 1953 on the Black Labour Relations Act. It was in the context of exclusion from the formal industrial relations system that black workers were to organise into trade unions.

African trade unions date from the period of protest during and after the First World War. Faced with rising inflation and accelerating labour migration, African workers began acting spontaneously in defence of their interests.

In 1955, the South African Congress of Trade Unions (SACTU) was formed as a predominantly African trade union federation drawing on the now defunct Council of Non-European Trade Unions (CNETU), but including among its affiliates the 'left' non-racial strand of the registered trade union movement formerly organised in the Trades and Labour Council. SACTU's alliance with the ANC and the Congress movement resulted in a novel redefinition of its trade union role along the lines of 'political unionism'. Faced by a weak power base in the factories and a hostile state and employers, SACTU chose to engage politically with nationalism as a means of transforming its small factory base.

The effect that SACTU's political unionism had on the growth of trade unionism during the 1950s remains a matter of debate. Some argue that the alliance led to the subordination of trade unions to the struggle for national liberation; others that the alliance facilitated the growth of trade unionism and enabled workers to influence the direction of the national democratic struggle. However, where trade unions were not given priority, as in most of the Transvaal, evidence points to the subordination of workers' interests: the 1957 stayaway — a trade union-led initiative around the pound-a-day campaign — was a great success. In contrast, the 1958 stayaway was a failure, in part because an essentially trade union campaign was transformed by the Congress Alliance into a broad protest, coinciding with the general elections and directed at influencing white parliamentary politics under the unrealistic slogan, 'The Nats must go'.[5]

By 1964, the resurgence of African trade union activity that characterised the late 1950s and early 1960s had been crushed. South Africa was to experience a decade of industrial peace. However, it was a decade in which the economy experienced a structural transformation financed by a massive influx of foreign capital; accelerated expansion of industry; a restructuring of capital and the growing concentration and centralisation of ownership. The extent of cartelisation by the late 1970s may be gauged by the information supplied by the Mouton Commission on monopolies in 1977. According to the Commission, a mere 5 per cent of the total number of firms in the manufacturing sector collectively accounted for 63 per cent of the sector's turnover; only 5 per cent of those in the wholesale and retail sector accounted for 69 per cent of turn-over; 5 per cent of those in construction accounted for 63 per cent of turnover; and 5 per cent in transport accounted for 73 per cent of turnover.

Coupled with these changes came a corresponding growth in the black working class which brought black workers firmly to the centre of the industrial stage. In particular, there was a growth in the number of semi-skilled black workers, as an organisational base for industrial unionism. As Hemson writes,[6]

> With the growth of monopoly capitalism and the concentration of production in large-scale, highly mechanised factories went a black proletariat neither differentiated by traditional skills, nor having experienced the benefits of reform. These are the conditions for a rapid advance in class consciousness as the political resistance to apartheid gains momentum.

By concentrating large numbers of workers in production, the material conditions for a new kind of shop floor-based trade unionism had been created by the early 1970s.

The mass strikes in January and February 1973 in Durban dramatically highlighted these changes, when an estimated 100,000 workers broke the decade of industrial peace by taking to the streets to demand wage increases. These strikes were to expose as inade-quate the existing system of dualistic control in the workplace. 'Enlightened' employers began to realise that a new system of control was required and that continued reliance on a system of racial despotism would exacerbate conflict. On the basis of employer recommendations the state amended the existing Black Labour Relations Act, introducing joint management-worker bodies called liaison committees.

Employers quickly embarked on an offensive to promote these committees, and between 1973 and 1975, the number of liaison committees increased from 118 to 1,751, the majority of which had been established at management's initiative. That they were no substitute for unions is attested by the number of strikes that broke out in establishments in which such committees had been formed, the most celebrated example being that of the Heinemann strike of 1976. The speed with which the liaison committee system was introduced is an index of the depth of the crisis of control in workplace relations. In contrast with the previous decade, when the number of African workers involved in industrial disputes never rose above 10,000 in any year, in a period of time between 1973 and 1976 the yearly figure for those involved in disputes ranged between 30,000 and 100,000 (in 1973).

In the early 1970s, the new independent unions eschewed political action outside of production. They wished to avoid the path taken by SACTU which was closely identified with the campaigns of the Congress Alliance in the 1950s and was destroyed or forced into exile along with the rest of the Alliance by state repression in the 1960s. Rather, the emerging unions devoted their attention to building democratic shop-floor structures around the principle of worker control, accountability and mandating of worker represent-atives, and to developing a working class leadership in the factories. This strategy was justified in two ways. Firstly, strong shop-floor organisation had a better chance of surviving state repression which would be directed in the first instance at 'leaders'. Secondly, at least until 1980-1, it could be argued that union organisation was so small and narrow that its political impact would have been insignificant, whilst at the same time these fledging unions had everything to lose by adopting a confrontationist stance.

However, while the growth of shop-floor unionism and factory struggles represented a necessary condition for the state and management to search for a different form of control to that of the liaison committee, it was not a sufficient condition. It was the out-break of urban unrest in 1976 that was to provide the final impetus to the search for new forms of control. Although organised labour remained aloof from the 'unrest', fearing suppression if they became involved in a 'political strike', it had become clear to employers and the state that consent within the black population needed to be widened. The initiative by leading industrialists Harry Oppen-heimer and Anton Rupert in November 1976 in establishing the Urban Foundation, with the clear objective of creating a black middle class, illustrates this strategy.

The state feared that the resurgence of popular-democratic struggle in 1976 would lead to the re-establishment of links between organised labour and the popular struggle similar to those in the 1950s and early 1960s. Sophisticated strategists for capital and the state had come to realise that a certain form of trade union recogni-tion could facilitate a separation of the 'politics of production' from 'global politics', thus hoping to weaken the role that organised workers could play in the national democratic struggle. Thus, banning what the state saw as the more political leadership — i.e. repression — was not inconsistent with attempting to control the unions from above by giving them statutory recognition — i.e. reform.

The solution envisaged by the Wiehahn Commission, which reported in 1979, involved the deracialisation of the established industrial relations system by incorporating black workers into the industrial council system. African unions, Wiehahn maintained, are not subject to 'protective and stabilising elements in [the present] system of discipline and control'. In part, they enjoyed greater freedom than registered unions in that they could participate in party politics and use their funds for any purpose they saw fit. It would be better, Wiehahn concluded, to recognise them at an early stage, in order to control the pace of union development.

The Wiehahn solution was clearly contradictory. The intention was to control the emerging unions by drawing them into the established industrial relations structures, in particular, the industrial councils, thus pre-empting the unions' attempts to establish a shop-floor presence. However, this required giving these unions official recognition, enabling them to gain more space in their attempt to move beyond the struggle for recognition to direct negotiations at shop-floor level. Recognition at plant level was not won without struggle in the post-Wiehahn period, but in the years immediately after Wiehahn, a new frontier of control was being defined as recognition agreements at plant level became increasingly common in most sectors of the economy.

Some unions — particularly the General Workers Union and African Food and Canning Workers Union — responded by refusing to register on the grounds that this ceded too much control to the state and contradicted the principle of worker control, and constituted the first step on the road to co-optation. Others, particularly the South African and Allied Workers Union (SAAWU), adopted a more fundamental stance, opposing any contact ('collaboration', as they saw it) with any state machinery. On the other hand, the Federation of South African Trade Unions (FOSATU) argued that registration allowed unions to exploit concessions made by the state in order to create further space. They simply refused to accept any restraint on organising activity and argued that co-optation could be prevented by continuing to enforce the original organisational principles of worker control, and by building democratic shop-floor structures. These differences were resolved in the process of struggle: the unregistered unions survived without official recognition; those that registered were not co-opted. Today, the issue of registration is seen by most as a tactical one.

While the Wiehahn-Riekert strategy set the tone of reform from above, the working class set the pace of resistance. In 1979, the seven month long strike in Cape Town at Fattis and Monis was won with community support in the form of a consumer boycott. This was followed by the Ford strike in Port Elizabeth after the local community leader, Thozamile Botha, was forced to resign from his job in the Cortina plant.

The strike gave rise to an important ideological and organisational division. The United Automobile Workers union (UAW), a parallel union of the coloured National Union of Motor Assembly and Rubber Workers of South Africa (NUMARWOSA), had organised the neighbouring Ford engine plant, and at the time of the strike, had only begun to organise at Cortina. Consequently, it was the Port Elizabeth Black Civic Organisation (PEBCO)-linked Ford Workers Committee (FWC) which took the lead in mobilising against the sacking of Botha. On the one hand, PEBCO and FWC began to present themselves in terms of the national democratic tradition and concentrated on building mass-based community organisations. The FWC, which later became the Motor and Components Workers Union of South Africa (MACWUSA), bitterly criticised UAW for neglecting the workers at Cortina and for failing to take up worker grievances in the community. (PEBCO and MACWUSA are now UDF affiliates.) On the other hand, UAW and NUMARWOSA (which has since merged to form the National Automobile and Allied Workers Union — NAAWU — the most powerful FOSATU union in the region), distanced themselves from the PEBCO-MACWUSA style of 'community unionism', criticising it for being populist and for neglecting workers' interests on the shop floor. The battle for hegemony between these two groupings exacerbated the structural division between home and work by preventing sustained union-community solidarity.

The action shifted back to the western Cape when a strike wave broke out between December 1979 and 1980. This provided the impetus for the eight-month Cape Town schools boycott. Running parallel to the schools boycott that spread throughout the country during 1980, a series of strike waves affected all of the major industrial centres, and even some rural areas. The eastern and western Cape were the most politically mobilised regions, where strikes, school boycots, bus boycotts, rent struggles, strike support campaigns, and the mushrooming of community organisations contributed to the emergence of a new political culture. By the end of the year, the trade union movement had, for the first time, begun to win what they had been struggling for since 1973: a base on the factory floor.

In 1981, there was a regional shift in community-based and worker struggles from the Cape to the Transvaal. Initially, activity focused on the East Rand, but later spread to the Vaal Triangle. These two areas contain some of the largest concentrations of industrial workers in the country. Rapid industrial growth was not accompanied by adequate township facilities. As a result, large numbers of workers live in hostels and shacks. It was these conditions that were to fuel worker grievances, leading to rapid mobilisation in these areas.

The most significant struggles were the two strike waves that hit the East Rand towards the end of 1981, and again during the first few months of 1982. Between July and November 1981, over 24,000 workers came out in over 50 different strikes. Possibly the most important strike during 1981 was at Colgate over the demand by workers to negotiate at plant level. This dispute was won in part because of the threat of a successful product boycott. In the metal industry alone, 25 'demonstration stoppages' took place during the second half of 1981, three-quarters of which were over 'control' issues such as demands for the removal of racist foremen or the reinstatement of dismissed workers. With the onset of recession in 1982, the conflict sharpened; what had begun as short demonstration stoppages were beginning to take on the characteristics of trials of strength as managements refused to negotiate wages at plant level, insisting on bargaining through the highly centralised and bureaucratic industry-wide industrial councils.

In April 1982 a decisive battle was fought at Scaw Metals, a key factory in the East Rand and a subsidiary of the giant Anglo-American Corporation. Ostensibly being a strike over a nominal interim demand for 10 cents an hour, the conflict at Scaw was to widen into a trial of strength over the workers' demand for plant-level bargaining. Trade union organisation was strongest in the factory shop-steward structures and management saw factory-level bargaining as a fundamental challenge to capital itself. The police were called in and all Scaw Metal workers dismissed. The union, the Metal and Allied Workers Union (MAWU), was forced into a tactical retreat, and a year later decided to join the industrial council. With the deepening recession during 1982, the retrenchment of a large number of active shop stewards and overall demoralisation as the heady atmosphere of direct action faded, it looked as if capital had won another round.

Despite set-backs, the recession did not prevent continued worker militancy on the shop floor. Whereas in 1982 and 1983, there were 394 and 336 strikes respectively, in 1984 there were 469. The number of working days lost increased by 200 per cent from 124,594 in 1983 to 378,712 in 1984. Industrial relations consultants were concerned that strikes were lasting longer and involving more workers than previously.

Trade union membership doubled between 1981 and 1985. Most importantly, a large proportion of the growth in trade union membership has taken place on the mines. The National Union of Mineworkers (NUM), founded in 1982, and drawing on concentrations of up to 40,000 workers on one mine, by mid-1985 claimed a paid-up membership of 100,000, and a signed up membership of double that number.

Growing side-by-side with this new force on the shop floor were new forms of working class organisation in the townships. Although first mooted in the wake of the 1976 Uprisings, shop steward councils were only to take root in the townships in 1981. Founded as a way of involving shop stewards in the organisation of unorganised factories, these councils spread rapidly during the 1981–2 strike waves. They brought together the different factories in an area and provided a focus for workers as a class, beyond their individual unions. This form of organisation developed most clearly on the East Rand.

At the centre of this social movement in the East Rand hostels was the migrant worker. Faced with rural collapse and growing retrenchment, these migrant workers found in the new unions a movement that was able to express their discontent and give direction to their energies.[7] This widening of the scope of union action beyond production to the sphere of reproduction — including demands for adequate pensions, maternity rights, housing and unemployment benefits — reflects the deepening crisis in the social formation as a whole.

However, the onset of the recession imposed constraints on this involvement in global politics, altering the conditions of struggle. Retrenchments took a heavy toll — in the metal industry, 2,000 per month were retrenched during 1983. The reserve army of unemployed, it was envisaged by capital, would be used to discipline those left in employment. In most sectors, profits have been squeezed, reducing employers' room for manoeuvre, with the result that strikes have tended to be longer and more bitter. Although union membership continued to increase and workers took more militant strike action, trade unions had to consider their actions very carefully so as not to endanger hard-won gains made on the factory floor. This was one of the reasons why the unions did not prioritise the development of structures and organisational forms appropriate for more direct political action on a national level. The recession also affected the 'community unions' because as they pursued their political objectives, less resources were available to maintain trade union organisation.

Nevertheless, the organisation of the unions, their large membership, the daily access to members and their location in strategic sectors of the economy, had by 1984 given the union movement greater capacity to mobilise power than any other organisation publicly active in South Africa. This is well illustrated by the ability in February 1982 of these unions to mobilise over 100,000 workers in the space of two days for a half-hour nation-wide stoppage after the death in detention of Dr Neil Aggett, Transvaal organiser of the Food and Canning Workers Union.

It was Aggett's death and the unions' united response which gave a new urgency to talks started in April 1982, designed to bring about one united national federation. In the event, unity was delayed due to organisational differences — over general versus industrial unionism — and over political line. By the end of 1984, there were three trade union groupings; the core industrial unions still engaged in the unity talks; and two groupings of general unions, the one affiliated to the UDF (the most important being SAAWU) and the other — the Azanian Confederation of Trade Unions (AZACTU) — in the black consciousness tradition, affiliated to National Forum. Since then the major industrial and general unions merged to form the Congress of South African Trade Unions (COSATU), which was launched in December 1985. The Council of Unions of South Africa (CUSA) decided to stay out of COSATU and instead opted to merge with AZACTU, now the National Council of Trade Unions, in October 1986 under a black consciousness ideological banner. Thus, whereas COSATU brings together the community-orientated and independent working class unions, CUSA-AZACTU brings together those unions that subscribe to a left-wing black consciousness ideology. The Trade Union Council of South Africa, the only pro-capitalist moderate union grouping with black membership, decided to disband in December 1986 because of declining membership. The various moves towards unity, re-alignment and disbandment were inextricably bound up with the central question facing the trade union movement: its relationship with the political struggle.

Trade unions and political struggle — the political dimension

The present conjuncture in South Africa is characterised by sustained political and economic crisis. The economy has been in recession since 1982, resulting in closures, retrenchments and mass unemployment, a falling rand which fuels internal inflation and threatens the balance of payments, and high interest rates which have prevented new investments and recovery. For the state, the effect has been to provoke a major fiscal crisis which in turn restricts its ability to finance 'reform'.

The crisis has been met with unprecedented levels of mobilisation and resistance in the factories and communities over economic and political issues: the highest strike levels in South African history, rent strikes, bus boycotts, school boycotts, consumer boycotts, anti-Constitution campaigns and stayaways became permanent features of the political terrain from 1984 onwards. Moreover, this phase of resistance has been marked by new organisational, ideological and political alignments, most clearly evident in November 1984 when unions, community organisations and student organisations joined together in the massive Transvaal stayaway (see Table 7.1).

The continuing debate over the relationship between trade unions and politics was to re-emerge in 1982. The Food and Canning Workers Union argued that while there is a need to get involved in community issues, a separate form of organisation is needed:[8]

> We do believe that separate forms of organisation are needed for these struggles. A trade union is not a community or political organisation. A union which tries to be a community or political organisation at the same time cannot survive.

At the same time FOSATU entered the debate with a keynote speech by General Secretary Joe Foster.[9] Foster's speech called for the building of a workers' movement, much more broadly defined than simple trade unionism; made provision for alliances and joint campaigning with other progressive organisations; and called on union members to get involved in community and political organisations. However, Foster went on to warn against unions being drawn into political action which was not worker-controlled

Table 7.1: Black worker stayaways, 1984-6

Area	Demands	Organisation involved	Employees' response	Date	Effectiveness	Actual duration
Sharpeville	Rent	Civic Associations/ shop stewards		3 September 1984	60%	1 day
Soweto	Solidarity on rents Police in townships	RMC		17 September 1984	35-65%	1 day
Springs	Student demands	Parent/Student Committee		22 October 1984	80%	1 day
PWV Area	Student demands Repression, cost of living and rents	Unions Students Community	No work, no pay except SASOL who dismissed all 6,000	5-6 November 1984	80% in unionised factories Approximately 800,000	2 days
Port Elizabeth	Retrenchments and petrol prices	PEBCO and PEYCO	No work, no pay	18 March 1985	90% Africans (Port Elizabeth) 36% Africans (Uitenhage)	1 day
Uitenhage	Solidarity for victims of repression	UYCO	No work, no pay	21-22 March 1985	98% Africans 16% Coloureds	2 days
East Rand	Solidarity stoppage over death of Raditsela in detention	CWIU and FOSATU	Dependent on form of action	14 May 1985	Partial and uneven. Up to 100,000 took some form of action	Up to 1 day stay-away on East Rand. Elsewhere short stoppages
Pietermaritzburg	Support of striking SARMCOL	MAWU	No work, no pay	18 July 1985	100%	1 day

Area	Demands	Organisation involved	Employees' response	Date	Effectiveness	Actual duration
Cape Town	Opposition to State of Emergency	Unclear	No work, no pay	10–12 September 1985	37% on 11 September. Overall unsuccessful	1 day
Nation-wide	Day of prayer	Bishop Tutu		9 October 1985	Unsuccessful	1 day
PWV area	Release of detained union leader Moses Mayikeso	MAWU	No work, no pay	5 March 1986	58%	1 day
Port Elizabeth/ Uitenhage	Commemoration of Sharpeville and Langa	UDF COSATU	No work, no pay. Also authorised leave	21 March 1986	98% African 82% Coloured (Uitenhage) 99% African 28% Coloured (Port Elizabeth)	1 day
Port Alfred	Conviction of a rapist	Port Alfred Womens Organisation		5 May 1986	100%	5 days
Country-wide	Recognition of May Day as a public holiday	COSATU and NECC	No work, no pay	1 May 1986	Transvaal 80% West. Cape 15% East. Cape 99.5% Natal 70%	1 day
Country-wide	Commemoration of Soweto Uprising and protest against the state of emergency	COSATU, UDF, NECC, CUSA, National Foundation	No work, no pay	16 June 1986	Transvaal 90% West. Cape 39% East. Cape 99.5% Natal 60–80%	1 day

Note: For full names of organisations, see Abbreviations listing.
Source: Labour Monitoring Group, *South African Labour Bulletin*, vol. 10, nos 6, 7, 8; vol. 11, nos 1, 2, 5.

but was 'populist' in character.

Foster's speech reaffirmed the principles of worker control, but now applied these to political action beyond production. However, the guidelines set down were of a general nature, allowing for very different interpretations: the criticism of populism reinforced a narrow 'workerism' in some quarters; the provision for alliances and community involvement was welcomed by those with national democratic leanings; whilst references to a 'workers' movement' were interpreted by the SACP as a form of syndicalism.[10]

The debate came to focus on whether or not trade unions should affiliate to the United Democratic Front (UDF), newly formed in 1983. Unions such as SAAWU and MACWUSA articulated a position which favoured affiliation on the grounds that workers were also members of the community, and that unions must also fight for their members' interests outside the sphere of production. They also argued that trade unions encompassed only a part of the working class, and further that a successful political challenge to the state demanded alliances with other social groups and the widest possible unity of those who are oppressed under apartheid. The GWU, on the other hand, asserted the need to ensure democratic structures and worker control. The argument was that the UDF was made up of activist-based organisations, with no structures of mandating and accountability. The trade unions would be swamped by a host of organisations — with equal voting power — but often little real membership. Furthermore, it was argued, the UDF represented a multi-class alliance, and its very style and language was at variance with the traditions established in the unions, and did not contribute towards working class leadership.

While these issues were being debated, new forms of organisation began to emerge on the ground. On the East Rand, the shop stewards councils spearheaded agitation against the destruction of shacks by the authorities. In the eastern Cape — and to a lesser extent in Natal and the western Cape — trade unions played a major role in the anti-tricameral election campaign in 1984. In the same year, FOSATU locals began to meet with student and youth organisations to exchange views. At the same time, community-based subsistence struggles led to the involvement of unionised workers — as in the case of the 18-month-long East London bus boycott — pointing to the possibility of a more direct role for unions in politics.[11]

However, these efforts remained localised and partial. In the main, trade unions did not develop a unified national approach to the question of political action. The movement remained divided in its approach: the community unions, particularly SAAWU, engaged in direct confrontation with the authorities (the Ciskei 'government' especially), whilst the industrial unions moved cautiously on to this terrain and at a local level. Foster's speech was not concretised, leaving a political vacuum and intensifying divisions inside the labour movement. Significantly, when the United Metal, Mining and Allied Workers of South Africa (UMMAWSA) split from the Metal and Allied Workers in June 1984, the break was justified in terms of MAWU's and FOSATU's alleged lack of political involvement and leadership.[12]

By the end of 1984, the industrial unions were facing numerous pressures that forced them to reconsider their organisational and political strategies. On the one hand, there was increasing militancy on the shop floor as strike levels escalated, while on the other, there was a need to consolidate their organisational capacity in the face of a deepening recession. In addition, the crisis in the townships and the general level of nation-wide political mobilisation was forcing unions to take an appropriate stand. Organised workers were demanding direct involvement in the struggle for political rights and urban change. However, in the absence of one united national trade union federation, there was no unified response to these pressures. Consequently, responses were shaped at a local level. This was clearly evident during the Transvaal and eastern Cape stayaways, where regional factors resulted in different outcomes. Whereas in the Transvaal, the unions were catapulted into a leading role in the stayaway, in the eastern Cape the unions chose to oppose the stayaway call. The underlying reasons for these differing outcomes bring into relief the possibilities and problems that lie ahead in any alliance between trade unions and the national liberation movement.

In the case of the successful two-day stayaway in November 1984, it involved co-ordinated action between trade unions and political organisations. It was the beginning of united mass action between organised labour and student and community organisations, with unions taking a leading role. For the trade union movement, it marked a decisive break with economism. Compared with previous stayaways, this one was the largest, with up to 800,000 workers staying away and 400,000 students boycotting classes. The sheer scale of the stayaway must be understood in terms of the build-up of conflict and struggle in three key spheres in the Transvaal: the townships, schools and factories. The occupation of the townships by the army was the catalyst that was to lead to the stayaway. The Congress of South African Students (COSAS) — the leading student organisation in the townships until its banning in 1985 — whose demands had not been met, wanted to widen the level of resistance in order to achieve its short-term goals. As a result, it called for the support of the UDF organisations and the trade unions. Responding to this call, Parent-Student Committees were formed in a number of townships. In the Transvaal between August and November 1984, the beginnings of a working relationship between community-student organisations and the trade unions were formed.

The Labour Monitoring Group's (LMG's) investigations at the time indicated that where trade union and community-student organisation coincided, the stayaway was most effective. Furthermore, 70 per cent of our sample of unionised establishments had a stayaway rate of over 80 per cent. There were two important features of the stayaway. Firstly, there was no weakening of the stayaway on day two, as had been anticipated by some observers. In the past, extended stayaways have failed, such as a call for a five-day stayaway in November 1976 which simply petered out. Secondly, there seems to have been no significant difference between the participation of migrant and township dwellers. In contrast with 1976, when migrant workers were mobilised against student protestors, many of these hostel dwellers, particularly on the East Rand, are now unionised.

While November 1984 was an historically important moment in which united mass action took place, during the coming months a number of obstacles and problems emerged which inhibited the realisation of this potential unity. Many of these problems came to the fore when the non-UDF unions opposed the PEBCO call for a Black Weekend consumer boycott (16–17 March 1985) and a stayaway (18 March 1985) as a response to the political and economic crisis in the eastern Cape. PEBCO identified the following issues: mass retrenchments, the merger between automobile enterprises controlled by Ford and Amcar (an Anglo-American subsidiary) and increased petrol prices, with the last becoming the final focus of the stayaway.

The non-UDF unions gave a number of reasons for opposing the stayaway at that time. In particular, their public statements were concerned that a call made by PEBCO — an African community organisation — would exclude coloured workers; a local response to what was a national problem was likely to be ineffective; there was inadequate consultation with the workers; and workers in smaller and unorganised establishments would be vulnerable.

In the event, the stayaway was successful among African workers but had limited success among coloureds (see Table 7.1). These differences reflect the reality of a divided working class — divisions which find organisational expression in the historic antagonism between PEBCO-MACWUSA and the FOSATU trade unions that goes back to the 1980 split. In addition, the recession — particularly severe in the automobile industry, which is concentrated in the eastern Cape — affected employed workers and unemployed workers in different ways. While unions such as NAAWU were concerned to consolidate their position — seeking to preserve jobs and the gains already made on the shop floor — unemployed workers, many of whom were members of the Port Elizabeth Youth Congress (PEYCO), played an important role in the mass protests in the townships.

A further obstacle that emerged was that the state's coercive response to the rising levels of mobilisation prevented the trade unions and the national political organisations from consolidating their structures. After the army occupied the townships, protest became increasingly militaristic as large numbers of youths began engaging the security forces in running street battles that claimed hundreds of lives. The militaristic voluntarism of the youth eclipsed the organisational concerns of the activists as the townships became 'ungovernable'. The first few months of 1985 constituted a period of intense urban conflict, leading eventually to the declaration of the State of Emergency on the 22 July.

The mobilisation of a conservative black petite bourgeoisie by Inkatha (a Zulu-based ethnic organisation under the leadership of Chief Gatsha Buthelezi and enjoying considerable though declining popular support) became an increasingly serious threat to mass-based trade union and UDF organisations during 1985. Inkatha's strength in the urban areas rests, it has recently been argued, on an alliance with a fraction of the black petite bourgeoisie, especially the traders, and those whose jobs rely upon Inkatha's wide patronage networks.[13] The organisation also retains a popular appeal for many workers, particularly those who are recently urbanised and/or retain considerable links with the land. However, the high level of involvement of contract workers in the November 1984 stayaway in the Transvaal suggests a critical weakening of Inkatha's influence amongst organised workers on the Rand. Forced to chose between loyalty to Inkatha — which opposed the stayaway — and the unions, many chose the latter. However, workers in

Natal are less likely to reject Inkatha if they are forced to choose, as they may well be with the launch of the Inkatha-backed United Workers Union of South Africa (UWUSA) on 1 May 1986.

Despite the obstacles to unity identified in this section, the foundations for sustained united mass action were being laid during this period by trade unionists, parents and community activists. State repression was to trigger a number of important protests of a joint kind. The solidarity action by 100,000 workers on 14 May 1985 was an example of successful workplace protest against state repression over the death of union leader Andries Raditsela. Another example was the successful two-day stayaway in March 1985 in Uitenhage over state repression and the Langa massacre in particular. Then, during 1986, over one million workers heeded nation-wide stayaway calls on May Day and June 16 (see Table 7.1). This growing willingness by the trade unions to take solidarity action with one another and with community groups was to culminate in the launch of COSATU in December 1985, the largest trade union federation in South African history.

COSATU rests upon an alliance of two major traditions of opposition to South Africa's system of racial capitalism — the one is shop floor-based and the other is linked to the national democratic movement. This was captured by Cyril Ramaphosa, General Secretary of the NUM, in his opening speech to the inaugural congress of the Federation: COSATU, he said, would take an active role in national politics in alliance with other progressive organisations, but such alliances must be on terms favourable to the working class.

By the end of 1985, the independent union movement had an estimated total paid-up membership of the order of 520,000. Membership was spread between three national federations — COSATU, CUSA and AZACTU — consisting of approximately 61 different unions. However, with an economically active population of ten million, the potential for new growth of the independent trade union movement is considerable. With a traditional trade union membership of nearly one million, South Africa can be said to have a total union membership (registered and unregistered) of approximately 1.5 million, comprising over 15 per cent of the total workforce. This gives South Africa the lowest percentage of workers unionised in the developed, capitalist world. Sweden with 88 per cent has the highest, followed by the United Kingdom (50 per cent), Germany (33 per cent), Japan (24 per cent) and the United States with 18 per cent. What is of particular interest is that, whereas union membership has steadily declined in recent years in most industrialised countries, in South Africa it has steadily grown. However, most of these unions are still small by Western standards, where the 'giant unions' of Europe and North America can represent up to two million members. A major challenge facing the independent union is to turn the relatively small unions into nation-wide industrial trade unions. The foundations for such a project have been laid in the motor, metal, retail, mining, paper, chemical, textile, food and transport sectors of the economy. In fact, the newly formed COSATU has made the slogan of 'one union, one industry' a high priority in its organisational activities in the coming years.

Table 7.2: Trade union organisation

	For 23 unions in our sample	1983 all unions
Number of shop stewards	12,462 (1 per 42 paid-up members)	6,000
Number of shop stewards councils/committees	1,443	—
Number of paid officials	306 (1 per 1,186)	—
Number of agreements	450 (?)	420
Number of workplaces organised	3,421 (?)	756

Source: Jon Lewis and Estelle Randall, 'Survey: the state of the unions'. *South African Labour Bulletin* vol. II, no. 2, Oct.–Dec. 1985; E.C. Webster, 'New Force on the Shop Floor' in *South African Review Two* (Ravan Press, Johannesburg, 1984).

The organisational depth of shop-floor organisations will greatly facilitate this task. By the end of 1985, the independent union movement had an organising presence in over 3,400 workplaces, covering largely factories and mines, but including newspapers, supermarkets, hotels and nursing homes. In 450 of these, formal agreements had been signed by the unions. Shop stewards and their committees have become the pivot of the organisational structures of these new unions. Structuring of these committees and their incorporation in the constitution of the unions was a significant innovation in South African trade unionism. Each department in the workplace elects a shop steward and there are now over 12,000 shop stewards in the independent unions. Their growing use of mediation and conciliation is providing black workers with meaningful access to the legal system at the grass roots level, possibly for the first time in South African history.

Conclusion

The central challenge facing the system of industrial relations in South Africa is that recognition of black trade unions, instead of depoliticising industrial conflict as pluralist theory promises, has led to the increasing politicisation of the workplace. This, I have suggested, arises from the exclusion of the black population from the political process and the deterioration in living standards during the recession. Of course, other industrialised countries have also had to adjust to economic decline through lay-offs and retrenchments and a permanent restructuring of the labour force. The crucial difference between South Africa and many other industrialised countries, it has recently been pointed out, is that organised labour, management and the state in these latter countries have an established tripartite structure that enables them jointly to alleviate the crisis. The newness of the system of collective bargaining, as well as the lack of legitimacy of the state, makes such bold corporatist solutions unlikely in the foreseeable future. Instead, Jaffee and Jochelson argue the lack of adequate education, housing, medical, unemployment and welfare benefits, coupled with rising prices and rents, has led the trade unions, in alliance with students and community groups, to play a leading role beyond the workplace in the struggle for democracy and political rights.[14]

The result of these economic and political conditions of labour in South Africa is the emergence of a trade union movement that is quite different in many respects, from the model of professional and bureaucratic union leadership that characterises industrial relations in advanced, industrialised countries. I have argued in this chapter that it is both patronising and wrong to see these unions as 'immature'. What we need to recognise is that a different kind of unionism has emerged — what I have called social-movement unionism.[15]

Social-movement unionism emerges in authoritarian countries such as the Philippines, Brazil and South Africa, where workers are excluded from the central political decision-making processes. It differs from conventional trade unionism in that it is concerned with labour as a social and political force, not simply as a commodity to be bargained over. As a result, its concerns go beyond the workplace to include the sphere of reproduction. Furthermore, it places a strong emphasis on democracy and workers' control.

Essentially, the concept of social-movement unionism recognises that the trade union has two faces — the one economic, the other social and political. When the black trade union movement re-emerged in the 1970s, it focused on the economic dimension: more recently, it has come to focus on the political and social dimensions as well.

The challenge now facing the black trade union movement is to blend these two faces of trade unionism.

Notes

1. Richard Allen Lester, *As unions mature* (Princeton University Press, Princeton, 1958), p. 2.
2. J.G.B. Maree, 'An analysis of the independent trade unions in South Africa in the 1970s' (unpublished PhD thesis, University of Cape Town, 1986).
3. See Rob Lambert for a discussion of these issues. 'Political unionism and working class hegemony: perspectives on the South African Congress of Trade Unions 1955-1965', *Labour Capital and Society*, vol. 18, no. 2 (November 1985), pp. 244-77. For a discussion of social-movement unionism see Peter Waterman, 'The international restructuring of labour and the rise of social movement unionism'. N.I.O. Kromiek no 34, Sept.-Oct., 1984.
4. Richard Freeman and James Medoff, 'The two faces of unionism', *The Public Interest* (1979).
5. Lambert, 'Political unionism'.
6. David Hemson, 'Trade unions and the struggle for liberation', *Capital and Class*, vol. 6 (Autumn 1976), no. 1-41.
7. A. Sitas, 'From grassroots control to democracy: a case study of the impact of trade unionism on migrant workers' cultural formations on the East Rand', *Social Dynamics*, vol. 11, no. 1 (June 1985), pp. 32-44.
8. Food and Canning Workers Union, 'Search for a workable relationship', *South African Labour Bulletin* (July 1982), pp. 30-40.
9. J. Foster, 'The workers' struggle — where does FOSATU stand?', *South African Labour Bulletin*, vol. 7, no. 8 (July 1982), pp. 67-86.
10. L.N. Mahlalela, 'Workerism and economism', *African Communist*, no. 104 (1986), pp. 25-32.
11. Mark Swilling, 'The East London bus boycott', *South African Labour Bulletin*, vol. 9, no. 5 (March 1986), pp. 45-74.
12. Mark Swilling, 'Workers divided: a critical assessment of the split in MAWU on the East Rand', *South African Labour Bulletin*, vol. 10, no. 1 (August-September 1984), pp. 99-123.
13. A. Sitas, 'Inanda, August 1985; "Where wealth and power and

blood reign worshipped goals'' ', *South African Labour Bulletin*, vol. 11, no. 4 (February-March 1986), pp. 85–122.

14. Georgina Jaffee and Karen Jochelson, 'The fight for jobs — union initiatives on retrenchments and unemployment', in South African Research Services, *South African Review Three* (Ravan Press, Johannesburg, 1986), pp. 51–78.

15. For a comparative treatment of this theme see R. Munck, *Third World Workers and the New International Labour Studies* (Zed Press, London, forthcoming).

8

Political Mobilisation in the Black Townships of the Transvaal

Jeremy Seekings

Introduction

16 June 1986 was the tenth anniversary of the shooting in Soweto of Hector Petersen and other peacefully protesting school students. A decade after 'Soweto', political mobilisation in South Africa's black townships had grown to unprecedented scale and importance, as residents have sought to change the terms of urban life.

South African historians have increasingly recognised that subordinate classes play an integral role in the shaping of processes of class formation, industrialisation, and urban transformation.[1] However, there has been an unfortunate failure to examine the social actors engaged in political protest in South Africa's black townships today.

Liberal scholars have been quicker than those in Marxist traditions to consider politics in the townships, but their focus on 'unrest' has been almost exclusively in terms of violent protest, failing to locate this in either a thorough analysis of township politics or any analysis of the South African political economy.[2] The concept of 'unrest', employed by liberal scholars, the newspapers, and the government, may give the impression of capturing the essence of township politics, but in fact makes it impossible to comprehend political process. Whilst on the one hand it is nebulous and seems all-embracing, on the other it suggests a homogeneity that bears little resemblance to the reality of diversity in township politics, and an incoherence that denies the playing out of concrete class interests. It also makes resistance seem natural through suggesting, as one liberal observer has himself pointed out, 'that these cycles of violence and counter-violence simply form part of the larger age-old political dilemma that plagues South Africa'.[3]

Marxist scholarship is only now beginning to catch up with the actors in South Africa's class conflict. Analysis until recently tended to locate the 'urban crisis' in terms of the supposed logic of underlying structural contradictions, rather than in uncertain processes of struggle. They often focused only on the responses of the state and capital, in areas such as urban rights, housing, transport, education, labour allocation and influx control, political representation, and labour law.

However, there is now emerging a body of work on political mobilisation in the townships. Most of this work focuses on specific (and visible) forms in which conflict has been manifested: for example, stayaways,[4] schools boycotts,[5] transport boycotts,[6] and consumer boycotts.[7] There is still, however, very little work on the social composition of protests, and the overall patterns and dynamics of township politics.[8] The effect of this is that politics often seems to revolve around a small number of key events, such as (in the Pretoria-Witwatersrand-Vaal (PWV) region) the Vaal Uprising in September 1984, the November 1984 stayaway, and the declaration of a State of Emergency in July 1985 and again in June 1986. There seems little to link events together.

In this chapter I seek to locate recent events in processes of political mobilisation in black townships[9] in the PWV region.[10] I focus primarily on the emergence and development of widespread resistance over the period 1982-4.[11]

Urban political analysis has recently benefited from criticism of the overly-structuralist Marxism of, for example, the early work of Manuel Castells.[12] One key aspect of this criticism has concerned the role of 'urban social movements' in political change. Whilst structuralist accounts deny movements any importance, seeing their existence, demands, and effects as determined by structural contradictions, critics have emphasised the need to study the movements if their demands and effects are to be understood.[13]

Many of the critics of structuralism, however, fail to shed the structuralist perspective completely. Whilst they do now consider local political protest, they interpret it in terms of its effects on political change, rather than considering the effects in terms of the protest. When, as is usually the case, the effects are identified as a homogeneous and coherent set, then it suggests a homogeneity and coherence to the mobilisation. Thus, for example, Castells himself has explicitly repudiated his earlier structuralism, and written a book full of rich detail on the development of urban social movements.[14] Yet whilst his descriptions of particular urban social movements document both diversity and complexity, his account of the development of each movement remains essentially predetermined by the movement's 'final' effects.[15]

In contemporary South Africa we can hope for, but do not know, the precise outcome of struggle. Whilst political activists at a national level espouse an interpretation of protest in terms of their goals of national political change, it remains clear that struggle is not unidirectionally aimed at national political rights. The demands and effects of struggle are shaped by such factors as the organisation, leadership, and composition of protests, and these are shaped by, *inter alia*, the experience of struggle. To understand the direction of change, it is necessary to examine the nature of mobilisation.

The South African experience therefore suggests several important questions for the study of the genesis and development of urban social movements. What is the nature of apparent acquiescence, and how and why does it give rise to visible mobilisation and resistance? What is the relationship between the diverse themes within 'a' movement? How valid is generalisation about 'a' movement, given its constituent diversity?

It is widely believed in South Africa that resistance constitutes 'a' movement. The assumed unity of mobilisations follows from the structural context and chosen political tactics and theory. The combination of residential concentration, of the racial aspect of oppression, and especially of the threat of removal in some cases, has indeed always generated some sense of 'community', and given some substance to the notions of a 'black experience' pervasive in the literature and of the primacy of national oppression in national democratic ideology and political rhetoric.

The structural context shapes not only the patterns but also the dynamics of township politics, as key structural influences change. Marxist analysis has identified the current context as one of crisis, and more particularly of an urban reproductive crisis. This crisis is exacerbated and in part caused by the fiscal crisis of the state, as it tries to ensure the reproduction of labour power on a daily and generational basis, of capitalist relations of production (including the means of extracting labour from labour power), and of a political, social, and cultural system that enables sustained and stable capital accumulation.

The notion of crisis is rather over-used in discussion of the state and capital. It is often unclear whether political protest is in response to or the cause of crisis, and just how much struggle, or restructuring by the state or capital, is necessary to distinguish a period of crisis from 'normal' periods. However, the state's fiscal crisis has been of key importance in the development of political resistance, with the reduction in the racially defined provision of urban public services, especially housing and township development (but also transport). During the late 1970s, the Administration Boards (later to become Development Boards) began running increasing deficits, and in response pushed up rents and service charges, passing on both their debts and the responsibility for rent increases to the new councils. The Riekert Commission claimed that it was vital that 'black communities . . . bear to an increasing extent a greater part of the total burden in connection with the provision of services in their own communities'.[16]

The most important effect of the state's fiscal crisis was on housing. In the mid-1960s, the state had virtually stopped building outside of the bantustans in order to bolster the bantustan strategy. This led to an escalating shortage of housing, estimated at 141,000 housing units by the Riekert Commission in 1977. The state's fiscal crisis has ensured that this shortage has since grown. By 1982, estimates went as high as 560,000 units (by the National Manpower Commission). Since 1981, the state's fiscal conservatism has been coupled with economic recession.

However, heightened grievances do not automatically lead to political mobilisation, which is not simply a response to the material conditions of life, but also to the perceptions of what is just and what is possible. The notion of justice in urban political protest has been identified by the English historian E.P. Thompson, who argues that each crowd action has 'some legitimising notion'.[17] In South Africa's townships, we can usefully combine Thompson's 'legitimising notions' with Castells's broader concept of 'urban meaning', referring to 'the structural performance assigned as a goal to cities in general . . . by the conflictive process between social actors in a given society'.[18] Particular legitimising notions are part of a broader perception of the desired meaning of urban space. Whilst residents demanded the realisation of use-values in township life, especially in terms of housing, so councillors and local state officials who were seen as opposed to such demands became legitimate targets for opposition as they thereby violated notions of justice.

Castells is mistaken, however, in assuming that the participants in his movements share a common, homogeneous and static perception of how the urban meaning should be redefined. The creation of an alternative vision of urban meaning is itself a key process in urban political change: mobilisations only constitute a movement when the diverse urban political cultures and perceptions of desired urban meaning converge.

In South Africa's townships, the historical diversity of urban political visions has reflected the complex and varied cultural mediation of the structural context. Over the period 1982–6, however, there has developed a common urban vision. This is the process which I begin to explore in this chapter. 'Communities' in the townships remain, to use Benedict Anderson's term, imagined.[19] However, that is not to deny notions of 'community' any political salience: their importance lies not in their existence, but rather in the nature of the process of their construction.

The origins of political mobilisation, 1977–83

At the root of conflict in the PWV townships is the built environment, i.e. the 'physical landscape' of houses, roads and railways, factories and offices, parks and pavements, schools and sewage systems. In the townships the most important of these has been the most basic — housing — although demands for other elements in the built environment are becoming more important as residents become more assertive.

The built environment is not only a key feature in the welfare of township residents, but is also a symbol of both the failures ad the perceived duties of the state. Furthermore, conflict over the built environment has emphasised the need for residents to secure control over the decision-making process and a claim on extra-township resources, both of which have led apparently narrow demands over the built environment to more overtly political demands. Thus, residents' struggles to redefine the township in terms of use-values have entailed chronic conflict with the state over both the broad political and the specific fiscal relationships concerning the built environment.

Township residents' discontent with the built environment prompted diverse responses. It widely provoked hidden forms of resistance (such as squatting or growing rent arrears), and populism on the part of some candidates for local government elections. During the period 1977–83, mobilisation developed as residents' perceptions of local councils changed. Active political protest, organisation, and direct action emerged. During 1984 mobilisation was transformed.

In this period 1977–83, most of the apparently prominent areas of local political mobilisation, however, did not clearly concern the built environment. Local activity was most often reported over national issues, within national organisational structures, including Inkatha, the Azanian People's Organisation (AZAPO), the National Forum, the United Democratic Front (UDF), the Congress of South African Students (COSAS), and the Release Mandela Campaign (RMC). Particular campaigns included the Free Mandela Campaign of 1980, opposition to the Koornhof Bills and the proposed new Constitution, and finally opposition to the black local authority (BLA) elections in the last two months of 1983. Also well reported was the escalation of sabotage activity by Umkhonto we Sizwe.

Local activity in parties contesting local elections held under the 1977 Community Councils Act in late 1978, and later under the 1982 Black Local Authorities Act, was well reported. Much less reported was the increasing mobilisation in extra-state local organisations, such as the old Evaton Ratepayers Association and the new Soweto Civic Association (SCA), Vaal Civic Association (VCA), Krugersdorp Residents Organisation (KRO), the Duduza Civic, and the East Rand People's Organisation (ERAPO). In most cases, the focus of their organisational activity concerned local housing issues. Hardly reported at all was spontaneous, intermittent, or informally organised resistance, especially over housing, but also over transport, food costs, and educational grievances.

National organisations were often credited with a considerably more important role than they played in practice, and the nature of local mobilisation has therefore often been hidden under the rhetoric and appearance of national political protest. Anti-election campaigns, for example, were very important in terms of linking local with national political objectives, and so contributed to the reshaping of local political consciousness and organisation. However, hostility to the councils and the low election polls should not be interpreted primarily in terms of demands for broader political representation, but rather in terms of local political dynamics, which generally revolved around the built environment.

The key role of the built environment has been reflected in state policy. The Stallardist doctrine, the planned townships of the 1940s and 1950s, constraints on construction outside the bantustans in the 1960s and 1970s, forced removals, the 1979 Riekert Report, and the attempted recommodification of housing,[20] have all been aimed at discouraging political protest as well as solving the financial problem of reproducing the labour force.

The most obvious conflict over the built environment from the

1940s through to the late 1970s concerned where people were permitted to live. The struggle over forced removals was not only a question of distances from the workplace, but also one of the standard of the built environment, and above all of urban meaning. Removals in the PWV have always been contested, and in a few cases (such as Alexandra, Evaton, and Munsieville) resistance or the threat thereof has served to prevent removal being effected.[21] Since the late 1970s, conflict has revolved around the standard and cost of the built environment within townships. Whilst the central state sought to use housing to achieve political objectives, it ironically ignored the links between housing and other aspects of state policy. Most importantly, it failed to gauge the political effects of the restructuring of the local state, and especially of transferring political and financial responsibility for the built environment. The transformation of passive into active resistance in the PWV townships was in large part the result of the political unviability of the Community Councils and their successors, the BLAs, which was itself the result of their responsibility for the built environment in the political economy of the early 1980s.

The Councils were caught in an overwhelming contradiction. Their revenue largely comprised rent and service charges, and state funds were only available for housing construction at economic rates of interest. However, increases in rents or charges were met with effective passive resistance from residents, either through a proliferation of shacks, increasing overcrowding, or through growing rent arrears. Revenue could therefore only be increased if:

(1) informal housing was controlled and/or taxed,
(2) rents were increased, and
(3) rent defaulters were evicted (and replaced by tenants who would pay the rent).

Such action would, however, remove any residual legitimacy that councillors enjoyed and could precipitate active resistance.

Administration Board officials recognised this danger and hoped that black councillors would be able to absorb and defuse the discontent. In 1978 the West Rand Administration Board delayed increasing rents until the three Community Councils in Greater Soweto had been elected. The Soweto Council announced the rent increase in August 1979; rents were to rise by 88 per cent in three stages over the following four months. In the resultant protest the Soweto Civic Association was launched, to co-ordinate opposition to the proposals, and the Council decided to defer the increase. Elections due in 1980–1 to Community Councils that were to be upgraded to BLAs were postponed, in the hope that the greater powers vested in the latter would prevent complete election boycotts. P.J. Riekert (then Chief Director of the Western Transvaal Administration Board) unambiguously recognised this, saying: 'These local authorities will serve to defuse pent-up frustrations and grievances against administration from Pretoria.'[22]

Councillors generally recognised the contradiction they faced and sought to achieve a remarkable balancing trick for as long as possible, essentially through demanding continued financial support from the central state. However, what in the short term amounted to successfully maintaining a balance, inevitably undermined their position in the medium term. The very success of residents in creating a space that was relatively free from the financial demands of the local state (and from its control) necessitated an escalating use of force if the local state were to preserve a 'balancing' revenue enabling some infrastructural development in the townships under existing legislation.

During the early 1980s these contradictions became more acute and Councils resorted with increasing frequency to coercive measures. In Katlehong, many new residents escaped rising rents (up by 60 per cent in 1978–80) and the rising shortage of housing by building shacks. The number of shacks (or 'umkhukhu', meaning chicken coops) rose from an estimated 3,000 in 1979 to 8,000 in 1980, 22,000 by early 1982, and 44,000 by mid-1983, with almost twice as many shacks as 'legal' houses. The Community Council in effect authorised this illegal accommodation, and so avoided losing support. As the shacks proliferated, however, the Council first sought control and finance by imposing a R3 levy, then raised the levy to R5, and finally, in November 1982, sent in the bulldozers to clear shacks. Action was also taken against shacks in Daveyton and Tokhoza.[23]

By the end of 1982 there was an estimated shortage of 35,000 houses in Soweto, and an estimated 23,000 families were living in 'zozos'. In May 1982, shack demolition began in Jabavu. Two thousand alleged illegal residents were arrested in massive pass raids in September. In February 1983, the Council began demolishing shacks in Orlando East. Despite resistance, including demonstrations and court action, the Soweto Community Council and West Rand Administration Board proceeded with shack demolition.[24]

In many cases, shack residents were able to circumvent the

Council's measures. In Katlehong,[25] 'As the Administration Board knocks down homes like a wave, workers jump ahead and around the wave and reconstruct their umkhukhu behind it.' Councils' growing alienation from residents was hastened by their perceived unreasonableness over procedures as well as over their actions. Thus, for example, Katlehong and Tokhoza councillors agreed to meet residents in February 1983, but failed to turn up.

Residents' struggles to define the townships in terms of use-values were evident in the determined words of a speaker at a Katlehong meeting in May 1983:[26]

> Let's come together. When they demolish ten shacks tomorrow we must build a hundred behind them. These people believe we should stay in a hostel. It's unchristian to stay alone without a family. The best way is to fetch our families from the homelands and come here. If we are cowards we will achieve nothing.

Rent increases also provoked widespread opposition. A surprise rent increase in April 1981 in Tembisa prompted residents to demonstrate outside the East Rand Administration Board offices. When police violently dispersed the protesters, and prevented public meetings to discuss the issue, residents rioted, causing an estimated R80,000 damage to Administration Board and Council property.[27]

The announcement of rent increases in West Rand townships similarly provoked opposition to the Councils and Administration Board. Protest meetings were held by the Mohlakeng Organisation of Civic Associations (MOCA) and KRO. At a mass meeting in Mohlakeng, which the mayor refused to attend out of concern for his safety, 3,000 residents decided not to pay until they had been given satisfactory reasons. One speaker told the meeting: 'You should not allow these people to dig holes in your pockets. They should first clean the streets, tar them, and electrify the township.'[28] In Kagiso, residents called for all councillors' resignations, and decided to boycott their businesses.[29]

Many councils refused to authorise the Administration Board-suggested rent increases. The Chairmen of the Ikageng and Orkney Community Councils were sacked by the West Rand Administration Board for refusing to agree to a 105 per cent increase in 1982.[30] However, where Councils held out for one year, they caved in to Board pressure the following year: for example, both the Mamelodi and Atteridgeville Community Councils refused to increase rents in 1981, but in 1982 backed down and allowed huge rises.

In some townships the issue that provoked protest was not rising rents, in a strict sense, but rather unwarranted increases in service charges. The distinction between rents and service charges is always a tenuous one, as there appears to be little link between service charges or capital expediture and the provision of services. In a number of PWV townships in the early 1980s, the state proposed costly development plans focusing on electrification and sewerage systems, with the cost, unsurprisingly, being passed on to residents.

In Duduza, the East Rand Administration Board proposed a so-called 'master plan' for the installation of a sewerage system to replace night buckets in 1982. The cost would be recouped over 20 years, with rents/service charges being increased by more than 100 per cent over the first three years. Residents, dissatisfied with their Council, formed a civic association in October. Discontent was not simply due to the cost of the development; rather, it arose from the state's violation of popular notions of justice. Duduza residents had been moved from the old Nigel location in 1964, and given the impression that their removal would facilitate prompt development. Until 1982, however, significant township development was not even on the state's agenda in Duduza, whilst the old location, now a 'coloured' township, had been developed. Residents were very aware that even before the proposed increases, they were paying the same rents/charges as people in other townships which already had sewerage, and had not apparently paid for its installation.[31]

When Community Councils were first elected in late 1978, they enjoyed some legitimacy. This was often based in councillors' roles as arbiters of justice and dispensers of patronage. According to one Tumahole resident:

> here were some sort of makgotlas. If you fought with your wife, you could be taken there, and they will sort out the problems. They were divided into wards. In the beginning, most of the cases were not handed over to the police, but were being solved by these makgotlas. Or if you have a relative living in the rural areas, and you want that relative to live in the township, this can be done through the councillors . . . Some people thought that the councillors can do things. Whenever you have a problem, they can solve it quickly. If you are divorced, and your wife wants to take the kids,

then the councillor can sort this out . . . .

According to another resident:

> The councillors were people who were just going to help with family disputes. Our people didn't think of them playing any active political role whatsoever, they were just like social workers, or marriage councillors. They will just say, 'we'll make sure the woman next door doesn't commit adultery with your husband'.

In Tumahole, this legitimacy had been substantially eroded by 1984. Most importantly, residents were growing disillusioned through the councillors' failure to convert their election promises and the escalating rents into tangible development in the township.[32]

As residents grew increasingly discontented with councillors throughout the region, allegations of Council corruption and mismanagement became rife, and corruption was accorded a symbolic importance. What had previously been seen as the appeal of patronage was transformed into the crime of corruption, as councillors crudely manipulated their control over trading licences, bursaries for students, and council funds in general, to favour themselves or their supporters. As one middle-aged Tumahole man put it: 'After someone is elected a councillor, all avenues are open to him' — literally true, as the first road in the township to be tarred linked the mayor's house to his supermarket.

Two separate motions of no confidence brought by disaffected members of the Lekoa Town Council, detailing examples of corruption by leading councillors, were both ruled out of order by the mayor on spurious grounds. One had spelt 'Lekoa' incorrectly, and the other referred to the 'Lekoa Town Council' as opposed to the 'Town Council of Lekoa', which is its official title. At the Delmas Treason Trial, even councillors called as state witnesses have admitted that knowledge of corruption was very widespread, and was a key factor in the Vaal Uprising and the specific hostility directed at leading councillors.[33]

Council corruption prompted resistance not only because it destroyed the image of responsible leadership upon which the Council system depended, but because the councillors were combining corruption with illegitimate actions over the built environment. Shacks were cleared and rent defaulters harassed, and rents were increased with the justification that this was to finance township development, whilst such development rarely materialised. Incidents of active protest before 1984 seem usually to have occurred when there was this combination of factors. In Katlehong, for example, the Council's demolition of shacks came soon after it had received R2 million for new offices, but was failing to address the huge housing shortage. The emergent critical opposition to incumbent councillors worked, in some cases, within the local government framework, allowing the Councils as institutions to retain some legitimacy.

In Alexandra, Sam Buti's Save Alexandra Party secured widespread support through its successful campaign for a reprieve for the township, and its populist plans for township development. In the 1983 Town Council elections, the party's candidates were elected unopposed. In Soweto, the official turnout of 10 per cent in the 1983 elections for the Soweto Town Council was higher than the turnout in 1978, probably due to the populist stand taken by the opposition Sofasonke Party. Sofasonke candidates promised rent cuts, leniency towards defaulters, permanent house ownership, and even the abolition of influx control for people born after 1945! Sofasonke had been formed to represent squatters in the late 1940s, and the Council's action against squatters in 1982–3 boosted its old populist appeal.[34]

In Mamelodi too, the Council retained a degree of legitimacy as a result of the radical populism of the Vukani Vulahmelo People's Party (VVPP). Formed in 1980, the VVPP opposed high rents, the 99-year leasehold, and slum clearance. The Party denounced financial irregularities, demanded low-cost housing, and even took the Administration Board to court. In 1983 the VVPP won the Town Council elections with a (relatively) high 28 per cent turnout.[35]

Populist rhetoric was insufficient to reconcile residents' demands and expectations concerning the built environment with what was possible under the existing local government framework. This became clear sooner in the larger townships, where the looser links between residents and councillors made the latter less accessible and less accountable. Rising discontent with the Councils, although they were the only elected government structures for township residents, was reflected in low voting in most areas during elections, the unwillingness of Councils and central state officials to hold new elections when they were supposedly due, and the formation of alternative township organisations which were opposed to councillors and the Councils.

In some townships, short-lived organisations emerged in the early 1980s: for example, the April 1981 protests in Tembisa led to the formation of a Tembisa Residents Action Committee. Intermittent and unsustained organisation gave way to more permanent organisation with the recognition that Councils did not have the power to change living conditions in the townships, and they could and should be effectively opposed. The belief in the viability of challenge was in part the result of the revitalisation of nationalist politics in the early 1980s.

The nature of protest organisations also changed. Early organisations tended towards conservatism and elitism. Mass and sustained mobilisation against the Councils only arose with their later failure to meet residents' demands over the built environment and their rising illegitimacy through corruption. Thus, whilst the narrowly based Committee of 10 was formed in Soweto in response to the inactivity of the Soweto Urban Bantu Council (UBC, or 'useless boys club') during 1976–7, the threatened rent increases in 1979 generated broader mobilisation that was reflected in the formation of the Soweto Civic Association.

The transformation of resistance, 1984

By early 1984, conflict between the Councils and residents over housing had become sufficiently acute for the transition from passive resistance to active protest and direct action to occur. This transition took place in many townships in the PWV during the second half of 1984. The three main political developments during that year were:

(1) Protests within secondary schools over educational grievances, with intermittent boycotts first starting in Atteridgeville in January, and later beginning in Soweto, Tembisa, Alexandra.

(2) Isolated and sporadic protests over the issue of housing, due to announced rent increases in mid-year, coupled with the very low level of legitimacy of Town and Community Councils; such protests began in July in Tumahole, and during August and September in the rest of the Vaal Triangle.

(3) The combination of discontent over housing and rents, mobilised school students, the illegitimacy of the Councils, and repression by the security forces, led to widespread resistance during August, exploding into the Vaal Uprising in the first days of September. Unprecedented

mobilisation and violent conflict later emerged widely through the PWV region.

As conflict over the built environment intensified during 1984, the growing crisis in many townships' high schools became increasingly important as grievances and participants interacted and together shaped emerging patterns of mobilisation. Whilst conflict over the built environment provided the fundamental impetus for resistance, students and ex-students played a major role in the revolt of the last three months of 1984, which continued through 1985.

During 1983 there had been isolated protests in individual schools over educational grievances: for example, students at Orlando High School in Soweto briefly boycotted classes in protest against the transfer of three highly regarded teachers, and at another high school, students protested against a dictatorial principal who tried to implement the Department of Education and Training's (DET) new age limits.[36] In Atteridgeville, simmering discontent during 1983 cystallised over the Christmas vacation over alleged irregularities in exam marking and the readmission of students. When school authorities ignored representations by the local COSAS branch, students at Saulridge High in January 1984 began the Transvaal's first sustained class boycott. Further demands were taken up, and intermittent class boycotts spread to five of the six high schools in the township by the end of February.[37]

The initial protests concerned purely educational grievances, and the students only boycotted when other channels for communicating their grievances were ignored, and then they only protested peacefully inside the schools. The move towards active protest in part reflected the growing level of resistance in the township as a whole. Discontent over the built environment and the failure of the Councils had led, in November and December 1983, to the formation of the Saulsville-Atteridgeville Youth Organisation (SAYO) and the Atteridgeville-Saulsville Residents Organisation (ASRO) to oppose elections for a Town Council.

Students were very soon made aware that the schools were not isolated from wider issues. Atteridgeville school protests were transformed by the unprovoked killing of a student, on school premises, by police in February. Parents were drawn into the dispute through their outrage at the killing, and participated in organising a peaceful funeral. The suspension of student leaders in April further intensified boycotts. The DET temporarily closed schools in late April, and completely so in mid-May. School or class boycotts continued for the rest of the year as a result of rising police harassment (often aided by school authorities) and the DET's refusal to meet key demands. Throughout the year the Town Council failed to make any significant attempt to solve the educational crisis or to restrain the police. This led to further discontent with councillors, and growing support for ASRO, which did try to help negotiations.

This pattern of events in Atteridgeville was repeated elsewhere. Students were radicalised, and drawn into broader township conflicts, by their experience of repression and of the intransigence of both school and township authorities. By August, the DET had closed schools in Alexandra, Daveyton, and Tembisa.

The announcement of rent increases by Councils throughout the PWV in May, June, and July, brought the rent and education issues together. In Atteridgeville, residents called on the councillors to resign, and ASRO sought legal assistance and successfully opposed the increases. In August, increased service charges were proposed, but these were also abandoned in September under pressure from residents and ASRO, in the face of escalating conflict in the Vaal and East Rand, the school boycotts, and the petrol-bombing of the mayor's house in August. Despite the abandonment of the proposed increases, many residents were unable to pay their rent. In early November, the Town Council stated that rent arrears stood at R300,000, and its budget deficit was now R2.9 million.

In Daveyton, 2,000 residents said they would not pay the increase. In Ratanda, the mayor called public meetings over the rent issue, but either failed to turn up or arrived drunk. Residents finally persuaded two councillors to address them at a meeting in August, at which it was resolved not to pay the increase. Three councillors resigned soon afterwards. A civic was formed, and over 1,000 people attended its first public meeting in September.[38]

The first township in which protests against the rent increases led to violent conflict during 1984 was Tumahole. In previous years, residents had been passive in the face of rent increases, but the 42 per cent increase announced in May 1984, on top of an identical percentage increase in the previous year, and together with rising unemployment and prices but stagnant incomes, provoked unprecedented opposition.[39] At public meetings, the Tumahole councillors were asked to explain why they had failed to fulfil previous years' promises that rent increases were to finance township development, and in particular high-mast lighting and sewerage.

The councillors did not answer these questions, and adopted a dismissive and uncompromising position. At a meeting with some of the younger residents, councillors were challenged over previous years' budgeting of over R150,000 for high-mast lights (each costing about R9,000), yet only one had been built. It transpired that this one light had in fact been donated by South African Breweries.

On 15 July, a march was held against the rent increase. Residents felt that a mass demonstration was the only way of making their outrage known. Possibly a majority of the township population marched through Tumahole with the intention of ending up at the community hall. Large numbers of police shadowed the marchers, and finally blocked the route, ordering them to disperse. Before the warning period was complete, the police fired tear gas and started sjambokking the dispersing marchers. Residents retaliated by burning and looting councillors' property. The police made over 50 arrests. One of those arrested was badly assaulted by police and died in custody.

The proposed rent increase was, for many households, literally unaffordable. How could a single woman, earning only R40 per month as a domestic worker, afford nearly R40 per month rent? However, the increases were also seen as deeply unjust, and the councillors were now seen as illegitimate. Although different people participated in the march for different reasons, the older residents seemed to have done so from a sense of indignation as much as simple deprivation. The police intervention was seen as unnecessary and illegitimate, and the attacks on the councillors' property was widely seen as justified retaliation. Although the initial rioters were younger residents (mostly in their twenties), the looters included many parents. The death in custody also provoked further outrage.

With the collapse of the Council's legitimacy, and the subsequent resignation of some of the councillors, it became likely that an alternative and more representative leadership would emerge. A mixture of old and young residents, unemployed and working, came to the fore. Strongly critical of the council system, they were to constitute the core of the Tumahol Civic Association launched in October 1984.

The formation of a popular civic required more than simply a leadership opposed to the Council system: it needed mass support, convinced of the viability of an alternative as well as of the bankruptcy of the Council. This support materialised as a result of activitists' success in opposing the proposed rent increase, whilst the remaining councillors continued to support the proposal.

The key event in this process took place on 10 September. Residents marched to the Development Board offices, held a stayaway from work, and closed most of the shops. A delegation met with the remaining councillors and Development Board officials, who finally agreed to maintain rents at their old level. No doubt the officials' willingness to make concessions was in large part due to the desire to avoid a repeat in Tumahole of the Vaal Uprising of the previous week, in the townships north of the Vaal. They may have felt that for the time being, the concession over rents was a small price to pay in a township that had demonstrated its potential volatility in July and August.

Regardless, this concession over rents was correctly seen in Tumahole as a victory for the embryonic civic (and the residents, of course) and a defeat for the Council and the Board. It was widely known that the councillors had tried to stop the meeting at the beginning; that the civic had secured the abandonment of the proposed increase, which the Council had not even attempted; and, at the end of the meeting, the police brigadier asked the delegation and not the councillors 'to appeal to the residents to disperse and return to their homes peacefully', and 'to remove all barricades and stones from the streets'.[40]

The events in Tumahole in July were soon overshadowed by events north of the Vaal river in September. The Vaal Uprising is widely identified as marking the beginning of the current wave of 'unrest' in South Africa, with direct action involving the killing of councillors and widespread destruction of property. The Uprising should be considered a key event, but not because of the use of violence as resistance (as in liberal and crude revolutionary interpretations). Its importance lies instead in the radicalisation of political cultures, because of the rent increases and the heightened repression by the security forces trying to contain intensified mobilisation. Repression polarised politics and legitimised violence, leading to the collapse of elected black local government and the consolidation of township resistance.

Whilst housing in the Vaal was not in crucially short supply, rents were very high and rising, as the Oranje Vaal Development Board (OVDB) sought financial self-sufficiency. Whilst the Vaal had been the fastest growing industrial region in South Africa during the 1970s, it was devastated by the recession of the early 1980s. The growing disparity between incomes and rents made housing a potentially explosive topic. As early as 1978, one study estimated that income in over three-quarters of Sebokeng households fell below a conservatively defined household subsistence level.[41] Between 1978 and the beginning of 1984, rents in the Vaal rose by over 400 per cent, making them over 20 per cent higher than in any other metropolitan area. By April 1984 the Lekoa Town Council admitted that 35,000 households, i.e. over half the total in the townships concerned, were in arrears on rent and service charges, with the Council's deficit for the first quarter of the year at over R1.5 million.[42]

The announcement that rents were to increase yet again in the townships on the north side of the Vaal river led the Vaal Civic Association to hold a series of weekend meetings during August to discuss rents. At mass meetings on 2 September, residents resolved to stay away from work in protest the following week, and to march to the OVDB offices the following day.[43] The march turned into a riot when, passing the house of a councillor, protesters called on him to resign and his guards, panicking, started shooting. Residents of all ages attacked the property of councillors and other shops with a reputation for over-charging, and four councillors were killed (three members of the Lekoa Town Council, and one in Evaton).

Ministers blamed the protests on agitators. According to Law and Order Minister Louis le Grange, 'I am not convinced that the rent increase was the real reason . . . There are individuals and organisations clearly behind what has happened in the Vaal Triangle.' Gerrit Viljoen blamed 'external elements', and even Piet Koornhof was moved 'to express my strongest displeasure to those who are behind these events and who are misusing innocent people and inciting them to chaos'.[44]

Others were more perceptive. Tjaart van der Walt, in his official report on the Uprising, described the rent increase as having been handled 'overhastily, unwisely, clumsily and insensitively' by the Council, and decided it was 'the final straw, the spark that caused the powder keg to blow up'.[45] Many councillors also recognised the root causes of conflict. Alexandra's mayor, Sam Buti, accepted that increasing rents[46] '. . . would throttle our people. It would be absurd if the development of Alexandra were to become a threat to our own people. The uprisings in black townships is tied to this same issue'.

Faced with the depth of opposition in the townships (and the consequent difficulties of using Councils as a route to political leadership), councillors across the PWV resigned. Before the end of November, at least 38 councillors had resigned in Ratanda,

Tsakane, Duduza, Evaton, Atteridgeville, Tembisa, Tumahole and from the Lekoa Town Council.[47] The threat of violent attacks on their lives and property had clearly provided an extra incentive, but no threat had yet developed in several of these townships. The following May, Atteridgeville councillor I Mosuma declared:[48] 'I now agree with the UDF for calling us puppets who are only good at evicting people who do not qualify to stay in Atteridgeville. We are sitting here with big agendas and doing nothing at all.'

The impression given in the media of events since September 1984 is one of violent conflict spreading from one township to another, with each 'hot spot' soon reclining into apparent passivity, soon replaced under the spotlight by another township. This picture confirms for many whites the government's allegations that violence is orchestrated by a central and revolutionary organisation.

Despite the broad sweep of capital accumulation, state oppression, and most recently progressive national organisation (through the UDF, COSAS, and FOSATU), the links between townships throughout 1984 remained poor and co-ordination almost non-existent. However, whilst incidents of violent confrontation can only be understood in terms of the history of each individual township (which, unfortunately, remains largely unknown outside of the township itself), it is possible to generalise about trends across townships. This is because the escalation to violent conflict has primarily arisen through heightened state repression. Generalisation is, therefore, in terms of the state's responses in the first instance, and only indirectly in terms of political processes within townships.

Levels of political mobilisation rose throughout the PWV region during late 1984, as reflected in the November 1984 stayaway, resignations by local councillors, and rising death tolls. During 1985 and early 1986, high levels of mobilisation were sustained and generalised, with chronic resistance through rent and consumer boycotts erupting on occasions into virtual civil war (perhaps the best reported example in the PWV being in Alexandra in early 1986). The range of magisterial districts in the PWV covered by the first State of Emergency, declared in July 1985, indicated the geographical scope of protest.

Behind this generalisation and entrenchment of resistance lay processes of radicalisation and convergence of political cultures. Educational grievances, rents, evictions, Councils, and repression were not seen as unconnected issues. Rents and evictions concerned moral, and therefore political, relations as well as economic problems, as discussed above. Educational grievances took on an importance outside of the schools when they too became disputes about who should hold the power to make key decisions. Heightened repression, as an overtly political response to discontent, tied all the issues together through developing the explicit political content in the moral economy or political cultures of township residents.

The experience of repression eroded any lingering legitimacy of the local state, polarised the townships between the supporters of the local state and the mass of more discontented residents, and broadened the latter group's demands. Rents and educational grievances could not be challenged without provoking a repressive response, and so mobilisation over these grievances led to mobilisation over the more fundamental issue of the power of the local state — i.e. who should control township administration and the instruments of repression. Two of the demands generated were the resignation of councillors and the withdrawal of troops from the townships. Higher rents were opposed not just because they could not be afforded and because they were not matched by development, as promised, but now also because, as protesters in the Vaal demanded: 'We won't be made to pay for our oppression.'[49]

In October, escalating state repression was made very apparent to Vaal residents by Operation Palmiet when 5,000 troops and 2,000 police sealed off and searched the Vaal townships house-by-house. The objective was variously described by the government as rooting out 'revolutionary . . . criminal and intimidatory forces', '[restoring] the situation to normal', and as ending lawlessness, or alternatively in terms of the demonstration of state authority. However, none of the 358 people arrested were charged under security legislation.[50]

The experience of successful progressive organisation served to combine with the experience of repression to cohere mobilisations into one movement. Participants realised that their grievances and demands were shared by many others and, more importantly, that they could act together with purpose. The convergence of political cultures constituted a growing homogenisation of residents' perceptions of an alternative definition of urban meaning. Castells suggests that[51]

> urban social movements . . . seem to develop around three major themes:
> (1) Demands based on collective consumption, that is goods and services directly or indirectly provided by the state.

(2) Defence of cultural identity associated with and organized around a specific territory.

(3) Political mobilisation in relationship to the state, particularly emphasising the role of local government.

Castells fails, however, to explore the interconnections between these three themes. In South Africa's black townships, political cultures have certainly not been static, with these changes both resulting from, and subsequently giving rise to, demands over collective consumption and local state power. The discourse and practice of politics have both shifted from quiescence to increasingly assertive forms of resistance and direct action. Mobilisations in the townships have recently come to constitute a 'movement' through the convergence and radicalisation of residents' demands.

However, whilst perceptions have converged, there obviously still remain diverse political cultures and diverse priorities in terms of changing the conditions of township life. These concern just how fundamental a political change is required in the short term, and what urban public services should be provided first.[52]

The first manifestation of the emerging active and radical solidarity was the Transvaal stayaway of 5–6 November.[53] According to the Labour Monitoring Group, 'The successful 2-day stayaway . . . marks a new phase in the history of protest against apartheid; the beginnings of united action among organised labour, students and community groups — with unions taking a leading role.' The initiative for the stayaway came from students, who sought older residents' support in their struggle in the schools, which was in danger of flagging as end-of-year exams approached. However, the impetus came from union leaders and regional political organisers (but not the regional UDF leadership). The demands reflected the coming together of diverse grievances: democratically elected SRCs, the abolition of the age limit and of corporal punishment, and an end to sexual harassment in the schools; the withdrawal of troops from the townships and the release of all detainees, no increases in rents, bus fares or service charges, and the reinstatement of workers dismissed by a local employer (Simba Quix). Students and union leaders had emphasised the basic similarity between their demands in the schools, and workers' demands in the workplace.

The number of workers involved in the stayaway is uncertain, with the LMG estimating a minimum of 300,000 and a maximum of 800,000. The number of students boycotting school was put by the government at 400,000. The stayaway was strongest in the East Rand, Vaal, and Atteridgeville, i.e. those areas which had seen greatest mobilisation and greatest state repression. The strongest support was in townships in which the state took unwarranted violent action on the eve of the stayaway — for example, in Duduza, where two residents had been killed by police at a funeral on 4 November. Support was weak on the West Rand, Mamelodi, and among commuters from the Bophutatswana townships.

Social composition of the movements

Different groups of residents have not all played identical roles in these processes of mobilisation. It is clear that young people have played a leading role in many of the most visible protests since mid-1984. This has led to some analyses suggesting that there are two 'poles' to township resistance, the so-called 'youth' and the 'workers'.[54]

Despite the extensive use of the term 'youth' in liberal and press analyses, it is unclear who these people really are. As a generational term, it presumably should comprise young workers, and young women doing household work, as well as the young unemployed and students. Youth congresses generally exclude students, but include residents up to quite a late age. In the case of the Soweto Youth Congress (SOYCO), the age limit was set at 38.[55] Many youth congress activists are therefore young workers. In the liberal and press usage, however, 'youth' seems to refer to anyone who engages in 'unrest' (i.e. violent conflict), most of whom are of course less than 38, but few of whom are in work.[56]

There are many reasons why younger generations are likely to play a major role in any protest. Firstly, there are simply very large numbers of young people. Secondly, both students and unemployed people, many of whom are young, have more time than their employed elders. Schools regenerate new cadres annually, and provide a relatively invulnerable nurturing space for organisational skills. Specific to South Africa's schools is the persistence and immediacy of educational grievances, and an accentuated sense of injustice in terms of both education and national politics. In the Vaal, students in the late 1970s were the most aware of Council corruption.[57] Finally, there emerged a widespread sense of elders having abdicated responsibility for political leadership, based on the reality of many parents having grown disillusioned, having accepted the 'imperative' of individual advancement through education rather than mass action, or remaining distracted by other structures including Councils and workplace-bound unions. This sense of role was no doubt influenced by the record of Soweto in 1976–7.

However, the interrelations between different age-groups in most townships defy any simple dichotomisation between 'workers' and 'youth'. In some cases there is an organisational gulf and even ill will between members of different age-groups, but generational differences seem to be the characteristics, and not the causes, of such divisions.

In Tumahole, students lacked the confidence to organise in the schools before mid-1984, but they had grievances, many of which were shared by their parents. Thus, for example, students were prevented from writing exams unless they wore the school uniform and paid school fees (although DET policy was officially more flexible), which hit poorer families, and the secondary school principal's overbearing manner antagonised parents as well as students. Where education is seen as a possible means of sons (and sometimes daughters) raising themselves out of their parents' poverty, parents are likely to be wary of disrupting school but also will be concerned with 'unreasonable' actions by principals.[58]

When Tumahole residents began protesting over rents, secondary school students participated. One explained his reasons:

> I was washing clothes in the yard when I saw many people marching in the next street. I went to see what was going on . . . I joined the march because I saw the placards against high rents. I thought that it was better if my parents spent that money on me. We had very little money to buy clothes and things. That is what encouraged me to join the rent issue.

Many students recognised the links between poverty and rents, and some saw an outlet for their frustrations. The students' participation was welcomed. In Tumahole, students and unemployed ex-students had a 'responsible' image with older residents. In 1980, a students organisation had been formed by former students to serve as a social organisation for students, a fund-raising welfare organisation in the township, and a medium for raising political topics. These three themes came together in drama productions. Younger residents' public spiritedness and their role in opposing councillors earned their elders' respect.

After the July protests, the students were more assertive in

219

school, overcoming their previous passivity and sense of powerlessness, and protesting over both educational and consciously political demands. A major factor in this transformation was their experience of conflict, first on 15 July, and later when educational grievances gave rise to violent confrontation between 20 and 21 August. The experience of arrest, and the sense of the need to revenge the death of comrades, brought formerly timid supporters openly into 'the struggle'. Students' experience of success, when the principal left Tumahole, underlined their new found power.

Parents were supportive of the students' own protests, although many feared the police reaction. When conflict turned violent, and students began petrol-bombing the houses of 'collaborators', older residents seem to have remained supportive. It was widely recognised that violence followed unprovoked police repression rather than preceding and, in some sense, provoking it. Moreover, the targets were precisely those people who had sacrificed legitimacy with older residents through the rent issue and subsequent repression, i.e. councillors and black police. Thus, when the Secondary School Board held the meeting with the parents to discuss school boycotts, and did not want to allow students to attend, the parents insisted that they be allowed to do so. At another meeting, a parent said that he wanted the children to go to school, to which a student replied: 'You go to school and experience what we are experiencing there, we are not going to school; if you want to go to school, give us your overalls, we will go to work, you can go to school.' Even the more cautious parents seem to have found this convincing. Perhaps parents are brought nearer to their children because of the high incidence of unemployment and low incomes.

In Tumahole, generational differences did not deepen to the point of tension. When primary school children became militant in 1985, parents were initially opposed to it; but unwarranted and indiscriminate police brutality seem to have changed parents' attitudes. In many townships, residents established parents committees to mediate in school disputes. A Tumahole Parents Committee was set up in 1984. According to someone who was not a member, 'Its purpose was to deal with the students' grievances, as the students did not want the school board, which they said was working with the principal and the authorities, never meeting their demands.' In KwaThema, a parent-student committee was formed in October 1984, and organised a local stayaway on the 22nd, which was an important model for the Transvaal stayaway between 5 and 6 November.

Duduza students first protested over the dismissal of a popular teacher, long after residents had taken up the sewerage issue and the councillors had been widely condemned. Here, as so often elsewhere, students became involved in protests outside the schools when they were subjected to unwarranted repression.[59] Similar processes have been identified in the western Cape.

As was the case in 1976 and 1980, containment and repression of opposition by the state accelerated mass support for protest and resistance. On numerous occasions actions by small groups of activists swelled into community response after violent security force responses . . .[60]

In some townships, parents initially reacted in a very hostile way to student protests, even forming vigilante groups to discipline the students. This was most common where students protested before older residents had themselves begun to mobilise. In most townships, however, the state's reaction to mobilisation (among students and older residents) led to greater support. One mother in Atteridgeville said (after the DET had closed the schools):[61]

We are all very depressed and concerned about the future of our children. We never thought it would go this far . . . But we as parents are partly to blame. The instigators are our children and we should have taken up matters that came out after the 1976 and 1977 boycotts.

The role played by younger residents has increased in visibility and importance during 1985–6 as,

(1) the pattern of political mobilisation has changed, and (2) active protest has spread to some previously quiescent townships through the medium of students.

The most important feature of the changing pattern of mobilisation has been the rising incidence of violent conflict. This has been primarily due to rising levels of state and vigilante repression, but has become rooted through the general process of polarisation whereby councillors and other identified 'collaborators' have become popularly legitimate targets for violent attack. Younger residents play a disproportionately active role in violent conflict, although this role is exaggerated in court appearances, as younger residents are more vulnerable to police harassment and charging. In some townships, there is a tension between militant residents tending towards the use of violence as a means of attaining immediate goals, and other equally militant residents tending towards organisational responses. In practice, there is no fine dividing line, but if these crude categories are accepted, it may often be the case that ex-students, whilst found in both groups, comprise a larger proportion of the former. In Tumahole, there was tension within the student leadership during 1984–5 that reflected this tension as well as personal rivalries.

Where consumer boycotts, for example, have been introduced in poorly mobilised townships, younger residents have assumed responsibility for 'supervising' them. If they have not been involved in mass participatory organisation (formal or informal), they have sometimes used violence or the threat thereof, rather than persuasion, to ensure solidarity. Thus, for example, in some Cape Town townships,[62]

> there had been increasing dissatisfaction on the part of many residents with the way in which the 'magabane' had 'monitored' the consumer boycott. They gave an example of how domestic workers . . . were forced to throw away groceries they had been given by their employers as it was assumed that the goods had been bought at 'white' shops. Others in the community had been forced to eat raw meat, detergent etc . . . It seems that the failure of the 'magabane' to explain the nature of these campaigns led to a conservative reaction on the part of some sections within the community.

Ekangala is a township with insignificant numbers of older students, because the population comprises families moved from Pretoria and East Rand townships, mostly with young children only. Whilst Ekangala residents have one very specific grievance, a high level of mobilisation shows how the social (and generational) composition of a township population shapes the form rather than the level of resistance.

The role of legitimising notions of justice in prompting protest is particularly clear in townships such as Ekangala, where the state has failed to fulfil the promises it made when it moved people to them. Dissatisfaction with the built environment led residents to form the Ekangala Action Committee, which successfully took up issues including rents and tariffs, shops and amenities, and the bus service to Ekangala. The issue to provoke unprecedented mobilisation, however, was the threat of incorporation into KwaNdebele and residents' experience of KwaNdebele-based vigilantes. Ekangala residents and even Ekangala Action Committee (EAC) activists were politically conservative, fully committed, for example, to negotiations and opposed to violence. However, the prospect of incorporation not only violated earlier promises made by East Rand Development Board officials, but also conflicted completely with their political culture. One of their objections to incorporation was their preference for 'location law' rather than the 'homeland system' — 'We are not a tribe', they wrote in a memorandum submitted to Pretoria. Rather than live in KwaNdebele, many of the residents were prepared to leave Ekangala together and occupy vacant land elsewhere on the East Rand.[63]

Women comprise one group of residents that is all too often ignored by both political activists and researchers, but they have not been inactive. They provided the initial impetus for rent protests and consumer boycotts in several townships. In Port Elizabeth, women 'were angry about police brutality, the state of the emergency, township conditions and the infighting between the UDF and AZAPO. The community's energy should be directed at the oppressors, they said.'[64] In addition, in Mamelodi, the Zakheni Women's Club played a central role in mobilising residents during 1984. It was women who constituted the core of the march to the Council offices in November 1985 to protest against high rents, the presence of troops in the township, and restrictions on funerals. Security forces dispersed the peaceful protesters, killing 13 in what became known as the Mamelodi massacre. It was outrage over this that generated solidarity behind Mamelodi's second consumer boycott.[65] In Duduza, women were especially prominent in meetings on the sewerage issue, because, as they complained, they were the people who had to empty the buckets. It was a woman who suggested direct action, taking the buckets to the administration offices, so that the township manager 'would feel the smell'.[66]

However, the initial impetus of women, and their specific concerns, have rarely been translated into a sustained organisational role. Women are possibly the least organised group of township residents, despite (indeed because of) the fact that they face specific problems, stemming from the sexual division of labour and the 'triple oppression', as women, as workers, and as blacks. Women are therefore likely to be under-represented in all township organisations except for specifically women's organisations, such as the

Zakheni Women's Club, based on a sexually defined constituency.[67]

Internal stratificaton within townships is becoming increasingly important with the growth of what is generally but perhaps not usefully called the black 'middle class'. The impact of stratification on township politics is examined in a separate paper, focusing on the shift from participation in local state structures to either involvement in violent reactionary activity through vigilantes, or participation in progressive organisation.[68]

Notes

The following abbreviations are used below:
SALB   *South African Labour Bulletin*
WIP   *Work in Progress*
SN   *SASPU National*
AP   *Africa Perspective*
RDM   *Rand Daily Mail*
WM   *Weekly Mail*

1. See especially: Shula Marks and Richard Rathbone (eds), *Industrialisation and social change in South Africa* (Longman, London, 1982); Belinda Bozzoli, (ed.), *Labour, townships and protest* (Ravan Press, Johannesburg, 1979), and *Town and countryside in the Transvaal* (Ravan Press, Johannesburg, 1983); Tom Lodge, *Black politics in South Africa since 1945* (Longman, London, 1983). I do not examine the nature of the 'revolt' of 1976–7, which, despite a now extensive literature, does not seem to have been fully unravelled. Outstanding questions include especially the interrelationship between different grievances, organisations, and social groups or classes in the townships concerned.

2. See contributions to the journal *Indicator SA*, especially: L. Schlemmer, 'Township unrest as seen by township residents', *Indicator SA*, vol. 2, no. 4 (January 1985); 'South Africa's urban crisis: the need for fundamental solutions', *Indicator SA*, vol. 3, no. 1 (Winter 1985); and 'Unrest: the emerging significance', *Indicator SA*, (Summer 1986); Graham Howe, 'Cycles of civil unrest 1976/84', *Indicator SA*, vol. 3, no. 1 (Winter 1985).

3. Howe, 'Cycles of civil unrest', p. 7.

4. Eddie Webster, 'Stayaways and the black working class: evaluating a strategy', *Labour, Capital and Society*, vol. 14, no. 1 (April 1981); Labour Monitoring Group, 'The November stayaway', *SALB*, vol. 10, no. 6 (1985); Mark Swilling, 'Stayaways, urban protest and the state' in South African Research Services, *South African Review Three* (Ravan Press, Johannesburg, 1986).

5. M. Bot, 'Schools boycotts 1984: the crisis in African education', Centre for Applied Social Studies, University of Natal, Durban (1985).

6. Jeff McCarthy and Mark Swilling, 'Transport and political

resistance' in *South African Review Two* (Raven Press, Johannesburg, 1984); and 'South Africa's emerging politics of bus transportation', *Political Geography Quarterly* (July 1985).

7. Ingrid Obery and Karen Jochelson, 'Consumer boycott: driving a wedge between business and the state', *WIP*, no. 39 (October 1985); Roland White, 'A tide has risen, a breach has occurred: towards an assessment of the strategic value of the consumer boycotts', *SALB*, vol. 11, no. 5 (April-May, 1986); J. Seekings, 'Workers and the politics of consumer boycotts, *SALB*, vol. 11, no. 6 (July, 1986).

8. For references on differentiation within townships, see: J. Seekings, 'Reform, repression, and the changing political terrain in South Africa's black townships', paper presented at the Review of African Political Economy conference, Liverpool, September 1986.

9. Although I use the term black, I am generally only concerned with the residents of 'African' townships, i.e. excluding townships defined in law as 'coloured' or Indian. This limitation reflects both my sources, and the real political differences resulting from what are, to some extent, 'racially' distinct processes of class formation and 'racially' defined political institutions.

10. My research subsumed an area that extends rather wider than the PWV as generally defined. It is necessary to include those settlements in the bantustans of Bophutatswana and KwaNdebele which lie within the complex of commuter labour markets of the Pretoria, the Rand, and the Vaal Triangle. My use of 'the PWV' therefore approximates to the state's proposed Development Region H.

11. The study of township politics is further discussed in J. Seekings, 'The anvil: the politics of township conflict, 1976–86', unpublished BA (Hons) dissertation, Department of Political Studies, University of the Witwatersrand, Johannesburg, February 1986.

12. Manuel Castells, *The urban question* (1972; Edward Arnold, London, 1977).

13. Cf. Chris Pickvance, 'From social base to social force: some analytical issues in the study of urban protest' in Michael Harloe (ed.), *Captive cities* (John Wiley, Chichester, 1977); Peter Saunders, *Urban politics: a sociological interpretation* (Hutchinson, London, 1979): Patrick Dunleavy, *Urban political analysis* (Macmillan, London, 1980); M. Castells, *The city and the grassroots* (Edward Arnold, London, 1983); Stuart Lowe, *Urban social movements: the city after Castells* (Macmillan, London, 1986).

14. Castells, *The city and the grassroots*.

15. Seekings, 'The anvil', part 1.

16. Quoted in Robin Bloch, 'All little sisters got to try on big sister's clothes: the community council system in South Africa', *AP*, no. 21 (1982), p. 50. Also see Bloch and Peter Wilkinson, 'Urban control and popular struggle: a survey of state urban policy', *AP*, no. 20 (1982); Simon Bekker and Richard Humphries, *From control to confusion: the changing role of the Administration Boards in South Africa, 1971–1983* (Shuter and Shooter, Pietermaritzburg, 1984); Jeff McCarthy, 'Progressive politics and crises of urban reproduction in South Africa: the case of rents and transport', paper presented to the African Studies Institute Seminar, University of the Witwatersrand, September 1985. The best account of recent changes in

the broad structural context is Billy Cobbett, *et al.*, Chapter 2 in this volume.

17. E.P. Thompson, 'The moral economy of the English crowd in the eighteenth century', *Past and Present*, vol. 50 (February 1971).

18. Castells, *The city and the grassroots*: p. 303.

19. Benedict Anderson, *Imagined communities* (Verso, London, 1983); cf. Kelwyn Sole, 'Culture, politics and the black writer: a critical look at prevailing assumptions', *English in Africa*, vol. 10, no. 1 (May 1983), for a criticism of the notion of community in black literature; also J. Seekings, 'The anvil', pp. 12–14.

20. The recommodification of housing has involved: the reintroduction of 30-year leasehold (1976) and later extension to 99-year leasehold (1978), the sanctioning of 'self-help' housing strategies (1980), the state's massive house-selling programme (1983), and most recently the introduction of freehold (1985); cf. Alan Mabin and Sue Parnell, 'Recommodification and working-class home ownership: new directions for South African cities?, *South African Geographical Journal*, vol. 65, no. 2 (1983); and Paul Hendler, A. Mabin and S. Parnell, 'Rethinking housing questions in South Africa' in *South African Review Three* (Ravan Press, Johannesburg, 1986), pp. 195–207.

21. Cf. Laurine Platzky and Cheryl Walker of the Surplus People Project, *The surplus people: forced removals in South Africa* (Ravan Press, Johannesburg, 1985).

22. Quoted in Bekker and Humphries, *From control to confusion*, p. 111. On Councils also cf. Bloch, 'All little sisters'; Heather Hughes and Jeremy Grest, 'The local state' in *South African Review One* (Ravan Press, Johannesburg, 1983), pp. 122–41; J. Grest and H. Hughes, 'State strategy and popular response at the local level' in *South African Review Two* (Ravan Press, Johannesburg, 1984), pp. 35–62.

23. 'Katlehong removals', *SALB*, vol. 8, no. 6 (June 1983); Swilling, 'The politics of working-class struggles in Germiston, 1979–83', unpublished History Workshop paper, University of the Witwatersrand, Johannesburg, February 1984; 'Shack City hopes are bulldozed to dust', *SN*, vol. 4, no. 1 (March 1983). On Daveyton and Tokhoza: 'Koornhof attempts to bring dummy Community Councils to life', *SN*, vol. 4, no. 4 (October 1983).

24. *SASPU Focus*, vol. 1, no, 3 (December 1982); *SN* vol. 4, no. 1, March 1983); Nigel Mandy, *A city divided: Johannesburg and Soweto* (Macmillan, Johannesburg, 1984), p. 235.

25. Baznaar Moloi, former Secretary of the Katlehong FOSATU Shop Stewards Council, quoted in Katlehong removals'. Alf Stadler has detailed the same responses in Soweto in the 1940s in 'Birds in the cornfield: squatter movements in Johannesburg, 1944–1947', *Journal of Southern African Studies*, vol. 6, no. 1 (October 1979).

26. Quoted in 'Katlehong removals'.

27. *SN*, vol. 2, no. 3 (May 1981).

28. *SN*, vol. 1, no. 3 (December 1982).

29. *City Press*, 20 April 1983.

30. *Star*, 14 February 1985.

31. Interviews conducted in Duduza by Menachemson and Seekings, April-May 1986; press clippings.

32. Seekings, 'The anvil', pp. 19–21. Makgotlas were 'traditional'

courts, widely discredited during the 1970s through the corruption of 'tradition', generally by councillors.

33. I am greatly indebted to Matthew Chaskalson for sharing his appreciation of the background to the Uprising, which he is currently researching. Notes: The Lekoa Town Council's jurisdiction covers the townships of Sebokeng, Bophelong, Boipatong, and Sharpeville (north of the Vaal), and Zamdela (south of the Vaal).

34. *SN*, vol. 5, no. 1 (March 1984); Mandy, *A city divided*, pp. 240–4. Sofasonke's leader, millionaire 'ET' Tshabalala, still tries to play a populist/patronage line, recently settling squatters on the Soweto golf course (for a small fee, of course).

35. Interviews with Mamelodi residents, conducted by Janet Hersch, Jochelson, and Seekings, April-May 1986; press clippings; Georgina Jaffee, 'Beyond the cannons of Mamelodi, *WIP*, no. 41 (April 1986), pp. 9–10. I am very grateful to Janet Hersch and Karen Jochelson.

36. *SN*, vol. 4, no. 3 (September 1983).

37. Interviews with Atteridgeville residents, conducted by Hersch and Jochelson, April-May 1986; press clippings.

38. Interviews with Ratanda residents by A. Creecey and others; press clippings, especially *SN*, vol. 5, no. 5 (September 1984), and vol. 5, no. 7 (December 1984).

39. Seekings, 'The anvil', pp. 31–40.

40. This is recorded in the official minutes for the meeting, drawn up by the OVDB; cf. Seekings, 'The anvil', pp. 62–4.

41. S. Bekker, 'The local government and community of Sebokeng', unpublished mimeo (1978).

42. On the background to the Vaal Uprising, see: evidence presented before the Delmas Treason Trial (1986); the Report of the Van der Walt Commission of Enquiry into Education for Blacks in the Vaal Triangle following upon the Occurrences of 3 September 1984 (1985). The range of factors involved can be seen in terms of the scale of the response proposed by the OVDB.

43. 'Vaal in flames', *SN*, vol. 5, no. 5 (September 1984); Johannes Rantete, *The third day of September* (Ravan Press, Johannesburg, 1984); Southern African Catholic Bishops Conference, *Report on police conduct during township protests, August-November 1984* (1985).

44. *RDM*, 5 September 1984, 7 September 1984, 25 September 1984.

45. Van der Walt Report. Although the Commission was set up to look into the educational crisis specifically, Van der Walt recognised that this could not be viewed in isolation. The Report was only published after a long delay, but parts were leaked earlier; cf. *WM*, 2 May 1986.

46. *Sunday Express*, 9 December 1984.

47. Thirty-three are listed in the *Star*, 16 March 1985, and I have added five from Tumahole. The actual number was certainly higher.

48. *Star*, 30 May 1985; see also Seekings, 'Reform, repression'.

49. 'Vaal in flames'.

50. *RDM* and the *Star*, 23 October 1984, *Star*, 27 October 1984, *RDM*, 2 November 1984; 'The townships are occupied', *SN* vol. 5. no. 7 (December 1984); also Gavin Cawthra, *Brutal force: the apartheid war machine* (IDAF, London, 1986), pp. 244–7.

51. Castells, *The city and the grassroots*, p. xviii.

52. One interesting survey in the eastern Cape suggests that 'petty bourgeois' grievances concern education and housing quality primarily, whilst blue collar workers' grievances are with high rents and charges, and the low quality of amenities and public transport. Cf. McCarthy, 'Progressive politics'.

53. Labour Monitoring Group, 'The November stay-away'; M. Swilling, 'Stayaways'. See also the COSAS pamphlet reproduced in *SALB*, vol. 10, no. 6 (May 1985), pp. 99-100.

54. For example, Stephen Gelb, Jon Lewis, M. Swilling and E. Webster, 'Working-class politics and national liberation in South Africa', unpublished mimeo (1985).

55. 'Soweto youth on the move', *SN*, vol. 4, no. 4 (October 1983).

56. L. Schlemmer's article 'Township unrest as seen by township residents' is based on surveyed responses to the following question: 'Why do you think that young people in the townships are behaving the way they do?'

57. Bekker, 'Sebokeng'.

58. Seekings, 'The anvil'; Seekings, 'A town where 14-year-olds battle police', *WM*, 25 April 1986.

59. See note 31.

60. Papers by Colin Bundy and M. Hall were reported in the *WM*, 25 July 1986.

61. *Evening Post*, 1 June 1984.

62. Nicholas Haysom, 'Mabangalala: the rise of right-wing vigilantes in South Africa', *Centre for Applied Legal Studies, University of the Witwatersrand, Johannesburg, Occasional Paper*, no. 10 (1986), pp. 108-16; Differential involvement in consumer boycotts is discussed in Seekings, 'Workers and the politics of consumer boycotts'.

63. Interviews in Ekangala, April-May 1986; newsletters of the Transvaal Rural Action Committee.

64. Obery and Jochelson, 'Consumer boycott', p. 13.

65. *SN*, vol. 6, no. 3 (December 1985); see note 35.

66. See note 31.

67. Cf. Seekings, 'Workers and the politics of consumer boycotts'.

68. Cf. Seekings, 'Reform, repression'.

9

State of Exile: The African National Congress of South Africa, 1976–86

Tom Lodge

The environment of exile politics is usually viewed as hazardous, sterile, corrosive and demoralising. Political groups which are forced out of their domestic terrain are understood to be especially vulnerable; loneliness, frustration, inactivity, hardship and insecurity generate ideological dissent, personality conflicts, and escapist delusions. Exile politicians are forced into a dependent relationship with their hosts and patrons, whose hospitality and generosity may be conditional and subject to capricious change. Survival and success in such an environment may depend on skills and talents quite different from those developed in the history of the movement before its departure from home. It could require ideological innovations which risk distancing it from its original social constituency. Exile is usually perceived as an experience which is inherently detrimental and problematic.

The understanding of exile as a term of trial for political organisations has been consolidated by the study of movements which have been especially badly affected by their displacement.[1] Outstanding in the studies of African exile politics is John Marcum's work based on the history of Angolan Nationalist organisations.[2] Marcum's analysis of the difficulties of exile has influenced many other academic commentaries.[3] Those historians of exile movements which have prospered or flourished have understood their success as being achieved despite the pitfalls of exile, usually as the result of the reinsertion of leadership and followers back within their native territory.[4]

The approach in this chapter is rather different. Here the subject is an organisation whose bureaucracy, structures and disciplined following exist outside its country, yet which has not only survived exile but has, it will be argued, been strengthened by the experience. The African National Congress (ANC) has been an exile body for over two decades. Its survival during the first phase of exile during which it was unable to initiate any significant political or military activity within South Africa has been described in an earlier essay by this author.[5] My concern here will be with its development in the post-1976 phase, in the ten years since the political reawakening inside South Africa represented by the Soweto Uprising. The ANC's activities inside the country since 1976 will not be detailed here: they lie outside the focus of this chapter, which deals with the ANC's external presence and functions. It is sufficient to state that accompanying the development of the exile movement over the last ten years, and contributing very significantly to its buoyant morale and diplomatic impact, has been the revival of an internal guerrilla insurgency. The guerrilla warfare, though still at a very modest level, has been steadily increasing its scope and effectiveness in quite exceptionally difficult circumstances. The tables below provide an indication of the present character of guerrilla activity.

Table 9.1: African National Congress guerrilla activity 1977–86: annual numbers of incidents

1977	23
1978	30
1979	13
1980	19
1981	55
1982	39
1983	56
1984	44
1985	136
1986 (to 30 June)	118

The insurgent campaign has succeeded in re-establishing the ANC as the predominant force in black African politics, even if its support is still mainly in the form of ideological inclination and emotional sentiment rather than organised membership.[6]

The apparent self-confidence and vitality of the ANC exiles at present is certainly partly attributable to the ANC's success in re-establishing a presence within the townships of South Africa; but it will have to be contended that this is not the whole story. The terrain of exile is not wholly disadvantageous for the development of a political movement. It can provide protection, security, powerful forms of external support, factors and conditions which facilitate

Table 9.2: *Guerrilla activity, July 1985 to June 1986: numbers of incidents*

Descriptions	1 July–31 December 1985	1 January–30 June 1986
Attacks on police or police facilities; police/Umkhonto clashes	25	50
Attacks on SADF personnel or buildings	6	0
Attacks on homeland politicians, community councillors, and other individuals	22	9
Land-mine explosions	6	11
Limpet mine attacks on economic infrastructure (mainly Electricity Supply Commission (Escom) sub-stations)	9	26
Limpet mine attacks on railway facilities	2	3
Limpet mine attacks or bombings on commercial premises used by civilians during business hours	1	4
Limpet mine or bomb attacks in or outside hotels or restaurants during business hours	0	4
Gunfire attacks on commercial premises during business hours	0	1
Grenades thrown in crowded business districts	1	0
Limpets in central business districts out of business hours	15	2
Limpets in or outside recreational facilities out of hours	0	2
Attacks on government or public buildings	1	0
Others/unspecified	0	5
TOTAL	88	117

the development of a form and quality of organisation unattainable in the precarious circumstances of opposition politics within the homeland.

What follows is a sketch of the bureaucracy which the ANC has created in a foreign environment. After examining the workings and functions of different sections of the ANC's organisation, the chapter will discuss in turn ANC diplomacy, the character of the ANC's leadership, and the recent development of ideology. The chapter concludes with an assessment of the political implications of the ANC's experience and formation during its period of exile.

The ANC's political and bureaucratic organisation is elaborate and extensive. At the summit of the movement is a 30-member National Executive Committee (NEC) elected and enlarged at the 1985 Kabwe Consultative Conference. The NEC had last been elected at a similar meeting in 1969, its membership augmented through co-option rather than election from an original group of nine to the 22 members on the eve of last year's elections. At Kabwe (Zambia) it was decided that consultative conferences should be held at five-year intervals and elections should accompany them. With many of its office-holders located in different countries, the NEC meets infrequently and everyday decisions are in the hands of a smaller working committee based in Lusaka (Zambia) and chaired by Oliver Tambo, or in his absence, the Secretary General, Alfred Nzo. NEC policy decisions are put into operation by two committees which are responsible for political (including trade union) and military activity within South Africa. A co-ordinating body supervises the work of these committees. All are subject to the authority of the NEC and were established in 1983 to replace the 'Revolutionary Council' which from 1969 had had the task of directing operations inside the Republic. In 1983 the Military Committee was chaired by Joe Modise, Commander-in-Chief of Umkhonto we Sizwe, while the first Chairman of the Political Committee was John Nkadimeng, General Secretary of the South African Congress of Trade Unions (SACTU).[7]

A secretariat, based in Lusaka since the early 1970s, employs thirty people in three sections, a President's Office, a treasury, and a division for external affairs. The external affairs section administers the ANC's diplomatic offices and representatives, a network which today embraces 22 countries, as well as the cultural, educational and health facilities which the ANC provides for its members. These include a complex of schools in Morogoro, southern Tanzania. The President's Office oversees the ANC's military establishment as well as its Information and Publicity Department.[8] Parallel though simpler structures exist for the Youth and Women's Sections, as well as SACTU which has its headquarters in Lusaka. Altogether 300 ANC people and their dependents are concentrated in Lusaka. Their numbers include the 80-man work-force on Chongella Estates, an old tobacco farm bought for the ANC by a Swedish development agency on which is grown much of the bureaucracy's food requirements (as well as crops for sale). Its 1,000 cattle graze peacefully in fields adjacent to a ranch owned by Anglo-American.[9] The ANC also runs a nursery school for children of people at the Lusaka headquarters. It provides food, health care and a uniform 14 Kwacha a month pocket-money to all members.

Estimates of the numbers of people involved in the exile movement vary. Observers disagree in particular about the size of the army, Umkhonto we Sizwe. Howard Barrell, a Harare (Zimbabwe)-based journalist whose writing is usually informed by ANC sources, suggested in a recent report that Umkhonto forces numbered 10,000, of which only 400 or so were operating inside South Africa.[10] American intelligence estimates are similar, though they categorise a larger number as being operational.[11] South African sources are more conservative, the Pretoria Institute of Strategic Studies assessing ANC strength at between 2,000 and 4,000.[12] In 1980, Steve Davis, an American scholar drawing upon interviews with ANC people, argued that the total ANC establishment numbered 9,000, of which 5,400 were military personnel (200–300 inside South Africa), and the rest being either administrative or educational.[13] ANC sources claim Umkhonto recruitment has increased very dramatically since September 1984[14] as an effect of the exodus of refugees from South Africa. The United Nations High Commission for Refugees distributes funds through the ANC for about 9,000 South African refugees,[15] so the higher estimates of ANC strength appear quite reasonable. Umkhonto we Sizwe is clearly the largest structure within the exile organisation and it seems sensible to begin any survey of the ANC's bureaucracy with an examination of Umkhonto's essential characteristics.

For the majority of the men and women who join the ANC's external organisation, joining the ANC means joining an army. Much of this army is accommodated in five training camps run by the ANC in Angola, two near Luanda, and the others in the north and north-east. Umkhonto recruits have been trained in Angola since 1977, before then most of the ANC's military instruction was conducted in Tanzania.[16] Umkhonto guerrillas often spend two years in Angola and a chosen elite supplements its basic training with advanced courses in the Soviet Union and the German Democratic Republic.

From the testimony of state witnesses and defectors at political trials, a fairly coherent picture of the contents of the military trained programme has emerged. ANC recruits join the organisation in territories neighbouring South Africa — most frequently Botswana or Swaziland — and after a screening process which is intended to weed out police agents, they are offered the choice of immediate military instruction or the completion of their academic education.[17] Only in 1985, at the Kabwe Conference, was experience of the military camps made compulsory for all ANC members. Prospective guerrillas, after their induction into the organisation and a few educational sessions concerning ideological essentials, are flown to Luanda, where they are placed in a reception camp. Here they receive introductory lessons in South African history and politics, lectures on explosives, map-reading and military tactics, as well as physical drilling and exercise sessions. Weapon-handling begins in a second camp; recruits are taught to handle automatic rifles, RPG 7 rocket-launchers, hand-grenades, as well as the light weaponry employed by the South African Defence Force. The instruction is usually supervised by Cubans[18] and its quality is excellent, according to South African police sources.[19] The trainees learn how to use explosives and deploy them in sabotage, they are taught the principles of clandestine organisation and communications, and they are instructed in guerrilla tactics as well as the military techniques employed in more conventional forms of welfare. The range of weaponry and equipment to which trainees are introduced is much wider than the variety actually used by Umkhonto in South Africa; apart from theoretical classes in the operation of heavy artillery, the Angolan trainees' programme has included lessons on the use of land-mines since 1977[20] — eight years before such devices were introduced into South Africa, as well as radio communications.

After the completion of basic guerrilla training, Umkhonto members are given more specialised courses, sometimes in a different camp: different programmes are arranged for rural and urban warfare, some people receive special training in ordinance and logistical support, and others (especially women)[21] graduate as couriers. The more proficient are sent to Europe, often to the Ukraine where they learn to handle more complicated weaponry:

Grad P rocket-launchers,[22] anti-tank weapons, mortars and heavy machine-guns — weapons which require a team to operate them and which are usually associated with mobile or conventional warfare rather than small-scale guerrilla operations. In Russia they learn more sophisticated sabotage techniques, as well as interrupting the curriculum with cultural excursions to collective farms, schools and factories.[23] Fully trained guerrillas are either immediately absorbed into operational duties or they are placed in holding camps and subjected to refresher courses.

At any one time, only a small proportion of trainees are involved in combat in South Africa. As yet it is a small-scale war; since the beginning of 1980 to mid-1986, the number of attacks carried out by Umkhonto totals less then 500. If each of these attacks was carried out by a different Umkhonto unit (which is not the case), then at most 2,000–3,000 Umkhonto people would by 1986 have had field experience — a minor proportion of their numbers. How are the rest deployed? Placing large numbers of men in holding camps for long periods of inactivity is an almost certain recipe for low morale and indiscipline. Reports of demoralisation and mutiny in ANC camps have been infrequent since 1977,[24] the year of resumption of guerrilla operations. It is likely that a proportion of trained guerrillas are used in the logistical support given to combat units — Umkhonto is organised on the basis of a very compartmentalised division of labour.[25]

The camps themselves require staffing and defending: Cubans and other non-South Africans provide technical expertise, but much of the direct instruction in all branches of the programme is given by Umkhonto members. Other ANC facilities require defending, especially in Front-line states. The training camps are supposed to provide their own food and each camp maintains a farm.[26] Then there is the possibility that those guerrillas not involved in the South African theatre may be engaged alongside MPLA troops fighting UNITA forces in Angola itself. Both UNITA spokesmen and ANC defectors have alleged that the ANC plays a role in the Angolan conflict.[27] It would not be the first time Umkhonto soldiers have fought on foreign soil; ANC units participated in joint offensives with ZAPU in 1967–8 and again in 1978–80.[28]

With the exception of those who go to Europe, the direct influence on them of their East European and Cuban instructors is confined to technical matters. Paralleling the military training is an extensive academic programme with a heavy emphasis on South African history, political economy and philosophy. The teaching is by South Africans, in the early stages of the development of the camps by eminent leaders of the ANC and the South African Communist Party (SACP), later on administered by the hierarchy of political commissars who provide a second element in the command structure of the camps from platoon level upwards. The academic programme includes courses in the history of South African resistance, ANC ideological principles, especially those associated with the Freedom Charter, the analysis of the South African economy and the basic essentials of Marxism-Leninism. Some of the political education was reportedly a cause of dissatisfaction among recruits for it reflected the ideology of a left-wing leadership which had emerged ascendent within the ANC during the 1950s and 1960s, and which was out of step with the intellectual background of recruits influenced by the Black Consciousness Movement of the early 1970s.[29] This does not seem to have been an enduring problem, probably because of the shift in black political culture within South Africa since 1976. Considering the location of the camps, the sources of externally supplied training and resources available to Umkhonto, and the strong association of the SACP with the Umkhonto hierarchy from its inception in 1961, it would not be surprising if the camps were an important source of radicalising impulse with the ANC as a whole.

Umkhonto operations and logistics are directed and administered through Botswana and other territories adjacent to South Africa, but the vulnerability of these countries, and their governments' attitudes to Umkhonto, rules out the development of large military bases by the ANC within their borders.[30] Umkhonto's command structure was until the 1984 Nkomati accord largely located in Maputo,[31] but that is no longer possible and leading Umkhonto officers seem to work for most of the time in Lusaka or in Angola. Political and military leadership within the ANC is closely intertwined, the three most senior Umkhonto officers are all members of the NEC, and at least one-third of NEC members have military experience.[32]

Umkhonto is a bureaucratically complicated, technically sophisticated and operationally effective organisation. Its training programme produces highly motivated and militarily accomplished combatants whose quality has been proven in the progress Umkhonto has made in developing an insurgent campaign inside the Republic.[33] It is still, though, largely an exile army: only quite recently has its organisational structure within South Africa advanced beyond individual and mutually isolated cells or units.[34]

Despite a formal commitment to democratic principles reflected in the absence of privileges associated with rank[35] as well as periodic attempts by military and political leaders to make themselves personally accessible to rank and file, the organisation is hierarchical, elitist[36] and disciplined.[37] This is in keeping with its East European models of external military inspiration and is also appropriate with a military organisation whose leaders conceive its future development as advancing through increasingly sophisticated phases of warfare. South Africa is a modern industrial state; the armed force which seeks to overcome its defences requires a matching bureaucratic and technological quality, and this is difficult to reconcile with prerequisites of democracy.

The second largest wing of the ANC's organisation also provides a haven for a substantial number of its youthful recruits. The ANC's educational establishment is situated in Morogoro, the isolated area in south-eastern Tanzania where the organisation used to have its guerrilla training camps. The need for the ANC to provide secondary schooling for its adherents became especially pressing in the wake of the Soweto riots when it began receiving large numbers of refugee school children. A school was first established in a few farm buildings on a 600-acre site in Mazimba, Morogoro, the land being donated by the Tanzanian government in 1977.[38] The following year the ANC created a Department of Education and Culture, a complex pyramid of committees which linked leading office bearers in the ANC, SACTU, Youth and Women's sections to the administration of the school.[39] Starting wth 50 students, by the end of 1980 student enrolment had increased to nearly 200, taught by 20 teachers. An elaborate building programme began in 1980 and three years later, 1,000 pupils were accommodated at Mazimba. Numbers seem to have stabilised since then: today the ANC community at Mazimba totals about 1,500, including teachers, administrative staff, and infants and primary school children.[40]

As well as the secondary school, the Solomon Mahlangu Freedom College (SOMAFCO), the complex houses the Charlotte Maxeke Child Care Centre,[41] a creche, a hospital and a maternity home, three small factories which supply furniture, clothing and food, a photographic laboratory and 800 hectares of farm land which make Mazimba self-sufficient in maize, sorghum and beans. SOMAFCO itself has well equipped classrooms, a library and several dormitory buildings. The planning and construction of the buildings were executed by ANC members, but the finance for the facilities came from outside. The single most important donors have been Swedish, both private and governmental, though Dutch anti-apartheid organisations and United Nations (UN) agencies have also given substantial support. In 1982 SOMAFCO's budget alone amounted to $5.5 million.[42] As well as externally derived financial support, the ANC has also begun to appeal for volunteer teachers; certain British Labour Party-controlled local education authorities recently announced plans to recruit and pay British teachers to work at Mazimba.[43]

Apart from the normal concerns of educationists, the teaching staff at Mazimba have two particular preoccupations. Firstly, there is the object of providing the ANC with people possessing the vocational skills required for government. In the words of SOMAFCO's principal, Comrade Njobe:[44]

We are thinking of educating to take over a country which is highly developed and therefore in our curriculum we stretch over ordinary academic subjects . . . to skills in the vocational and technical fields — commercial skills, secretarial skills and all skills along those lines.

Secondly, the curriculum itself and the way in which the school is administered are calculated to strengthen the influence of certain political and social principles. Thus, for example, considerable emphasis is placed on 'bridging the gap between mental and manual labour' — teachers and students spend several hours each week working on the farm. As far as is possible, the school stresses material self-sufficiency. Amongst the various subjects taught is a course on the 'Development of society'. Corporal punishment is prohibited. Student representatives participate in the deliberation of the School Administrative Committee.[45] Students run the hostels and also contribute to disciplinary decisions. To quote Njobe again: 'We are teaching to destroy all tendencies towards stratification of societies into exploiting classes. We would like to create a school of comradeship.'[46]

The ideas are of course very similar to those which are orthodox within the educational system of the ANC's host, and major benefactor, Tanzania. Over the seven years of the centre's existence, donors have clearly remained impressed, for the ANC has apparently gained a reputation for 'honest and competent use of resources'.[47] Scandinavian aid, which is principally directed at the ANC's educational projects, has increased rapidly: nearly $12 million was received by the ANC from Norway and Sweden in the course of 1985.[48] In 1986 $20 million is expected from these sources.[49]

The ANC's resources do not stretch to tertiary education. In 1983 it was estimated[50] that nearly 1,500 ANC members were being trained in British, European and American universities. This represents an impressive proportion of the total membership of the exile organisation. There are sizeable groups of students attending institutions in Holland, East Germany and the United States. Communist countries seem to have been especially significant in supplying to the organisation technical skills: agriculturists, paramedical workers and engineers. The wide variety of higher educational systems experienced by people destined to occupy senior positions within the movement is likely to ensure that it remains subject to eclectic intellectual influences. Regional educational committees in different parts of the world where there are concentrations of ANC students do provide one means of regulating the ideological predisposition of the student diaspora. Within the facilities at Mazimba, this is the task of political commissars appointed to the governing committees.

From 1977 the ANC has become predominantly an organisation of young men and women surmounted by senior echelons of soldiers and bureaucrats whose exile had in many cases preceded the births of their new disciples. The townships exodus in the couple of years following the Soweto Uprising brought to the ANC a mass of vigorous recruits whose intellectual development had been unaffected by the ideological tradition represented by the older ANC leaders. Davis, writing in 1981, refers to the 'neo-Africanism' of the post-1976 recruits and their impatience with the heavy emphasis on class analysis in the education received in the camps.[51] In 1950 the victory of ZANU in the Zimbabwean Chimurenga was rumoured to have reinforced the questioning within the rank and file of the ANC's customary political alignments.[52] Ian Smiley, writing in *The Times* in June 1983, reported that the ANC was contemplating a restoration of 'a more traditional black African image'.[53] In the same year, Tom Karis, an authoritative analyst of the ANC, suggested that the abolition of the Revolutionary Council and its replacement with committees more directly subject to the NEC may have been intended to emphasise the prominence of Africans in the organisation.[54] In the case of the ANC's African leaders, their manner and bearing as diplomats and, increasingly, statesmen, conflicted with the sartorial expectations of the teenage graduates of Soweto street battles. Oliver Tambo, an essentially unpretentious man, is not in the habit of donning combat fatigues on public occasions and this has allegedly been a source of some grumbling among ANC student communities.[55]

Administrative measures such as the provision of educational programmes or a political commissariat can help to bridge the gulf between different generations and echelons of ANC membership but they can only be part of the solution. Since 1981, which the ANC designated as the 'Year of the Youth', a conscious effort has been put into fostering an ideological base for young people. The Youth Section was re-invigorated at a special conference at Mazimba in 1982 under the leadership of Umkhonto cadres. The predominantly military role young people play inside the ANC was a theme which influenced much of the discussion:[56]

> . . . ANC youth have to fully come to terms with the fact that we are at war inside South Africa and we are not just here outside the country . . . It also means that membership of Umkhonto we Sizwe is, not only for those who are 'less educated' — intellectuals are needed in the field of battle. We are not talking about the 'battle of ideas' but the actual armed confrontation. We need engineers, scientists, technicians etc.
> — in the past we tended to concentrate on social sciences but now there is a shift in our ranks towards natural sciences.

The 15-man Youth Secretariat is apparently composed of men and women said to be 'steeped in conspiracy' and 'clandestine methods' with a reputation for fearlessness earning for them 'a good deal of respect from the older leaders'.[57] By the mid-1980s, though, the 'young lions' had left 'neo-Africanism' a long way behind them: many of their leaders were said to have joined the Communist Party as well as the ANC,[58] and an extensive process of discussion and debate preceded the election at Kabwe of the ANC's first 'non-racial' National Executive.[59]

Since 1980, of course, the ANC's youthful intake is being shaped by a popular political culture in which Black Consciousness is no longer pre-eminent. In South Africa the most powerful influences are being supplied by the burgeoning trade union movement, as well as the massive federation of local community and youth organisations led by the United Democratic Front (UDF). The UDF has itself been radicalised since its inception, partly as a result of the absorption into its leadership structures of the men from

Robben Island, the pioneers of the first Umkhonto guerrilla offensive of 1961-5. Today the ANC's ideas and iconography are intrinsic to South African black teenage subculture; and ideological disaffection with the 'second wave' of post-1984 recruitment is rather unlikely.

The original purpose of the ANC organisation which began to be built outside South Africa after 1960 was diplomacy, and this still remains one of the most important functions of the ANC's bureaucracy. Diplomacy is a vital sphere of ANC activity. It can secure financial and other forms of assistance in such a way as to minimise reliance on a single or narrow range of foreign allies. International legitimacy is crucial for the ANC in a conflict which already involves many powerful external interests. With foreign goverments poised to implement various sanctions against South Africa, the extent to which the ANC is recognised by these powers as being popularly representative has become all the more important. Most recently ANC diplomacy has assumed a fresh dimension, that of defining or developing the movement's relationship with a variety of interest groups and organised bodies inside the Republic.

The ANC receives its military equipment from the Soviet Union and other allied states. As we have seen, these countries also give military training and various forms of tertiary and vocational education of selected groups. The German Democratic Republic prints ANC and SACP literature. The assistance is significant for the ANC but does not represent massive allocations of these states' resources. Much of the weaponry is fairly old and unlike other insurgent armies in Southern Africa (for instance, SWAPO or UNITA) the ANC's arsenal consists largely of automatic rifles, hand-grenades, mines and sidearms. The ANC receives very little cash from Warsaw Pact donors.[60] It is accorded with hardware which no other states (with the exceptions, perhaps, of China and one or two African countries) are willing to supply, hospitality and recognition. ANC representatives in Eastern European countries are granted diplomatic status and treated with elaborate courtesy. It is a relationship of long standing: key ANC leaders visited the socialist bloc during the 1950s and the channel of military assistance was opened in 1962. Obviously the alliance with the SACP helped to keep it open without being a necessary condition for it. The affinities developed by the ANC in the international Cold War tensions of the 1950s and early 1960s also helped to bring it into alignment with the ideologically similar MPLA and Frelimo of Angola and Mozambique, establishing a relationship with both which was to be very helpful later on.

To what extent socialist bloc-derived help is reciprocated by the ANC is difficult to say. It is true that the ANC is supportive of Soviet positions in foreign policy: Tambo, for example, in his presentation of the NEC report at Kabwe, indicated sympathy for Soviet perceptions of issues in Afghanistan and Czechoslovakia — but neither is of vital concern to Southern African politics. It is likely that socialist donors place less value on such formal gestures of rhetorical courtesy than on the development of several generations of soldiers, technocrats and scholars now holding high office in the ANC who can be expected to have been intellectually influenced by their training in socialist institutions.[61]

Western-derived aid is of considerable importance to the ANC and probably needs more diplomatic effort to secure and maintain. The ANC has an international network of offices, though these are modest establishments, and the representation of the ANC in public is often allocated to fairly junior people. The ANC does not maintain a vast cadre of diplomats, but the few whom it does deploy in the United States, Western Europe and, since 1984, Australia, are extremely able.[62] In these countries the ANC has traditionally benefited from the activities of local anti-apartheid or anti-racist pressure groups; and in the case of the British anti-apartheid movement, the ANC had a role in its establishment and continues to work very closely with its leadership.

Britain has always been a centre of ANC diplomatic work and this is logical. Britain's links with South Africa are stronger than any other foreign power, there is an expatriate community of 50,000 South Africans living in Britain, and a long history of contact between left-wing and liberal British politicians and their black South African counterparts. The ANC's headquarters was once situated in London and a large number of older ANC and SACP members are permanently resident in Britain.[63] The long-established ANC presence in Britain is beginning to reap dividends. Quite apart from symbolic gestures of recognition — freedom of several British cities for Nelson Mandela and his statue on the bank of the Thames — the ANC has begun to have contacts with both the Foreign Office and Conservative politicians and has been promised more substantial favours by the Labour Party. ANC spokesmen use a language and have a manner which seems to evoke a warm public response in Britain: this is partly a reflection of the skill of their representatives, but it is also the result of familiarity and common elements of culture.[64]

Notwithstanding the lobbying experience of Mfanafuthi Makatini, their seasoned UN representative, the ANC's position in the United States is less certain. Until recently ANC presence in America was limited largely to students. Official American hostility to Marxism and the lack of American experience in dealing with radical anti-colonial movements used to ensure that ANC contact with US politicians was slight or inconsequential. Nevertheless the ANC has had a considerable impact on non-government circles. Oliver Tambo began what has become a succession of meetings with, or addresses to, multinational corporation executives from 1981. In 1982 the New York group of ANC activists had succeeded in attracting considerable media attention through pickets of 'tribal' musicals and were being asked to check and advise on forthcoming productions of South African related material.[65] The ANC presence in the USA was at least sufficiently developed to enable it to be cast in a leading role when the disinvestment campaign exploded on college campuses in 1984. This has now compelled the present US administration grudgingly to concede a degree of official contact with ANC representatives.

The Front-line states apart, the ANC seems to accord Africa rather a low priority in its diplomatic agenda. It is represented in only a sprinkling of African states outside of Southern Africa. African aid, with the exception of Zambia, Tanzania and Ethiopia, is usually administered through the Organisation of African Unity, and as Oliver Tambo has often publicly indicated, it is neither dependable nor substantial.[66] It is in Africa in which the ANC is chiefly confronted with the presence of a competitor, the Pan-Africanist Congress, which is still able to influence public and official perceptions in (at the least) Nigeria, Zimbabwe and Libya. The most important help which the ANC obtains from any foreign power is of course the accommodation provided by Zambia, Angola and Tanzania, but this today is the outcome of a relationship which is of a much deeper and more intimate character than that characterised by diplomacy. The ANC's relationship with other Front-line states is more problematic because of their vulnerability to South African pressure. Outstanding in its absence from the various expressions of congratulatory support from foreign governments and organisations at Kabwe was any mention of a greeting from Mozambique.[67] The ANC's experience in Mozambique, and the way it was kept ignorant of the events which culminated in the signature of the Nkomati pact, is a telling instance of the uneven quality of its African diplomacy.[68] It serves as a reminder of just how important diplomatic activity can be, especially in the case of a foreign country with the potential to influence South African events and with a non-committal approach to the ANC — the United States and Britain are two such examples.

The ANC's usual diplomatic work has been augmented by the beginning of a new phase of formal contacts with South African groups. Since September 1985 the Lusaka or Harare offices have entertained at least a dozen deputations. Beginning with a group of business men led by the Anglo-American Chairman, these have included representatives of the Progressive Federal Party, the Soweto Parents' Crisis Committee, the Federated Chamber of Industries, the National Convention Movement, Roman Catholic and Protestant churches, the Kngwane Inyandya movement, the Congress of South African Trade Unions, the National Union of South African Students, and the National African Federated Chambers of Commerce (NAFCOC) and the University of Cape Town. In some cases, as with the white business men, these talks have been exploratory, to elicit from the ANC its position on particular issues. In the case of COSATU and NAFCOC, intentions may have been more ambitious: both represent constituencies which may favour the ANC's accession to power, subject to certain assurances. In the case of Inyandya and the SPCC, visiting the ANC was a significant political statement: in Inyandya's case, setting it apart from other homeland-based groups; and with the SPCC, in endorsing its attempt to represent and lead the school children boycott movement.

These contacts are obviously beneficial for the ANC: they help to confirm its ascendency in black South African politics and open up the possibility of eroding the South African government's support base within the white community. They have their problematical dimension, though. Commenting on the talks, a SACP Politbureau document observed:[69]

> . . . a political readjustment in the ruling power block which favours its liberal bourgeoisie wing would undoubtedly create better objective conditions for the continuing struggle by the revolutionary forces to achieve the aims of national democratic revolution.
>
> Tactically, what flows from this?
>
> On the one hand we are justified in helping by all means (including talks) to advance the process of breaking the cohesion and unity of the ruling class and to isolate and weaken its most racist and politically reactionary class brothers . . .

We must expose their objective of co-opting forces from among the oppressed in order to frustrate the achievements of the main aims of the national democratic revolution.

We must not play into their hands by working out compromises (or being seen to work out compromises) for some hypothetical negotiating table . . .

Nor must a genuine desire to project a public image of 'reasonableness' tempt us to paddle softly on the true nature of the liberation alliance and its revolutionary socio-economic objectives.

At the same time we must not mechanically dig in our heels against any future possibility of negotiation with bourgeois forces.

The difficulty for the ANC leadership is that in such a process it can become increasingly difficult to distinguish between a tactical position and one representing a principle. This is especially the case when the ANC leadership itself is eclectically diverse and lacks a detailed conception of such issues as the precise role the state would play in the economy in a liberated South Africa. There is also the problem that whatever the intentions of the participants in such talks, these cannot always be easily communicated. This difficulty has obviously been worrying the ANC leadership:

[there is the] possibility that our movement will be in contact with levels of the ruling circles . . . that it has never dealt with before . . . [it is] vital [that we] should be of one mind about this development . . . to ensure . . . it does not have a negative effect on the development of the struggle.[70]

ANC spokesmen do seem to have made some allowances for the preoccupations and special concerns of their partners in these various talks. The key question for both business men and Western governments has been the extent and nature of economic nationalisation advocated by the ANC. Oliver Tambo and other ANC leaders have insisted on their commitment to a mixed economy, and have suggested that the level of private enterprise which would be a matter of debate, not something, to quote Tambo, that 'we . . . envisage fighting in the street over'.[71] The same point, incidentally, was made by Joe Slovo in his speech at the 65th anniversary celebrations of the SACP in London: ' . . . the continuing drive towards a socialist future . . . could well be settled in debate rather than on the streets'.[72] Oliver Tambo at the September 1985 meeting with South African business men speculated that ANC nationalisation measures might be limited to a 51 per cent state shareholding. This moderation well may be the reflection of principled beliefs rather than a tactical negotiating ploy: even the SACP has a theoretical commitment to a transitional phase of national democracy.[73] Nevertheless, ANC ambivalence on economic issues is out of step with more radical economic philosophies which prevail inside South Africa: UDF leaders proclaim the virtues of a 'peoples' dictatorship' in which private ownership would be restricted to boutiques and barber's shops.[74] Clearly, this was not the vision which Sam Motsuenyane and his colleagues in NAFCOC brought away with them from Lusaka.[75]

The ANC, like any other organisation in such a situation, uses different language for different constituencies. The gentle and courteous language of diplomacy and discussion with outsiders contrasts sharply with the strident and jargonised prose employed in its journal, *Sechaba*. In its radio broadcasts to South Africa, presumably directed at a popular audience, the language is especially harsh:

> The regime's police and soldiers who have been massacring our people in millions over the years still return to their homes and spend comfortable nights in the warmth of their beds . . . They must be haunted by the mass offensive. We must attack them at their homes and their holiday resorts just as we have been attacking their bootlickers at their homes. This must now happen to their white colleagues. All along it has only been the black mothers who have been mourning. Now the time has come that all of us must mourn. White families must also wear black costumes. [Domestic servants must play] a leading role. They know where their employers keep their weapons and they are the ones who can devise plans of transferring the ownership of these weapons.[76]

The issue of towards just whom violence should be directed seems to be one over which there is disagreement in the ANC. Reddy Mazimba, the ANC representative in Harare, was attributed with the injunction that 'White parents would have to go to the graveyards when the ANC's offensive reached white areas and white schools',[77] a threat which was swiftly repudiated by the ANC's Lusaka office.[78] ANC leaders maintain that white civilians *per se* will not be targets of attack, only incidental victims of 'crossfire'.[79] Joe Slovo referred to recent limpet mine explosions which killed or hurt civilians at bus stops and a Wimpy Bar as 'diversions and blemishes'.[80] Even within the narrower field of diplomacy, the ANC employs variations in rhetoric: in the United States its personalities describe the organisation as 'a community of love and justice [on a] pilgrim's road to freedom' and speak of their admiration for the values enshrined in the American Constitution,[81] while in a different context they proclaim their 'natural alliance with the Soviet Union and the world socialist system as a whole'.[82]

Such alterations of language and tone are inevitable and necessary in an organisation which has to preserve a balance between the requirements of loyalty and gratitude to its military patrons, assuaging the potential hostility of Western governments, and reassuring liberal allies within capitalist democracies, while at the same time retaining and expanding support within a heterodox collection of constituencies inside South Africa. They only represent a threat to the ANC's integrity if they open up ideological and strategic divisions within leadership or between leadership and following. As yet this does not appear to be a serious risk, but it should be bourne in mind that the ANC's leadership is socially and ideologically an eclectic one. I will conclude this survey of the exile organisation by looking briefly at the composition of its leadership and the different political traditions it represents.

The men and women elected at the Kabwe conference can be placed in four categories, each of which represents a significant group within the organisation. Firstly, there are the people whose political experience dates back to the nationalist revival of the ANC Youth League in the 1940s and who predominated in the mass-based militant populist campaigning of the 1950s. Oliver Tambo is representative of these, a former attorney and school teacher, whose moderate philosophy and disinterest in economic questions dates back to a period when the ANC's ideology expressed the concerns of a class alliance which had strong roots in the African middle class. Of the same age as the veterans of populist nationalism are the working-class leaders of the 1940s and the 1950s, many of them former trade unionists and SACTU office holders, and some of them also office holders within the Communist Party. John Nkadimeng, the late Moses Mabhida and also Joe Slovo (never in fact a trade unionist but currently the Chairman of the SACP) can be placed in this group. More radical in their socio-economic ideals, they nevertheless share many common areas of experience with the older nationalists: the decades of open multi-class and multi-communal campaigning of the 1950s, an aversion to extreme degrees of violence, the patience and caution of long years of exile, a dislike of utopian sectarianism,[83] and other elements of a common political outlook.

Then there are two younger groups. A considerable proportion of NEC leaders spent its politically formative years in the politics of violent and clandestine action of the 1960s, when the ANC's methods had of necessity to be those of a conspiratorial and clandestine elite. Within the country the ANC was reconstituted underground and was in the process considerably radicalised. Some of these men — Mac Maharaj and Jacob Zuma are two such cases — underwent lengthy prison sentences in Robben Island for their role in the first Umkhonto campaign. Meanwhile, a fourth group of young men left the country to join the ANC in exile. Virtually the whole of their political experience has been in the external bureaucracy. Simon Makana, Francis Meli and Thabo Mbeki, all students who completed their academic training at foreign universities, were all representative of this category.

The younger men have matured in an ANC which for them has always been a revolutionary organisation, and despite the self-control and diplomatic restraint which they are often called upon to exercise, they are likely to be less conciliatory and more radical in their attitudes.[84] They are presently being joined by a fresh influx of potential leaders from the post-1980 era of open working-class mobilisation inside South Africa, who have brought with them the politics of a conflict which increasingly is popularly perceived in the terms of class polarisation.

Many external commentaries devote a great deal of attention to the extent to which the SACP influences the ANC leadership. This is very difficult to quantify with any precision — the SACP keeps the identity of most of its membership secret. This is partly the consequence of the engrained habit of always functioning in hostile terrain, but also because of the sensitivity of SACP involvement in the affairs of the ANC in the context of both African and Western hostility to Communists. Of the 30 NEC members, less than a quarter can be authoritatively said to be SACP members, though there is evidence which suggests that the SACP influences several others as well. As has been argued above, life experiences are at least as important as formal political affinities in determining the ideology of different members of the NEC (and presumably the ANC as a whole).

Two other points are relevant to the evaluation of SACP influences. Firstly, recent SACP documentation suggests that the manpower resources of the Party are very stretched at the moment and this has inhibited the degree to which the Party could function as a deliberate and unified presence within the wider liberation movement. Between 1983 and 1985, for example, the Central Committee had not held a single meeting.[85] Secondly, adherence to Marxism is by no means confined to Communists within the ANC. Both well-educated recruits from South Africa and the graduates of Western European universities are influenced by an intellectual background in which Marxism is a powerful constituent. Interestingly, Thabo Mbeki, a British- and US-trained economist, and one of the more radical young NEC members, was criticised in a Zimbabwean newspaper recently for his 'incomplete study of the South African Communist Party and the African-Communist'. Mbeki was taken to task by this contributor for allegedly aserting that the SACP was responsible for the 'shelving' of socialism.[86]

African nationalism, Christian liberalism, clandestinity, technocracy, Communist popular frontism, Western Marxism and indigenous working-class radicalism, as well as residual elements of the Black Consciousness Movement, are constituents in the ANC's complicated ideological recipe. Within this mixture, individual ideological identities are very difficult to chart and plot. There are, though, several issues which provide observable differences of emphasis and even implicit disagreement. Two to which I have already referred are the nature of the violence employed by ANC guerrillas, and the ingredients in the ANC's projection of a mixed economy. A third, which in future diplomatic activity may become accentuated, is the question of how the conflict will ultimately be resolved. Three years before his death, Moses Mabhida provided a clue which illuminated different perceptions between SACP revolutionaries and the wider movement on the mechanics of transition:

> [There is] one issue, on which the Party [the SACP] follows Communist doctrines in preference to the [Freedom] Charter's proposals. The issue is concerned with the nature of the State organisation to be established after the democratic seizure of power. In our opinion it will be necessary to destroy the apparatus of the racist state and replace it with new political institutions to safeguard the revolution and clear the way for a new social order.[87]

Obviously the form of 'seizure' (a favourite word in ANC phraseology) will be a decisive factor in the attainment of such a goal.

There do seem to be two different perceptions within the ANC regarding how transference of political power is likely to take place. On the one hand is the scenario favoured by Umkhonto strategists (probably irrespective of political affiliation). In this case, the denouncement of the struggle is conceived in terms of an overwhelming general insurrection:

> Armed insurrection, in some form or other, rather than guerrilla warfare, but often as a culmination of guerrilla warfare, is the classic method of making a revolution. There appear to be two main categories into which insurrections fall — the spontaneous mass uprising, as in Iran, and the planned uprising, as in Petrograd, October 1917. These stand at either end of a scale of varying possibilities.
>
> In the first category there is no prearranged plan or date, with an entirely unexpected, even extraneous event sparking off the conflagration. In such a situation, revolutionaries struggle to gain control, and organise the seizure of power.
>
> In the second category, insurrection is deliberately timed as the final move in a carefully prepared plan of revolutionary action — in which the balance of forces has been finely calculated. The Bolsheviks struggled to gain control over the forces unleashed by the February Revolution, as an unexpected event, and directed these forces to the planned seizure of power in October 1917. What we can be sure about is that every revolution which must depend for its ultimate support demands an active revolutionary situation before insurrection can be safely launched. It also needs a movement which has the forces and means powerful enough to overthrow the existing order.[88]

In emphatic contrast with this almost millennial vision is the practical *realpolitik* of the diplomats. Oliver Tambo has asserted on several occasions that the ANC's main objective lies not 'in a military victory but to force Pretoria to the negotiating table',[89] an argument elaborated by Thabo Mbeki:[90]

> The call you make to people is the same, saying you are not prepared to negotiate, that you must intensify the offensive.

But in the course of that offensive it is clear that one of the
most important things is breaking up of the power structure
. . . Even the army will have its problems because it is a con-
script army subject to all the pressures that the general public
is subject to. There are 'homeland' leaders also subject to
pressures and we hope that more of them will desert Botha's
camp as well. Out of this you will get a re-alignment of forces.
We are not talking of overthrowing the government but of
turning so many people against it that it would be forced to
do what Ian Smith had to do.

This should not be understood as a division between 'radicals'
and 'moderates', but rather a difference separating realists from
romantics, both of which categories may embrace a variety of
ideological inclinations. For Marxists as well as revolutionaries, the
advantages of inheriting as advanced industrial state relatively
unscathed by civil warfare are obvious enough. When the Commonwealth Eminent Persons' Group presented the possibility of a
non-violent accession to power, the ANC leadership's response was
unexpectedly, even receptively, uncertain.[91] For revolutionaries,
guerrilla insurgency is by no means the only safeguard against the
revolutionary process (to cite the historical analogy used by the
SACP) stopping short at a February without 'moving into an
October,'[92] not with the reappearance in South Africa of a massive
working-class political movement.

This chapter began with the contention that the ANC has been
not only unharmed by the pressures and trauma of exile but has actually prospered because of it. Below the shelter afforded by sympathetic
governments, the organisation has developed resources well beyond
the capacity of internally based South African political movements.
It has been able to offer to its partisans an hermetic world which has
taken its moral and physical authority to heights that vastly exceed
those of a political party. But then, as Oliver Tambo has frequently
argued, the ANC 'is not a political party, it is a national movement'.[93] It is an army, an educational system, a department of
foreign affairs, a mini-economy, a source of moral hegemony — in
short, a government. Despite the manifest insecurities of dependence
on weak countries unable to protect the organisation from the hostility
of the South African Republic,[94] despite the modesty of its material
assets,[95] and despite the human suffering which produced it and
continues to inform every facet of its existence, it is a state in exile,
and only in exile could such a state have been constructed.

Notes

1. See for examples: Sheridan Johns, 'Obstacles to guerrilla warfare: a South African case study', *Journal of Modern African Studies*, vol. 2, (1973), pp. 267–303; Kenneth Grundy, *Guerrilla struggle in Africa*, no. 7 (Grossmann, New York, 1971); Richard Gibson, *African liberation movement* (Oxford University Press, Oxford, 1971).

2. John Marcum, The exile condition and revolutionary effectiveness: Southern African liberation movements' in Christian Potholm and Richard Dale (eds), *Southern Africa in perspective* (Free Press, New York, 1979); John Marcum, *The Angolan revolution: volume 11: exile politics and guerrilla warfare* (The MIT Press, Cambridge, Mass., 1978).

3. Including my own. See my analysis on the exiled Pan-Africanist Congress in Tom Lodge, *Black politics in South Africa since 1945* (Longman, London, 1983). pp. 305–17.

4. For this perspective see: Barry Munslow, *Mozambique: the revolution and its origins* (Longman, London, 1983); and Basil Davidson, *In the eye of the storm* (Longman, London, 1972).

5. Lodge, *Black politics*, pp. 296–304.

6. For details of the urban guerrilla campaign from 1977 to date: Tom Lodge, 'The African National Congress in South Africa, 1976–1983: guerrilla war and armed propaganda', *Journal of Contemporary African Studies* (Pretoria), vol. 3, nos 1–2, 1983–4, pp. 153–80; Tom Lodge, 'The ANC in 1982' in South African Research Services, *South African Review One* (Ravan, Johannesburg, 1983), pp. 50–4; Tom Lodge, 'The ANC is 1983' in South African Research Services, *South African Review Two* (Ravan Press, Johannesburg, 1984), pp. 21–5; Tom Lodge, 'Mayehlome! — let us go to war!: From Nkomati to Kabwe, the ANC January 1984–June 1985', *South African Review Three* (Ravan Press, Johannesburg, 1986), pp. 226–47; Tom Lodge, 'The Second Consultative Conference of the ANC', *South Africa International* (Johannesburg), vol. 16, no. 2 (October 1985), pp. 80–97; Tom Lodge, 'The ANC, Kabwe and after', *International Affairs Bulletin* (Johannesburg), vol. 10, no. 2 (September 1986), pp. 80–97.

7. 'South Africa: people's war now', *Africa Now*, August 1983, pp. 21–2; House of Commons, Foreign Affairs Committee, Minutes, 29 October 1985, *The situation in South Africa*, testimony of Oliver Tambo, p. 1.

8. *Sowetan* (Johannesburg), 12 February 1986.

9. Ibid.

10. *Weekly Mail* (Johannesburg), 18 July 1986, p. 8.

11. Cited in the *Sunday Star* (Johannesburg), 19 January 1986.

12. Ibid.

13. Stephen Davis, *Season of war: insurgency in South Africa, 1977–1980* (Fletcher School of Law and Diplomacy, Tufts University, Medford, Mass., 1982), p. 207.

14. Howard Barrell, 'Exiles swell ANC ranks', *New Africa*, March 1986. Barrell cites 'reliable estimates' of 7,000 for the size of the Umkhonto trained forces before the exodus.

15. *Cape Times* (Cape Town), 11 May 1984.

16. See John D. Nelson, 'Some external aspects of internal conflict

within South Africa', unpublished PhD dissertation, George Washington University, 1975, p. 193. Umkhonto's Tanzanian camp today accommodates only trained men.

17. Captured ANC activists as well as defectors sometimes claim that they were beguiled into joining the ANC with promises of scholarships and then compelled to join Umkhonto. Such allegations have become less common; this may reflect ANC recruiting successes and the wider acceptance by black South Africans of the legitimacy of political violence.

18. According to one ANC defector, nine Cubans were present at one camp which otherwise had an ANC complement of 450. Testimony of Jeffrey Boshigo to the Subcommittee on Security and Terrorism of the United States Senate, 24 March 1982, mimeo (henceforth Denton committee hearings).

19. See, for example, the statement by Lieutenant Colonel Jack Buchner, cited in the *Star*, 13 May 1982.

20. Boshigo's testimony. Denton committee hearings. According to Ephraim Mfalapitsa, another witness in the Denton committee hearings, the Umkhonto command intended to initiate a rural land-mine offensive based from Botswana as early as 1981. Mfalapitsa's own defection apparently thwarted this.

21. The vast majority of Umkhonto cadres who have been tried in South African courts have been men but recent trials suggest the pattern in changing.

22. First used by the ANC in South Africa in an attack on Voortrekkerhoogte military base near Pretoria in 1981.

23. The numbers involved in Russian and Eastern European training are quite large. Boshigo's group numbered 60 altogether and short training periods in Europe are a fairly common factor in the experiences of guerrillas who are later captured and put on trial in South Africa. For a general description of Russian training facilities based on trial testimony, see the *Star*, 17 May 1984.

24. Camp mutinies in Tanzania and Angola were reported in 1984 and 1985 (*Star*, 18 March 1985 and *Rand Daily Mail*, 23 April 1984), the one a reaction to the Nkomati Accord set-back by guerrillas impatient for action, and the other related to dissatisfaction with living conditions. That there were reasons for rank-and-file dissatisfaction was obliquely acknowledged by Oliver Tambo ('We are a force', *Sechaba*, October 1984). However if discontent and tension were endemic problems, this would have been more apparent at the Kabwe conference of which we now have quite a detailed picture. No reports suggest camp demoralisation on the scale which existed in the late 1960s (see the *Star*, 'Big troubles in ANC guerrilla camps', 22 December 1968), and which came to a head at the 1969 Morogoro conference (for reference to tensions at the Morogoro conference, see Joe Slovo, *The African Communist*, no. 95 (1983).

25. See Davis, *Season of war*, p. 368. As well as divisions with specialised military functions — ordinance, rural guerrilla activity, sabotage — different groups are assigned to financial, transport and other administrative operations.

26. The *Financial Mail* of 8 June 1984 reported the camps as agriculturally self-sufficient. Poor food has in the past been the most frequent

source of morale and disciplinary problems. In 1967-9 Zambian-based diplomats claimed that Umkhonto units in local ANC camps conducted 'food raids' in the surrounding countryside (Nelson, 'Some external aspects', p. 203).

27. Testimony of Elizabeth Matube in State vs. Sipho Binda, 19 August 1985. UNITA claims vary. Savimbi has suggested that the ANC has several thousand soldiers committed to anti-UNITA operations (The *Citizen*, Johannesburg, 7 May 1986). A UNITA brigadier was more conservative, claiming the ANC to have deployed three battalions, 600 men, alongside FAPLA forces (The *Citizen*, 20 May 1986).

28. References to joint ZAPU-ANC operations, 1978-80: The *Washington Post*, 2 January 1984; The *Star*, 12 April 1984; Mfalapitsa testimony, Denton committee hearings. At the end of the Zimbabwean conflict, 100 ANC guerrillas reported to guerrilla reception points.

29. See Davis, *Season of war*, pp. 182-9.

30. Neither the Zimbabweans nor the authorities of Botswana are prepared to tolerate any military-linked activity by the ANC. The transport of guerrillas and arms across their territories has to be clandestine. The Swazis are openly hostile to the ANC.

31. In 1982 a Mozambican intelligence official defected to South Africa, bringing with him a document which he claimed to be an official agreement between the Mozambique government and Umkhonto representatives. In return for Mozambican provision of field equipment, transport base areas and houses, the ANC would hit targets of strategic significance to the Mozambican economy. There is no evidence that such plans were ever implemented and whatever help the Mozambican government provided came to an end in April 1984 (*Scope*, Durban, 18 March 1983). It does seem likely that Maputo was an important operational centre for Umkhonto. ANC and SACP publications have conceded that among the casualties of the SADF raid on ANC houses in Matola were several experienced Umkhonto officers (see, for example, the profile of Motso Mokgabudi in *Umsebenzi*, vol. 2, no. 1 (1986)).

32. The three leading Umkhonto Officers are Joe Modise, Commander-in-Chief; Thembi Chris Hani, Political Commissar; and Joe Slovo, Chief of Staff.

33. The training seems to be weakest in educating prospective combatants in the techniques of clandestine operation. A significant number of Umkhonto cadres have been arrested in South Africa as a result of their own indiscretions. Careless driving is especially one cause for them attracting police attention. On the other hand the fact that Umkhonto units are able to survive in the field undetected for increasingly lengthy periods suggests that this may not be a universal problem.

34. Since mid-1984 Umkhonto units have been recruiting and training activists within the country. Several trials have suggested that a command structure located within South Africa co-ordinates the activities of different groups of units. South African police were prepared to concede this at the beginning of 1986 (The *Citizen*, 18 March 1986).

35. All reports suggest that the spartan regime of the training camps is shared by everybody within them. Promotion within the Umkhonto hierarchy seems to be the reward of combat experience and quite high

ranking Umkhonto officers continue to be deployed in the field. Even defectors' accounts do not suggest that a hierarchy of privilege exists within the ANC.

36. Within Umkhonto there are elite combat units, such as the Special Operations Unit (see The *Weekly Mail*, 11 April 1986; The *Citizen*, 22 May 1986); R. Kasrils in *Sechaba*, May 1986). As we have seen, Umkhonto training is graded according to ability and potential of different trainees, and the graduates of Angolan camps are regarded overall by the ANC leadership as the officer corps of a future peoples' army.

> We have to bear in mind the fact that the comrades we are training outside constitute the core of our army. They are the organisers and the leaders of the mass army that we have to build inside the country. They are our officer corps, we cannot deploy them forever as combat units. They are our officer corps. For obvious reasons, no army in the world fights with combat units composed of officers (Documents of the Second National Consultative Conference of the African National Congress, p. 35).

37. Police sources claim that a harsh disciplinary system prevails which includes a prison camp in Quartro, Angola (The *Star*, 17 May 1984). Such reports should be treated with reserve. Nevertheless, changes instituted at the Kabwe conference suggest a disciplinary regime which may have been resented in the camps. One of the two former NEC members who failed to be re-elected was Andrew Masondo, National Political Commissar and Head of Security. The conference established a grievance procedure to act as a check on the abuse of leadership authority. On the more positive side Umkhonto discipline has had the effect of restraining units in the field from attacking civilian targets. It is not clear whether the recent series of attacks on shopping arcades and commercial premises is the effect of a breakdown in discipline or rather, as Howard Barrell has argued (*Weekly Mail*, 18 July 1986), the result of units in the field being given greater tactical autonomy.

38. *Sechaba*, August 1979; The *Herald* (Harare), 4 September 1985.

39. Ibid.

40. 'A people's education', *SASPU National* (Braamfontein), April 1986.

41. 'Childcare: imperative for our future', *Sechaba*, November 1982.

42. *International Herald Tribune*, 12 September 1985.

43. The authorities concerned were those of Brent, Haringey and ILEA. The help is at the ANC's request. The *Star*, 23 November 1985.

44. 'Interview with Njobe', *Sechaba*, February 1980.

45. *SASPU National*, April 1986.

46. *Sechaba*, February 1980.

47. *SASPU National*, April 1986.

48. *International Herald Tribune*, 17 August 1985.

49. Ibid., 12 September 1985.

50. *Financial Mail* (Johannesburg), 8 June 1984, citing Davis in Harpers, December 1983.

51. Davis, *Season of war*, pp. 182-9.

52. Ibid., p. 182.

53. 'A new and bloodier image for the ANC?', *The Times*, 27 June 1983.

54. T. Karis, 'Revolution in the making: black politics in South Africa',

Foreign Affairs, Winter (1983–4,) p. 395.

55. Testimony of Elizabeth Matube, State vs. Sipho Binda, 1985. This defector's claim has been corroborated by similar complaints from informants of the author who remain loyal to the ANC.

56. 'Impressions of the ANC youth conference', *Sechaba*, November 1982.

57. The *Sowetan*, 21 October 1985.

58. The *Sunday Star*, 20 October 1985. Leaders of the Youth Section delegation to an international youth festival in Moscow found in Soviet achievements evidence 'of the superiority of socialism over capitalism' (Nyawuza, in *Sechaba*, October 1985, pp. 18–19).

59. See H.J. Simons, 'The Freedom Charter, equal rights and freedom' in *Selected writings on the Freedom Charter* (Sechaba Publications, London, 1985), p. 105.

60. According to Oliver Tambo when he met South African business men in September 1985.

61. Francis Meli, for example, the author of an historical PhD dissertation on the history of the Comintern, written at the University of Leipzig in the 1960s. Today he edits *Sechaba*. The obituary in *Sechaba* (January 1982) of a leading personality in the Women's section, Nomvana Shangaia, refers to the ten years she spent in the USSR undergoing medical training.

62. This is a reputation they have enjoyed since the 1960s. See Nelson, 'Some external aspects', p. 200.

63. Western European recognition is by no means confined to Britain. ANC representatives are given semi-official status in Scandinavian countries (in which they receive government aid), were signatories to the Geneva Convention in 1980, and have had several meetings with European Economic Community officials (The *Star*, 10 September 1985, and 26 September 1985).

64. The *Star*, 4 February 1982.

65. Both *Sechaba* and the *African Communist* are edited in London.

66. See Tambo's criticisms of the OAU, reported in *The Times*, 11 August 1984.

67. See list of greetings in *Documents from the Second Consultative Conference of the ANC*, pp. 60–1.

68. Joseph Hanlon, *Mozambique: the revolution under fire* (Zed Books, London, 1985), p. 261.

69. SACP Politburo document released to South African journalists by the South African State President's Office, 12 June 1986.

70. *Documents from the Second Consultative Conference*, p. 36.

71. 'A conversation with Oliver Tambo of the ANC', *Cape Times*, 4 November 1985.

72. 'Communist blueprint for South Africa', *Guardian Weekly*, 17 August 1986, p. 9.

73. Peter Hudson, 'The Freedom Charter and socialist strategy in South Africa', *Politikon*, vol. 13, no. 1 (June 1986), pp. 75–90.

74. See Raymond Suttner and Jeremy Cronin, *Thirty years of the Freedom Charter* (Ravan Press, Johannesburg, 1986).

75. See *Business Day* (Johannesburg), 30 May 1986; and 'ANC in favour of private property says Motsuenyane', *Weekly Mail*, 1 July 1986, p. 5.

76. Reported in The *Guardian*, 20 October 1985.

77. The *Star*, 28 May 1985.

78. Ibid.

79. See for example Oliver Tambo's statement to the House of Commons Foreign Affairs Committee, *The situation in South Africa*, minutes, 29 October 1985, p. 6.

80. Joe Slovo interviewed on the BBC World Service, 4 July 1986.

81. Tom Karis, 'Revolution in the Making', pp. 394–5; and Joe Leyleveld, quoted in The *Star*, 3 November 1983.

82. Leyleveld, ibid.

83. See for example 'Conference expels left-wing deviationists', *Sechaba*, August (1985), for a detailed history of the ANC's treatment of a group of Trotskyite dissenters.

84. For instance, contrast Thabo Mbeki's position in relation to black entrepreneurs with that of Nelson Mandela, as expressed in the 1950s:

Thus black capitalism instead of being the antithesis is rather confirmation of the parasitism with no redeeming features whatsoever, without any extenuating circumstances to excuse its existence (Mbeki in *Selected writings on the Freedom Charter*, p. 48).

The breaking up and democratisation of these monopolies will open up fresh fields for the developments of a prosperous Non-European bourgeois class. For the first time in the history of this country the Non-European bourgeoisie will have the opportunity to own in their own name and right mills and factories and trade and private enterprise will boom and flourish as never before (Nelson Mandela, 'In our lifetime', *Liberation*, no. 19 (June 1956), p. 6).

85. 'Inner Party Bulletin' taken by South African Defence Force members raiding ANC facilities in Gaborone in June 1985, and later given to South African journalists.

86. *Zimbabwe Herald*, 28 November 1985.

87. Moses Mabhida, speech to ANC youth conference, Morogoro, 17–23 August 1982, *African Communist*, no. 92, First Quarter (1983).

88. Ronnie Kasrils, 'People's war, revolution and insurrection', *Sechaba*, May 1986.

89. *Financial Mail* (Johannesburg), 17 January 1986.

90. *Observer* (London), 2 March 1986.

91. An ANC representative at the Nassau conference appeared willing to contemplate the possibility of a truce proposal (The *Star*, 25 October 1985). ANC preconditions for negotiation with the South African authorities seemed to soften significantly in the days which immediately succeeded the SADF raids on ANC buildings in Zimbabwe, Zambia and Botswana (*Business Day*, 'EPG peace package is still on the rails', 21 May 1986).

92. SACP Politburo document.

93. House of Commons, *The situation in South Africa*, p. 4.

94. Witness the recent deportation of ANC members from Lesotho. There, is a long list of assassinations of prominent ANC people in the Frontline states. A plot to kill the Lusaka-based leaders reported by Howard Barrell (*Sunday Tribune* (Durban), 19 December 1982) has at least been

partially corroborated by defector testimony (see statement by Ephraim Mfala, Denton commission hearings, p. 19).

95. The ANC's reputed overall budget of $100 million in 1983 (*Financial Mail*, 8 June 1984) is comparable with that of the reformist business group, the Urban Foundation, and minute when contrasted with, for example, the 1981 South African military budget of $2.76 billion (*Washington Post*, 2 January 1984).

10

Images of the Future and Strategies in the Present: The Freedom Charter and the South African Left

Peter Hudson

Introduction

There can be no gainsaying the importance of the Freedom Charter[1] in contemporary South African politics. Although over 30 years old, a *de facto* obligation appears still to exist on all political organisations struggling to transform the South African state to define their position *vis-à-vis* the Charter. The Charter is, moreover, the *clef de voute* of the alliance between the South African Communist Party (SACP)[2] and the African National Congress (ANC), one of the most significant political alliances in South Africa today. In its programme the SACP identifies itself as belonging to the National Liberation Alliance headed by the ANC. The objective of this alliance is national liberation, the 'main content of which is the national liberation of the African people' (SACP, 1962). This strategic alliance is based on the fact that the SACP, *qua* communist party, does not pursue socialism as an objective separate from national liberation, but rather, sees the latter as the necessary vehicle for the attainment of the former. Over and above this strategic alliance, members of the SACP belong to, and occupy very important positions within, the ANC *qua*, in this case, not communists but nationalists.[3] The central objective of this chapter is, firstly, to elucidate the theoretical basis of this strategic alliance; and secondly, to consider some recent critiques of this strategy developed from within the South African left.

The theoretical basis of the political alliance between the SACP and the ANC is to be located, it is argued, in the identification by the SACP, in its official programme, of South Africa as a colonial society 'of a special type' and in its subscription to the theory of national democratic revolution (see SACP, 1962). A few years later, the ANC itself, in the course of what has been referred to as its 'continuing leftward turn' (see Davies *et al*, 1984, p. 289), formally endorsed, at the Morogoro conference held in Tanzania in 1969, the theory of colonialism of a special type and its strategic corollary in the South African context, the theory of national democratic revolution (see Turok, 1970, p. 145). The recent regrouping and mobilisation, through the formation of the United Democratic Front (UDF) in 1983, of political forces opposed to apartheid and the South African state, and which identify with the Congress tradition, has resulted in a renewed interest in, and reliance upon, this theoretical and strategic perspective (see, for example, Anon, 1983; Anon, 1983; and Anon, 1986).

The theory of national democratic revolution is therefore central to the strategies of many of the most important political organisations opposed to the South African state and apartheid. The unifying role of the Freedom Charter in the struggle against apartheid, in particular its role as the corner-stone of the alliance between the SACP and the ANC, is, it will be argued, dependent upon its interpretation in the terms of this theory.

The SACP's endorsement of the Freedom Charter is *prima facie* surprising. The first clause of the Charter demands that 'The people shall govern'. It would be wrong, however, to construe the Charter a calling for nothing more than the establishment of a classical bourgeois democracy, as it contains a series of clauses which call for wide-ranging economic reform in South Africa. On the other hand, these stop far short of calling for the elimination of private property in the means of production. A recent commentator has argued that 'the language of the Charter combines the liberal ideals of the Enlightenment and the social ideals of the modern welfare state' (Fine, 1986, p. 38).

The principal economic clauses of the Freedom Charter referred to above call for the 'national wealth' of South Africa to be 'restored to the people'; for the ownership by 'the people as a whole [of] the mineral wealth, the Banks and monopoly industry'; for the control of 'all other industry and trade . . . to assist the well being of the people'; for 'all people [to] have equal rights to trade where they choose, to manufacture and to enter all trades, crafts and professions'; for the ending of 'restrictions of land ownership on a racial basis'; and for the redivision 'of all the land . . . amongst those who work it'. At most what is called for there is the nationalisation of certain economic resources. There is no reference to the socialisation of the means of production, and the principle of private property in the means of production is certainly not impugned. What, then, makes it possible for the SACP, *qua* communist party, to endorse the Freedom Charter?

The answer to this question is to be found, firstly, in the SACP's analysis of the nature of South African society; and secondly, in the specific interpretation of the Freedom Charter which it advances on the basis of this analysis. According to the SACP, such is the nature of South African society that the transition from capitalism to communism in South Africa cannot follow the classical model (see SACP, 1962). It will, it argues, under South African conditions first be necessary to establish a 'national democracy', which is defined as a transitional form of society which is neither capitalist nor socialist. On the theory of 'national democratic revolution' to which the SACP subscribes, the establishment of a national democracy inaugurates a rupture with capitalism and a non-capitalist path of development which, however, is not socialist (see ibid.).

Socialism is itself, in the lexicon of Marxism-Leninism, a transitional form of social structure, and what is therefore being proposed by the SACP is a revision of the classical Marxist-Leninist model of revolution (see Lenin, 1963; Marx, 1974, and Balibar, 1977). The classical model defines socialism as the period during which capitalism is being transformed into communism. Marx and Lenin argue that this transformation cannot occur immediately, and necessarily takes the form of a process. During this process, control over the means of production is progressively withdrawn from the class of capitalists and vested in the hands of the 'associated producers' (Marx, 1967, p. 820). The hybrid, transitional form of society whose existence is coterminous with the duration of this process is referred to as socialism.

The classical capitalism-socialism-communism sequence is thus replaced in the SACP's programme by the sequence capitalism-national democracy-socialism-communism. Although the SACP acknowledges that the Freedom Charter is not a socialist document, it is able to endorse it because it identifies the model of society adumbrated there as a 'national democracy', i.e. as a non-capitalist transitional form of society.

The theory of national democracy and of national democratic revolution is at the heart of the current strategy of the SACP. Furthermore, the adhesion of the SACP to this theory is a *sine qua non* condition of the ANC — South African Communist Party alliance. Its political importance cannot therefore be underestimated. One searches in vain, however, both in the official programme of the SACP, as well as in other expositions of its strategy, for a comprehensive account and defence of it.[4] In order to fill this lacuna, the historical origins and logic of the theory, which was developed by the international communist movement during the 1950s, are reconstructed in what follows. An historical and theoretical excursus is thus called for before we consider the specific way in which the SACP applies this theory to South Africa and uses it to interpret the Freedom Charter.[5] Thereafter, another perspective on the transition to socialism in South Africa, which is sharply critical of the national democratic strategy, will be identified and briefly discussed.

National democracy — the genealogy and logic of a concept

From the Seventh Congress of the Comintern in 1935 until 1947 (excepting the period of the German-Soviet pact of 1939 to 1941) the international communist movement pursued a strategy of alliance with all social sectors and states which were anti-fascist. This expressed itself, *inter alia*, in the pre-war Popular Fronts, in the wartime 'Grand Alliance' of the USSR, the USA and Great Britain, as well as in anti-fascist alliances during the war. At the close of the war this strategy was maintained and resulted in the formation of governments of national unity and reconstruction (in which communist parties participated) in France and Italy during the immediate post-war 'honeymoon' period (1945–1947) (see Zhukov, 1969; Birchall, 1975; Claudin, 1975; and Spriano, 1985).

The theory of 'the two camps' advanced by Zhdanov in his report to the conference of nine communist parties in Poland in 1947, at which the formation of the Cominform was announced, led, however, to a fundamental change in strategy.[6] On Zhdanov's analysis of the international conjuncture (developed largely in response to the 'Marshall Aid' offensive of the United States, the world was bifurcated into two implacably antagonistic 'camps', the 'anti-imperialist democratic' camp and the 'imperialist anti-democratic' camp. In such a highly polarised world, there was no place for the politics of alliance and unity practised by the international communist movement during the previous decade and a 'left turn' ensued. According to the 'switch' of 1947, the communist parties in the colonial, semi-colonial and dependent countries were to eschew alliances formed with the national bourgeoisie during the preceding period. Moreover, in the dualistic perspective of Zhdanov's analysis, countries which had recently acquired independence under the aegis of the national bourgeosie were consigned to the camp of imperialism and their claims to neutrality and national autonomy rejected as specious.

This analysis was before long to be replaced, however, by a novel approach to the question of communist strategy and socialist transformation in the colonies and ex-colonies, based on the concept 'national democracy'. The 'switch' of 1947 had not resulted in an increase of communist influence in the underdeveloped (colonial, semi-colonial and dependent) countries. In addition, the behaviour of nationalist regimes, often dominated by the national bourgeoisie, in many newly independent countries was increasingly incompatible with their conceptualisation in the theory of 'two camps'. Their quest for independence and non-alignment showed itself to be more than mere rhetoric, and many of them, moreover, initiated far-reaching social and economic reforms. Not only did the Zhdanovite schema seem empirically inconsistent with developments in the underdeveloped world, but it was also politically unfruitful both for the Soviet Union on the international plane and for numerous communist parties in underdeveloped countries.

The analysis of the nature of underdeveloped societies gradually changed, as did the strategy pursued *vis-à-vis* such societies by the Soviet Union and by local communist parties. The Soviet Union ceased demeaning decolonisation as merely formal and began to recognise it as an essential prerequisite for the full emancipation of the colonies. It began to acknowlege the authenticity of the claim by many newly independent countries to be non-aligned and strove in co-operation with them to construct a 'zone of peace' by bracketing together the 'socialist camp' and the non-aligned countries against the advanced capitalist imperialist countries. The identification of the national bourgeoise in the underdeveloped world as being compelled by its 'class nature' to ally itself with international finance capital was also eventually jettisoned.

By 1956 the dominant view was highly critical of the 'sectarian errors' made in the past concerning the role of the national bourgeoisie *vis-à-vis* the perpetuation of imperialist domination and underdevelopment on the one hand, and national liberation on the other (see Sovetskoye Vostokovendeniye, 1969). Now it was argued that the interests of the national bourgeoisie in the underdeveloped world lay in the formation of an alliance with the working class, the petite bourgeoisie and the peasantry, in order to struggle with them against imperialism. Ex-colonial societies under the rule of the national bourgeoisie ceased to be perceived by the international communist movement as irrevocably integrated into the 'imperialist anti-democratic camp'. It was acknowledged that the national bourgeoisie could oppose imperialism, lead the ex-colonies to real national autonomy and initiate programmes of economic development. Constitutional political independence was no longer seen as bogus but as a necessary precondition for a more extensive autonomy (see Kruschev, 1969). However, such political independence had to be complemented by a series of economic measures if the newly independent nations were to achieve a balanced and autonomous economic growth, considered necessary if they were to eventually consummate their autonomy. These measures included: the nationalisation of foreign-owned enterprises and financial institutions, or at least their subjection to strict control by the state; the creation of state-controlled enterprises; and the introduction of state economic planning (see Tabarin, 1975; and Chirkin and Yudin, 1978).

The possibility of economic growth in ex-colonial social formations (and thus of real national autonomy) came no longer to be seen as contingent upon the prior destruction of capitalism. In fact, it was argued that capitalist ownership of the means of production should at this stage be maintained as it still had a positive contribution to make to economic development.

It seems . . . that it would hardly be expedient to put a total ban on the development of private capital, even in countries which have already moved further than others along the path of social progress. The public sector is not yet able to guarantee a country the necessary goods. So great is these countries' backwardness that it is necessary to use all available resources, under state control, of course, for economic development. Total prohibition of private capital might also do political damage. The revolution is at a democratic stage. This would be a sectarian policy, which might result in the defeat of the progressive forces and ultimately in the victory of imperialism (Tyagunenko, 1969, p.340).

. . . the restructuring of social relations [in such societies] is accompanied by a simultaneous extension of the private sector . . . experience . . . shows that when subjected to government controls the private sector can contribute to the development of the economy (Tabarin, 1975, p. 66).

Moreover in practice, state control of foreign-owned enterprises can take many different forms in national democracies. In some cases, where it is deemed in the interests of the national economy, this is construed as involving the encouragement of foreign investment via the granting of certain privileges to foreign investors, such as tax exemptions or the provision of raw materials on preferential terms (see Chirkin and Yudin, 1978).

The specific developmental strategy associated with the construction of such a 'multi-structural' (Kridl Valkreiner, 1983, p. 85) economic system (in which elements of private capitalist ownership of the means of production still have an organic and significant role to play) was identified as an example of the 'non-capitalist road' towards socialism and societies engaged on such a path of development were conceived as 'transitional social structures' (Tabarin, 1975, p. 305), neither capitalist nor socialist. Similarly, the state in societies of this type is neither capitalist nor socialist, but reflects 'the interests not of any one particular class, but of the widest strata of the population of the newly-free nations' (Tyagunenko, 1966, p. 65). Such forms of social structure and of the state were, it was felt, novel *vis-à-vis* the conceptual corpus of classical Marxism. Here was a state which, it was argued, could not be defined as a dictatorship of either the bourgeoisie (a capitalist state) or the proletariat (a socialist state), and a social structure in which the respective positions of the dominant and dominated classes had been so altered as a result of state economic intervention and control that it was no longer capitalist but not yet socialist either.

In order to fill what was considered to be a significant (conceptual) breach in Marxism-Leninism, the concept 'national democracy' was introduced to name such forms of society and state. The growing international links between the Soviet Union and the ex-colonial world received a doctrinal basis and justification through the introduction of this concept. In the declaration of the meeting of 81 Communist and Workers' parties in Moscow in 1960, the term 'national democracy' was formally introduced into the theoretical repertoire of the international communist movement in order to designate that category of ex-colonial (and dependent) countries which could be identified as engaged on a non-capitalist path of development in opposition to imperialism and towards national autonomy. A national democracy is defined in the declaration as committed to the strengthening of national independence, land reforms in the interests of the peasantry, abolition of the remnants of feudalism, extirpation of the economic roots of imperialist rule, the limitation and ousting of foreign monopolies from the economy, the foundation and development of a national industry, the raising of the standard of living of the population, democratisation of public life, and an independent, peace-loving foreign policy (Declaration of the Second Conference of 81 Communist and Workers' Parties, 1960).

In such countries, local communist parties should not, it was argued, aim in the first instance at the socialist transformation of society. This is because of the 'very low level of development of the productive forces and social production' (Tabarin, 1975, p. 309) in these countries and the consequent political immaturity and insignificance of the proletariat (Starishenko, 1969, p. 193). The working class is thus viewed, in most cases, as incapable of initiating and sustaining a struggle aimed at socialist revolution. Local communist parties should not, however, forgo the objective of socialist revolution, but should instead aim to construct 'a new social structure transitional to socialism . . . [via] the implementation of a complex set of socio-economic measures' (Tabarin, 1975, p. 305). They should aim in other words for a 'gradual development of revolution, stage by stage, [for] non-capitalist development towards socialism' (Tyagunenko, 1969, p. 340).

The establishment of a national democracy in an ex-colonial country and the pursuit of a non-capitalist path of development are seen as creating conditions propitious for an eventual transition to socialism and should therefore be supported by communist parties in the underdeveloped world. The industrialisation strategy of national democracies is held to alter their social composition in favour of the proletariat:

Since national industries are still too weak, there are not the necessary conditions for a revolution. At this moment, then, it is necessary to wait for the national bourgeoisie to mature, since they clearly cannot appear overnight . . . With a strong bourgeoisie there is a strong proletariat (Brookfield, 1981, pp. 132, 133).

At the same time, such states establish cultural and political conditions under which communist parties can be formed (if not already in existence) and acquire a hegemonic role amongst the proletariat (and its allies). The interests of the national bourgeoisie and the working class are thus conceived as converging in underdeveloped societies. The national bourgeoisie has an interest in the struggle against the international capitalist monopolies, which seek to stifle its growth. It has, moreover, an important role to play in what is referred to as the 'non-capitalist' path of development. Capitalist ownership of the means of production is an integral feature of this mode of development. The forms of state intervention which are part of this 'non-capitalist' path of development are not seen as in conflict with the interests of the national bourgeoisie or with capitalist property ownership. On the contrary, a large and energetic state sector in the economy is conceived in the theory of national democracy as the best defence available to the national bourgeoisie against the international monopolies (ibid., p. 132).

In the mid-1970s, the term 'national democracy' was replaced by the term 'socialist orientation'. This terminological substitution was introduced in order to remedy what was felt to be the 'non-socialist' connotation of the term 'national democracy' (Kridl Valkreiner, 1983, p. 97; Craig Nation, 1984, p. 30; and Steele, 1984, p. 171). In substance the concept itself remained unaltered. A socialist-oriented society, like a national democracy, is defined as pre-socialist. In the document released by the first meeting (attended by the SACP) of the Communist Parties of Tropical and Southern Africa in 1978, states of socialist orientation are defined, *inter alia*, by the fact that they pursue policies aiming at 'the gradual creation of the political, material, social and cultural preconditions for the transition to building socialism' (Declaration of the First Meeting of Communist Parties of Southern and Tropical Africa, 1979).

Internal colonialism, national democracy and the Freedom Charter

The SACP recognises that in a very crucial respect, contemporary South Africa differs significantly from the societies for which the theory of national-democratic revolution was initially developed. The forces of production are more developed in South Africa and the proletariat is neither small (*vis-à-vis* other classes and sectors), nor politically insignificant (see SACP 1962; and Denga 1985): 'There is no doubting that the material prerequisites for socialism exist in South Africa: a certain level of industrialisation, socio economic contradictions and the force to carry out the revolution (the working class)' (Denga, 1985, p. 65).

Why should the theory of national democratic revolution be applied to South Africa? The answer to this question is to be found in the characterisation by the SACP of South Africa as an 'internal colonial' society, or alternatively, as a 'colonialism-of-a-special-type' (see SACP, 1962).

The existence in South Africa of a state which has the form of a racial dictatorship is best understood, it is argued, as an instance of colonialism. On the other hand, colonial domination in South Africa is distinctive in that unlike elsewhere, it occurs within the boundaries of a single political territory. In South Africa the white nation is, on this analysis, identified as the colonial power, and the politically oppressed blacks as the colonised. This has two signifi-cant consequences. Firstly, the colonial subjection of all blacks has the effect of inhibiting the emergence within the black proletariat of a class consciousness. The black worker, it is argued, perceives his/her place in society, and defines his/her social identity, not in class but in racial terms. This is because of the specific articulation of racial and class relations of domination in South Africa:

Production relations [in South Africa] express more than mere economic relations; they also reflect the political position of the various sections of society . . . Therefore, the nature of exploitation manifests itself first and foremost in the context of the place [the black worker] occupies in the racial equation, in the specific way production relations manifest themselves under internal colonialism. He therefore not only sees his position on the factory-floor through the colonial screen, but also identifies with the rest of this number who belong to the lower 'caste'. This is not a false consciousness but a reflec-tion of the most immediate contradiction within South African society — between the oppressed people and their rulers (Denga, 1985, p. 65).

Secondly, common subjection to racial-national domination is said to result in a convergence, amongst the colonised, the nationally oppressed, of economic class interests (see SACP, 1962). The immediate economic interests of black capital owners, members of the middle class, and black workers are, on the internal colon-ialism analysis of South Africa, all opposed to the maintenance of apartheid, and this further promotes national consciousness over class consciousness.

The absence of a proletariat conscious of itself *qua* proletariat, of its specific class interest in the construction of socialism, means that the classical Marxist-Leninist schema of socialist revolution cannot be applied in South Africa. The structure of South African society is thus identified as inhibiting the emergence of a necessary subjective condition of socialist revolution. Just as in other colonial situations, here too there can be no question of the transition to socialism being immediate and direct. It must be preceded by a national-democratic struggle leading to a national-democratic revolution. Then, and only then, will it be possible to put the transition to socialism on the immediate political agenda.

Although more than 20 years have passed since the adoption by the SACP of its official programme, *The road to South African freedom*, it has not wavered in its adhesion to the analysis and strategy contained there. In a recent issue of its theoretical organ, the *African Communist*, the indispensability of the national-democratic stage as a preliminary to the transition to socialism was vigorously re-endorsed.

> . . . we should move away from such superficial and not well-thought-out formulations as that the national-democratic stage will be a 'short phase', a 'formality', or an 'unnecessary bother'. We need to grapple with the implications of this process — the national democratic revolution — more so that the revolution in Africa, Zimbabwe lately, do indicate that this process has a momentum of its own, perhaps even stages one has to go through before it is possible to talk of transition to socialism. Perhaps we need to relook at the suggestion of the Comintern about 'An Independent Nature Republic as stage towards a workers' and peasants' republic' . . . Incidentally a workers' and peasants' republic is not the same thing as a 'socialist republic' — it is a stage towards socialism and therefore the Comintern seems to have had in mind a number of stages in the revolution. This is not to suggest that our theories of a two-stage revolution are wrong — even the first stage might have to be divided into phases. We need to guard against the simplification of complicated processes (Nyawuza, 1985, p. 59).

The repeated insistence of the SACP that the working class

must and will play a 'leading role' in the struggle for national liberation, and that this will ensure an 'uninterrupted' movement towards
socialism', should not be misunderstood (see SACP, 1985a, b). Far
from impugning its attachment to a 'stagist' conception of socialist
transition in South Africa, the above argument in fact presupposes
such a conception, for were national liberation and the transition
to socialism no different, it would be entirely otiose.

Read through the prism of the theory of national-democratic
revolution and the colonialism-of-a-special-type analysis of South
Africa, it is not difficult to interpret the principal clauses of the
Charter as comprising national-democratic demands. As has been
explained above, in terms of the theory of national-democratic
revolution, a national-democratic state is more opposed to foreign
political and economic domination, more anti-colonialist and anti-
imperialist, than anti-capitalist. At the same time anti-imperialism
is not exhausted by the struggle for political emancipation. It also
involves striving for the restitution to the colonised nation of its
wealth via the nationalisation of large, foreign-owned monopoly
capital. Once the thesis, based on the colonialism-of-a-special-type
analysis of South Africa, that the white population of South Africa
should be identified as a colonising nation, is accepted; and once
it is borne in mind that monopoly industry, the principal financial
institutions and the mineral wealth were (and still are, very largely)
white-owned, then the Freedom Charter's call for their nationalisation appears as a national-democratic demand. Thus even though
the Freedom Charter does not call for the destruction of capitalism
in South Africa and does not refer, even implicitly, to socialism,
the SACP is able to endorse it, and thereby enter into an alliance
with the ANC because in its view, the model of a future South
African adumbrated there represents a necessary stage, viz. the stage
of national democracy, that must be traversed before there can be
any transition to socialism (and eventually communism), in South
Africa.

Working-class autonomy and the struggle for socialism

It would be incorrect to assume that the analysis of South Africa
outlined above, and the political strategy flowing from it (in which,
as we have seen, the Freedom Charter plays a pivotal role), enjoys
the support of all on the South African left. One of the more
important critiques of the national-democratic strategy to have

emerged in recent years is contained in the keynote address delivered by the Federation of South African Unions' (FOSATU) General Secretary, J. Foster, at the 1982 Second Annual Conference of FOSATU (Foster, 1983, p. 99). What distinguishes this critique of the national-democratic strategy and makes it more politically significant than many other attacks on it is the fact that Foster was speaking as the General Secretary of the largest non-racial trade union federation then in existence (100,000 signed-up members at the end of 1981), and the first non-racial trade union federation to operate in a non-clandestine manner in South Africa since the South African Congress of Trade Unions (SACTU) in the early 1960s.

The essence of Foster's argument is that there has never existed in South Africa what he describes as a 'working-class movement'. By this he means 'a number of different organisations — trade unions, co-operatives, political parties and newspapers — that all see themselves as linked to the working class and furthering its interests' (ibid., p. 101). Such movements exist and constitute 'powerful social forces' in the advanced industrial societies, both capitalist and socialist. In South Africa on the other hand, the working class has not been able to constitute a 'working-class movement' in the above sense. Instead, militant trade unions in South Africa have tended to subordinate the struggle to secure specifically working-class interests to the more general struggle against apartheid. However, broadly based popular movements aimed at the overthrow of oppressive political regimes cannot by their very nature and objectives, contends Foster, 'deal with the particular and fundamental problems of workers' (ibid., p. 107). Foster goes further and suggests not only that such movements are unable to address specifically working-class issues and interests, but also that there exists a very real danger 'that the popular movement [may be] hijacked by elements who will in the end have no option but to turn against their worker supporters' (ibid., p. 107).

The gravamen of his critique, then, is that in canalising all its energies into the struggle against apartheid, the working class in South Africa runs the risk of eventually merely serving the ends of non-proletarian black classes who desire the destruction of apartheid and the deracialisation of capitalism in South Africa, but who have no interest whatsoever in the specific problems of the working class, and who in fact are opposed to seeing the construction in South Africa of a society in which 'workers . . . control their own destiny' (ibid., p. 101).

Foster's conclusion, therefore, is that although the working class should participate in the wider political struggle against apartheid, workers should at the same time 'strive to build their own powerful and effective organisation' (ibid., p. 107). The South African working class needs, in other words, to construct a 'working-class movement', it needs its own political organisation and its own political voice. The conditions necessary for the emergence of such a 'working-class movement' have, he argues, been created by the last 20 years of rapid economic growth in South Africa. As a result of this, a much larger and better-educated industrial proletariat has been created which is highly concentrated in very large corporations. Moreover, and very importantly, the 'links — [of these workers] — with past identities are all but broken so that more and more a worker identity is emerging' (ibid., p. 105).

On the other hand, this rapid economic growth has also meant that the position of the capitalist class in South African society has itself changed. This class will no longer, argues Foster, be able to 'hide behind Apartheid' (ibid., p. 105) to the same extent as previously. The existence of these new conditions, whilst favourable for the emergence of a 'working-class movement', does not, however, entail that it will automatically emerge: on the contrary, insists Foster, it must be constructed.

Foster's address was interpreted by some as a call for the creation of a new political party in South Africa, representing above all the interests of the South African working class, a new working-class party. Unsurprisingly, it was perceived by the SACP as a direct challenge to its claim to be precisely that — viz. a political party whose *raison d'être* is the prosecution of the specific interest of the South African working class, i.e. the construction of socialism in South African (see Toussaint, 1983; Nhere, 1984; and Vuk'ayibambe, 1985).

Nowhere in his address does Foster refer to the SACP, and the clear implication of his argument (which largely explains this resounding silence) is that the SACP has disqualified itself as the representative of the interests of the South African working class as a result of its pursuit of a national-democratic strategy. Such a strategy involves, as we have seen, that the struggle for socialism be postponed until after the establishment of a national democracy: or, to express this slightly differently, according to this strategy the struggle for national democracy is the form which, under current conditions, the struggle for socialism must assume in South Africa. In terms of this strategy, the specific interests of the working class are best served precisely by its focusing its energies on the struggle to destroy apartheid and establish a form of society based on the model of the Freedom Charter, a national democracy, rather than here and now striving to establish a socialist society. For Foster, the submersion of the working class in the general struggle to destroy apartheid amounts to the subordination of its specific interests to those of other politically oppressed black classes and as a consequence undermines the working-class struggle for socialism. For the SACP, on the other hand, it is only by initially giving priority to and privileging the struggle for national democracy, for the realisation of the Freedom Charter, over the struggle for socialism, that socialism will ever be established in South Africa.

Although Foster's analysis clearly implied that it was self-defeating for the working class to consider the Freedom Charter as the lodestar of its struggle, he did not mention the Charter by name. However, in some recent interventions in the debate over socialist strategy in South Africa, which are in broad agreement with many of the positions expressed by Foster, the content of the Charter itself is found wanting *vis-à-vis* the demands and possibilities of the contemporary conjuncture (see Innes, 1985; Fine, 1986; and Innes, 1986). Even in 1955, when the Charter was endorsed by the Congress of the People at Kliptown, trade unionists were, it is held, dissatisfied, 'as it offered little in the way of a workers' vision of a future South Africa' (Innes, 1986, p. 13). In this respect the inadequacy of the nationalisation clauses of the Charter is cited. In the absence of explicit reference to and emphasis on workers' control, 'nationalisation is not necessarily a socialist demand . . . and is quite compatible with capitalism' (ibid., p. 36). Similarly, the absence of any reference in the Freedom Charter to the right of workers to strike is identified as a capital and revealing omission. The Charter falls, it is concluded, 'short of goals which are fundamental to the workers' movement' (ibid., p. 15).

Conclusion

From the perspective of the colonialism-of-a-special-type analysis of South Africa, these criticisms of the Freedom Charter and of the national-democratic strategy are without weight. The claim that the national-democratic strategy and the Freedom Charter do not prioritise the specific interests of the working class can be dismissed as trivial because they were never intended to do so. Moreover, in terms of the conception of South African society embodied in the colonialism-of-a-special-type analysis, the working class should not — and moreover cannot — give priority to the struggle for specifically working-class interests. The route to socialism (and eventually communism) in South Africa is necessarily, on this analysis, via national democracy.

Underlying the strategic dispute discussed above are two very different conceptions of the nature of South African society. The thesis that the rapid economic development of the last 20 years has resulted in the primacy, amongst the working class, of a class identity over a national or racial identity is central, as we noted above, to Foster's analysis of contemporary South Africa, his critique of the national-democratic strategy and his call for the formation of a new workers' party. The SACP, for its part, continues to stress that South Africa is a colonial society (albeit of a special, internal, type), and that the experience of national oppression still has a very significant effect on the consciousness of all black South Africans, including members of the working class, which must be taken into account in the formulation of political strategy. Foster, it is charged, 'underplays, almost to the point of extinction, the continuing existence of national oppression, which provides a fertile soil for continuing — perhaps even growing — national consciousness and national unity' (Toussaint, 1983, p. 42). As a consequence, he and all those who endorse his analysis

> . . . do not understand the significance of the national-democratic revolution . . . They have not perceived the interaction between national and class oppression which gives South African revolutionaries the specific strategic tasks laid out in the programmes of the ANC and the SACP (Nhere, 1984, p. 79).

Notes

Acknowledgement: The author would like to thank *Politikon* for permitting the re-publication of an earlier version of this article.

1. The origins of the Freedom Charter lie in the perception by the ANC leadership in 1953 that a comprehensive programme of demands was needed in order to give more focus and structure to its struggle against the South African state. 'Freedom volunteers' throughout South Africa set about collecting demands which were then collated and eventually appeared as the

Freedom Charter. This was endorsed by the Congress of the People at Klip-town in the Transvaal in 1955. See Lodge (1983) and Suttner and Cronin (1986) on the origins of the Freedom Charter.

2. The CPSA was formed in 1921. In 1950 it dissolved itself because it did not consider itself adequately prepared for the clandestinity imposed on it by the Suppression of Communism Act of 1950. It was reformed, underground, in 1953 as the South African Communist Party (SACP). The official programme of the SACP was adopted at the Sixth National Conference held in Johannesburg in 1962. See SACP, 1962.

3. It has in fact been estimated that nearly half of the ANC's national executive belong to the SACP. See Laurence, 1986, p. 14; and Wallington, 1986, p. 8.

4. This has been remarked by other commentators (see du Toit, 1981, p. 190), du Toit, however, is apparently unaware that the more comprehensive account he desires is available elsewhere.

5. This should be kept separate from the role of the members of the SACP in the formulation of the Freedom Charter. With respect to this, Joe Slovo has in a recent interview discussed, apparently for the first time, his clandestine participation in the actual writing of the Freedom Charter (see Frankel, 1985, pp. 16-17).

6. Cattel, 1963; Dallin, 1963; Dinerstein, 1963; Lowenthal, 1963; Morison, 1964; Carrerre d'Encausse and Schram, 1969; Klinghoffer, 1969; Ojha, 1970; Cohen, 1972; Kapur, 1972.

References

Anon (1983) Colonialism of a special kind and the South African state. *Africa Perspective, 23*, pp. 75-94

—— (1983) National Democratic Struggle, *Social Review, 24-25*, pp. 9-17

—— (1986) National Democratic Struggle. *Isizwe — The Nation — Journal of the United Democratic Front, 11* (2), pp. 27-35

Balibar, E. (1977) *On the dictatorship of the proletariat.* New Left Books, London

Birchall, I. (1975) *Workers against the monolith.* Pluto Press, London

Brookfield, H. (1981) *Interdependent development.* Methuen, London

Carrere d'Encausse, H. and S. Schram (1969) *Marxism and Asia.* Allen Lane, London

Cattel, D. (1963) The Soviet Union seeks a policy for Afro-Asia. In K. London (ed.), *New nations in a divided world.* Praeger, New York, pp. 163-80

Chirkin, V.Y. and Y.A. Yudin (1978) *A socialist-oriented state: instrument of revolutionary change.* Progress Publishers, Moscow

Claudin, F. (1975) *The communist movement.* Penguin, Harmondsworth

Cohen, H.D. (1972) *Soviet policy toward black Africa.* Praeger, New York

Craig Nation, R. (1984) Soviet engagement in Africa, motives, means and prospects. In R. Craig Nation (ed.), *The Soviet impact in Africa.* Lexington Books, Toronto

Dallin, A. (1963) The Soviet Union: political activity. In Z. Brzezinski (ed.), *Africa and the communist world.* Oxford University Press, London

Davies, R. and D. O'Meara (1983) The state of analysis of the South

African region: issues raised by South African strategy. *Review of African Political Economy, 29*, pp. 64-76

—— and S. Dlamini (1984) *The struggle for South Africa — a reference guide to movements, organisations and institutions.* Zed Books, London

Declaration of the Second Conference of 81 Communist and Workers' Parties in Moscow (1960), in R. Lowenthal (1963) National democracy and the post-colonial state. In K. London (ed.), *New nations in a divided world.* Praeger, New York

Declaration of the First Meeting of Communist Parties of Southern and Tropical Africa (1979) For the freedom, independence, national rebirth and social progress of the peoples of tropical and Southern Africa. In *The yearbook of international communist affairs*, Hoover Institute Press, Stanford

Denga (1985) Botha's reforms have not changed 'Colonialism-of-a-special-type'. *African Communist, 100*, pp. 67-72

Dinerstein, H. (1963) Soviet doctrines on developing countries: some divergent views. In K. London (ed.), *New nations in a divided world.* Praeger, New York

du Toit, D. (1981) *Capital and labour in South African class struggle in the 1970s*, Kegan Paul, London

Fine, B. (1986) The Freedom Charter: a critical appreciation. *South African Labour Bulletin, 11* (3), pp. 38-42

Foster, J. (1983) The workers' struggle: where does FOSATU Stand? *Review of African Political Economy, 26*

Frankel, G. (1985) White communist who wants to end apartheid with a gun. *Guardian Weekly* (Manchester), 28 July

Innes, D. (1985) The Freedom Charter and workers' control. *South African Labour Bulletin, 11* (2), pp. 35-42

—— (1986) Worker politics and the popular movement. *Work in Progress, 41*, pp. 14-17

Kapur, H. (1972) *The Soviet Union and the emerging nations.* Michael Joseph, London

Kase, F. (1968) *People's democracy.* A.W. Sijthoff, London

Klinghoffer, A.J. (1969) *Soviet perspectives on socialism.* Farleigh Dickenson University Press, New Jersey

Kridl Valkreiner, E. (1983) *The Soviet Union and the Third World.* Praeger, New York

Kruschev, N. (1969) Debates of the 20th Congress of the Communist Party of the Soviet Union. In H. Carrere d'Encausse and S. Schram (eds), *Marxism and Asia.* Allen Lane, London

Laurence, P. (1986) Just how powerful is the Communist Party — the spectre of the red funeral flags. *Weekly Mail* (Johannesburg), 11 April

Lenin, V.I. (1963) The state and revolution. In his *Selected works*, Progress Publishers, Moscow

Lodge, T. (1983) *Black politics in South Africa since 1945.* Ravan Press, Johannesburg

Lowenthal, R. (1963) National democracy and the post-colonial revolution. In K. London (ed.), *New nations in a divided world.* Praeger, New York, pp. 56-75

Mandela, N. (1977) In our lifetime. In T. Karis and G. Carter (eds), *From protest to challenge — a documentary history of African politics in South Africa 1882-1964.* Hoover, Stanford, pp. 245-50

Marx, K. (1967) *Capital, vol. III*. International Publishers, New York
—— (1974) Critique of the Gotha Programme. In D. Fernbach (ed.), *The First International and after*. Penguin, Harmondsworth
Morison, D. (1964) *The USSR and Africa 1945-1963*. Oxford University Press, London
Nhere, R. (1984) The dangers of legal Marxism in South Africa. *African Communist, 99*, pp. 75-93
Nyawuza (1985) New 'Marxist' tendencies and the battle of ideas in South Africa. *African Communist, 103*, pp. 45–61
Ojha, I.C. (1970) The Kremlin and Third World leadership: closing the circle?. In W. Raymond Duncan (ed.), *Soviet policy in developing countries*. Ginn Blaisdell, Massachusetts
Potekhin, I.J. (n.d.) The Stalinist theory of colonial revolution and national movement in tropical and South Africa. In *Communist policy towards Africa*, Research and Microfilm Publications, New York, pp. 1-22
South African Communist Party (SACP) (1962) *The road to South African freedom*. Ellis Bowles, London
—— (1985a) The South African Communist Party holds its Congress. *African Communist, 101*, pp. 5-7
—— (1985b) The new Constitution adopted by our 6th Congress is another milestone. *African Communist, 102*, p. 46
Sovetskoye Vostokovendeniye (1969) Text 2 Section X. In H. Carrere d'Encausse and S. Schram (eds), *Marxism and Asia*. Allen Lane, London
Spriano, P. (1985) *Stalin and the European communists*. Verso, London
Starishenko, G. (1968) Article in *Kommunist*, September 1962, cited in A.L. Klinghoffer, *Soviet perspectives on African socialism*. Fairleigh Dickenson University Press, New Jersey
Steele, J. (1984) *The limits of Soviet power*. Penguin, Harmondsworth
Suttner, R. (1984) 'The Freedom Charter, the peoples' charter in the nineteen-eighties' (26th T.B. Davies Memorial Lecture). University of Cape Town Press, Cape Town
—— and Jeremy Cronin (1986) *Thirty years of the Freedom Charter*. Ravan Press, Johannesburg
Tabarin, E.A. (ed.-in-chief) (1975) *Neocolonialism and Africa in the 1970s*. Progress Publishers, Moscow
Toussaint (1983) A critique of the speech — 'Where does FOSATU stand?' *African Communist, 35*–45
Turok, B. (1980) *Revolutionary thought of the twentieth century*. Zed Books, London
Tyagunenko, V. (1966) *Bypassing capitalism*. Novoste Press Agency, Moscow
—— (1969) On the necessity for a realistic analysis of the revolution in the developing countries. In H. Carrere d'Encausse and S. Schram (eds), *Marxism and Asia*. Allen Lane, London
Vuk'ayibambe (1985) Revolutionary trade unions and the tasks of the Party. *African Communist, 103*, pp. 94-8
Wallington, P. (1986) How leftist is the ANC? *Business Day* (Johannesburg), 12 May
Wolpe, H. (1983) Apartheid's deepening crisis. *Marxism Today*, January pp.3-6
Zjukov (1969) The aggravation of the crisis of the colonial system. in H. Carrere d'Encausse, and S. Schram (eds), *Marxism and Asia*. Allen Lane, London, pp. 261-3

11

Beyond Apartheid:
Pathways for Transition

Philip Frankel

The last three years have seen the burgeoning of what is undoubtedly the most pronounced political crisis in recent South African history. Since the beginning of the present round of unrest in the Vaal Triangle riots of September 1984, the daily death-count through political violence has risen to a point at which, according to some commentators, South Africa is firmly locked into a state of low-intensity, if undeclared, civil war. A massive destruction of property has taken place over the last three years through a mixture of sabotage and anomic violence. This has, in some areas of the eastern Cape and Transvaal culminated in an almost complete collapse of government and community services. All evidence suggests that the present conflict is likely to spread rather than diminish in the foreseeable future — conceivably in a way which sweeps away many of the established features of the system of apartheid.[1]

The incomparable severity of the forces shaking the South African political and economic order is partially attributable to the unprecedented level of international involvement in South African affairs at the present moment. While the current crisis is essentially the legacy of internal developments, especially 40 years of National Party rule, the last year to 18 months has seen at least a partial shattering of the widely disseminated fiction of South Africa as a highly encapsulated and self-sufficient economic entity. Many of the adjustments made to apartheid over the last three years predate the decision of the international economic community to institute sanctions and curbs on capital inflows to the Republic: nonetheless, a good proportion of change in state rhetoric and policy over the last 18 months is linked to the coincidence between massive international economic and political pressure which is a hallmark of the present crisis. With continued restrictions on the movement of investment capital and an acceleration in the sanctions campaign following recent US and EEC decisions, global economic influences are likely to remain prominent, if not decisive, in shaping state choices between the poles of further isolation or, at the other extreme, conceding South African membership of an interdependent world with moral requirements for race relations and political order sharply at variance with the cardinal postulates of apartheid. Any prognosis for the future is clearly related to the degree to which the South African government is prepared to concede some measure of sovereignty to superior world opinion in the face of external economic pressure.

This is not to say, as spokesman for the state have reiterated, that the major decisions governing South Africa's future will be taken abroad. On the contrary, any realistic scenario for the years to come must also take into account the extent to which the fervency and pitch of domestic opposition to apartheid have rapidly escalated and expanded since the last months of 1984. 'Black power', despite the predilections of overseas observers, is still incapable of overthrowing the political system. Yet the countervailing ability of the white minority to monopolise the content and pace of the socio-political agenda is nonetheless disintegrating into reactive-type responses, as political initiatives are seized by the black opposition on both the labour and township fronts. In the black townships in particular, the current state of 'permanent insurrection' (to use the widely employed terminology) reflects an unparalleled wave of either passive or active community solidarity which, unlike 1976, has mushroomed out from a youthful constituency to cut across generational, ethnic and class divisions in the process of generalising dissent over a wide range of social and political issues. This is particularly the case in communities in which the experience of state violence exercised by the military or police has raised the political quality of rent, school, labour and consumer boycotts to a premium. These various boycotts, with their capacity to intervene in the domestic concerns of even the most non-political of black township dwellers, are a source of both community solidarity and popular political education. Inasmuch as they draw attention to the structural characteristics of the overall system, it has become increasingly difficult for the state to exercise control, either by manipulating the divisions among its opponents, or through inducing compliance by incremental-type co-optive action.

There are major differences between the present character of black rebellion and its predecessors. In both its organisational characteristics and geographic dispersal, for example, the present unrest poses unfamiliar challenges to a state accustomed to dealing with relatively isolated and unco-ordinated township conflicts. In contrast with 1976, when the organisational foundations of black protest were relatively weak, present actions against the state are firmly rooted in a complex, if nascent, network of civic, youth and community structures which have emerged in even the smaller and more isolated of black areas.[2] Successive States of Emergency have only partially succeeded in neutralising these new centres of opposition, with their potential to forge links between township and industrial protest. In a number of areas of the Transvaal and eastern Cape, the new instruments of 'people's power' have already effectively displaced the established black local authorities, both in the black public imagination and in the daily administration of the townships. In these circumstances of ostensible 'dual power', a considerable degree of South Africa's immediate future at the crossroads of evolution and revolution turns on the extent to which the state either can or cannot enter into some sort of fruitful negotiation with the new grassroots black organisations.

The extraordinary combination of powerful internal and domestic pressure on the state does not, however, presume the present political order disintegrating along the apocalyptic lines sketched by generations of South African commentators. On the contrary, inasmuch as it is possible to label the complex configuration of forces in contemporary South Africa, what we are witnessing is basically a Gramsci-like situation of interregnum, homeostasis or equilibrium, in which the inability of dissidents to overthrow the hegemony of the state is countered by the incapability of the state to eliminate dissidence completely. In this complex configuration of stalemated power relations and open-ended possibilities, there are four basic pathways along which South Africa can conceivably proceed into the immediate future.

State reform

The technical and organisational base of the South African state is likely to remain firm into the immediate future, independent of internal or internationally induced stress; and, in the circumstances, there is still some space for the present pattern of state reform to accelerate, broaden and deepen in dealing with the fundamental issues related to the redistribution of political power. Sanctions, it should be added, will inevitably injure the economy in the long run — if effectively applied. In the intervening period, however, there are good grounds for believing that the economy will actually survive and possibly prosper, with assistance from rising gold prices and the initial positive impact of import substitution. On the internal front, the state has indisputably vast and untapped reserves of force which, if insufficient to build the conditions of legitimacy necessary to long-term political stability, can nevertheless be applied to buy time for state reform. This would basically involve depriving the black political opposition of the essential resources of leadership and organisation necessary to convert township protest into a coherent nation-wide movement capable of overthrowing the entire political system.

A purely reformist pathway into the immediate future is, however, fraught with considerable difficulty. State concepts of power-sharing and those of its opponents are basically at odds. While there is considerable evidence pointing to positive changes in white political attitudes toward socio-political change in recent years, white South Africa is still largely incapable of bridging the gap between its own conception of what constitutes 'reform' and the broader expectations adhered to by representative black leaders. The language, philosophy and concrete categories of state action still tend to define black participation as an end in itself, whereas the discourse in oppositional circles defines participation as a means for the substantive transfer of power. In the circumstances, there are outstanding and quite fundamental divisions over the power which the state is willing to concede and the power demanded by its opponents.

Present state policy is, in addition, relatively inchoate to a degree which precludes any sort of consistent reform policy capable of legitimising some widely-acceptable variant of the present order in the relatively short space of time available to the present system. Within the ruling elite, the principle of rulership remains inviolable and there are few signs of a breakdown in the political self-confidence identified by some theorists as critical in creating a proto-revolutionary power vacuum. White government and society has nevertheless lost the clear sense of political direction inherent in the 'Total Strategy' of three to four years ago, and there appears to be no strategy at all to deal with the present crisis. This is candidly conceded by highly placed government officials, most of whom will readily admit to the drying-up of the well of reform-type confederal and consociational ideas behind the rationalising public jargon. The tortuous debate within the state over complicated forms of geographic and racial confederalism is, for the most part, more indicative of a desperate anarchy of opinion than of a sustained search for solutions.[3] It is a measure of this confusion that the daily conduct of economic and political policy is increasingly shifting, incremental and dominated by crisis-to-crisis considerations.

Conflicts within the state which preclude the development of some sort of transcending reform strategy and vision are today altogether more complicated than the ideological struggle between 'verligtes' and 'verkramptes' characteristic of an earlier phase of state responses to growing black pressure. The standard ideological divisions between conservatives and 'liberals' remain a factor in the power struggles within the state bureaucracy, the security apparatus and the ruling party. Yet technocratic and organisational variables have increasingly come to supplant the classic clashes of ideological principle which have dominated the history of the National Party at least since the early 1960s. As the state has begun to flounder in shaping adequate programmes to deal with the accumulating social agenda, dangerously idiosyncratic and bureaucratic factors have intervened in the process by which 'reform' is defined and applied. This is particularly evident, for example, in relations between the 'verligte' Department of Constitutional Development (under the imperium of Mr Heunis), and elements within the state security apparatus (i.e. the police and military), whose intention is to rationalise the existing system along managerial lines rather than to dabble with relatively far-reaching plans to federalise (or consociationalise) power.[4]

The whole process of reform is complicated by the progressive erosion of the moderate centres in white and black politics under the stresses of political and racial polarisation. This is not to imply that there are no longer constituencies for evolutionary change among white political interests and the upwardly mobile segments of the Indian, coloured and black communities. The private sector has also emerged as an important actor for accelerated state reform as a result of its natural inclination to modulate the process of change as a means of protecting the economic system from political rupture.[5] The state is experiencing considerable difficulty, nonetheless, in capitalising on these natural allies for reform as a result of its internal ideological and organisational divisions, which preclude it from effectively examining the sacrosanct principles of political apartheid in a way which allows for the translation of rhetoric into policy-making action. Tasks of this nature, however pressing, demand a degree of leadership, foresight, insight and sheer political courage of an order sadly lacking, individually or collectively, in today's top government circles.

Negotiation

The relative paralysis of central government has encouraged the emergence of a variety of white groups external to the state which have partially appropriated the banner of reform and begun to exert pressure on government to support the general principle of an overall negotiated settlement. Within the ranks of this multi-ideological 'peace movement' are to be found the churches, organisations such as the End Conscription Campaign, and — pre-eminent in the category — the Progressive Federal Party (PFP) and significant elements of the private sector. While the withdrawal of the PFP from the parliamentary network is a matter of acute ideological debate within the Party following the resignation of van Zyl Slabbert, the recent decision of the Party to devote more attention to its extra-parliamentary activity in fostering a climate of negotiation represents an important strategic shift into terrain previously exclusive to the United Democratic Front (UDF).[6] The rapid, if sometimes reluctant, politicisation of the private sector over the last 18 months has important implications for power relations within the white elite in the near and distant future. Most business activity as a pressure group has previously been confined to the State President's Economic Advisory Council. In the last 18 months, however, major employer organisations, such as the Urban Foundation, the Association of Chambers of Commerce (ASSOCOM), and the Federated Chamber of Industries (FCI) (if not the Afrikaanse Handelsinstituut) have begun to press for accelerated political change and negotiations about the post-apartheid South Africa in a way which signifies a far more assertive political stance on the part of capital since the early 1960s. The recent decision on the part of the state to replace the pass laws with a policy of positive 'orderly urbanisation', the desegregation of central business districts and pressure for the abolition of the Group Areas legislation, are very much the result of private sector activity in the face of a threatening economic and political climate. To the extent that business can convince central government of the necessity to end the State of Emergency and release political prisoners, it could emerge as a vital force in creating a climate conducive to negotiation.

There is, however, a number of factors which together largely preclude a negotiated settlement as an option for South Africa — at least in the short term. In the first place, it is government policy to denigrate the ANC as a representative component of any such settlement — even though it has been manifestly clear for some years that any viable arrangement for a post-apartheid South Africa must necessarily include the ANC as being primary amongst black organisations. The release of Nelson Mandela and other political prisoners is clearly not on the state agenda while the National Party seeks to rebuild support on its right, and the ANC is clearly reluctant to suspend the armed struggle *at least* before the termination of the State of Emergency. This is not to ignore a number of forces at work within the ANC which continue to foster the principle of negotiated settlement.[7] These include a residual commitment to principles of passive resistance on the part of the older generation of ANC leaders, as well as a keen strategic sense that a lengthy and damaging race war would vastly complicate an eventual ANC inheritance of power. Nonetheless, ANC leaders cannot conceivable enter into open negotiations with the state as long as its leaders are detained and troops and police continue viciously to enforce state control in the townships. To do so is both philosophically and personally abhorrent to virtually the entire ANC leadership, a number of whose older and more moderate elements are also engaged in protecting their internal power base against the more militant claims of a new generation of post-1976 activists. In the circumstances, ANC policy on negotiation remains limited to dealing with various white groups — business men, students and members of the established churches — each of whose pilgrimages to Lusaka exposes raw divisions within the white elite and adds to the lustre and legitimacy of the Congress as an instrument of alternative government.

Similar considerations dominate the prospects for an 'internal' dialogue between the ruling National Party, the UDF and Inkatha. Chief Buthelezi is clearly attracted to the prospect of acting as kingmaker between the state and the ANC, but is unlikely to make a clear political choice regarding service on the government's new National Statutory Council (NSC) until there is clarity regarding the powers of this new body at the apogee of its constitutional vision for South Africa. State reactions to the proposals of the Indaba for a non-racial regional option in Natal are also likely to be crucial in weaning Inkatha into some sort of alliance.[8] It is questionable, in addition, whether any black leader, aside from Mandela, has a nation-wide power base, even though individuals such as Buthelezi, Bishop Tutu and a number of lesser figures in the UDF enjoy powerful specific constituencies. This means that even if the state were capable of inducing one of these individuals to the negotiation table, it would have to include other representative black leaders if subsequent dialogue is to be meaningful. Whether this is possible is by no means apparent in the light of divergent political interests and historic tensions between the UDF and Inkatha. Even if it were, it is politically suicidal for any black leader of stature to enter into discussions with the state, apart from tight pre-conditions related to the termination of the Emergency, the release of Mandela and the total dismantling of apartheid as a precursor to a fundamental redistribution of political power.

Given the highly emotive connotations of 'collaboration' in current black political circles, no respectable black leader can conceivably justify dealing with the state in any form, without government first putting its own house in order. Yet the likelihood of government taking the initiative to do so to a degree acceptable to even the more moderate of its critics is unlikely, given the psychology of state leadership, in which negotiation on terms other than those prescribed by existing constitutional plans is seen as tantamount to political surrender. Taken in conjunction with the political ascendency of the Afrikaner right over the last five years, it is most unlikely that the immediate future will see National Party leaders making the dramatic gestures and policy changes appropriate to setting in motion effective negotiation over the major power questions.

The various white groups outside the state and the National Party cannot, in addition, fully substantiate their political credentials in a way which could create impetus for round-table talks about a post-apartheid South Africa. Both the private sector and the PFP have periodically represented themselves in the role of mediating change at some sort of national convention; yet neither possesses sufficient influence within the dominant power structures of Afrikanerdom, or in black society, effectively to market negotiation between the major power blocs. While the PFP could eventually emerge to hold the balance of parliamentary power following the electoral rise of the Conservative Party and major defections on the left of the Nationalists, its current ability to perform the role of mediator is compromised by internal leadership and policy struggles which reinforce its image of pusillanimous, if well-intentioned, white liberalism, across the political spectrum. The pretensions of the business community to act as a communications bridge between the state and the ANC is also constrained by state intolerance of business intervention in the political process, and by fairly substantial differences of principle between the ANC and South African capital over the structural features of a future post-apartheid economy. While the Freedom Charter at the centre of the ANC's vision of the future is sufficiently flexible to suit a variety of social purposes, there is an outstanding and deep divide between the unbridled free market philosophy of South African business and the social-democratic conceptions for economic change articulated in the ANC programme.[9] There is also, understandably, little support in the ANC for the federalist ideas of the PFP as political ends rather than the means for transferring social power.

The various difficulties bedevilling the politics of negotiation are indicative of the much deeper structural problems which face peaceful evolution in present-day South Africa. South Africa currently displays many of the classically dangerous features of the famous J-curve to revolution in which state-cultivated expectations of reform are dashed against state actions which inhibit the following of policy to its logical conclusions.[10] Botha, as Bishop Tutu has pointed out, has had the foresight to open the gates of change but not the courage to step through them. In the process, the townships have become crucibles of frustration and bitterness, where 'normal' levels of despair are rubbed raw by daily doses of state violence. In these conditions, the state is perceived as both obdurant and illegitimate. Indeed, with mounting evidence that the security forces are acting with considerable latitude and independence from the central state, there is some element of suspicion that the civil authorities may be the wrong people with whom to talk. Such an atmosphere is generally not condusive to the polite requirements of a workable national convention — short of both black and white leaders reining-in their respective forces. Whether they are able to do so is also a moot point. As ANC and government leaders privately concede, a situation may be in the offing in which neither the state nor the black opposition can effectively manage what has become, in many instances, an authentically spontaneous township dynamic.

Any genuine negotiation exercise must, despite marked polarisation, evoke participation by political interests on both the left and right of the political mainstream. Attitudes toward dialogue in both UDF and ANC are undoubtedly shaped by the fact that the state is under unprecedented pressure. While the leadership of both organisations is realistic enough to appreciate that the present system is still far from tottering, it makes strategic sense at this point to take a relatively hard position on negotiation, the occurence of which will inevitably diminish this pressure. It is, of course, in the realm of the fantastic to envision the white parties of the far right engaging in any dialogue involving the transfer of power referred to in official ANC or UDF communications — least of all in present circumstances where the Conservative Party (CP) (and to a lesser extent, the Herstigte Nasional Partei (HNP) and Afrikaanse Weerstands Beweging (AWB) are riding what appears to be the tide of white reaction. The National Party government itself has taken an ambiguous position on regional negotiations, in both Natal and the eastern Cape, and is clearly reluctant to come to the negotiating table unless it is in the dominant position of setting the agenda.[11] The state is, on the whole, determined to maintain control over any initiatives leading to negotiation — including, it appears, the various 'local options' advanced by a number of municipal power groups as consistent with government commitments to consociationalise the devolution of power.[12] The intention of the state to proceed with ethnically based Regional Services Councils of its own creation, as well as recurrent announcements that there is a range of 'non-negotiables' related to group rights — most of which touch the fundamentals of power — leads one to conclude that the state still needs to be persuaded of the value of negotiation over the central issues in a crisis-ridden South Africa.[13]

Closure

The time for negotiation, may, ironically, be premature, despite the deeply divided nature of contemporary society. White South Africa, as some commentators note, may need to be squeezed much more tightly in both the political and economic arenas before it takes negotiation seriously. This is clearly recognised in the punitive logic of economic sanctions, which are designed, at least in part, to tighten the screws on white South Afica with a view to bringing it to the negotiation table. Most internal black leaders also concede, however reluctantly, that further pressure needs to be exerted on the white community before it can be expected to negotiate seriously on the fundamentals of redistributed power. Among the more militant opposition groups in the black townships, there is also a tendency to exaggerate 'people's power', and a consequent belief that verbal intercourse with the state is undesirable and/or unnecessary.

In practice, the South African state remains overwhelming if not pristine in its access to power. The implementation of sanctions has also paradoxically consolidated state power, at least in the short term, by expanding the range of freedom of the state to act with impunity in the face of global pressure. As the threat of economic action has become a reality, there is less incentive for decision-makers to reference their actions against a restraining world opinion. It is more than coincidental that the growth of international hostility over the last six months corresponds with what is undoubtedly the most ferocious, consistent and enduring state onslaught on opposition movements in South African history. This has not entirely eliminated black dissidence, yet much of the evidence gleaned from the second State of Emergency indicates that severe damage has been wrought to the organisational networks carefully and laboriously constructed during the early 1980s. The relative short-term success of the Emergency in stifling the means, if not the spirit, of black resistance, is also an important source of political power for the extremist fragments of the white elite, within the state and in the broader social process. Since the inception of the current crisis in September 1984, there has been a strong body of opinion on the right of the National Party and within the state bureaucracy (especially in the Ministry of Law and Order, the South African Police (SAP) and the upper/middle ranks of the military) which has favoured what might be termed a 'closure option' in dealing with the multiple challenges to white power. The Emergency, assisted by the siege psychologies developing among the white elite as a reaction to accelerating sanctions, has added inestimably to the political influence wielded by these reactionary elements in the process through which public policy is defined and implemented.

Given the rising tide of 'closure' as a pathway along which South Africa can conceivably move in the forseeable future, it is necessary to define the notion more closely. Firstly, despite appearances, closure does not necessarily imply the cessation of reform or the reinstitutionalisation of the various legal and administrative mechanisms which have conventionally sustained classical apartheid. With the exception of the political parties and movements of the ultra-right (i.e. the CP, HNP and AWB), whose power base is circumscribed by a relative absence of downward mobility in white society at present, no political group within the white minority subscribes to the idea of reversing reform in the sense of reintroduced apartheid. In essence, closure implies *imposed* rather than negotiated reform, whose character and content is determined exclusively by the political interests which already have access to central state power.

Closure in this sense implies, secondly, that the timetable and nature of state reform are matters to be dealt with within South Africa, according to national interests defined by the central government. While the intention of economic sanctions is to allow the global community extra leverage in assisting the process of change, the consequence of sanctions will be — at least in the short to medium term — the engendering of a tenacious and belligerent siege psychosis on the part of white South Africa whose very nature excludes external 'interference' with a vengeance. Various South African officials have already given notice on this score in the light of international moves to economically isolate the Republic.

Thirdly, closure involves a reorganisation of the modalities of state power to enable the dominant elite to withstand the inevitable domestic and international reaction to what appears to be a half-hearted form of state-sponsored 'revolution'. On the economic front, the South African government has rapidly moved toward devising a national economic plan to circumvent sanctions by reshaping and (where possible) reducing dependence on the world economy. On the political front, 1986 has seen significant developments aimed at centralising power as an integral part of constructing a more effective and rational authoritarian system. The imposition of severe restrictions on media reporting of civil unrest, the replacement of elected provincial assemblies with state-controlled executives and the articulation of a nation-wide system of Joint Management Committees (JMCs) responsible to the all-powerful State Security Council, are ominously significant.[14]

It is already clear that a number of social, as opposed to ideological, interests have a vested stake in some version of closure. While the reactions of the ultra-right to moves in a closure direction are largely rooted in xenophobia tailored to the racial interests of downwardly mobile white classes, there are other elements in elite society which will benefit from moves to impose reform, centralise power and pull up the drawbridge against international opinion. These include groups among capital who will initially benefit from state policies of import-substitution; the export sector, whose competitiveness has already increased with the declining convertibility of the rand; mining interests likely to capitalise on world anxiety at blockages on the outflow of strategic minerals; and investment capital, which has already begun to pump liquidity reserves into the market created through disinvestment by multi-national capital. Both the military and technocratic elements within the state bureaucracy will accumulate political influence with the centralisation of government structures.

What is less clear however, are the more long-term consequences of closure, apart from the fact that the economic and political reorganisation of South African society along siege lines is likely to be relatively irreversible in the short to medium term. In the first instance, one of the primary rationalisations of closure — i.e. that it will create the appearance and possible substance of stability eventually to defuse the hostility of international financial circles — represents a massive misjudgement of the intensity of world criticism; and this is likely to increase rather than decrease with the passing of time, unless the state moves towards a system of genuine non-racial power-sharing. While it is equally misconceived to underrate the hard, conservative and materialist impulses beind corporate involvement in South Africa, it is difficult to envision a return to the capital investment patterns of mid-1984 — unless the South African state can guarantee political and economic stability, at minimum. As we have suggested, this is predicated on the existence of a vigorous broadly acceptable, but unlikely programme of political reform.

Effective closure also requires a uniformity of purpose, a level of political mobilisation and a measure of state co-ordination which is clearly beyond the resources of a diverse and developing South Africa. In the short term, closure can, and probably will, engender some measure of internal instrumental support, as various interests within the state and capital move to exploit the various political and economic advantages of siege status. The ability of the state to co-opt black opposition could also increase to the extent that a number of non-racial structures are created within the overall central framework at local and regional level. Over the long term, however, closure is not a viable option due to the level of integration between the South African and world economy. South Africa is neither developed enough for relative self-sufficiency, nor underdeveloped enough to support a primitive economy in isolation from the international system. Given the fundamental and concurrent problems of mass unemployment, rising inflation and the lack of structural investment, economic growth is unlikely to meet rising social demands after an estimated four to five-year post-sanctions mini-boom unless there is a renewed flow of capital imports.

While the role of gold prices is an important variable, given its centrality to the economy, the support of business for closure is likely to diminish after an initial outburst of confidence and enthusiasm. Closure is also unlikely to address the legitimacy crisis of the state, even while it enhances the capability of government to organise and use power. In the circumstances, the 'permanent insurrection' of the present will continue sporadically in a way which fuels the forces of repression. It has been widely noted that the military has become progressively involved in the civil political process since the mid-1970s. Endemic crisis since 1984 and the present movements towards closure have further eroded civil-military distinctions in the social process. This has culminated in the recent activation of the National Security Management System — undoubtedly the most highly institutionalised network of civil-military co-operation in defence of white power in South African history. The 'consequence of militarisation', it has been noted, 'is more militarisation'.[15] The consequence of closure may be more closure and, in the process, a far more authoritarian and brutally militarised version of the present system.

Revolution

This leads in turn to the fourth and potentially most violent of the various scenarios postulated by analysts — i.e. some cataclysmic series of revolutionary events occurring in the forseeable future, leading through a bloody race war to the displacement of the white monopoly over power. It is argued here, however, that despite the prognostications of legions of commentators that white rule will eventually terminate in this fashion, a fully fledged civil war along race lines is unlikely in the next five to ten years — at least not a civil war in the dramatic terms sketched by the more apocalyptically minded observers. In part this has to do with force as the basic denominator in any revolution, and, more particularly, with the largely untapped ability of the South African state to use sufficient coercion to rule, if not govern legitimately, into the immediate future.

This is not to say, it must be emphasised, that state capacity for hard-fisted coercion is either infinite or limitless. Extended township violence concurrent with a full-scale war on the Angolan border will severely strain the security forces along the classic lines described by various theorists of revolutionary warfare.[16] The growing reliance of the South African Defence Force (SADF) on conscripted manpower for township control is also a matter of concern to both military planners in the Joint Defence College and civil planners who see economic growth as dependent on the optimal use of skilled white manpower. The increased adoption by township communities of rent, school, consumer and bus boycotts to express protest also suggests the emergence of sites of resistance at which it is difficult to deploy pure military power effectively.[17] With increased integration between withdrawal-type politics in the community and labour struggles on the industrial front, the state will undoubtedly experience growing difficulty in using the putative force at its disposal.

Revolution is, however, a two-way street, involving interaction between those who hold and those who contend for power.[18] As a result, revolutions are made as much by elites as by the popular interests opposing them. In this regard, it is important to note that the social base of the white state remains relatively unified, strong and self-sufficient — notwithstanding defections to left and right in the discourse over the nature and strategies of change in a post-apartheid direction. Emerging siege conditions against the background of white history, politics and the culture mythologies which rationalise race rule will for some time head off the sense of elite demoralisation identified by various theorists as precursors of classical forms of revolution.

White South Africa, if still far from questioning the legitimacy of its power, has nevertheless made a number of tactical errors in the process of protecting its base in recent years. Reform has been painfully slow (measured by any standards), but not slow enough to inhibit rising popular expectations. The state has generally failed to capitalise on a number of political opportunities since the beginning of the 1980s; and, caught between past and present — its cultural obligations as a white institution and the demands of survival which require non-racial reorganisation — it has failed to strike out decisively in either direction. In so doing, it has alienated both its conservative supporters — some of whom in the AWB or HNP talk of a 'restorative revolution' to corporatise the state or re-establish the classical apartheid of the 1950s — and, perhaps more importantly, the mainstream moderates of black society who most keenly feel the symptoms of relative deprivation.

The current State of Emergency has, as we have intimated, largely succeeded in its intention of disrupting the township civic and youth structures erected since 1976. As a consequence of sheer exhaustion and an estimated 42,000 detentions since early 1985, black protest is partially grinding down from the high of mid-1986 in a way which will allow the state some breathing space to implement its current plans for upgrading social facilities as a means of purchasing instrumental support.[19] The progressive organisations at the national level, in the unions and the township communities have subsequently begun to organise for a protracted struggle. At the same time, the largely indiscriminate character of state repression since June 1986 has also succeeded in eliminating some of the most viable conflict-moderating structures in the black areas, with the inevitable result that community power has now tilted away from the older black moderates to far more militant elements in a variety of eastern Cape and Transvaal townships. In the circumstances, black middle-class society — the great white hope — increasingly finds itself in the classic nutcracker between people and state in a way which demands political choices.[20] Given the onslaught of the state on the civic and youth organisations (some dominated by the middle class), many have irreversibly turned away from the notion of the reasonably peaceful reform of the present order. The demonstrable inability of the state to restore normality in the townships is also important to moderate black opinion. Revolutions proceed from the perception that the state is weak.[21] With the persistence of unrest, a growing, if immeasurable, proportion of the strategic black middle class has clearly begun to consider whether it makes any sense to support an apparently crumbling regime as a matter of long-term political interest.

None of the foregoing presumes an inevitable revolution. The state still has a measure of co-optive capacity geared to the class interests of privileged fragments in black society, while the SADF has a massive and largely unused armoury of sophisticated technologies of violence which can partially compensate for the illegitimacy of the system in the worst of all possible situations. There is some evidence of strain in the command and control channels running from the centre to the periphery of the state security apparatus after two years of endemic civil violence. Current township protests measured against the reserves of police and military power are nevertheless little more than an irritant. In the last analysis, the failure of the SADF or the SAP to extinguish protest completely is attributable more to political constraints than to military weakness. There is considerable evidence that the security forces have also acted to turn internal conflicts within the townships to their own advantage. In most cases this involves recruiting vigilantes from the black unemployed, the petite bourgeoisie or others with vested class interests in the *status quo* as a supplementary source of power.[22] In the final analysis, revolutions seldom occur while the military sides with the state — they never fail when it does not — and it is inconceivable that the white-commanded security forces will desert to the enemy, given the racial and class ties binding them to elite society.[23]

This situation does not constitute grounds for complacency on the part of the white elite: on the contrary, developments within the townships have become the reference point for the international community in determining its economic and political responses to South Africa. The country cannot hope to alleviate its pariahdom, with all of the accompanying political and economic consequences, unless government can come up with more creative and equitable political solutions for the black areas other than simply unleashing its police and military units. The current round of disturbances will also not trickle away, given their distinguishing features (noted above), and are likely to change as black protest is taken out of isolation in the townships into the central business, industrial and residential areas of the major white cities in the forseeable future.

The geographical location of the majority of townships lends itself to their surrounding and penetration by the security forces. Yet it is ANC strategy to 'take the struggle into the kitchens and bedrooms of the white ruling class', and one can expect future developments in this direction. In general, it is impossible for a society at South Africa's level of development to encapsulate conflict in a particular area of social or geographical activity. The black trade unions have, for example, organised unprecedented industrial resistance over the last two years — and it is unlikely that the Congress of South African Trade Unions (COSATU) will not capitalise on the opportunities presented by an increasingly dissatisfied urban population (squeezed between economic retrogression and governmental recalcitrance), in the process of building political resources at the nexus between industrial and community struggles in the foreseeable future.[24] It is out of this conjuncture that popular solidarity and power will emerge to steer South Africa along a painful and violent, if not necessarily revolutionary, course in the years to come.

It is generally accepted that South Africa is at a watershed in its political history — somewhere between classical apartheid with its rigid racial separation, and a new society whose precise dimensions are unknown. While most writers also agree that 'post-apartheid' South Africa will be shaped by the social processes from which it is born, there is also considerable uncertainty as to the nature and timing of the transition. Short of the now-evident fact that the transition is bound to involve substantial violence in one form or another, the immediate future of South Africa involves the interaction of so many indeterminate variables as to make prediction naïve and/or foolhardy. The capacity of the state judiciously to balance coercion with reform; the extent to which oppositional movements build popular support, institutions and leadership resources to develop strategies to exploit the contradictions inherent in 'dual power' situations in various areas of the country; the interweaving and co-ordination of labour and community struggles; the role of the private sector in moderating state reactions to these conflicts and assisting in the implementation of policies geared to curbing structural unemployment; the development of township infrastructures and new representative political institutions; the loyalty of the military in conditions of persistent instability; world political and economic reaction to the pace of change in South Africa — these are just some, but by no means all, of the factors in a complex equation.

In circumstances which correspond to Gramsci's notion of an interregnum, no single one of the four pathways or scenarios that have been sketched can conceivably encapsulate the dynamic reality of contemporary South Africa. Negotiation at regional or local level still represents a pathway to the future, although it is readily evident that the range of issues around which to develop consensus is fast narrowing under the impact of racial polarisation. Many of the 'advanced symptoms of revolution' are present in contemporary South Africa, but there is a variety of crucial catalysts or 'accelerators' which need to lock into the relations between the incumbents of state power and their challengers before revolution in the true sense becomes a conceivable reality.[25] State reform is likely to continue, but it will be reform of a unilateral character, determined by those already in power. Meanwhile, closure — or some variant of closure determined by the structural features of South Africa as a differentiated actor in the global political economy — will become more evident.

A number of factors are particularly important within this complex of shifting and often contradictory social forces. In the first place, executive action by the state could conceivably tip the balance between the various options in the course of the next 12–18 months. While closure is likely to be the predominant but not exclusive modality into 1988, if not longer, changes in executive leadership could make a substantial difference to the character of events thereafter. Many of the features of state reform, including what many commentators regard as a 'paralysis' in current state responses to township developments, bear the hallmark of P.W. Botha. Even if the behaviour of large-scale social organisations is clearly irreducible to idiosyncratic factors, the disappearance of Botha from the political scene, by death or retirement in the forseeable future, will substantially change the landscape of state policy. The period since the advent of the Botha administration has in general witnessed a massive centralisation of power in the executive office, and this implies that any successor to Botha will be strategically and uniquely placed to tip the delicate balance between closure, reform, negotiation and revolution — particularly if the next 12–18 months sees further reorganisations of state structures to suit the centralised requirements of a closure-type siege society. In the circumstances, it can make an extraordinary difference whether a conservative Jan de Klerk, a 'verligte' Chris Heunis or a more 'liberally'-minded Pik Botha emerges triumphant from the succession struggles already in motion.[26]

Power struggles within the National Party must also be seen against the wider backdrop of the differentiation of Afrikanerdom, one of whose consequences has been to reduce the ruling party caucus from a primary institution of government to an important institution *inter pares*.[27] The emergence of a new and powerful generation of technocrats in the state bureaucracy is an important development in this context, with major implications for the short- to medium-term future.[28] The projection of technocratic power at the highest levels of state policy making is one of the strongest constraints on the implementation of closure advocated in the more ideologically belligerent of conservative Afrikaner circles. This suggests that while a variety of technocratic skills within the state is currently being deployed in the erection of siege-type political and economic structures, these could become a brake on the further development of a South African siege-type society once the inevitable point is reached at which it is evident that closure as a pathway carries more costs than benefits.

Technocratic formulae for constitutional change could emerge at the foundations of a reinvigorated reform programme, even though, as a number of writers correctly note, these formulae often provide a pseudo-scientific justification for the maintenance of established systems of power.[29] There are, it must be conceded, enormous conceptual, sociological and political problems confronting

present state plans for constitutional change. The tricameral Parliament, as even its erstwhile supporters now concede, is an institutional monstrosity which will have to be scrapped, or fundamentally restructured, if the state is to secure even a modicum of 'non-
white' support for its future reform plans.[30] Yet as has already
been intimated, important constitutional initiatives have been set
in motion at the regional and local levels, initiatives which technically provide for multiracial decision-making and the redistribution
of resources in a way which confounds South African political
experience and administrative practice.[31] If the technocrat:cally
minded elements in government can force through a package con-
taining state recognition of a non-racial regional authority (such
as that proposed by the Natal Indaba); a modified and equally non-
racial version of the proposed Regional Services Councils; the lifting
of the State of Emergency and the release of political prisoners; the
elimination of remaining racist legislation in the form of the Group
Areas, Land and Population Registration Acts — then those government elements could create a powerful momentum among the
remainder of representative black moderates for participation in
negotiations concerning the design of political structures at the
national level.

Whether this can be done depends on the interaction between
a variety of political groupings with the capability of shaping state
policy. Under the oscillating conditions of the present stalemate,
the local and international business community could be of considerable importance in punishing *and* rewarding certain forms of
change to tip the balance between reform and retrogression. The
economic dimensions of the current crisis have already enlarged
the political role of the private sector, and this could continue at
various levels into the immediate future. To the extent that capital
is unwilling or incapable of communicating accelerated change at
the highest levels, supporters of siege and closure in the bureaucracy
and ruling National Party will increasingly come to occupy the
terrain upon which policy is formed and implemented. To the
degree that the international economic community persists in
withholding credibility from policies of reform initiated by the
moderates in government, it will encourage the psychologies of
withdrawal which have already led the more reactionary elements
of the state in the direction of closure.

Developments in black politics over the next year to 18 months
are also crucial. As already indicated, one of the most significant
features of the current crisis is the extent to which it has impacted

on the mood of the black middle classes. With the state now unable to 'normalise' life in the townships, many moderate blacks are now unable or unwilling to declare their support for a negotiated settlement without risk to their social and physical existence. It remains to be seen whether state action can partially reverse this tendency, at least in part by conceding to the well-known popular demands — the termination of the emergency, the release of political detainees, the withdrawal of the military from the townships, and a fixed timetable on the part of government for the elimination of all forms of racial discrimination on the road to genuine power-sharing. To the extent that the state cannot meet the basic demands, the central issue concerns the extent to which the national liberation movement can equip itself with the leadership, popular unity, organisational means and coercive muscle to confront government directly at the various sites of popular struggle.

Any realistic prognosis for the next year or two must ultimately recognise the enormity and interconnection between the various forces working against conflict resolution. At the level of state leadership, there are few grounds for optimism that policy will move speedily to operationalise the consociational/federalist ideas bandied about in a variety of governmental and white political circles. At a time when dramatic and highly visible action by government is necessary to defuse domestic and international pressure, the ruling party continues to trim its sails to the right and reform putters along on the margins of the central questions of political power. Continuing unrest will in all probability feed the forces of reaction and closure — despite private sector overtures to the state along the lines of the recent Bryntirion 'summit'.[32] The international credibility crisis facing South Africa is also unlikely to abate to pre-1985 levels, particularly if government continues to wield sticks over carrots in controlling political developments into the immediate future. Nor is there likely to be a dimunition of black protest in the face of continued state violence.

Political conflict in South Africa is essentially over power and privilege. These are matters which are technically negotiable in a way which religious or ideological conflicts (the grand clashes of world views) are not. A further year or two of 'violent equilibrium' does not in itself cancel out for the indefinite future the possibility of some sort of negotiated settlement over redistributed power. A continued fermentation of the revolutionary pressures at work in the country nonetheless narrows the options. Five years of political and economic stress may, in principle, induce the 'hawks' in white society to contemplate negotiation as the only response to further violence and conflict. The intervening period must inevitably sap the power of the remaining 'doves', in both the black and white communities. Quite apart from the economic costs of sanctions, protracted conflict must eventually undermine governmental confidence to the classic threshold where the state, devoid of psychological and physical resources, lacks the sheer motivation to govern. In these conditions of 'power deflation', the more militant of black opposition movements will press their strategic advantage to demand radical transformation,[33] and in this eventuality, the politics of negotiation may be redundant. When the white elite turns to real negotiation about post-apartheid, to paraphrase Alan Paton, black South Africans may long since have turned to revolution. History has, of course, little regard for the wrong choices at the right time, or the right choices in the wrong circumstances. Least of all is it tolerant of opportunities lost and choices made too late.

Notes

1. On the township crisis, see, *inter alia*, J. Grest and H. Hughes, 'State strategy and popular response at the local level' in South African Research Services, *South African Review Two* (Ravan Press, Johannesburg, 1984); R. Bloch and P. Wilkinson, 'Urban control and popular struggle: a survey of state urban policy', *Africa Perspective*, no. 20 (1982); K. Helliker, 'The South African townships: social crisis and state policy', unpublished Masters thesis, University of Newfoundland, 1985.

2. See Na-iem Dollie, 'The National Forum' in *South African Review Three* (Ravan Press, Johannesburg, 1986); Jo-Anne Collinge, 'The United Democratic Front' in *South African Review Three* (Ravan Press, Johannesburg, 1986); Howard Barrell, 'The United Democratic Front and National Forum: their emergence, composition and trends', in *South African Review Two* (Ravan Press, Johannesburg, 1984).

3. Among the extensive literature on consocation and federation as pathways to the South African future, see Laurence J. Boulle (ed.), *Constitutional reform and the apartheid state: legitimacy, consociationalism and control in South Africa* (St Martin's Press, New York, 1984); Roger Southall, 'Consociationalism in South Africa: the Buthelezi Commission and beyond', *Journal of Modern African Studies*, vol. 21 (March 1983); Newell Stultz, 'Interpreting constitutional change in South Africa', *Journal of Modern African Studies*, vol. 22, no. 3 (September 1984); Murray Forsyth, *Federalism and the future of South Africa* (South African Institute of International Affairs, Johannesburg, 1984).

4. Michael Evans, 'Restructuring: the role of the military' in *South African Review One* (Ravan Press, Johannesburg, 1983); Kenneth Grundy, *The rise of the South African security establishment: an essay on the changing locus*

of state power (South African Institute of International Affairs, Johannesburg, 1983); Kenneth Grundy, *The militarisation of South African politics* (I.B. Taurus, London, 1986); Philip Frankel, *Pretoria's Praetorians: civil-military relations in South Africa* (Cambridge University Press, Cambridge, 1984); Philip Frankel, 'South Africa: the politics of police control', *Comparative Politics*, vol. 12, no. 4 (July 1980).

5. On the contemporary role of the private sector in the political process, see Merle Lipton, *Capitalism and apartheid* (David Philip, Cape Town, 1986).

6. *Financial Mail* (Johannesburg), 21 November 1986.

7. Robert Fatton, 'The African National Congress of South Africa: the limitations of a revolutionary strategy', *Canadian Journal of African Studies*, vol. 18, no. 3 (1984); Tom Lodge, 'The African National Congress, 1983' in *South Africa Review Two* (Ravan Press, Johannesburg, 1984).

8. John D. Brewer, 'The modern Janus: Inkatha's role in black liberation' in Institute of Commonwealth Studies, *The societies of Southern Africa in the 19th and 20th centuries, vol. 12* (ICS, London, 1981); John Brewer, 'The membership of Inkatha in KwaMashu', *African Affairs*, vol. 84, no. 334 (January 1985); Roger J. Southall, 'Buthelezi, Inkatha and the politics of compromise', *African Affairs*, vol. 80, no. 321 (October 1981); Gerhard Mare and Georgina Stevens, *An appetite for power: Buthelezi's Inkatha and the politics of 'loyal resistance'* (Ravan Press, Johannesburg, 1986).

9. The controversy over the meaning and nature of the Freedom Charter is discussed, *inter alia*, in Raymond Suttner, 'The Freedom Charter: the people's charter in the nineteen-eighties', *South Africa International*, vol. 15, no. 4 (April 1985); Community Resources and Information Centre, *Until we have won our liberty: thirty years of the Freedom Charter* (Community Resources and Information Centre, Johannesburg, 1985); Peter Hudson, 'The Freedom Charter and socialist strategy in South Africa', *Politikon*, vol. 13, no. 1 (June 1986).

10. James C. Davies, 'The J-curve of rising and declining satisfactions as a cause of some great revolutions and a contained rebellion' in H.D. Graham and T.R. Gurr (eds), *The history of violence in America* (Praeger, New York, 1969); James C. Davies, 'Toward a theory of revolution', *American Sociological Review*, vol. 27, no. 1 (February 1962).

11. For the so-called 'Indaba' in Natal, J. Beall, 'The Natal option: regional distinctiveness within the national reform process'; D. Glaser, 'Regionalisation: the case of Kwa-Natal', papers presented at the 17th Annual Congress of the Association for Sociology in Southern Africa, University of Natal, Durban, July 1986.

12. The 'local option' in contemporary South Africa is the subject of numerous recent works, including Neil Dewar, 'Municipal government under the new South African Constitution: who gets what, where, who decides and who decides who decides?', *Social Dynamics*, vol. 11, no. 2 (December 1985); J. Grest and H. Hughes, 'The local state' in *South Africa Review One* (Ravan Press, Johannesburg, 1983).

13. On the proposed Regional Services Councils, M. Bennett *et al.*, *Servicing the nation* (Centre for Applied Social Sciences, Durban, 1986).

14. *Weekly Mail* (Johannesburg), 3 October 1986.

15. Eric A. Nordlinger, *Soldiers in politics: military coups and governments*

Prentice-Hall, Englewood Cliffs, NJ, 1977), p. 207.

16. Joseph Hanlon, *Apartheid's second front: South Africa's war against its neighbours* (Penguin Books, Harmondsworth, 1986).

17. R. White, 'A tide has risen, a breach has occurred: toward an assessment of the strategic value of consumer boycotts', *South African Labour Bulletin*, vol. 11, no. 5 (1986); J. McCarthy and M. Swilling, 'Transport and political resistance: bus boycotts in 1983' in *South African Review Two* (Ravan Press, Johannesburg, 1984); K. Jochelson, 'Rent boycotts', *Work in Progress*, no. 44 (1986); C. Reintges, 'The changing dynamics of political opposition: the Joint Rent Action Committee', paper presented to the 17th Annual Conference of the Association of Sociology in Southern Africa, University of Natal, Durban, July 1986.

18. Harry Eckstein, 'On the etiology of internal wars', *History and Theory*, vol. 4, no. 2 (1965).

19. Max Coleman and David Webster, 'Repression and detentions in South Africa' in *South African Review Three* (Ravan Press, Johannesburg, 1986).

20. On the black middle class, Peter Hudson and Mike Sarakinsky, 'Class interests and politics: the case of the urban African bourgeoisie' in *South African Review Three* (Ravan Press, Johannesburg, 1986).

21. See Lyford Edwards, *The natural history of revolution* (University of Chicago Press, Chicago, 1929).

22. Tom Lodge and Mark Swilling, 'The year of the Amabuthu', *Africa Report*, vol. 31, no. 2 (March-April 1986); Nicholas Haysom, *Mabangalala: the rise of right-wing vigilantes in South Africa* (University of the Witwatersrand Centre for Applied Legal Studies, Johannesburg, 1986).

23. Frankel, *Pretoria's Praetorians*.

24. On the labour movement, see: Johan Maree, *The independent trade unions, 1974–84* (Ravan Press, Johannesburg, 1986); Alan Fine and Robyn Rafel, 'Introduction: trends in organised labour' in *South African Review Three* (Ravan Press, Johannesburg, 1986); Steven Friedman, *Building tomorrow today: African workers in trade unions, 1970–1984* (Ravan Press, Johannesburg, 1986); Douglas Hindson, 'Union Unity' in *South African Review Two* (Ravan Press, Johannesburg, 1984); Jon Lewis, *Industrialisation and trade union organisation in South Africa* (Cambridge University Press, Cambridge, 1984).

25. Mark Hagopian, *The phenomenon of revolution* (Dodd Mead, New York, 1974).

26. *Star* (Johannesburg), 17 October 1986.

27. On changes in contemporary Afrikanerdom, see Craig Charney, 'Restructuring white politics: the transformations of the National Party' in *South Africa Review One* (Ravan Press, Johannesburg, 1983); Willem de Klerk, *The second revolution: Afrikanerdom and the crisis of identity* (Jonathan Ball, Johannesburg, 1984).

28. Heribert Adam, 'Minority monopoly in transition: recent policy shifts of the South African state', *Journal of Modern African Studies*, vol. 18, no. 4 (December 1980); Grundy, *The rise of the South African security establishment*.

29. D. Posel, 'Language, legitimation and control: the South African state after 1978', *Social Dynamics*, vol. 10, no. 1 (June 1984).

30. On constitutional developments, Dennis Austin, 'The Trinitarians: the 1983 South African Constitution', *Government and Opposition*, vol. 30, no. 2 (Spring 1985); David Welsh, 'Constitutional changes in South Africa', *African Affairs*, vol. 83, no. 331 (April 1984).

31. The growing literature on regionalism in the South African context includes Wolfgang Thomas, 'Regional development in a federal South Africa', *Development Southern Africa*, vol. 1, no. 3 (August 1986); and Buthelezi Commission Report, *The requirements for stability and development in KwaZulu and Natal* (2 volumes) (H. and H. Publications, Durban, 1982).

32. *Financial Mail* (Johannesburg), 31 October 1986.

33. On 'power deflation', see Chalmers Johnson, *Revolutionary change* (Little Brown, Boston, 1966).

12

Select Bibliography on South Africa

Noam J. Pines

Adam, Heribert (1971) *Modernising racial domination*, University of California Press, Berkeley
—— (1973) 'The rise of Black Consciousness in South Africa', *Race*, vol. 15, no. 2, pp. 149–65
—— (1975) 'Conflict and change in South Africa' in Donald G. Baker (ed.), *Politics of race*, Saxon House, London
—— (1976) 'Ideologies of dedication vs. blueprints of expedience', *Social Dynamics*, vol. 2, no. 2, pp. 83–91
—— (1979) 'Three perspectives on the future of South Africa', *International Journal of Comparative Sociology*, vol. 20, no. 1–2, pp. 122–36
—— (1980) 'Minority monopoly in transition: recent policy shifts of the South African state', *Journal of Modern African Studies*, vol. 18, no. 4, pp. 811–26
—— (1983) 'Outside influence on South Africa: Afrikanerdom in disarray', *Journal of Modern African Studies*, vol. 21, no. 2, pp. 235–51
—— (1984) 'Racial capitalism vs. capitalist non-racialism', *Ethnic and Racial Studies*, vol. 7, no. 2
—— and Hermann Giliomee (1979) *Ethnic power mobilised: can South Africa change?* Yale University Press, New Haven
—— and Kogila Moodley (1986) *South Africa without apartheid: dismantling racial domination*, University of California Press, Berkeley/Maskew Miller Longman, Cape Town
Adedian, Iraj (1984) 'The public sector and income distribution in South Africa during the period 1970–1982', *Social Dynamics*, vol. 10, no. 2, pp. 49–60
African National Congress (1985) *Selected writings on the Freedom Charter*, ANC, London
Alexander, Neville (1985) *Sow the wind*, Skotaville Publishers, Johannesburg
Aluko, Olajide and Timothy M. Shaw (1985) *Southern Africa in the 1980s*, Allen and Unwin, London
Anderson, E.W. and G.H. Blake (1984) *The Republic of South Africa as a supplier of strategic materials*, South African Institute of International Affairs, Johannesburg
Austin, Dennis (1985) 'The Trinitarians: the 1983 South African Consti-

Select Bibliography

Barrell, Howard (1984) 'The United Democratic Front and National Forum: their emergence, composition and trends' in South African Research Services, *South African Review Two*, Ravan Press, Johannesburg 1984, pp. 6–20

Bekker, Simon Bailey and Richard Humphries (1985) *From control to confusion: the changing role of Administration Boards in South Africa, 1971–1983*, Shuter and Shooter, Pietermaritzburg

Belknap, Timothy (1985) 'Laboring under apartheid', *Africa Report*, vol. 30, pp. 57–62

Bell, R. Trevor (1985) 'Issues in South African unemployment', *South African Journal of Economics*, vol. 53, no. 1, pp. 24–38

—— (1986) 'The role of regional policy in South Africa', *Journal of Southern African Studies*, vol. 12, no. 2, pp. 276–92

Benson, Mary (1986) *Nelson Mandela: the man and the movement*, Norton, New York

Bhana, Surendra and Brigdal Pachai (eds) (1984) *A documentary history of Indian South Africans*, David Philip, Cape Town

Bohmer, Elizabeth Wilhelmina (1985) *A bibliographical and historical study of left radical movements and some alleged left radical movements in South Africa and Namibia, 1900–1981*, University of Stellenbosch Institute for the Study of Marxism, Stellenbosch

Bonner, Philip L. (1985) 'Trade unions: where does South Africa stand?', *Energos*, vol. 12, pp. 4–13

Boulle, Laurence J. (ed.) (1984) *Constitutional reform and the apartheid state: legitimacy, consociationalism and control in South Africa*, St Martin's Press, New York

Bowers, Cathy and Alison Cooper (1986) *U.S. and Canadian investment in South Africa*, Investor Responsibility Research Center, Washington D.C.

Bozzoli, Belinda (1981) *The political nature of the ruling class: capital and ideology in South Africa, 1890–1933*, Routledge and Kegan Paul, London

—— (ed.) (1983) *Town and countryside in the Transvaal*, Ravan Press, Johannesburg

—— (ed.) (1987) *Class, community and conflict: South African perspectives*, Ravan Press, Johannesburg

Brewer, John D. (1981) 'The modern Janus: Inkatha's role in black liberation' in Institute of Commonwealth Studies, *The societies of Southern Africa in the 19th and 20th centuries*, vol. 12, ICS, London, pp. 11–107

—— (1985a) 'The membership of Inkatha in KwaMashu', *African Affairs*, vol. 84, no. 334, pp. 111–35

—— (1985b) 'Official ideology and lay members' beliefs in Inkatha', *Politikon*, vol. 12, no. 1, pp. 57–63

—— (1986) *After Soweto: an unfinished journey*, Clarendon Press, Oxford

Buroway, Michael (1982) 'State and social revolution in South Africa', *Kapitalistate*, vol. 9, pp. 93–122

Buthelezi Commission Report (1982) *The requirements for stability and development in KwaZulu and Natal*, 2 vols, H. and H. Publications, Durban

Callaghy, Thomas M. (ed.) (1983) *South Africa in Southern Africa: the intensifying vortex of violence*, Praeger, New York

Callinicos, Alex and John Rogers (1977) *Southern Africa after Soweto*, Pluto Press, London

304

Cameron, R. (1986) 'The rhetoric and reality of local government Reform', *Social Dynamics*, vol. 12, no. 1, pp. 70–80

Carter, Gwendolen M. (1980) *Which way is South Africa going?* Indiana University Press, Bloomington

Cell, John W. (1982) *The highest stage of white supremacy: the origins of segregation in South Africa and the American South*, Cambridge University Press, Cambridge

Charney, Craig (1983) 'Restructuring white politics: the transformations of the National Party' in South African Research Services, *South African Review One*, Ravan Press, Johannesburg, pp. 142–54

Cilliers, S.P. and C.J. Groenewald (1982) *Urban growth in South Africa 1936–2000*, Department of Sociology, University of Stellenbosch

—— and L.P Raubenheimer (1986) *Patterns of migration and settlement in rural South Africa*, Department of Sociology, University of Stellenbosch

Coleman, Max and David Webster (1986) 'Repression and detentions in South Africa' in South African Research Services, *South African Review Three*, Ravan Press, Johannesburg, pp. 111–36

Collinge, Jo-Anne (1986) 'The United Democratic Front' in South African Research Services, *South African Review Three*, Ravan Press, Johannesburg, pp. 248–66

Commonwealth Group of Eminent Persons (1986) *Mission to South Africa: the Commonwealth Report*, Penguin Books for the Commonwealth Secretariat, Harmondsworth

Community Resources and Information Center (1985) *Until we have won our liberty: thirty years of the Freedom Charter*, CRIC, Johannesburg

Cooper, Carole (1983) 'The established trade union movement' in South African Research Services, *South African Review One*, Ravan Press, Johannesburg, pp. 204–17

Cooper, Linda and Dave Kaplan (1983) *Reform and response: selected research papers on aspects of contemporary South Africa*, University of Cape Town, Rondebosch

Curtis, Fred (1984) 'Contradiction and uneven development in South Africa: the constrained allocation of African labour-power', *Journal of Modern African Studies*, vol. 22, no. 3, pp. 381–97

Danaher, Kevin Drew (1985) *In whose interest? A guide to United States-South African relations*, Institute of Policy Studies, Washington, D.C.

Davenport, T.R.H. (1986) *South Africa: a modern history*, 3rd edn, Macmillan South Africa, Johannesburg

Davies, Robert H. and Dan O'Meara (1984) 'Total Strategy in Southern Africa: an analysis of South African regional policy since 1978', *Journal of Southern African Studies*, vol. 11, no. 2, pp. 183–211

—— and Sipho Dlamini (1984) *The struggle for South Africa: a reference guide to movements, organisations and institutions*, 2 vols, Zed Press, London

Davis, Dennis and Mana Slabbert (eds) (1985) *Crime and power in South Africa: critical studies in criminology*, David Philip, Cape Town

De Klerk, Willem (1984) *The second (r)evolution: Afrikanerdom and the crisis of identity*, Jonathan Ball, Johannesburg

Dewar, Neil (1985) 'Municipal government under the new South African Constitution: who gets what, where, who decides and who decides who decides?', *Social Dynamics*, vol. 11, no. 2, p. 37–48

Dollie, Na-iem (1986) 'The National Forum' in South African Research Services, *South African Review Three*, Ravan Press, Johannesburg, pp. 267–77

Evans, Michael (1983) 'Restructuring: the role of the military' in South African Research Services, *South African Review One*, Ravan Press, Johannesburg, pp. 42–9

—— (1986) *The Front-line states, South Africa and Southern African security, military prospects and perspectives*, University of Zimbabwe, Harare

Fatton, Robert (1984a) 'The African National Congress of South Africa: the limitations of a revolutionary strategy', *Canadian Journal of African Studies*, vol. 18, no. 3, pp. 593–608

—— (1984b) 'The Reagan foreign policy toward South Africa: the ideology of the new Cold War', *African Studies Review*, vol. 27, no. 1, pp. 57–82

—— (1986) *Black Consciousness in South Africa: the dialect of ideological resistance to white supremacy*, State University of New York Press, Albany

Fenrick, Joseph C. (1966) *South African politics and race relations: selected bibliography of books and articles published since 1961*, Library of Congress, Legislative Reference Service, Washington, D.C.

Fine, Alan and Robyn Rafel (1986) 'Introduction: trends in organised labour' in South African Research Services, *South African Review Three*, Ravan Press, Johannesburg, pp. 1–19

Forsyth, Murray (1984) *Federalism and the future of South Africa*, South African Institute of International Affairs, Johannesburg

Frankel, Philip H. (1980a) 'South Africa: the politics of police control', *Comparative Politics*, vol. 12, no. 4, pp. 481–99

—— (1980b) 'The politics of poverty: political competition in Soweto, *Canadian Journal of African Studies*, vol. 14, no. 2, pp. 201–20

—— (1980c) 'Consensus, consociation and co-optation in South African politics', *Cahiers d'Études Africaines*, vol. 20, no. 4, pp. 473–94

—— (1981) 'Political culture and revolution in Soweto', *Journal of Politics*, vol. 81, no. 3, pp. 831–49

—— (1984) *Pretoria's Praetorians: civil-military relations in South Africa*, Cambridge University Press, Cambridge

Frederickson, George (1981) *White supremacy: a comparative study in American and South African History*, Oxford University Press, New York

Friedman, Steven (1987a) *Black politics at the crossroads*, South African Institute of Race Relations, Johannesburg

—— (1987b) *Building tomorrow today: African workers in trade unions, 1970–1984*, Ravan Press, Johannesburg

Gann, Lewis H. and Peter Duignan (1980) *Why South Africa will survive*, Croom Helm, London

Gastrow, Shalag (1985) *Who's who in South African politics*, Ravan Press, Johannesburg

Geldenhuys, Deon Johannes (1984) *The diplomacy of isolation: South African foreign policy making*, Macmillan South Africa, Johannesburg

Gerhart, Gail M. (1978) *Black power in South Africa*, University of California Press, Berkeley

Giliomee, Hermann (1982) *The parting of the ways: South African politics 1976–82*, David Philip, Cape Town

—— (1986) 'Afrikaner nationalism and the fable of the Sultan's Horse', *Energos*, vol. 13, p. 28–48

—— and Lawrence Schlemmer (eds) (1985) *Up against the fences: power, passes and privilege in South Africa*, St Martin's Press, New York/David Philip, Cape Town

Greenberg, Stanley B. (1980) *Race and state in capitalist development*, Yale University Press, New Haven/Ravan Press, Johannesburg

—— (1981) 'Economic growth and political change: the South African Case', *Journal of Modern African Studies*, vol. 19, no. 4, pp. 667–704

Grest, Jeremy and Heather Hughes (1984) 'State strategy and popular response at the local level' in South African Research Services, *South African Review Two*, Ravan Press, Johannesburg, pp. 35–62

Grundy, Kenneth W. (1983a) *The rise of the South African security establishment: an essay on the changing locus of state power*, South African Institute of International Affairs, Johannesburg

—— (1983b) Soldiers without politics: blacks in the South African armed forces, University of California Press, Berkeley

—— (1986) *The militarisation of South African politics*, I.B. Tauris, London/Indiana University Press, Bloomington

Hanf, Theodor, *et al.* (1981) *South Africa: the chances of peaceful change*, Rex Collings, London/Indiana University Press, Bloomington

Hanlon, Joseph (1986) *Apartheid's second front: South Africa's war against its neighbours*, Penguin, Harmondsworth

Harries, Patrick (1985) 'Modes of production and modes of analysis: the South African Case', *Canadian Journal of African Studies*, vol. 19, no. 1, pp. 30–7

Harrison, David (1981) *The white tribe of Africa*, British Broadcasting Corporation, London

Harsh, Ernest (1980) *South Africa: white rule, black revolt*, Monad Press, New York

Hatchen, William A. and C. Anthony Gifford (1984) *The press and apartheid*, University of Wisconsin Press, Madison

Haysom, Nicholas (1986) *Mabangalala: the rise of right-wing vigilantes in South Africa*, University of the Witwatersrand Centre for Applied Legal Studies, Johannesburg

Hill, Christopher R. (1983) *Change in South Africa: blind alleys or new directions?*, Rex Collings, London

Hindson, Douglas C. (1984) 'Union unity' in South African Research Services, *South African Review Two*, Ravan Press, Johannesburg, pp. 90–107

—— and Marion Lacey (1983) 'Influx control and labour allocation: policy and practice since the Riekert Commission' in South African Research Services, *South African Review One*, Ravan Press, Johannesburg, pp. 97–113

Hirson, Baruch (1979) *Year of fire, year of ash*, Zed Press, London

Hudson, Peter (1986) 'The Freedom Charter and socialist strategy in South Africa', *Politikon*, vol. 13, no. 1, pp. 75–90

—— and Mike Sarakinsky (1986) 'Class interests and politics: the case of the urban African bourgeoisie' in South African Research Services, *South African Review Three*, Ravan Press, Johannesburg, pp. 169–85

Hughes, Heather and Jeremy Grest (1983) 'The local state' in South African Research Services, *South African Review One*, Ravan Press, Johannesburg, pp. 122–41

Human Sciences Research Council (1985) *The South African society: realities and future prospects*, HSRC, Pretoria

Hund, John and Hendrik van der Merwe (1986) *Legal ideology and politics in South Africa*, Centre for Intergroup Studies, University of Cape Town, Rondebosch/University Press of America, Lanham, MD

Huntington, Samuel P. (1981) 'Reform and stability in a modernising, multi-ethnic society', *Politikon*, vol. 8, no. 2, pp. 8–26

Innes, Duncan (1984) *Anglo-American and the rise of modern South Africa*, Heinemann, London/Monthly Review Press, New York/Ravan Press, Johannesburg

—— (1986) 'Monetarism and the South African crisis' in South African Research Services, *South African Review Three*, Ravan Press, Johannesburg, pp. 290–302

Jacobs, Gideon F. (ed.) (1986) *South Africa: the road ahead*, Jonathan Ball, Johannesburg

Jaffee, Georgina and Karen Jochelson (1986) 'The fight to save jobs: union initiatives on retrenchment and unemployment' in South African Research Services, *South African Review Three*, Ravan Press, Johannesburg, pp. 51–67

James, Wilmot G. (1986) 'Nolutshungu's South Africa', *Social Dynamics*, vol. 12, no. 1, pp. 43–8

—— and Lieb Loots (1985) 'Class and income inequality, South Africa 1980', *Social Dynamics*, vol. 11, no. 1, pp. 74–83

Johnson, R. W. (1977) *How long will South Africa survive?*, Macmillan, London

Johnstone, Frederick A. (1976) *Class, race and gold*, Routledge and Kegan Paul, London

Kallaway, Peter (ed.) (1984) *Apartheid and education*, Ravan Press, Johannesburg

Kane-Berman, John (1979) *South Africa: a method in the madness*, Pluto Press, London (originally published by Ravan Press, Johannesburg, as *Soweto: black revolt: white reaction*, 1978)

Kaplan, David (1983) 'South Africa's changing place in the world economy' in South African Research Services, *South African Review One*, Ravan Press, Johannesburg, pp. 158–70

Karis, Thomas G. (1983–4) 'Revolution in the making: black politics in South Africa', *Foreign Affairs*, vol. 62, pp. 378–406

—— and Gwendolen M. (eds) (1972) *From protest to challenge*, 3 vols, Hoover Institution Press, Stanford

Keenen, Jeremy (1983) 'Trickle up: African income and employment' in South African Research Services, *South African Review One*, Ravan Press, Johannesburg, pp. 184–92

—— (1984) 'Agribusiness and the Bantustans' in South African Research Services, *South African Review Two*, Ravan Press, Johannesburg, pp. 318–26

Kuper, Leo (1974) *Race, class and power*, Duckworth, London/Aldine, Chicago

—— (1977) *The pity of it all: polarisation of racial and ethnic relations*, Duckworth, London/University of Minnesota Press, Minneapolis

Select Bibliography

Lambley, Peter (1980) *The psychology of apartheid*, Secker and Warburg, London

Lawrence, John C. (1979) *Race propaganda and South Africa*, Victor Gollancz, London

Leach, Graham (1986) *South Africa*, Routledge and Kegan Paul, London/ Century Hutchinson, Johannesburg

Leape, Jonathan, Bo Baskin and Stefan Underhill (1985) *Business in the shadow of apartheid: U.S. firms in South Africa*, Lexington Books, Lexington, Massachusetts

Leatt, James, Theo Kneifel and Klaus Nürnberger (eds) (1986) *Contending ideologies in South Africa*, David Philip, Cape Town

Legassick, Martin (1985) 'South Africa in crisis: what route to democracy?', *African Affairs*, vol. 84, no. 337, pp. 587–603

Leger, Jean, Judy Maller and Jonny Myers (1986) 'Trade union initiatives in health and safety' in South African Research Services, *South African Review Three*, Ravan Press, Johannesburg, pp. 79–96

Lelyveld, Joseph (1986/1985/1986) *Move your shadow: South Africa black and white*, Michael Joseph, London/Times Books, Division of Random House, New York/Jonathan Ball, Johannesburg

Leonard, Richard (1983) *South Africa at war*, Lawrence Hill, Westport

Lewin, Julius (1963) *Politics and law in South Africa: essays on race relations*, Merlin Press, London/Monthly Press Press, New York

Lewis, Gavin (1986) *Between the wire and the wall: a history of South African 'coloured' politics*, David Philip, Cape Town

Lewis, Jon (1984) *Industrialisation and trade union organisation in South Africa*, Cambridge University Press, Cambridge

Lijphart, Arend (1986) *Power sharing in South Africa*, Institute of International Studies, University of California, Berkeley

Lipton, Merle (1985/1986) *Capitalism and apartheid*, Gower, Aldershot/David Philip, Cape Town

Lodge, Tom (1983a) *Black politics in South Africa*, Ravan Press, Johannesburg

—— (1983b) 'The African National Congress, 1982' in South African Research Services, *South African Review One*, Ravan Press, Johannesburg, pp. 50–4

—— (1984) 'The African National Congress, 1983' in South African Research Services, *South African Review Two*, Ravan Press, Johannesburg, pp. 21–5

—— (1986) ' "Mayihlome! — let us go to war!": from Nkomati to Kabwe, The African National Congress, January 1984-June 1985' in South African Research Services, *South African Review Three*, Ravan Press, Johannesburg, pp. 226–47

—— and Mark Swilling (1986) 'The year of Amabuthu', *Africa Report*, vol. 31, no. 2, pp. 4–7

Lombard, Johannes Anthonie (1978) *Freedom, welfare and order*, Bembo, Pretoria

Low, Allan (1986) *Agricultural development in Southern Africa: farm household-economics and the food crisis*, James Currey, London/David Philip, Cape Town

Lumby, Anthony B. and M.D. North-Coombes (eds) (1984) *A bibliographical guide to South African economic development*, University of Natal Department of Economic History, Durban

McGrath, Michael (1984) 'Global poverty in the South African economy', *Social Dynamics*, vol. 10, no. 2, pp. 38–48

—— 'Economic growth and distribution of racial incomes in the South African economy', *South Africa International*, vol. 15, no. 4, pp. 223–32

Magubane, Bernard Makhosezwe (1979) *The political economy of race and class in South Africa*, Monthly Review Press, New York

Mann, Michael (1986) 'Shifts in dominant ideology in contemporary South Africa', *Africa Perspective*, N.S. vol. 1, no. 1, pp. 68–83

Marcum, John (1982) *Education, race and social change in South Africa*, University of California Press, Berkeley

Maré, Gerhard (1986) 'The new Constitution: extending democracy or decentralising control?' in South African Research Services, *South Africa Review Three*, Ravan Press, Johannesburg, pp. 208–22

—— and Georgina Hamilton (1987) *An appetite for power: Buthelezi's Inkatha and the politics of 'loyal resistance'*, Ravan Press, Johannesburg

Maree, Johann (1987) *The independent trade unions, 1974–1984*, Ravan Press, Johannesburg

Marks, Shula, (1986) *The ambiguities of dependence in South Africa: class, nationalism and the state in twentieth century Natal*, Ravan Press, Johannesburg

Marquard, Leo (1971) *A federation of Southern Africa*, Oxford University Press, London

Mathews, Anthony S. (1971) *Law, order and liberty in South Africa*, Juta, Cape Town

Maylam, Paul (1986) *A history of the African people of South Africa from the early Iron Age to the 1970s*, Croom Helm, London/St Martin's Press, New York/David Philip, Cape Town

Millar, Thomas Bruce (1985) *South Africa and regional security*, South African Institute of International Affairs, Johannesburg

Moodie, Thomas Dunbar (1975) *The rise of Afrikanerdom: power, apartheid and the Afrikaner civil religion*, University of California Press, Berkeley

Mothlabi, Mokgethi (1984) *The theory and practice of black resistance to apartheid: a social ethical analysis*, Skotaville, Johannesburg

Nasser, Martin (1984) 'Report on black employee attitudes to capitalism', University of South Africa School of Business Leadership, Pretoria

Nattrass, Jill (1986) 'The South African economy: the year 2000 from the 1986 viewpoint', *Energos*, vol. 13, pp. 14–17

Noer, Thomas, J. (1985) *Cold War and black liberation: the United States and white rule in Africa 1948–1968*, University of Missouri Press, Columbia

Nolutshungu, Sam C. (1982) *Changing South Africa: political considerations*, Manchester University Press, Manchester/David Philip, Cape Town

Odendaal, André (1984) *Vukani Bantu! The beginning of black protest politics in South Africa to 1912*, David Philip, Cape Town

O'Dowd, Michael (1974) 'South Africa in the light of the stages of economic growth' in Adrian Leftwich (ed.), *South Africa*, Allison and Busby, London

O'Meara, Dan (1983) *Volkskapitalisme: class, capital and ideology in the development of African nationalism, 1934–1948*, Cambridge University Press, Cambridge/Ravan Press, Johannesburg

O'Meara, Patrick (1981) 'South Africa, mobilisation, revolt and crisis',

Canadian Journal of African Studies, vol. 15, no. 3, pp. 567–70

Omond, Roger (1985) *The apartheid handbook*, Penguin, Harmondsworth

Orkin, Mark (1986) *Disinvestment, the struggle, and the future: what black South Africans really think*, Ravan Press, Johannesburg

Pines, Noam J. (1985) 'Approaches in political science to the study of development', *Development Southern Africa*, vol. 2, no. 1, pp. 26–37

Platzky, Laurine, on behalf of the National Committee Against Removals (1986) 'Reprieves and repression: relocation in South Africa' in South African Research Services, *South African Review Three*, Ravan Press, Johannesburg

—— and C. Walker, for the Surplus People Project (1985) *The surplus people: forced removals in South Africa*, Ravan Press, Johannesburg

Posel, Deborah (1983) 'Rethinking the "race-class debate" in South African historiography', *Social Dynamics*, vol. 9, no. 1, pp. 50–66

—— (1984) 'Language, legitimation and control: the South African State after 1978', *Social Dynamics*, vol. 10, no. 1, pp. 1–16

Price, Robert M. and Carl G. Rosberg (eds) (1980) *The apartheid regime: political power and racial domination*, Institute of International Studies, Berkeley/David Philip, Cape Town

Rantete, Johannes (1984) *The third day of September: an eyewitness account of the Seboking Rebellion of 1984*, Ravan Press, Johannesburg

Rhoodie, Nic (1983) *Intergroup conflict in a deeply segmented society*, Human Sciences Research Council, Pretoria

Rich, Paul B. (1984) *White power and the liberal conscience: racial segregation and South African liberalism 1921–60*, Ravan Press, Johannesburg

Rotberg, Robert I. and John Barratt (eds) (1980) *Conflict and compromise in South Africa*, Lexington Books, Lexington, Mass./David Philip, Cape Town

Saul, John S. (1986) *South Africa: apartheid and after*, Westview, Boulder

—— and Stephen Gelb (1981) *The crisis in South Africa: class defense, class revolution*, Monthly Review Press, New York

Saunders, Christopher (1986) *The making of the South African past: historians on race and class*, David Philip, Cape Town

Savage, Michael (1977) 'Costs of enforcing apartheid and problems of change', *African Affairs*, vol. 76, no. 304, pp. 287–302

Schlemmer, Lawrence (1984) *Black worker attitudes, political options, capitalism and investment in South Africa*, University of Natal Centre for Applied Social Sciences, Durban .

Shrire, Robert A. (1982) *South Africa: public policy perspectives*, Juta, Cape Town

Simkins, Charles E.W. (1984) 'Society', *Energos*, vol. 10, pp. 108–21

—— (1986) *Reconstructing South African liberalism*, South African Institute of Race Relations, Johannesburg

Sincere Jr, Richard E. (1984) *The politics of sentiment: churches and foreign investment in South Africa*, Ethics and Public Policy Center, Washington, D.C.

Sizwe, N. (1976) *One Azania, one nation: the national question in South Africa*, Zed Press, London

South African Institute of Race Relations (SAIRR) *Race Relations Survey* (annual), SAIRR, Johannesburg

South African Research Services, *South African Review* (annual), SARS, Johannesburg

Southall, Roger J. (1981) 'Buthelezi, Inkatha and the politics of Compromise', *African Affairs*, vol. 80, no. 321, pp. 453–81

—— (1983) 'Consociationalism in South Africa: the Buthelezi Commission and beyond', *Journal of Modern African Studies*, vol. 21, pp. 77–112

—— (1982/1985) *South Africa's Transkei: the political economy of an 'independent' bantustan*, Heinemann, London/Monthly Review Press, New York

Stadler, Alf W. (ed.) (1984) *The creation and distribution of wealth*, Senate Special Lectures, University of the Witwatersrand, Johannesburg

—— (1987) *The political economy of modern South Africa*, Croom Helm, London/David Philip, Cape Town

Stultz, Newell M. (1979) *Transkei's half loaf: race separatism in South Africa*, Yale University Press, New Haven

—— (1984) 'Interpreting constitutional change in South Africa', *Journal of Modern African Studies*, vol. 22, no. 3, pp. 353–79

—— (1985) *Thinking about South Africa from afar*, South African Institute of International Affairs, Johannesburg

Suttner, Raymond (1985) 'The Freedom Charter: the people's charter in the nineteen-eighties', *South Africa International*, vol. 15, no. 4, pp. 233–52

—— and Jeremy Cronin (1986) *Thirty years of the Freedom Charter*, Ravan Press, Johannesburg

Swilling, Mark (1986) 'Stayaways, urban protest and the state' in South African Research Services, *South African Review Three*, Ravan Press, Johannesburg

Thomas, Wolfgang H. (1986) 'Regional development in a federal South Africa', *Development Southern Africa*, vol. 3, no. 1, pp. 356–79

Thompson, Leonard M. (1985) *The political mythology of apartheid*, Yale University Press, New Haven

—— and Andrew Prior (1982) *South African politics*, David Philip, Cape Town

Todes, Alison, Vanessa Watson and Peter Wilkenson (1986) 'Local government restructuring in South Africa: the case of the western Cape', *Social Dynamics*, vol. 12, no. 1, pp. 49–69

Turok, Ben (1974) 'South Africa: the search for a strategy' in Ralph Miliband and John Saville (eds), *The Socialist Register 1973*, Merlin Press, London

Uhlig, Mark (1984) 'The coming struggle for power in South Africa', *New York Review of Books*, 2 February, pp. 27–31

Vale, Peter (1983) 'Pretoria and Southern Africa: from manipulation to intervention' in South African Research Services, *South African Review One*, Ravan Press, Johannesburg, 7–22

Van den Berghe, Pierre L. (ed.) (1979) *The liberal dilemma in South Africa*, Croom Helm, London

Van der Merwe, Hendrik W. and Robert A. Schrire (1980) *Race and ethnicity*, David Philip, Cape Town

Van Vuuren, D.J. and D.J. Kriek (eds) (1983) *Political alternatives for Southern Africa*, Butterworth, Durban

Van Vuuren, Willem (1985) 'Domination through reform', *Politikon*, vol. 12, no. 2, pp. 47–58

Van Zyl Slabbert, Frederick (1985) *The last white Parliament*, Jonathan Ball, Johannesburg

—— and Jeff Opland (eds) (1980) *South Africa: dilemmas of evolutionary change*, Institute of Social and Economic Research, Rhodes University, Grahamstown

—— and David J. Welsh (1979) *South Africa's options*, David Philip, Cape Town

Villa-Vicencio, Charles and John W. de Gruchy (eds) (1985) *Essays in honour of Beyers Naudé*, David Philip, Cape Town

Walshe, Peter (1970/1971) *The rise of African nationalism in South Africa*, Hurst, London/University of California Press, Berkeley

Wassenaar, Andreas D. (1977) *Assault on private enterprise*, Tafelberg, Cape Town

Webster, Eddie C. (1984) 'New force on the shop floor' in South African Research Services, *South African Review Two*, Ravan Press, Johannesburg, pp. 79–89

—— (1986) *Cast in a racial mould: labour process and trade unionism in the foundries*, Ravan Press, Johannesburg

Wellings, Paul and Anthony Black (1986) 'Industrial decentralisation under apartheid: the relocation of industry to the South African periphery', *World Development*, vol. 14, no. 1, pp. 1–38

Welsh, David J. (1982) *South Africa: power, process and prospect*, inaugural lecture, University of Cape Town, Rondebosch

—— (1984) 'Constitutional changes in South Africa', *African Affairs*, vol. 83, no. 331, pp. 147–62

Wilson, Francis and Mamphela Ramphele (1987) *Towards reconstruction in Southern Africa*, David Philip, Cape Town

Wisner, Frank (1984) 'Southern Africa: an American perspective today', *South Africa International*, vol. 14, no. 3, pp. 467–75

Woods, Donald (1979) *Biko*, Penguin, Harmondsworth/Vintage, New York

Woodward, Calvin A. (ed.) (1986) *On the razor's edge: prospects for political stability in Southern Africa*, Africa Institute of South Africa, Pretoria

Wright, Harrison M. (1977) *The burden of the present: liberal-radical controversy over South African History*, Rex Collings, London/David Philip, Cape Town

Yudelman, David (1983) *The emergence of modern South Africa: state, capital, and the incorporation of organized labour on the South African gold fields, 1902–1939*, Greenwood, Westport, Conn./David Philip, Cape Town

Zille, Helen (1983) 'Restructuring the industrial decentralisation strategy' in South African Research Services, *South African Review One*, Ravan Press, Johannesburg, pp. 58–71

Index

churches' attitude to reform 283
Civic Action 123-4
  information-gathering and
  124
civil war 128-34, 140-1, 215,
  278, 291
Clewlow, W. 63-4
closure 287-91, 295-6
  definition of 288-9
Co-operation and Development
  Department (DCD) 15, 36
Co-ordinating Council 102
Coca-Cola 70
Coetsee, K. 138
colonialism, South African 268,
  270
coloured
  conscription issue 125-6
  labour preference 23
  minority, local government
  for 88, 92-3
  population 2
Cominform 262
Comintern 262
commandos 137-8
commissions of inquiry 66
communism 123
Communist Parties of Southern
  and Tropical Africa 267
Communist Party (SACP)
  236-7, 240, 246-9, 275n2
  alliance with ANC 259-62,
  270
  Freedom Charter and 259-62
  strategy 262-3, 268-70, 273-4
community
  councils 94-7, 202-9;
    corruption 207
  guard forces 106
  organisations 8-9, 202-4, 206
  unions 180, 184, 188-9
Community Agency for Social
  Enquiry 152-3
commuters
  black 22-3
  cross-border 13-14
confederalism 6-7, 10
Confederation of South African
  Trade Unions (COSATU)
  184, 192-3

Congress of Non-European
  Trade Unions 177
Congress of South African
  Students (COSAS) 190, 210
Congress of South African
  Trade Unions (COSATU)
  148, 163-4, 244, 294
conscription 125-6, 292
  resistance to 134-6
Conservative Party 78, 285,
  287
consocialisationalism 6, 10, 17,
  30, 38, 282, 298
Constitutional Development
  Department 282
Constitutional Development and
  Planning Department
  (DCDP) 10, 15, 17, 23, 33,
  34, 36, 44, 102, 104-5
  dismantled 108
constitutional reform 61,
  63-5, 78, 82, 101-4, 154,
  296-7
  business attitude to 80-1
constitutional restructuring
  30-7, 47
consumer boycotts 134, 181,
  185, 190, 198, 222-3, 279,
  292
controls of black population 2
Convention Alliance 155
Cooper, C. 163
Council of Unions of South
  Africa 184
Creation of Employment
  Opportunities, White Paper
  on 23
credit rating 76
crisis 1984-6, 10-18
Croeser, G. 29
Croeser Committee 100
Crossroads 23
currency, floating 73, 75, 77

Davis, S. 233, 239
de-racialisation, administrative
  41
decentralisation 78
  economic 27-30, 41-2, 68, 71
deconcentration areas 25-7, 28-9

317

319